Soft Innovation

Soft Innovation

Economics, Product Aesthetics, and the Creative Industries

Paul Stoneman

OXFORD
UNIVERSITY PRESS

OXFORD
UNIVERSITY PRESS

Great Clarendon Street, Oxford OX2 6DP

Oxford University Press is a department of the University of Oxford.
It furthers the University's objective of excellence in research, scholarship,
and education by publishing worldwide in

Oxford New York

Auckland Cape Town Dar es Salaam Hong Kong Karachi
Kuala Lumpur Madrid Melbourne Mexico City Nairobi
New Delhi Shanghai Taipei Toronto

With offices in

Argentina Austria Brazil Chile Czech Republic France Greece
Guatemala Hungary Italy Japan Poland Portugal Singapore
South Korea Switzerland Thailand Turkey Ukraine Vietnam

Oxford is a registered trade mark of Oxford University Press
in the UK and in certain other countries

Published in the United States
by Oxford University Press Inc., New York

British Library Cataloguing in Publication Data
Data available

Library of Congress Cataloging in Publication Data
Library of Congress Control Number: 2009931633

Typeset by SPI Publisher Services, Pondicherry, India
Printed in Great Britain
on acid-free paper by
MPG Books Group, Bodmin and King's Lynn

ISBN 978–0–19–957248–9 (hbk.)
ISBN 978–0–19–969702–1 (pbk.)

1 3 5 7 9 10 8 6 4 2

Contents

Contents

Acknowledgements

This work was only made possible by funding from the National Endowment for Science Technology and the Arts (NESTA), for which I am most grateful. A shorter, edited version of the work has been previously published as *Soft Innovation*, by NESTA, London, in April 2009. I would particularly like to thank Hasan Bakhshi of NESTA for his stimulating criticism in the production of this volume. He has been much more than just a passive funder. I would also like to thank Ernie Lee, Sunila Lobo, Daine Nicolaou, Taman Powell, Sotiris Rompas, Diane Skinner, and Ye Zhou (all WBS doctoral students at the time) for their contributions to data collection; Eleonora Bartoloni and Amid Mourani for inputs to Chapter 11; Temi Abimbola, Scott Dacko, and Simon Collinson of the MSM group at WBS, Peter Swann from Nottingham Business School, and Bruce Tether of Tanaka Business School for comments on an earlier draft; and providers of comments received at presentations at the Royal Economic Society Annual Conference 2008 and at a presentation at the Manchester Innovation Institute. Of course, all errors that remain are the responsibility of the author alone.

List of Figures

List of Tables

List of Abbreviations

ABI	Annual Business Inquiry
AHRC	Arts and Humanities Research Council
BERD	Business Enterprise R&D
CAPEX	Capital Expenditure
CIS	Community Innovation Survey
DAT	Digital Audio Tapes
DBERR	Department of Business, Enterprise and Regulatory Reform
DCMS	Department for Culture, Media and Sports
EPO	European Patent Office
GDP	Gross Domestic Product
GVA	Gross Value Added
HD	High Definition
IDBR	Inter-Departmental Business Register
IFPI	International Federation of the Phonographic Industry
IPR	Intellectual Property Rights
MOR	Middle of the Road
OECD	Organisation for Economic Co-operation and Development
PIMS	Profit Impact of Market Strategies
RCD	Registered Community Design
SCC	Sales Contingent Claims
SOC	Standard Occupational Classification
SKU	Stock-keeping Unit
SMEs	Small and Medium Enterprises
SUV	Sport Utility Vehicle
TPP	Technological Product and Process
USPTO	US Patent and Trademark Office

1

Introduction

1.1 Purpose

At its heart this book is about innovation and the innovation process. It may, on the way, consider culture and the cultural industries, aesthetics, creativity and the creative industries, and a number of other similar areas of study, but the common point of interest is innovation. Much of the existing economic literature on innovation has taken a particularly technological/ functional viewpoint as to what sort of new products and processes are to be considered innovations. One main purpose of the book is to argue that there is a type of innovation, here labelled soft innovation, primarily concerned with changes in products (and perhaps processes) of an aesthetic or intellectual nature, that has largely been ignored in the study of innovation prevalent in economics. Examples of innovations that, as a result of this refocusing, are here placed at the centre of the analysis include the writing and publishing of a new book; the writing, production, and launching of a new movie; the development and launch of a new advertising promotion; the design and production of a new range of furniture; and architectural activity in the generation of newly built form designs. The realization of the existence of soft innovation means that not only is innovation more widespread than previously considered but may also take a different form than commonly considered.

The idea of soft innovation is not completely new (see, e.g., Marzal and Esparza [2007] and the past work of Tether [2006] related to design) but in this research the idea is taken further than before by detailing the definition, clarifying issues of significance, contrasting soft innovation with other types of innovation, exemplifying the sort of activities that are brought into the purview of innovation analysis, exploring the connection with product differentiation, and providing some measurements of the rate and extent of soft innovation. In addition, the book explores whether the standard tools of economic analysis that have been used in the past to analyse innovation can also be applied to soft innovation, with what effect, and with what lessons for policy.

An obvious starting point is the definition of innovation. Schumpeter (1950) defined innovation to encompass new products, processes, raw materials, management methods, and markets, and characterized the technological change process as involving three stages – invention, innovation, and diffusion. These three stages of the Schumpeterian trilogy may well interact and demonstrate feedback. Although, for Schumpeter, innovation was a term used to encompass just one stage in the overall process it is now a term used widely to encompass all three stages of the technological change process and everything that it involves.

For the purposes of this volume, innovation in a 'global' sense is defined to occur when new products, processes, raw materials, and management methods are first introduced to an existing or new market. In order to be complete, and given current discussions of hidden innovations (see NESTA [2007]), equivalently, in a non-market context, innovation is taken to also occur when new products, processes, raw materials, and management methods are first introduced to non-market institutions. Innovation may also occur in a 'local' sense when a particular institution introduces new products, processes, raw materials, and management methods in an existing or new market activity for the first time, although others may have done so at an earlier date.

Prior to innovation in a global and maybe local sense, there will have been a process by which new products and processes are brought in to the market. This process will encompass a process of invention – the generation of new ideas – and probably selection and development. This may involve advances in knowledge and may or may not involve basic and applied research, design activities, and development expenditure. It will frequently concern the embodiment of new ideas into physical products. Not all new ideas will become innovations; many may be too expensive to develop, offer poor market prospects, or be technologically unsuitable. However, every global innovation will require prior generation and development. It is not always obvious what label to use for such activities. It might be labelled invention but that seems too narrow. It might be thought of as R&D but as will be shown later this is too technologically orientated. Here the activity is considered to be 'the innovation-generating process', noting that the output of this process, innovation per se, does not occur until the changes being generated come either to the market or are used for the first time. Generating innovations thus involves much more than invention alone.

The third stage of the Schumpeter trilogy is diffusion – the process by which global innovations, that is, new products, processes, and services, spread across their potential domestic and overseas markets (or across and within non-market institutions). It may be considered that, to some degree at least,[1] the diffusion process is another way of characterizing local innovations that follow global innovations. Not all advances will spread: some may, some may not. Over time early innovations may be replaced by later innovations, which in due course will also be replaced. There is always an issue as to where the boundary of an innovation is to be defined so as to, for example, distinguish between a new product and an improved product, but such issues are usually treated in an ad hoc manner.

The key issues addressed in the study of innovation in the past (see, e.g., Stoneman [1995]), and thus a guide to the matters to be addressed here, have been:

1. The measurement of: the rate and extent of innovation; the level of activity in the innovation-generating process (including measures of inputs such as R&D spending, and outputs such as patents registered or scientific papers published); the extent and rate of diffusion of innovations; and the interpretation of different measures.
2. The determinants of the rate and direction of innovation and diffusion usually building upon an assumption of profit-seeking firms and rational consumer behaviour, encompassing such issues as to why some firms, households, industries, and countries show faster or slower innovation and diffusion than others and the impact of market structure in the process.
3. The impacts of innovation and diffusion on outputs, productivity, employment, firm performance, trade, and, more than anything else, on economic welfare.
4. Policy, considering whether there is a rationale for government intervention in the innovation-generating and diffusion processes and if so what instruments can be used in such intervention?

Given the basis of the soft innovation concept, its analysis overlaps considerably with the analysis of other topics that are closely related but are not quite the same. Following are a few examples.

---

[1] To the extent that it is inter-household or inter-firm diffusion that is being discussed as opposed to intra-household or intra-firm.

The arts. Soft innovation does encompass innovation in or based on the arts but it may also occur beyond the boundaries of the arts. Also much of the study of the arts does not emphasize the dynamics of (i.e. innovation in) the sector. For example, in the extensive *Handbook of the Economics of Art and Culture* by Ginsburg and Throsby (2006), despite its impressive nature, innovation is not a prime concern.

Economics and culture. Throsby (2001) addresses the relationship between economics and culture. This is relevant when we talk of theories of value and the economics of creativity, but his analysis extends to encompass the interaction between economics and the cultural environment, cultural and economic approaches to related issues, and the cultural industries that are much more borderline to our concerns.

The copyright industries. This is a term that defines those sectors that rely most upon copyright as means to enforce intellectual property rights (see, e.g., Gantchev [2004] and Theeuwes [2004]). Copyright may be important for soft innovation, but it may be important for other innovations as well. Soft innovations may also be important beyond the copyright industries.

The knowledge economy. This is a generally vague term that is designed to capture the increasing role that knowledge, rather than things, plays in the world economy (see the informative web site of Danny Quah, econ.lse.ac.uk/~dquah/tweirl0.html.) An increasing role for soft innovation may be part of this changing picture but is neither the same nor a major part of the focus of such literature.

Intangible investments. Recently discussions of the knowledge economy have centred upon measurement issues relating to intangible capital (e.g. Haskel [2007]). This literature emphasizes the increasing role of intangible assets in the economy and the difficulties in measuring their extent (see H M Treasury [2007]). Although it has a similar philosophical basis, the overlap with soft innovation is limited.

Design. Design (Tether 2006) is an activity that is close to soft innovation but soft innovation is a wider concept. Design, for example, would not encompass new books, music, or theatre whereas the definition of soft innovation does so.

Creativity. Creativity (Howkins 2001) is the generation of new ideas, wherever this happens, and relates closely to our topic. However, soft innovation does not only encompass creation but also the turning of those ideas into marketable products. Moreover, creativity is also involved in other types of innovation and is thus not unique to soft innovation. For a discussion of the link between creativity, design, and innovation, see DTI (2005).

The creative industries. These industries are defined more precisely in the next chapter, but this term is currently being used to encompass the arts and media sectors (see, e.g., DCMS [2006]). However, soft innovation impacts beyond the boundaries of these industries. Moreover, much of the study of the creative industries does not emphasize the dynamics of the sector.

Prior work by Richard Caves (2000) on the creative industries does overlap with, although does not fully encompass, what is done here. Caves (2000) indicates in a masterful way how economic incentives, uncertainty, and contracts interact in the creative industries as an explanation as to why those industries are organized as they are and perform as they do. In his own words, he has

sought to widen the perspective on what economics can contribute to understanding "art worlds". Economics has more to offer than just the doleful message that costs "of humdrum inputs of the artist's sustenance" must be covered for a creative work to be viable. It can supply an understanding of why art worlds are organised the way they are. It draws on the logic of contracts (and their enforcement) and industrial organisation, supplemented by some propositions of how consumers behave in markets for creative goods. The explanatory power of this apparatus demonstrates that art worlds, while not all organized alike, all are ordered according to the same coherent process. (p. 365)

Caves (2000) devotes an entire chapter to innovation (chapter 13 on innovation, fads, and fashions). However, that chapter, as might be assessed from the title, scratches only the surface as compared to the manner in which it has been dealt with here. Caves (2000) also argues specifically with respect to innovation that:

Another explicable set of differences among art worlds arises in the nature and extent of innovation . . . The fixed cost of realising an innovation is an obvious factor . . . Another distinguishing factor lies in the subjective tastes of artists taking part in the innovative process. . . . Sometimes too the creative innovator devises successful innovation in performing technologies as well. . . . Finally innovation depends upon the insulation that the established canon enjoys from changes in the social and physical context that surrounds consumer demands for creative goods.

It has generally not been the main interest of the economics of innovation to study such intra-firm details of the innovative process: for example, how research teams work together, or the best ways to manage information workers, or the details of the pay and incentive structures in the production of innovations. This study has largely been left to management academics and to sociologists. Perhaps it has also been felt that the issues that arise by such an enquiry are also no different from those that arise in the non-innovation context. In not pursuing such intra-firm issues this current volume is no different from much of the earlier literature.

Despite this, it is worth keeping in mind two principal precepts that Caves (2000) considers as fundamental to the creative industries. The first is that there may be an 'art for art's sake' agenda at work, which means, for example, that economic actors may not always behave in the apparently rational manner predicted by standard economic theory, and may perhaps trade wealth for aesthetic satisfaction. The second is the principle that 'nobody knows', which implies that the commercial success of a creative vision cannot be known or pre-tested (and thus uncertainty is inherent).

Although there are obvious parallels, the study of soft innovation carves out a niche that differs from the traditional analysis of innovation in economics and also from all of the aforementioned.

1.2 An overview

This monograph has three parts. Part I is concerned with attempts to define and measure the extent and nature of soft innovation. This has been covered in four chapters. Chapter 2 introduces the issues and provides a more complete argument as to why soft innovation, conceptually, is important. Chapter 3 provides a macroeconomic perspective and attempts to provide some feel for the extent of such innovation in the economy as a whole and the economic activities that are built upon it. Chapter 4 is the first of two chapters that take a microeconomic view encompassing three creative industries – publishing, music, and video games – to provide a detailed pattern of invention/creation, embodiment, and diffusion of soft innovations. Of particular interest are product variant launch patterns, the lifetime of product variants, and how other types of innovations interact with soft innovation. Chapter 5 is the other chapter that takes a microeconomic view and explores the role of soft innovation in three industries outside the creative industries: food, pharmaceuticals, and finance. This part of the book is designed for the layman and does not necessitate any prior economic training. The examples provided are mainly based in the United Kingdom, but examples from other countries have also been used.

Part II is directed towards the economic analysis of soft innovation. It contains certain technical economic material and therefore requires more of the reader. Chapter 6 explores the extent to which soft innovation can be usefully modelled as an economic process driven by economic incentives and subject to economic rationality, and also the extent to which the use of tools and techniques commonly employed in the standard economic analysis of innovation (see, e.g., Stoneman [1995]) is still relevant in this context. One particular finding is that the analysis of soft innovation calls for approaches that are more commonly used to analyse product differentiation and this brings these two areas of study much closer together than has previously been the case. Chapters 7 and 8 consider alternative models of the supply and demand of (diffusion of) soft innovations relying heavily on models of product differentiation. Chapter 9 addresses issues related to risk and uncertainty, focusing on the choice between corporate innovation strategies of small-numbers nurturing vs. letting a thousand flowers bloom. Chapter 10 explores the role of intellectual property rights in the process of soft innovation and the extent to which the standard analysis is appropriate and can provide insight or requires modification.

Part III is concerned with impacts and implications and has an intermediate level of complexity. Chapter 11 addresses the private returns to investment in soft innovation, Chapter 12 considers policy issues, and Chapter 13 summarizes, draws implications, and gives indications for future directions of research.

For those readers who like to know in advance what they will find in the following pages, the ensuing paragraphs provide a reasonably non-technical summary of the arguments and findings. To begin with, the main source of economic growth is technological change and innovation. To date, however, in economics at least, the concept of innovation has primarily been centred around the scientific or technical, with the significance of new products and processes being judged upon the basis of improvements in functionality (technological product and process [TPP] innovation). Innovation that encompasses the artistic, formal (as in the contrast between form and function), intellectual, or aesthetic, has largely been ignored in the mainstream literature on innovation. At the very centre of this analysis is a form of innovation called 'soft innovation', which defines changes in goods and services that impact primarily on these aspects rather than on functional performance.

Soft innovation is mainly concerned with product innovation and product differentiation. Emphasizing product differentiation allows, in contrast to standard analysis, that innovation may: (*a*) involve changes that are horizontal in nature, and, as such, soft innovation may involve differences from the status quo and not just improvements, and (*b*) be vertical in nature and thus may (also) involve reductions in quality rather than just improvements (if price also falls more than proportionately). The emphasis upon product differentiation also means that economic analysis designed for exploring (static) models in differentiated markets can be brought to bear upon dynamic questions related to innovation. Innovation in terms of new product launches in such markets may reflect either movements towards equilibrium or changes in the equilibrium.

Two main types of soft innovation are detailed: the first involves changes in products in the creative industries while the second involves changes in the aesthetic/intellectual dimensions of products in other industries. The launch of new books, recorded music, and game titles are examples of the former; the launch of new food, and pharmaceutical and financial service products are examples of the latter.

At the macro level, indicators of soft innovation include the number of creative employees in different sectors, the extent of design activity, and headcounts of registered trademarks. The difference between the latter and indicators of R&D spending is considered as potentially the most useful on account of both concept and data availability. It is shown that the extent of soft innovation in the creative and other industries is extensive, probably greater than that indicated by measures of formal R&D activity, and is growing faster than TPP activity. Across industries, the apparent balance in innovative effort between sectors after taking account of soft innovation is also shown to be much more even than reliance upon measures of TPP innovation alone would suggest.

At the micro level, industry-specific indicators concerning the numbers of new product variants introduced are used with certain advantages such as the identification of the rate of significant innovation being claimed for a specific measure that tracks the share of the sales of best-sellers that were recently introduced into the market. In the creative sector, the indicated rates of innovation are high with a considerable number of new products or titles being launched and the churning of best-sellers in the studied markets being very fast. This reflects a pattern quite different to the usual suggestion that innovation occurs at a rate of about 2.5 per cent per annum (a measure based on indicators of labour productivity growth). There is a suggestion that the rate of soft innovation as indicated by market churn has been speeding up in some markets but not all.

Outside the creative sector, the measurement of soft innovation is hampered by data availability. It is once again possible, however, to observe extensive soft innovation as reflected in new product launches that do not reflect changed functionality. This is especially prevalent in the food industry but can also be found in the banking and pharmaceutical sectors. The study of generics in pharmaceuticals suggests that soft innovation activity may be the larger part of innovative activity in that industry. However, the data is not conclusive as to whether the rate of soft innovation is getting any faster.

All the data at differing levels of aggregation indicates that rates of soft innovation are high and that such innovation is widespread and extensive. It is therefore argued that the failure of the traditional literature to ignore such innovation causes much innovation activity in the economy to be left out. This is not to say that TPP innovation is not important, for it is, both by itself and as a basis for much soft innovation. It is, however, at least debatable that to concentrate solely on TPP innovation and to ignore soft innovation provides only a limited and biased picture of total innovative activity.

Although useful in many ways, the standard literature on the determinants of technological innovation is found not completely suitable to the analysis of soft innovation. This is primarily due to (*a*) the fact that soft innovation is mainly concerned with the introduction of new product variants and thus models with differentiated products are most appropriate and (*b*) the difficulties in conceptualizing, in the context of soft innovation, a basic component of standard models that relates expenditure on R&D to the extent of any advance.

Existing models of product differentiated markets are thus adapted to allow for a number of different scenarios that reflect some of the characteristics of products that may embody soft innovation. These include issues such as whether production and innovation coincide, whether the product is durable or not, whether the service flow requires hardware and software, and whether there are standards and compatibility issues. Of particular interest (because it fits the examples of books, recorded music, and video games) is the consideration of models where product variants are usually only bought once and continuation of the market depends on the continual launching of new product variants. It is also emphasized that the market outcome reflects the interaction of both supply and demand (their separate treatment is just a matter of ease of analysis). Considerations of uncertainty (and optimal launch strategies) as well as appropriability and IPR are also undertaken.

From the several models it can be derived that the list of factors that are important to the innovation process include the level, and particularly changes in, costs of generating and developing innovations, fixed costs of production, variable production costs, the number of suppliers, uncertainty and reactions to it, rivalry and excludability and the institutional IPR environment, the allocation of buyers' preferences, buyers' knowledge bases, buyers' price and technology expectations, and the nature of the product.

The theoretical analysis also shows that, as with much analysis concerned with TPP innovation, there is no guarantee that free markets will produce a welfare optimal outcome. The outcome may involve either too much or too little variety and innovation. The market failure thus identified can come from a number of sources. One general source is that there are positive and negative externalities in the market that drive a wedge between private and social incentives. Other factors such as creative destruction effects and the standing on shoulders effects also have a role to play. Considerations of uncertainty (and optimal launch strategies) as well as appropriability and IPR extend such arguments to matters of missing markets and the need for and effectiveness of different means of protecting intellectual property rights.

An attempt is made to look into the impact of soft innovation on firm performance in more detail as a proxy for producer surplus. It is shown that the existing literature, not surprisingly, is dominated by TPP-based approaches and, although such approaches can and have been applied to soft innovations using soft innovation proxies such as headcounts and trademarks, it is argued that such approaches are not ideal. Instead a number of successful soft innovations are presented as examples that show that soft innovation may stimulate firm performance and increase producer surplus.

Given the potential benefits of soft innovation it is only natural to consider whether governments can speed up or extend such activity. However speeding up is not necessarily welfare desirable. The real issue concerns whether markets will or will not, unaided, produce the welfare optimal outcome. The literature considered shows that this question cannot be answered irrefutably in either direction. Market failure is thus not a strong ground on which to base policy intervention.

Alternatively, international comparisons of soft innovation performance may be used by governments as a basis for policy. It is shown that the United Kingdom is not the international leader (although not a major laggard) in soft innovation. However, if intervention is to be based on relatively poor international performance, the problem is in getting a handle on why domestic performance is not good enough. Looking at returns to the Community Innovation Survey provides some insight into barriers to innovations and may be argued to support certain policy interventions. There is also only limited evidence on the potential effectiveness of policies. Some comments are also made on government support on the grounds of art for art's sake.

It is argued that there may be a foundation for supporting several policies such as tax incentives to soft innovation, government funding of soft innovation projects, government finance for soft innovation, labour market intervention, stimulating market contestability and facilitating the setting of standards. In the recent past, UK policy (and that of many other countries), has associated innovation with science and technology and R&D, and has devised policies aimed at these. This approach excludes consideration of soft innovation although soft innovation is a major part of the innovation map. Policy now needs to be rebalanced to include the total of innovative activity and not just part of it.

Suggested further research encompasses the dissemination of the idea that soft innovation is important, extensive, and capable of economic analysis and merits considerably more attention than has been the case in the past; further data collection relating to soft innovation and its prevalence; and further theoretical analysis of soft innovation, especially the link between models of product differentiation and innovation.

Part I

The Nature and Extent of Soft Innovation

2
Defining Soft Innovation

2.1 Introduction

This chapter is primarily concerned with detailing the concept of soft innovation, exploring its nature, and how it differs from other types of innovation, discussing its significance and introducing issues of measurement and incidence. The chapter also introduces a number of terms that are either related to, or of utility in, the further analysis presented later. This chapter defines soft innovation, but prior to doing so proceeds by first defining product, process, organizational, and marketing innovation in order to reveal where the soft innovation concept is new and adds to the picture of total innovative activity. The two faces of soft innovation are discussed and the means of judging significance explored. Soft innovation is argued to be related to product differentiation. The relationship of soft innovation to science, research and development (R&D) and patenting are also considered before conclusions are drawn. Two appendices are provided to detail the creative industries and to discuss measures of the impact of innovation on economic welfare.

2.2 Product, process, and organizational innovations

In order to define soft innovation, it would be useful to begin with some definitions relating to the more commonly recognized types of innovations. The definition of innovation provided by Schumpeter (1950) encompasses new products, processes, raw materials, management methods, and markets. A series of editions of the *Oslo Manual*, produced under the aegis of the Organisation for Economic Co-operation and Development (OECD – the first of which was published in 1992 and the latest in 2006

[OECD 2006]), have provided the yardstick by which statisticians and economists in most OECD and other countries have operationalized this definition in order to measure innovation and innovative activity.[1] In combination with the *Frascati Manual*, OECD (2002), which gives indications of how to measure R&D, the guidelines embodied therein provide the foundations upon which innovation surveys have been conducted and on which data on innovation and R&D have been collected for international comparison and national usage. In some countries they even provide the basis on which activities may be judged to attract R&D tax relief. A main argument in this book is that, even with recent extensions, the Oslo (and Frascati) manual definitions still do not adequately encompass, or sufficiently emphasize, soft innovation activities. As a result, collected data may portray a distorted picture of overall innovative activity in the economy.

Over time the *Oslo Manual* has been refined and its guidelines revised. Early versions concentrated on technological product and process innovation (TPP) in goods, which was then expanded to cover services (see, e.g., Tether [2003]). In the latest OECD (2006) manual the 'technological' label has been dropped but for ease of reference product and process innovations as defined by OECD (2006) will continue to be called technological (product and process) or TPP innovations. Organizational innovation was later included and finally, in the 2006 edition, marketing innovation (a variant of the definition of which was previously included in organizational innovation) has been separately identified. The 2006 manual now describes innovation as follows:

An innovation is the implementation of a new or significantly improved product (good or service), or process, a new marketing method, or a new organisational method in business practices, workplace organisation or external relations. (p. 46)

The definition of product innovation provided in Chapter 3 of OECD (2006) is:

A **product innovation** is the introduction of a good or service that is new or significantly improved with respect to its characteristics or intended uses. This includes significant improvements in technical specifications, components and materials, incorporated software, user friendliness or other functional characteristics. (p. 48)

In the manual, product innovations include both the introduction of new goods and services and significant improvements in the functional or user characteristics of existing goods and services. *New* products are goods and

---

[1] There are other definitions but they are neither as widely used nor as well detailed as the OECD guidelines. We thus concentrate here on those OECD guidelines.

services that differ significantly in their characteristics or intended uses from products previously produced by the firm. The development of a new use for a product with only minor changes to its technical specifications may also be a product innovation. *Significant improvements* to existing products can occur through changes in materials, components, and other characteristics that enhance performance. Product innovations in services can include significant improvements in how they are provided (e.g. in terms of their efficiency or speed), the addition of new functions or characteristics to existing services, or the introduction of entirely new services. Although design is an integral part of the development and implementation of product innovations, design changes that are not seen as involving a significant change in a product's functional characteristics or intended uses are considered by the manual *not* to be product innovations. Thus, to be termed a product innovation, by these definitions, any change (with respect to either goods or services) must involve either newness or significance as indicated by the impact on the product's functional or performance characteristics.

Process innovation is defined by the OECD (2006) as follows:

A **process innovation** is the implementation of a new or significantly improved production or delivery method. This includes significant changes in techniques, equipment and/or software. (p. 49)

Process innovations can be intended to decrease unit costs of production or delivery, to increase quality, or to produce or deliver new or significantly improved products and may involve the techniques, equipment, and software used to produce goods or services. Process innovations include new or significantly improved methods for the creation and provision of services. They can involve significant changes in the equipment and software used in services-oriented firms or in the procedures or techniques that are employed to deliver services. Process innovations also cover new or significantly improved techniques, equipment, and software in ancillary support activities, such as purchasing, accounting, computing, and maintenance. It is worth noting that, once again, for a change to be considered an innovation it must involve newness and/or a significant change in terms of impact on the functional or performance characteristics of the process.

Organizational innovation is defined thus:

An **organisational innovation** is the implementation of a new organizational method in the firm's business practices, workplace organisation or external relations. (p. 51)

Organizational innovations can be intended to increase a firm's performance by reducing administrative or transaction costs, improving workplace satisfaction (and thus labour productivity), gaining access to non-tradable assets (such as non-codified external knowledge), or reducing costs of supplies. The distinguishing features of an organizational innovation compared to other organizational changes in a firm is the implementation of an organizational method (in business practices, workplace organization, or external relations) that has not been used before in the firm and is the result of strategic decisions taken by management.

Organizational innovation per se does not play any further significant role in this volume and thus we pay little further attention to it except that, when first introduced by the OECD, the concept of organizational innovation included an activity called 'marketing innovation' that was defined to encompass implementation of changes in marketing concepts or strategies (e.g. packaging or presentational changes to a product to target new markets) and new support services to open up new markets, etc. In OECD (2006) these activities are removed from the definition of organizational innovation and incorporated into a more widely defined concept of marketing innovation which we discuss further below.

In order to illustrate the extent to which firms undertake the different types of innovation thus far identified, using the pre-2006 definition of organizational innovation, Table 2.1 provides some indications of the frequency of TPP and organizational innovation in the United Kingdom. Sourced from Battisti and Stoneman (2009) and based on data from the fourth UK Community Innovation Survey, several indicators of TPP innovation (the first three) and organizational innovation (the latter four) are listed alongside the proportions of the 16,383 sample firms that have undertaken such innovation in 2002–4.

As may be seen, both TPP and organizational innovations are used by about 20 per cent of the sample, although 'MACHINE' use is found more commonly. It was found by Battisti and Stoneman (2009) that, using the Kendall's tau-b correlation coefficient (a non-parametric measure of association based on the number of concordances and discordances in paired observations) for the seven innovation variables, that the pair-wise degree of association between adoption activities is significantly different from zero, indicating that the decision to adopt one innovative practice is not independent of the decision to adopt another innovative practice, and the adoption of all practices is correlated with the adoption of all others.

Table 2.1 TPP and organizational innovations, sample adoption (%), United Kingdom, 2002–4

Innovation variable label	Definition	Adopting firms (%)
PRODINOV	Whether a product innovation (new to the enterprise or to the market or a significantly improved good or service) has been introduced on the market between 2002 and 2004.	20
PROCINOV	Whether a process innovation (new to the enterprise or to the market that significantly improved methods for the production or supply of goods and services) has been introduced between 2002 and 2004.	29
MACHINE	Whether advanced machinery, equipment, or computer hardware or software to produce new or significantly improved goods, services, production processes, or delivery methods has been acquired between 2002 and 2004.	47
STRATEGY	Whether a new or significantly changed corporate strategy has been implemented between 2002 and 2004.	19.9
MANAGEMENT	Whether advanced management techniques, e.g. knowledge management systems or Investors in People, has been implemented between 2002 and 2004.	17.6
ORGANIZATION	Whether major changes to the organizational structure, e.g. introduction of cross-functional teams or outsourcing of major business functions, have been implemented between 2002 and 2004.	22.6
MARKETING	Whether changes in marketing concepts or strategies (e.g. packaging or presentational changes to a product to target new markets) or new support services to open up new markets have been implemented between 2002 and 2004.	23

2.3 Soft innovation: the definition

Despite the apparent widespread nature of product, process, and organizational innovation revealed in Table 2.1, there are many other innovative activities in the economy that are not covered by the above OECD categorizations. The prime reason for this is that the definitions of innovation provided by the OECD emphasize changes in functionality[2] as a, if not the, major characteristic of innovation. This seems inappropriately

---

[2] In an alternative reading of the OECD manual one could argue that another main requirement is a connection to science and technology.

limiting. For example, the world economy has changed much in recent years. The advent of information technology (IT) and the apparent decline of agriculture and manufacturing as sources of employment in the developed world have led to the coining of a number of different descriptive terms for the new state, e.g. the Information Economy, the Knowledge Economy, and the Weightless Economy. Each of these terms is supposed to reflect the greater importance of the trading of knowledge and information as opposed to things. In addition, services now form a growing part of all modern developed economies and they are often weightless or unembodied. It would seem that with the move away from trading in 'things' towards trading in 'ideas' to ignore certain changes because they are not functional may be to ignore an increasingly important innovative activity and to mistakenly exclude a major dynamic aspect of modern economies.[3]

In addition, although the creative process for new films or new music may be as costly as for new drugs (the costs of new movies now frequently exceeding $200 million) and involve similar activities as the R&D process in the pharmaceutical industry (e.g. creative thought, experimentation, selection, testing, market appraisal), the latter under the OECD definition would be considered innovation while the former would not. This seems illogical. Moreover to rule out some developments as innovation because they are not functional would seem to rule out much of the dynamic activity in industries such as the fashion industry.

Setting aside the requirement for functional change and instead considering newness as basic requirement of innovation brings into play as innovation many activities that would have previously have been ruled out. Examples include:

1. The writing and publishing of a new book
2. The development and recording of a new CD
3. The writing, rehearsing, and staging of a new theatre production
4. The writing, production, and launching of a new movie
5. The development and launch of a new advertising promotion
6. The development and launch of a new clothing line
7. The development and launch of some new financial instruments

---

[3] A definition of innovation alternative to that of the OECD that seems to have become popular recently (and appears to have at least been disseminated from the Department of Trade and Industry [DTI 2003]) is that innovation is the 'successful exploitation of new ideas'. Put in this way, there is no reason why the product of exploiting new ideas should be restricted to functional improvements and thereby exclude non-functional change. At the risk of overkill, another way of putting this is that innovation is about improving economic well-being by the use of new knowledge, and new knowledge is not just reflected in functionality.

8. Design and production of a new range of furniture
9. Architectural activity in the generation of new built-form designs
10. Design activities relating to motor vehicles

A number of earlier researchers have also drawn attention to non-functional innovations. Bianchi and Bartolotti (1996) define what they call 'formal' innovation *'which is innovation that changes product form without any necessary changes in product functions and production methods'*. They consider that the new form 'exalts the aesthetic or symbolic content of the product'. They associate such innovation with fashion and design goods. Cappetta et al. (2006) talk of 'stylistic innovation', defined by them as the change in the aesthetic and symbolic elements of goods and services, applying the approach to a longitudinal empirical study (1984–2002) in the fine fashion industry.

Postrel (2004) has taken this argument much further and beyond fashion and design goods. She argues that aesthetics is an increasingly important element of our society and people are concerned not only with function but also with how things look and feel. Examples of aesthetic changes include clothing, cars, make-up, plastic surgery, hairstyles, restaurants, and graphic design. She contrasts this with prior consumer focus on functionality and convenience but argues that pleasure is no less important than usefulness. Once again there is a contrast between the functional and the aesthetic.

Swan et al. (2005) confirm the importance of aesthetics (as compared to functionality) in product demand. They cite evidence that practitioners realize the importance of visual or aesthetic design in consumer choice; for example, they state that in the automobile industry one of the most important aspects for body design is how light will reflect off the surface of a car, and that the aesthetics of luxury automobiles are critical to their consumer appeal. They also find that product aesthetics can affect product evaluation and that portraying a quality image influences consumer product evaluation, even if the appearance has no bearing on the functional performance of the product. In a related way Hagtvedt and Patrick (2008) specifically address the issue of how the presence of visual art (on, e.g., packaging) has a favourable influence on the evaluation of consumer products.

Marzal and Esparza (2007) argue that there are industries that experience aesthetic innovations which occur when novelty is conferred on a product in terms of visual (broadly, sensory[4]) attributes. This can be compared with the new functions that are often considered to be conferred by technological change. As a result of aesthetic innovation a product can be perceived as being radically different and can displace earlier products.

---

[4] For example smell, see Morrin and Ratneshwar (2000).

They consider that the key characteristics of aesthetic innovation are that it increases the perceived value of the product and satisfies customer demands concerning taste, social image, and preference for novelty; does not provide new functionality to the product; does not alter the way a product is used; and may make use of new technologies or materials, but not necessarily. They also draw a number of analogies with other terms that have been proposed for what they call aesthetic innovation including design innovation and stylistic innovation. The key distinguishing characteristic is however once again the contrast between the aesthetic and the functional.[5]

In the light of the above discussion, and in particular dissatisfaction with an approach to innovation that emphasizes function at the expense of form or aesthetics, a new concept, soft innovation, as a contrast to the OECD innovation concepts, is defined here.

Soft innovation is innovation in goods and services that primarily impacts upon aesthetic or intellectual appeal rather than functional performance.

Because a word is often used to mean different things and aesthetic is one such word, some definitional clarity is useful. First, aesthetic is considered here to encompass issues wider than the concept of beauty and artistic experience and in particular visual beauty to which it may be restricted. The *Online Etymology Dictionary* refers to aesthetic as popularized in English by translation of Immanuel Kant, and used originally in the classically correct sense 'the science which treats of the conditions of sensuous perception'. Today, sensory is a more appropriate word than sensuous and it is this meaning that has been adopted here. Aesthetic is thus taken as encompassing not only sight but also touch, smell, and sound. For the purposes of completeness, the definition of soft innovation is also extended to include products that appeal to the intellect, such as books.

Soft innovation thus defined may occur in any industrial sector or market. Most soft innovation will involve the introduction of new goods or services but new processes (or production methods) that have different aesthetics are not ruled out (e.g. some green wind energy technologies have undesirable noise effects and are not visually appealing). However,

---

[5] They also argue that the definition of aesthetic innovation should exclude minimal changes which do not substantially alter the product image, because the magnitude of the change should also take into consideration the economic efforts and results (a change of colour, for instance) involved. According to this definition, an aesthetic change would be considered innovative if it makes the product be perceived as new or different. These changes must entail substantial modifications to the product's formal structure; thus, changing the colour of the product or its ornamentation would not constitute an innovation, but would be classified as 'other aesthetic changes'.

new processes are played down here and new products are instead empha-sized. New products may be targeted at consumers when the demand arises from households (and perhaps government) at home and overseas or producers when demand arises from firms (including perhaps govern-ment) at home and overseas. Producer demands for new products and processes may differ in their nature from consumer demand in that one might think that producer demand would be less concerned with aesthet-ics; however, observation of the architecture of office blocks in the world's major cities indicates that aesthetics may well be an important aspect of producer demand patterns as well as consumer demand patterns (the latter is well illustrated in Higgs et al. [2008]).[6] Soft innovations also may be one-off or mass market, and be either storable or non-storable.

2.4 The two faces of soft innovation

It is useful to distinguish between two main types of soft innovation.[7] The first type is innovation in products that are not generally considered func-tional in nature but instead offer aesthetic appeal, i.e. appeal to the senses or the intellect. The introduction of any new aesthetic product or product variant is taken to be a soft innovation. Examples are music, books, film, fashion, art, video games, etc. Such products are to be found particularly in those industries that in recent practice are called the 'creative industries', encompassing culture, media, and the arts, a sector shown to be of consid-erable size (see, e.g., DCMS [2006], Andari et al. [2007], and Appendix A2.2). It is clearly inappropriate to attempt to apply a concept of innovation based on functionality to innovation in such industries. In the past in most economic analyses of innovation these industries and their products have been ignored.[8] Thus, for example, despite the huge financial impact and considerable sales of the work of J. K. Rowling (the Harry Potter books and

---

[6] Also see Bakhshi et al. (2008) which discusses the use of the output of the creative industries in the innovation of non-creative sectors.

[7] For a similar approach, see Taylor (2005), Unweaving the Rainbow, at http://cihe-uk.com/docs/AHRCUnweaving the Rainbow.pdf

[8] In marketing, Venkatesh and Meamber (2006) look at cultural production and the cre-ation, diffusion, and consumption of cultural products. They address the nature of cultural production, including the roles that producers, cultural intermediaries, and consumers play in the process; emerging perspectives and ideas on cultural production; aesthetics and art in cultural production; new epistemologies concerning postmodernism and posthumanism as related to cultural production; and the implications of the cultural production processes for the marketing aspects of cultural industries.

resulting films), this work has not been considered (in economics) to be an innovation. This is undesirable.

The second type of soft innovation is aesthetic innovations in industries the output of which is not aesthetic per se but functional.[9] Although there is some literature on product innovations relevant to such markets, e.g. Trajtenberg (1990), only recently has there been any emphasis on the aesthetic aspects of such functional products, e.g. Tether (2006), DTI (2005), and Cox (2006). In addition to their functionality, products in such industries may have many non-functional characteristics. These will encompass the basic senses of sight, touch, taste, smell, and sound, e.g. the appearance of furniture, the sound of a car exhaust, the taste of a meal, the smell of flowers in a garden design, and the touch of a sheepskin rug. Innovation may well impact on the way functional products affect these senses and such innovation cannot be presumed to be encompassed by the description 'functional'. Many new products of this kind will, however, offer both soft and functional innovations, for example a new model of car will offer better miles per gallon, top speed, fuel consumption, etc. but also new colours, new shape, new sounds, etc.

This second type of soft innovation may to some degree at least be encompassed by the OECD concept of marketing innovation. Marketing innovation is defined by the OECD as follows:

A **marketing innovation** is the implementation of a new marketing method involving significant changes in product design or packaging, product placement, product promotion or pricing. (p. 49)

The manual explains that marketing innovations as now defined are innovations with the objective of increasing the firm's sales by means of better addressing customer needs, opening up new markets, or newly positioning a firm's product on the market. The distinguishing feature of a *new marketing method* is the implementation of a method not previously used by the firm, and must be part of a new marketing concept or strategy that represents a significant departure from the firm's existing marketing methods. New marketing methods can be implemented for both new and existing products.

Significant changes in *product design*[10] refer to changes in product form and appearance that do not alter the product's functional or user

---

[9] Bakhshi et al. (2008) detail links in innovation between the creative and non-creative sectors.

[10] Although design is an integral part of the development and implementation of product innovations, design changes that are not seen as involving a significant change in a product's

characteristics. They also include changes in the packaging of products such as foods, beverages, and detergents, where packaging is the main determinant of the product's appearance. An example of a marketing innovation in product design is the implementation of a significant change in the design of a furniture line to give it a new look and broaden its appeal. Innovations in product design can also include the introduction of significant changes in the form, appearance, or taste of food or beverage products, such as the introduction of new flavours for a food product in order to target a new customer segment. Changes in *product placement* primarily involve the introduction of new sales channels, examples being the introduction for the first time of a franchising system, of direct selling or exclusive retailing, and of product licensing. Innovations in *product promotion* involve the use of new concepts for promoting a firm's goods and services. For example, the first use of a significantly different media or technique – such as product placement in movies or television programmes, or the use of celebrity endorsements – is a marketing innovation. Another example is branding, such as the development and introduction of a fundamentally new brand symbol. Innovations in *pricing* involve the use of new pricing strategies to market the firm's goods or services, but those new pricing methods whose sole purpose is to differentiate prices by customer segments are not considered innovations.

However, a clear distinction on the basis of functionality is drawn between marketing innovation and product innovation. The manual argues:

The main distinguishing factor for product and marketing innovations is a significant change in the product's functions or uses. Goods or services which have significantly improved functional or user characteristics compared to existing products are product innovations. On the other hand, the adoption of a new marketing concept that involves a significant change in the design of an existing product is a marketing innovation but not a product innovation, as long as the functional or user characteristics of the product are not significantly changed. As an example, clothes produced using new fabrics with improved performance (breathable, waterproof, etc.) are product innovations, but the first introduction of a new shape for clothes intended for a new group of customers or to give the product a higher degree of exclusivity (and thus allow for a higher mark-up compared to the previous version of the product), is a marketing innovation. (p. 56)

---

functional characteristics or intended uses are considered by the manual not to be product innovations. However, they can be marketing innovations. Routine upgrades or regular seasonal changes are also not product innovations.

Introducing this concept of marketing innovation is a major change in the OECD definition of innovation because, for the first time, it brings within, and gives credibility to, a definition of innovation which includes 'significant change in the design of an existing product but where the functional or user characteristics of the product are not significantly changed'. The introduction by the OECD of the marketing innovation concept means that it now accepts that innovation no longer requires a change in functionality or product performance. More realistically, an innovation can exhibit just aesthetic change rather than functional change. This is support for the view that soft innovation, as defined in this book, has relevance.

However, the OECD concept only includes the second of the two types of soft innovation defined, i.e. aesthetic innovations in industries the output of which is not aesthetic per se but functional. It has not been extended to include the first type, encompassing new products in industries where the output is inherently aesthetic. To encompass all such aesthetic changes necessitates defining a concept of innovation that is similar to, but differs from, the OECD marketing innovation concept. That is the soft innovation concept defined here, with soft innovation of the second kind encompassing marketing innovation.

One may go as far as to argue that once soft innovation is included within the set of innovative activity, it is very difficult to conceive of any large parts of a modern economy that are not experiencing extensive, continuous innovative activity. Most products are being either enhanced functionally or changed aesthetically, and processes of production (physical and managerial) are also changing. Even in areas where change may not be expected, e.g. in commodities or basic food production or utilities, product, process, aesthetic, and organizational innovations are now commonplace. With soft innovation included, it is in fact difficult to conceive that the study of innovation should be considered, as currently, as just an add-on to the standard economic analysis of static systems. It would in fact appear that in a modern economy innovation is all-pervasive and that the study of static systems misses the essence of such economies.

Despite the importance and relevance of the soft innovation concept there are still practical issues, where, in practice, the line has to be drawn between a functional and a soft innovation. For example, with a personal service, is a more pleasant transaction a functional innovation or an improved aesthetic dimension to the trade? This problem is especially severe where the product is functional rather than aesthetic. One significant point, however, is that the inclusion of marketing innovation leads one naturally to consider that the distinctive but intangible quality encompassed by the concept of brand image[11] (which again can not really be considered as relating to functionality) is an aspect of product aesthetics.

Particular examples of the advantages that result from the extension of the innovation concept to encompass soft innovation include:

1. The inclusion as innovation of the dynamic process that includes the biannual round of fashion shows, restocking of shops, and changing of buyer's apparel which in fact may be much more innovative than activities in industries involved with the more traditionally considered technological product and process innovation.
2. The inclusion of changes in appearance, sound, and smell of cars as innovation. This implies that consumer choice between, for example, one sport utility vehicle (SUV) and another is not purely based on functionality or more precisely that a later model is only preferred to an earlier model because of its improved functionality. For example, as any Jaguar driver will know, the current (at the time of writing in early 2009) XJ8 in terms of functionality is far superior to the earlier model, but the company was criticized for failing to change the appearance of the car sufficiently when changing functionality and as a result suffered in the market. Similarly many people still would love to own a Jaguar E-type – this cannot be based on functionality. Of the many millions spent by car companies on innovations, only a certain amount will be related to comfort, performance, and efficiency; further amounts will be spent on design, smell, colour choice, exhaust note, the sound made by the closing door, the shape of the grill, the angle of the headlights, the extent of the chrome, etc. (i.e. aesthetic appeal or soft innovation).
3. The realization of links between soft and functional innovation. For example, the demand for DVD players may well be dependent on the quality of films available, as the demand for MP3 players may be related to music available. It is well documented how the demand for flat-screen television has been boosted by football events, and so the list continues. Even if there is no direct technological link, the demand for

---

[11] Defined by the American Marketing association as 'the perception of a brand in the minds of persons. The brand image is a mirror reflection (though perhaps inaccurate) of the brand personality or product being. It is what people believe about a brand - their thoughts, feelings, expectations'. (www.marketingpower.com/mg-dictionary-view339.php). See also Bennett (ed.) (1995).

certain hardware products will be related to the quality of aesthetic material embodied in the products of the aesthetic industries.

4. The possibility of arguing that some soft innovation activities may act as the foundation for entire industrial sectors such as publishing, textiles, and cinema.

5. Consideration of the extent to which some industries are reliant on a continuous flow of aesthetic innovations. For example, if no new titles ever appeared, one may predict that books' sales and publishers' revenues would diminish greatly and the industry would be poorer, employ fewer, and, even with process improvements, be of much lesser importance. Publishing may be one of a number of industries for which soft innovation is a *sine qua non* in that many or most existing products have a limited total lifetime sale. The music industry has a similar story. Recording companies and studios continuously seek new artists and new songs to tempt the buying public. Bands rise and fall. Orchestral interpretations rise and fall. New songs are written, produced, and sold and are replaced. This is again a process where the continuing flow of new material maintains the sales of the industry and without those sales the industry would be much smaller.

2.5 Soft innovation and product differentiation

In the economics literature on technological change as a whole, there has been only limited interaction between the concepts of product differentiation and innovation. This is a stance that one has to put aside in order to properly analyse soft innovation.

In the main, product differentiation activities per se have not been considered innovative activities, although, on occasion, it has been considered that some innovative products are different from existing products (see, e.g., Greenstein and Ramey [1998]) and there is a stream of US-based work emphasizing product innovation (see, e.g., Bresnahan and Gordon [1997]). In addition there is a line of literature within new growth theory that explores models of continually expanding variety (see, e.g., Acemoglu [2009, p. 448]).

In order to clarify discussion, and throughout the book from this point on, the term 'product' will be used to define the goods/services being purchased, e.g. books, CDs, video games, painkillers, and chocolate bars. Particular embodiments, e.g. pre-recorded DVDs of films of Harry Potter and Ben Hur, will be considered to be product variants. Different media are taken to encompass similar content embodied in different products, e.g. one may acquire a recording of Aida on vinyl, cassette, CD, DVD, or MP3. Hardware and software are defined so as to encompass respectively equipment and content.

Product variants are said to be differentiated when two or more goods or services are essentially or generically the same, but can be individually identified, either through performance or aesthetic appeal, or are preferred differently by and between consumers on the grounds of those consumers' tastes or preferences. Thus, for example, cars are a differentiated product in terms of design, colour, size, speed, power, hard- or soft-top, etc. Similarly railways and airlines offer different classes of travel. Recorded music offers a vast choice of differentiated recordings, and there is an enormous choice of differentiated books on the market. Clothes are as much differentiated as furniture, food, restaurants, financial instruments, and insurance policies. In fact differentiated products are the norm.

There are two recognized types of product differentiation in the literature – vertical and horizontal (Tirole 1988).

Two product variants are considered vertically differentiated if, at a given price, all buyers prefer one rather than the other. In such a case the two goods can be objectively ranked in terms of quality. A classic example is first-class versus second-class rail travel.

Two product variants are considered horizontally differentiated if at a given price one is preferred by some consumers and the other preferred by others. In this case, the variants cannot be ranked objectively in terms of quality, but only subjectively. An example is milk chocolate versus plain chocolate.

Note that although a newly introduced vertically differentiated product variant can be judged better or worse than existing products, this is not possible with a new horizontally differentiated product variant which may be judged better by some and worse by others without an obvious quality ranking.[12] Thus, once product differentiation is allowed, a new variant will be a different but not necessarily an improved variant, and there will be no necessary correspondence between innovation (new product variants) and 'improvement'.

---

[12] Bentley et al. (2007), taking a very different line to that taken here, suggest that turnovers in 'pop charts' for records, baby names, and dog breeds can all be explained by the random copying of cultural variants between individuals with occasional innovation. To the economist such cultural factors might be considered the foundations that determine preferences but such foundations are not considered here.

It appears to be implicit in the OECD definitions of innovation that, unless a new product is in a completely different category to existing products, for a new product variant to be defined as a product innovation it must be vertically differentiated from other products in the market.[13] It also appears that to be considered as innovative any new product variant must have a functional improvement and the possibility that the introduction of a lower-quality vertically differentiated product may also be an innovation is ignored. The authors of the OECD definitions do not appear to define the introduction of new horizontally differentiated product variants as innovation. In fact in the second edition of the *Oslo Manual* (OECD 2002), new models of complex products, where changes were 'minor' in a technological sense, were considered to be product differentiation and then ruled out as innovation. Here it is argued instead that (*a*) horizontal product differentiation (which it has been shown may improve economic welfare for some or all by offering more desired products and more variety; see, e.g., Dixit and Stiglitz [1977]; Brynjolfsson et al. [2003]) is also innovative, which considerably broadens the scope of activities considered to be innovative and (*b*) a vertical innovation need not show functional improvement if it has a sufficiently lower price.

Thus, not only should aesthetic changes be considered as innovations, but also those changes may be horizontal or vertical in nature and, moreover, if vertical, may even offer lower quality rather than higher quality.

2.6 Judging the relative significance of soft innovations

Many new aesthetic and non-aesthetic products, processes, organizational changes, and marketing methods are introduced in economies over time. But not all such changes will be of significance. The various Oslo manuals have quite rightly tried to separate significant from non-significant innovations, offering guidelines as to how significance is to be judged. These manuals have emphasized the extent of change in functionality as the key to measuring significance.

As an economist, the primary or ultimate means by which one evaluates change is on the basis of the impact of that change on economic welfare (at the date of innovation or later), and that is the criterion of significance

[13] However, it does not necessarily follow that a new vertically differentiated product has to be a TPP innovation. This would only be so if the vertical differentiation arose from technological performance characteristics, whereas it may also arise from aesthetic characteristics.

chosen here. Appendix A2.1 to this chapter details the reasoning as to how changes in economic welfare are indicated by changes in producer and consumer surplus (and other related matters). It makes no difference with this approach whether the innovation represents a horizontal or vertically differentiated product or product variant; it is still the impact on welfare that is to be measured. The impact may come from either or both the supply and demand side of the market. For example, if a soft innovation has a large impact on the demand curve, it will have a large impact on welfare and will be considered significant, whereas if it has little impact it will be considered not significant.

The welfare consequences of the introductions of new products has recently[14] received theoretical and empirical attention from economists (in particular see Bresnahan and Gordon [1997]; Nevo [2001]; Hausman and Leonard [2002]). Petrin (2002) is a good example of how this approach can be formally applied. He estimates the change in consumer welfare in the United States from the introduction of the minivan (people carrier in European terminology) and infers the changes in producer surplus, with the results that suggest that in this case the introduction generated large welfare gains for consumers (calculated to be US$2.8 billion in 1982–4 prices over the five years 1984–8 inclusive) and a surplus for the innovators (of US$105 million on a similar basis) but partly at the expense of others. Other papers, mainly US based, focus on buyer benefits from new products in traditional markets covering a range of goods, including automobiles (e.g. Feenstra [1988]; Berry, Levinsohn, and Pakes [1993]), computers (Bresnahan 1986; Greenstein 1994), health care technology (Trajtenberg 1989), breakfast cereals (Hausman 1997a), telecommunications services (Hausman 1997b), cable television (Goolsbee and Petrin 2001), and cellular phones (Hausman 1999). In addition, Bresnahan (1986) and Brynjolfsson (1995) have looked at welfare gains from investments in IT as has Prince (2007).

In the current context there will be no specific attempts to calculate the welfare pay-offs from particular technologies. The data is not available for such exercises and in any case the thrust of the current work is to argue a wide case for the importance of soft innovation rather than a narrow case of the importance of single innovations. The welfare impact criteria is however a vital one. In the absence of actual measures of welfare impacts, throughout this work the impact on consumer and producer surplus of a given new product or product variant will be taken to be indicated by the

---

[14] Although the Social Savings approach, which is very similar, goes back further (see, e.g., White [1976]).

sales and/or market share realized by that product or product variant. It is termed the 'market impact criterion'[15] here and it is discussed further in Appendix A2.1.

Recommending a market impact test is in direct contrast to the current emphasis being placed on the long tail in the markets for creative products (Anderson 2006).[16] The long-tail approach argues that recent changes in technology, such as digitalization,[17] have enabled suppliers to stock a wider selection of titles more cheaply with the result that titles of limited popularity may remain available longer in the tail of sales. These titles in turn can collectively command a larger market share than previously. Brynjolfsson et al. (2003) show how the increased variety available can increase consumer welfare. More relevantly here, Brynjolfsson et al. (2007) argue that traditional markets exhibit an 80/20 rule i.e. the top selling 20 per cent of products represent 80 per cent of sales. By analysing data collected from a multi-channel retailing company, they showed empirical evidence that in the Internet channel, this rule needs to be modified to a 72/28 rule in order to fit the distribution of product sales in that channel. Although a significant change, this does not seem sufficient to invalidate approaches used in chapters later where significant innovations are those that are ranked in the top ten, twenty, or fifty best-sellers and the total number of products in the market are in the thousands or even millions.[18]

The *Oslo Manual* approach to judging the significance of product and process innovation (it is not made clear how one is recommended to judge the significance of marketing and organizational innovation) has largely relied on functionality to measure significance, relating for example to 'technical specifications, components and materials, incorporated software, user friendliness or other functional characteristics'. The greater the functional advance, the more significant is the innovation considered to be. This metric cannot be employed when looking at soft innovation as the advances there are aesthetic and not functional. Of course TPP innovation could alternatively be judged by the market impact test. It is clear

[15] The market impact test has the further benefit of indicating as of most significance those innovations that are most widely diffused in the market with the extent of the market impact being spread over time in accordance with the diffusion pattern. This neatly ties together the second and third stages of the Schumpeter trilogy.

[16] The contrast is such that in discussion the approach used here has been called the fathead approach.

[17] Brynjolfson et al. (2006) identify how on the supply side e-tailers' large and centralized warehousing allows for more offerings, while on the demand side, search engines and sampling tools are allowing customers to find products outside their normal area.

[18] Also at the time of writing the finding is being challenged. See entertainment.timesonline.co.uk/tol/arts_and_entertainment/music/article5380304.ece

that what is significant on a functionality test may not be significant on a market impact test. An obvious example is that Concorde was functionally significant but had an insignificant market impact. In addition a functionally significant advance in an insignificant sector may be market (welfare) irrelevant, whereas a minor functional advance in a large sector may have a considerable market (welfare) impact.

Other alternative views of significance may also be employed. For example, one may employ a measure of scientific significance that represents the contribution to knowledge of an advance. This is often implemented in science by the use of peer review and citations to judge significance of a piece of work. Of course what may be scientifically significant is not necessarily (or even likely or designed to be) of market significance, e.g. advances in astronomy. Scientific significance is of course of little relevance when considering the importance of soft innovations.

Another alternative view of significance is artistic significance. Just as it may be judged that one functional advance is more functionally significant than another, so it may be argued that one aesthetic advance is more artistically significant than another, e.g. Elvis was more significant than the Beatles, or Van Gogh was more significant than Andy Warhol. However, unlike with science, internal metrics for judging artistic significance are less well established. It may be possible to devise internal metrics,[19] in fact several metrics, such as, for example, influence on others, the number of imitators, or the extent of copying have been suggested; however, currently there seems to be no agreed metric that an external observer would be able to employ. Moreover, rankings by artistic significance rarely make allowance for horizontal artistic differentiation. In fact, some commentators, e.g. Carey (2005), offer a counter view where it is argued that that there are no absolute criteria of value and there are no independent canons of taste in the arts.

Even if it were possible to rank by artistic significance, there is no reason why artistic significance and market impact will correspond. Galenson (2005) argues that for major artists that there is a correlation between prices and artistic importance, and that the most highly priced art is made by the greatest artists.[20] However, this is contentious and although

[19] Although on the whole I am somewhat sceptical about these possibilities. The existence of such a metric means, for example, that one can say that in some ways white is better than black or soft is better than hard, and that seems unacceptable.

[20] Bowness (1989) argues further, but in a similar way, that one can see four progressive steps in the fame of an artist: peer recognition, critical recognition, patronage by dealers and collectors, and public acclaim. Making a distinction between artists who produce work for public art galleries or museums ('geniuses') and the artist who produces work for the marketplace ('journeyman'), it is further argued that it is only the museum artists whose work generates exceptional prices.

it may apply to fine art it is unlikely to generally be the case that artistic significance and market impact will correspond.[21] Hutter and Throsby (2008) argue that in fact there is a basic distinction between economic and cultural value. For example, it has been suggested that the market (demand) impact of another Rocky film (of very limited artistic significance) may be much greater than another film of Hamlet (of much greater artistic significance), and the market impact test would surely suggest that the former is more significant than the latter. It has also been suggested that the Harry Potter books are derivative and not artistically innovative although they have had great market success and the market impact test would consider them to be very significant. These interpretations are correct. From an economic welfare point of view, society makes its choices of how to spend its money and in the absence of invidious interpersonal comparisons of utility these choices reflect that the total welfare gains from the less artistic exceed those from the more artistic. In fact the approach which judges significance by market impact is similar to the approach of Cowen ([2000]; see also Cowen [2006]) who 'rather than trying to use aesthetic criteria to order art works on a high/low spectrum', examines how economic incentives affect the artist's choice of audience.

The choice of the market impact criterion of significance has generated more argument in seminar presentations than any other part of this book. In particular the 'arts' community has expressed considerable opposition to the approach and appears to prefer instead to judge significance on the basis of some artistic metric (although which metrics they refer to is not clear). There is this some hint of the 'art for art's sake' argument which suggests that the value of artistic advances cannot be measured in monetary terms. Rather than trying to resolve an argument that probably cannot be resolved, the view taken here is that the market impact approach is one well suited to economic analysis which is what this volume employs. The use of other tests of significance may well involve different approaches that are not pursued here.

Having selected an indicator of significance, the next stage is to be clear as to what precisely is covered by the term 'innovation'. The choices are twofold. First, innovation could be considered anything that is new, and then significant innovation is anything that is new with a significant market impact. Second, one may define anything that is new and significant (in terms of market impact) as innovation. For the purposes of exposition below the former approach is chosen. Thus, innovation is

---

[21] Ashenfelter (2008) and Ali et al. (2008) make a similar case on quality and prices with respect to fine wines.

considered anything that is new, and those innovations with most impact are called 'significant innovations'. It is also useful to term the introduction of new horizontally and vertically differentiated products as horizontal product innovation and vertical product innovation respectively.[22] Innovation may thus encompass the introduction of a new horizontally differentiated product, a new higher-quality vertically differentiated product, and also, and often ignored, a new lower-quality vertically differentiated product that could be very significant if its price is low enough.

2.7 Science

In order to gain some insight into the data available about innovation and the innovation-generating process it is necessary to clarify a few more terms. This section looks at science and the science base. The national science and engineering base is generally defined to include:

- The university system
- The support system for basic research
- Public good R&D activities – funding programmes and institutions generally directed towards areas such as health, the environment, and defence
- Strategic R&D activities – funding programmes and institutions directed towards 'pre-competitive R&D' or generic technologies
- Non-appropriable innovation support – funding programmes and institutions directed towards research in areas where it is difficult for individual enterprises to appropriate sufficient benefit from their own in-house research
- The specialized technical training system

The extent of scientific effort is generally measured by the value of the inputs to the activity. Funding for such activities performed in the science and engineering base in the United Kingdom for 2003/4 is £5,486 million (including a small sum for support of the arts and humanities).

Innovation may be considered conceptually to be different from science, but the usual distinction made is that between science and

---

[22] These definitions are to be distinguished as different from those currently being used in the new growth theory literature (Jones 1999) where the vertical innovation process is defined as the introduction of a better-quality version of existing products and/or of their production processes and the horizontal innovation process is defined as the creation of completely new product lines. While the former is similar to the definition here the latter is not.

technology. There have been many attempts to define such a distinction, of which some offering a view whereby science in some sense precedes technology, providing the knowledge base upon which technology feeds and creates new producers and processes. This view is, however, somewhat discredited as being too associated with a linear view of innovative activity.

Rather than taking the linear approach, the view of Dasgupta and David (1994) that science is what scientists do, whereas technology is what technologists do, is more convincing. The apparent circularity of this definition becomes clear when it is further argued that scientists' and technologists' activities are governed by different incentives, the former by peer review and esteem and the latter by private profit-seeking. Thus, whereas scientists undertake research in order to gain esteem through publications and dissemination, technologists seek to gain profits through secrecy and market exploitation. The implication is that science has different objectives as compared to technology and moreover is less market oriented. It would thus make little sense to attempt to judge the significance of, or measure the output of, scientific activity by its market impact as the market is either (*a*) distant in time or (*b*) not relevant to the criteria driving the scientific activity. Aghion et al. (2005) extend this argument by contending that academic science allows scientists to freely pursue their own interests and can be indispensable for early-stage research, but the ability of the private sector to direct scientists towards higher pay-off activities makes it more attractive for later-stage research. It is implicit in this view that science and arts will be potential sources for soft innovations.

2.8 Research and development

International standards for the measurement of R&D were first put forward forty years ago in the *Frascati Manual*. The third and the latest edition of that manual, OECD (2002), deals exclusively with the measurement of human and financial resources devoted to research and experimental development (R&D). The formal definition of R&D is as follows:

Research and experimental development (R&D) comprise creative work undertaken on a systematic basis in order to increase the stock of knowledge, including knowledge of man, culture and society, and the use of this stock of knowledge to devise new applications. (p. 30)

Note that the definition covers both science and technology, i.e. basic research, applied research, and experimental development, and by including the phrase 'knowledge of man, culture and society' thereby includes the humanities and social sciences.

It is important to realize that the definition of R&D excludes a number of innovation activities.[23] In particular the manual states that it excludes 'other innovation activities' defined as

all those scientific, technical, commercial and financial steps, other than R&D, necessary for the implementation of new or improved products or services and the commercial use of new or improved processes. These include acquisition of technology (embodied and disembodied), tooling up and industrial engineering, industrial design n.e.c., other capital acquisition, production start-up and marketing for new and improved products. (p. 33)

The basic criterion for distinguishing R&D from related activities is the presence in R&D of an appreciable element of novelty and the resolution of scientific and/or technological uncertainty, i.e. when the solution to a problem is not readily apparent to someone familiar with the basic stock of common knowledge and techniques for the area concerned. (p. 34).

The reason for quoting at length is that these definitions require that R&D involves 'the resolution of scientific and/or technological uncertainty' and excludes 'industrial design . . . and marketing for new and improved products'. Thus, expenditure on activities that are not devoted to either science (including the arts and the social sciences) or to technological product and process innovation (i.e. excluding marketing innovations and organizational innovation) is not to be counted as R&D expenditures. This view is reinforced by the discussion in the manual regarding the R&D activities in the mechanical engineering industry:

In small and medium-size enterprises . . . there is usually no special R&D department, and R&D problems are mostly dealt with under the general heading 'design and drawing'. If calculations, designs, working drawings and operating instructions are made for the setting up and operating of pilot plants and prototypes, they should be included in R&D. If they are carried out for the preparation, execution and maintenance of production standardisation (e.g. jigs, machine tools) or to promote the sale of products (e.g. offers, leaflets, catalogues of spare parts), they should be excluded from R&D. (p. 35)

---

[23] Although even now there is discussion of how R&D should be defined and measured. A recent aspect of this discussion relating to the intangible aspect of R&D can be found in Galindo-Rueda (2007) and Haskel (2007). The Bureau of Economic Analysis (BEA) and the National Science Foundation (NSF) argue that Gross Domestic Product (GDP) would be nearly 3 per cent higher each year between 1959 and 2004 – US$284 billion higher in 2004 – if R&D spending were treated as investment in the US national income and product accounts (National Science Foundation 2007).

The manual proceeds to discuss more fully the problems of identifying R&D in services and argues that

[d]efining the boundaries of R&D in service activities is difficult, for two main reasons: first, it is difficult to identify projects involving R&D; and, second, the line between R&D and other innovative activities which are not R&D is a tenuous one. Among the many innovative projects in services, those that constitute R&D result in new knowledge or use of knowledge to devise new applications, in keeping with the definition [above]. . . . In many cases, R&D findings in service industries are embodied in software which is not necessarily innovative from the technical point of view but innovates by virtue of the functions that it performs. (p. 48)

The outcome of this discussion is that the definition of R&D is not confined to the manufacturing sector, but also encompasses services production and delivery and, includes both science and/or basic research. However, expenditure on those activities that have an aesthetic rather than a techno-logical or scientific component, and which we have called soft innovation (including product differentiation, activities such as design, and other aspects of marketing innovation), are not defined as R&D and are thus presumably not reflected in the data on R&D expenditure. The process of generating soft innovation is thus not measured in the R&D statistics. To the extent that this is so, R&D data, which has long been a key policy metric, gives an underesti-mate of total innovative activity and provides an unbalanced picture of overall innovative activity.

For background purposes, Table 2.2 provides data on Business Enterprise R&D (BERD) carried out[24] by industry in the United Kingdom in the period 1997–2005 in fixed prices (source www.dti.gov.uk/files/file22143.xls). It might be noted that the manufacturing total has varied between about £10 and £10.5 million in 2005 prices after 2000. Employment generated by R&D in the business enterprise sector for 2005 is estimated to be 147,000. With the additional funding for R&D performed in the science and engineering base the UK's gross domestic expenditure on R&D was £21.8 billion. This represents an increase, in cash terms, of 7 per cent from the level recorded in 2004. In real terms gross domestic expenditure on R&D increased by 5 per cent between 2004 and 2005. In 2005, expenditure on R&D was 1.76 per cent of gross domestic product, an increase on the previous year (ONS 2007a). In addition to BERD, the other performers of R&D were government (£1.3

---

[24] An interesting distinction to be always held in mind with R&D figures is that between spending and performance. R&D may be funded from the United Kingdom but performed overseas (out of the United Kingdom). National spending on R&D may thus not equal total R&D performed. Similarly funding by government and enterprise may not equal R&D performed by government and enterprise. Useful indicators of differences can be found in Bulli (2008).

Table 2.2 Business enterprise R&D in the United Kingdom, 1997–2005, current and 2005 prices

	CASH TERMS (£ million)								
	1997	1998	1999	2000	2001	2002	2003	2004	2005
TOTAL	9,556	10,133	11,302	11,510	11,978	12,469	12,677	12,816	13,410
Manufacturing: total	7,608	8,142	8,995	9,231	9,622	9,697	9,791	10,073	10,300
Chemicals	2,831	2,926	3,253	3,528	3,646	3,758	3,750	3,831	3,925
Mechanical engineering	709	730	712	776	782	850	775	818	802
Electrical mechanical	1,181	1,320	1,335	1,558	1,519	1,360	1,317	1,248	1,277
Transport equipment	990	1,020	1,235	1,094	1,020	1,047	995	934	895
Aerospace	893	1,039	1,237	1,091	1,320	1,370	1,652	2,005	2,197
Other manufacturing	1,004	1,108	1,222	1,183	1,335	1,312	1,302	1,237	1,204
Services	1,652	1,668	1,972	1,905	2,126	2,499	2,643	2,516	2,892
Other: total	295	323	335	374	230	273	244	227	217
Agriculture & forest; fishing	84	102	115	135	121	147	136	..	127
Extractive industries	44	41	42	46	38	45	41	36	43
Electricity, gas, & water	30	140	137	160	41	46	36	21	15
Construction	38	39	41	34	30	35	30		33

	REAL TERMS (2005 PRICES, £ million)								
	1997	1998	1999	2000	2001	2002	2003	2004	2005
TOTAL	11,536	11,929	13,042	13,098	13,314	13,444	13,274	13,059	13,410
Manufacturing: Total	9,184	9,585	10,380	10,504	10,695	10,455	10,252	10,264	10,300
Chemicals	3,418	3,445	3,754	4,015	4,053	4,052	3,926	3,904	3,925
Mechanical engineering	856	859	822	883	869	916	811	834	802
Electrical machinery	1,426	1,554	1,541	1,773	1,688	1,466	1,379	1,272	1,277
Transport equipment	1,195	1,201	1,425	1,245	1,134	1,129	1,042	952	895
Aerospace	1,078	1,223	1,427	1,241	1,467	1,477	1,730	2,043	2,197
Other manufacturing	1,212	1,304	1,410	1,346	1,484	1,415	1,363	1,260	1,204
Services	1,994	1,964	2,276	2,168	2,363	2,694	2,767	2,564	2,892
Other: total	356	380	387	426	256	294	255	231	217
Agriculture, forestry, & fishing	101	120	133	154	134	158	142		127
Extractive industries	53	48	48	52	42	49	43	37	43
Electricity, gas, & water	157	165	158	182	46	50	38	21	15
Construction	46	46	47	39	33	38	31		33

Source: ONS (2007)

billion), research councils (£1.1 billion), higher education (£5.6 billion), and private non-profit organizations (£0.5 billion).

2.9 Patenting

Patenting is a means by which inventors may protect their intellectual property rights for a proscribed period of time. Frequently the extent of

TPP innovations is measured by the level of patenting activity, sometimes supplemented with data reflecting payment of renewal fees as an indicator of quality. In the United Kingdom, only advances of an industrial nature can be patented (these advances may not even encompass all of TPP activity). Aesthetic improvements cannot be patented. Although there are other instruments that may be used for IPR protection of soft innovation (see Chapter 10), this means that one definitely cannot use patent data to measure soft innovation. Outside the United Kingdom, in say the United States, the picture is a little different. In the United States, utility patents may be considered the same as UK patents and will not encompass soft innovations. However, there are also design patents in the United States that may enable some soft innovations to be patented. These design patents match UK and EU design rights (see Chapter 10).

2.10 Conclusions

This chapter has defined soft innovation as comprising of innovations that have an impact on aesthetic or intellectual appeal. Two faces of soft innovation have been identified: innovation in aesthetic products and aesthetic innovation in products that are primarily functional. The definition includes changes in products that impact on sensory perception encompassing sight, touch, smell, sound, and the intellect. Comparisons have been drawn with the OECD-defined concepts of (technological) product and process innovation, organizational innovation, and marketing innovation, and it was argued that such prior constructs do not cover all of soft innovation and in particular innovation in aesthetic products. However, the concept of marketing innovation does include some portion of the soft innovation concept and thus both validates considering changes of an aesthetic nature as innovation and provides some rationale for considering soft innovation as relevant.

It has been observed that many soft innovations will be embodied in new differentiated products and the chapter proceeded to draw a distinction between horizontal and vertical soft innovations. Basically an innovation is considered as something that is new; however, just because something is new it is not necessarily significant.

The significance of a soft innovation is determined by its market impact as opposed to the standard OECD criterion of changed functionality (or other criteria such as scientific or artistic significance). The market impact criterion allows that the significance is determined by the impact of the innovation on the sum of producer and consumer surpluses.

The argument can of course be turned around. If it is accepted that significant innovations are those that have a significant impact on economic welfare, then because economic welfare arises not just from functionality but also from aesthetic and intellectual dimensions of products, it is natural to consider soft innovation as important as TPP innovation.

As the cultural industries are the main source of aesthetic products and thus a main source of soft innovation Appendix A2.2 provides some definitions and indicators of the size of that sector in terms of number of businesses (7.2 per cent of the register in 2005), value added (7.3 per cent of GDP), growth of value added (5 per cent p.a.), exports (4.3 per cent of the total), and employment (in excess of 1 million jobs). Although this does not reveal the whole footprint of soft innovation, it becomes immediately clear that economic activities related to such innovation will be quantitatively significant.

Some parts of those activities that are termed soft innovation here have been identified by other names by previous authors (e.g. formal innovation or artistic innovation). By bringing all such innovations under a common label, the potential total extent of such activity can be realized. Moreover, common categorization of the different activities being discussed emphasizes the extent to which ignoring such activities can bias the picture of the direction and extent of total innovation activity in the economy. The potential for under-recording of overall innovation if soft innovation is ignored, as it has largely been to date, is extensive. In addition if all innovation is considered to be functional or at the TPP end of the spectrum, then attitudes to innovation and innovation policy will be too blinkered and actual soft innovation activity, its future potential, and perhaps its need for support will be ignored (mainly in favour of TPP innovation) and probably at the cost of a potential loss of economic well-being.

For these arguments to carry weight, however, it is necessary to show not only that soft innovation exists as a concept but that it also quantitatively significant. Chapters 3–5 therefore consider the means by which the extent of soft innovation may be more precisely quantified or measured and also provide some indicators using the metrics suggested.

APPENDIX A2.1

THE MARKET-BASED APPROACH TO VALUING THE SIGNIFICANCE OF SOFT INNOVATION

A2.1.1 Introduction

Economics is a very broad subject and brings under its wings a wide range of different approaches. Thus, even if one only looks at the innovation literature there are approaches using ecological economics, Austrian economics, evolutionary economics, and others. Here, however, primarily as a reflection of by far the largest school of economics, the approach concentrates on the school that is called 'neo-classical'. The fundamentals of this school are that firms and consumers are rational, with firms pursuing profits and consumers maximizing utility; that utility and production functions exhibit the required convexity (declining marginal utility and marginal productivities with appropriate scale economies); and that markets clear with equilibrium between supply and demand. The material in this section can be found in most basic economics textbooks (a good example is Pindyck and Rubinfield [1998]).

In such a neo-classical world, without any uncertainty and with perfect competition (all players, whether on the demand or supply side, are price takers and individual behaviour cannot affect the market outcome), firms will supply to the market in such a way that at any price they will choose an output level that equates price and marginal cost of production and buyers will demand an amount that brings the marginal utility of an extra unit of consumption equal to the price. The resultant demand and supply curves are drawn in Figure A2.1.1 and market clearing under the law of only one price (different outcomes are possible[25]) ensures that price and output in this market will equal $(P_1 Q_1)$.

Economics measures 'value' in a market in relation to welfare. The total net welfare generated in the market at $(P_1 Q_1)$ is the difference between the sum of the utility gains of all purchasers and the total opportunity costs of the resources utilized to make output Q_1 (including intra-equilibrium purchases), which is measured by the sum of two areas. The first, termed 'consumer surplus' is the area between the demand curve and the line where price equals P_1 (ACE) that measures the extent to which buyers get utility gains from consumption in excess of the

---

[25] For example, Leslie (2004) shows how Broadway theatres discriminate with tickets and may charge different prices to different customers.

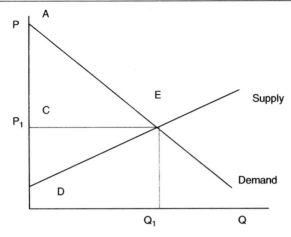

Figure A2.1.1 Market equilibrium: competition

(equilibrium) price they pay for the product. The second, called 'producer surplus' (or profits), is the area between the supply curve and the line where price equals P_1 (CDE) and measures the extent to which producers get revenues greater than the resource costs of that production. The sum of producer and consumer surplus (AED) is a measure of the welfare contribution of this product to total economic welfare and a measure of 'value' of the product.

The market price P_1 equals the opportunity cost (marginal cost) of the resources used to produce *the final unit purchased* as well as the marginal gain to social welfare (the welfare of society as a whole) as measured by *the utility gain of the marginal buyer* and thus equals the marginal welfare contribution provided by the last unit made and consumed.

The first obvious implication of this approach is that if one considers price as a measure of the 'value' of a product, then even in a competitive market, as modelled here, price and value will only be equal at equilibrium, and that too only in a marginal sense with price equal to the marginal utility gain of the marginal consumer and also equal to the marginal opportunity cost of the marginal resources used. Except in exceptional circumstances, the total value to society of the product (the sum of consumer and producer surplus) cannot be implied from the price alone. Price and 'value' are synonymous in a marginal but not in a total sense.

In the absence of competition the relationship of price and economic value is more complex. Assume that the demand curve is as before, but, as it is often common to do, assume the marginal cost of production (*MC*) is a constant and marginal cost equals average cost (*AC*). If the market were competitive the price would equal marginal cost (*MC*), profits would be zero and the welfare generated would be equal to the area under the demand curve at $P = MC$. Assume, however,

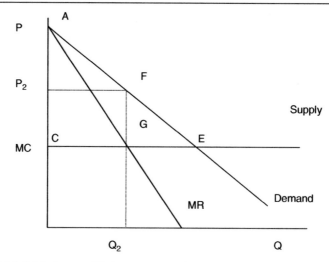

Figure A2.1.2 Market equilibrium: monopoly

that there is only one supplier of this product and that supplier maximizes profits by setting a price such that marginal revenue equals marginal cost, with market clearing at P_2Q_2 (see Figure A2.1.2).

Under monopoly the market price will be higher than under competition and output lower (in this example the output level is half that under competition). The marginal unit is sold at price P_2 at which price marginal revenue equals marginal cost. Thus under monopoly the price still equals the marginal utility gain of the marginal buyer but that is now greater as fewer units are being sold, and thus the marginal unit provides greater marginal utility to the marginal buyer than under competition. However, the market price no longer equals the opportunity costs of the marginal resources used to produce that final unit of output, instead the price exceeds that amount. Thus, the equality of price and opportunity costs is only a property of competitive markets.

Under monopoly, the sum of consumer (area AFP_2) and producer surpluses (area P_2FCG, which would be zero under competition in this case of constant costs) including the welfare gain of intra-marginal buyers, that is the welfare contribution or economic value, is the area AFGC which is less than it would be under competition. The difference relative to the competitive position is the triangle EFG which is usually called the monopoly welfare loss triangle.

In essence the total value of a product as encompassed by economic analysis equals the sum of consumer and producer surplus, that is the utility gain to consumers and profit gains to producers from the existence of the product. This value will depend upon the shape of the supply and demand curves and also whether the market is monopolized or competitive. At the margin, however, the marginal value from having one extra unit of the product available equals the price under competition which in turn equals the marginal opportunity costs of production; but in the absence of competition the price although still equal to the marginal utility gain of the marginal consumer will exceed the marginal opportunity cost of production and so the marginal values differ on both the supply and demand sides.

A2.1.2 Soft innovation and the demand curve

For illustrative purposes soft innovation in its very simplest form can be described as the innovation (e.g. a redesign of a non-aesthetic product) that makes a product more desirable to consumers and increases the utility from consumption of that product and thus the consumers' willingness to pay. Such changes may have an impact on all consumers when the change entails what is described as vertical product differentiation (or innovation), or on only some when the change is what is described as horizontal product differentiation or innovation.

For the sake of simplicity, let us assume that an aesthetic improvement in the product of a monopolized industry shifts the demand curve to the right. Assuming the cost curve does not change, there will be a new equilibrium in which the market price will be either as before or higher, consumer surplus will increase, and producer surplus will be either as before or greater. In other words economic welfare will have increased. The aesthetic improvement can be valued by this increase in welfare. Note that in general the increase in welfare (the sum of the increase in consumer and producer surpluses) will be greater than the increase in producer surplus, and thus the profit gains alone may offer an incentive to innovate that is too small from a welfare point of view, i.e. less than the social value of the gain.

It is not simple to formally extend this reasoning to competitive markets, for markets with differentiated products will not be competitive in the normal sense. However, one might argue that each supplier in a differentiated product industry may be considered a monopolist in the supply of its own differentiated product, with competition from other such products reflected in the firm-level demand curve faced. Soft innovation (by one firm) will shift the firm's demand curve to the right, and, pursuing the logic shown in Figure A2.1.2 (unless the slope of the demand curve is changed), price will (holding MC constant) be higher, output will be higher, and producer and consumer surpluses will both be higher. Economic welfare will again be increased. Note however that once more the gain in profits (consumer surplus) will be less than the gain in total welfare.

In each case, soft innovation increases welfare. The value of the innovation equals the difference in welfare (the sum of consumer and producer surpluses) with and without the innovation. That gain however is usually less than the producer surplus (although if an innovation allows monopolization that might not be so).

A2.1.3 Soft innovation and the supply curve

It is less common, but soft innovation may (also) cause the cost curve to move. The movement may be such that the new product is more expensive to produce, in which case the gain in economic welfare (and producer surplus) will be reduced. This would be the case if the new product is more difficult to make or involves more resources. Alternatively a new product could be cheaper to produce (or that the soft innovation is a process innovation that lowers costs) which will reinforce the demand effects and generate greater increases in economic value or welfare. Neither possibility however is sufficiently complicated to merit further particular discussion.

A2.1.4 The significance of soft innovation

Soft innovation may have an impact on either the demand or the supply side of the market and as it does so the market price, output, and economic welfare will change. An innovation that has a significant impact on the market will have a significant impact on welfare and as such will be of significant value. As we are unable to measure this welfare impact, throughout this volume we instead substitute a market impact test in which sales (e.g. of a product variant) will be used as a proxy for the welfare gain, and higher-selling innovations will be considered to have a greater impact than lesser-selling innovations. It is worth noting, however, that that the market impact test will reflect both the demand and supply side of the market and not just the demand side and thus sales are not always going to be a valid proxy for welfare impact (i.e. changes in the sum of consumer and producer surplus). For example the sales may be gained by a loss-making price. However, in the absence of detailed knowledge of product variant prices, cost functions, and consumer utility functions, which may enable more precision, the sales measure is a useful approximation.

APPENDIX A2.2
THE CREATIVE INDUSTRIES

A2.2.1 The creative industries, an introduction

In a growing general literature (see, e.g., Higgs et al. [2008]), a particular set of industries is attracting more attention than has previously been the case. It is appropriate as well that these industries are given special attention in this book. Although not the only source and definitely not the only users of soft innovations, it is clear that there are a set of industries that are at the heart of the process of soft innovation. These industries have a number of potential labels, but the term 'creative industries' now tends to be quite widely used. This appendix provides some definitions and discussion of these industries as well as some indicators of their size and relative importance in the economy as a whole.

In the United Kingdom, the Department for Culture Media and Sports (DCMS) has undertaken much work related to classification and measurement of the creative industries, and this material has been used here. The reader is referred to http://www.culture.gov.uk for fuller details. In addition, estimates of key economic indicators are available through publications such as DCMS (2006). Further, recent data on employment in the sector is available from Higgs et al. (2008). There is also a growing body of material relating to measures of the creative sector in other economies (e.g. Statistics New Zealand [2006]). However, it should be stated that there is considerable discussion as to appropriate measures and boundaries (see Andari et al. [2007]) and thus all numbers presented here come with a health warning.

The DCMS definitions initially describe a set of industries that are termed the 'cultural sector', encompassing seven 'activities':

- Audio-visual (includes film, TV, radio, new media, and music)
- Books and Press
- Heritage (includes museums, libraries, archives, and historic environment)
- Performance
- Sport
- Tourism
- Visual arts

On the basis of which three 'sub-sectors' are defined:

- The arts (includes galleries, architecture, design, and crafts)

- Creative industries (the audio-visual domain plus books, the press, performance, and the visual arts)
- Sport and tourism

Data on the cultural sector is collected through the Standard Industrial Classification (SIC 2003), which is based principally on output defined as the result of an industrial process, for example 'the wholesale and retail trade' or 'manufacturing industries', rather than the final market. Thus, using the SIC to describe industries that are understood in terms of their market is problematic. Often, one can only identify elements of a particular cultural domain; these then have to be artificially re-aggregated. The printing and publishing industry is illustrative of the difficulties faced, as the SIC considers the industry to be producing printed and other related output. There is no mention in the list of activities of that industry of those activities behind the material that is actually being printed or reproduced, e.g. writing. That is because the creation of material to be printed or published is classified as taking place in SIC 92, Other Community Social and Personal Service Activities, rather than in printing and publishing. Within publishing itself one may thus observe TPP innovations, such as the introduction of new printing methods, different manuscript transfer methods, or different distribution methods; or soft innovations such as repackaging of a previous edition. What one would not find is the activity that leads to the writing of a new volume of Harry Potter. Table A2.2.1 reproduces the DCMS Table of Industries considered as the cultural sector.

Table A2.2.1 The cultural sector

VISUAL ART	FUNCTION
52.48/6 Retail sale in commercial galleries – new code in SIC 03	Dissemination
52.50/1 Retail sale of antiques, including antique books – previously retail of second-hand goods in stores	Dissemination
74.20/1 Architectural activities	Creation
74.87/2 Specialty design activities including fashion, interior, graphics – previously included in 74.87/2 SIC 92	Creation
74.87/3 Activities of exhibitions and fair organizers	Exhibition/reception
92.31/9 Other artistic and literary creation and interpretation	Creation
NFW Production of craft-based artefacts	Making
NFW Manufacture of relevant capital goods (e.g. artists paint and materials)	Making
NFW Galleries, craft fairs, antique markets	Exhibition/Reception
NFW Sale and resale of antiques at auction	Dissemination
NFW Education and training for fine arts, crafts, architecture, arts press, and criticism, etc.	Education/understanding
PERFORMANCE	
92.31/1 Live theatrical presentation	Making
92.32 Operation of arts facilities	Exhibition/reception
92.34/1 Dance halls and dance instructor activities	Exhibition/reception
92.34/9 Other entertainment activities, n.e.c. including circus production, puppet shows, rodeos, activities of shooting galleries, firework displays, etc. (also includes training of circus animals)	Exhibition/reception

NFW Playwriting, scenography	Creation
NFW Education and training for theatre, dance, circus, mime, puppetry; criticism, etc. (92.34/9 includes animal training for circuses)	Education/understanding

AUDIO-VISUAL

22.14 Publishing of sound recordings	Making
22.31 Reproduction of sound recordings	Making
22.32 Reproduction of video recordings	Making
22.33 Reproduction of computer media	Making
24.64 Manufacture of photographic chemical material	Making
24.65 Manufacture of prepared unrecorded media	Making
32.1 Manufacture of electronic valves and tubes and other electronic components	Making
32.20/2 Manufacture of TV and radio transmitters	Making
32.3 Manufacture of TV and radio receivers, sound or video recording or reproducing apparatus, etc.	Making
33.40/3 Manufacture of cinematographic equipment	Making
36.3 Manufacture of musical instruments	Making
51.43/1 Wholesale of records tapes, CDs, videos, and playback equipment	Dissemination
51.43/9 Wholesale or radios and TVs and other electrical appliances nec	Dissemination
51.47/5 Wholesale of musical instruments	Dissemination
51.47/6 Wholesale of photographic goods	Dissemination
52.45 Includes retail sale of TV goods and radios	Dissemination
52.48/2 Retail sales of photographic, optical and precision equipment and office supplies	Dissemination
72.21 Software publishing	Dissemination
72.22 Other software consultancy and supply	Creation
74.40 Advertising	Creation
71.40/3 Renting of radios, TVs, video recorders, and DVD players	Dissemination
71.40/4 Renting of records and other pre-recorded media	Dissemination
71.40/5 Renting of video tapes and DVDs	Dissemination
74.81/2 Portrait photographic activities – previously other portrait photographic activities	Creation
74.81/3 Other specialist photography	Creation
74.81/4 Film processing – previously coded in 74.81/9 SIC 92	Creation
74.81/9 Photographic activities NEC	Creation
92.11/1 Motion picture production on film or video tape	Creation
92.11/9 Other motion picture and video production activities	Creation
92.12 Motion picture and video distribution	Dissemination
92.13 Motion picture projection	Exhibition/Reception
92.20/1 Radio activities	Creation
92.20/2 Television activities	Creation
92.72/1 Casting activities included previously 92.72 other recreational activities NEC SIC 92	Creation
NFW Publishing of leisure software	Making
NFW Production of new media or multimedia	Making
NFW Retail of recorded music, film, video, and leisure software	Dissemination
NFW Picture and film libraries and archives	Archiving/Preserving
NFW Education and training for broadcast, film, music, games; criticism related to all, etc.	Education/Understanding
NFW Screenplay and film development	Creation
NFW Leisure software design/development	Creation
NFW Research and development	Creation

(Continued)

Table A2.2.1 Continued

BOOKS AND PRESS

22.11 Publishing of books	Making
22.12 Publishing of newspapers	Making
22.13 Publishing of journals and periodicals	Making
22.15 Other publishing	Making
22.21 Printing of newspapers	Making
22.22 Printing nec	Making
22.23 Bookbinding– previously bookbinding and finishing SIC 92	Making
22.24 Pre-press activities – previously plate making and composition SIC 92	Making
22.25 Ancillary activities related to printing – previously other activities relating to printing SIC 92	Making
24.30/2 Manufacture of printing ink	Making
52.47 Retail sale of books, newspapers	Dissemination
52.50/9 Retail sale of other second-hand goods.	Dissemination
92.40 New agencies activities	Making
Literary and book fairs and festivals	Exhibition/reception
Education and training for journalism, creative writing, printing, publishing; literary press and criticism, etc.	Education/understanding
Activities of literary creation	Creation

HERITAGE

92.51 Library and archive activities	Dissemination
92.52/1 Museum activities	Exhibition/reception
92.52/2 Preservation of historical sites and buildings	Archiving/preserving
92.53 Botanical and zoological gardens and nature reserve activities	Exhibition/reception
NFW Heritage, museum and tourism services (refer to technical report for further information)	Creation
NFW Conservation science; painting, manuscript, book, textile, and furniture restoration	Archiving/preserving
NFW Education and training aspects	Education/understanding

SPORT

36.40 Manufacture of sports goods	Making
52.48/5 Retail sale of sports goods games and toys	Dissemination
71.40/1 Renting of sporting and recreational equip	Dissemination
92.61/1 Operation of ice rinks and roller-skating rinks	Exhibition/reception
92.61/9 Operation of sports arenas and stadiums NEC	Exhibition/reception
92.62/1 Activities of racehorse owners	Making
92.62/9 Other sporting activities nec	Making
92.72/9 Other recreational activities nec	Exhibition/Reception
93.04 Physical well-being activities	Exhibition/Reception
NFW Training, instruction, education, media, etc.	Education/Understanding
NFW Design, development of sports programmes and events	Creation
NFW Activities of gyms and health clubs	Making

TOURISM

34.20/3 Manufacture of caravans	Making
36.50/1 Manufacture of professional and arcade games	Making
55.10/1 Hotels and motels with restaurant (licensed) – previously 55.11/1	Making
55.10/2 Hotel and motels with restaurant (unlicensed) – previously 55.11/2	Making
55.10/3 Hotel and motels without restaurant – previously 55.12	Making
55.21 Youth hostels and mountain refuges	Making
55.22 Camping sites including caravan sites	Making

55.23/1 Holiday centres and villages	Making
55.23/2 Other self-catering holiday accommodation	Making
55.23/9 Other tourist or short-stay accommodation	Making
55.30/1 Licensed restaurants	Making
55.40/1 Licensed clubs	Making
62.20/1 Non-scheduled passenger air transport	Dissemination
63.3 Activities of travel agencies and tour operators	Creation
92.33 Fair and amusement park activities	Exhibition/Reception
92.71 Gambling and betting activities	Exhibition/Reception
NFW Education and training of service providers, etc.	Education/Understanding

Of the industries in the cultural sector only some are of interest here. Excluding sport and tourism from the cultural sector yields a definition of 'the creative industries' (the definition is slightly wider in scope than that used above) encompassing advertising, architecture, art and antiques, crafts, design, designer fashion, video films and photography, music and the visual and performing arts, publishing, software, computer games and electronic publishing, radio, and TV.

A2.2.2 The number of creative businesses

As illustrated in Table A2.2.2, the DCMS data indicates that in 2005 there were an estimated 117,500 businesses in the Creative Industries on the Inter-Departmental

Table A2.2.2 Numbers of businesses in the creative industries, United Kingdom, 1997–2005

Year	Adv	Arch	A & A	Des	VFP	MVPA	Pub	SC & EP	R & TV	TOTAL[1]
1997	10,400	3,400	1,500	1,400	4,800	32,600	7,000	49,500	2,300	**112,900**
1998	10,300	3,300	1,600	1,300	5,500	32,500	6,800	52,600	2,300	**116,200**
1999	10,000	3,400	1,700	1,300	6,000	32,200	6,800	55,700	2,700	**119,800**
2000	10,000	3,300	1,800	1,300	6,500	32,500	6,700	56,700	3,000	**121,800**
2001	10,100	3,100	1,800	1,300	6,800	32,600	6,700	56,100	3,400	**121,900**
2002	10,100	3,000	1,800	1,300	7,400	32,300	6,700	55,800	3,600	**122,000**
2003	10,100	3,500	1,800	1,300	7,900	31,500	6,700	53,700	4,000	**120,500**
2004	9,800	4,100	1,700	1,400	8,000	30,100	6,500	49,100	4,200	**114,900**
2005	9,900	4,700	1,700	1,400	8,600	29,000	6,700	51,200	4,400	**117,500**

Source: http://www.culture.gov.uk

Note: The codes for the abbreviations in the table are:

Adv	Advertising
Arch	Architecture
A & A	Art and antiques
Crafts	Crafts
Des	Design
Fash	Designer fashion
VFP	Video film and photography
MVPA	Music and the visual and performing arts
Pub	Publishing
SC & EP	Software, computer games and electronic publishing
R & TV	Radio and TV

Business Register (IDBR). This represents 7.2 per cent of all companies on the IDBR, although the true proportion of enterprises that are in the creative industries is likely to be higher as certain sectors such as crafts contain predominantly small businesses. Around two-thirds of the businesses in the creative industries are contained within two sectors: software, computer games, and electronic publishing (51,200 companies) and music and the visual & performing arts (29,000 companies).

A2.2.3 Output and exports in the creative industries, United Kingdom

Using the DCMS definitions, Table A2.2.3 details gross value added in current and 2000 prices, growth in value added at fixed prices, and also exports for the creative industries. The data indicate that in 2004 in the United Kingdom the creative industries accounted for 7.3 per cent of Gross Value Added (GVA), having grown by an average in real terms of 5 per cent per annum between 1997 and 2004 compared to an average of 3 per cent for the whole of the economy over this period. Three sectors showed above-average growth across all the creative industries: software, computer games & electronic publishing (9 per cent p.a.), radio & TV (8 per cent p.a.), and art & antiques (7 per cent p.a.). Exports by the

Table A2.2.3 Output and exports in the creative industries, United Kingdom

Year	Adv	Arch	A & A	Crafts	Des	Fash	VFP	MVPA	Pu	SC & EP	R & TV	TOTAL*
GVA at current prices (£ million)												
2000	6,100	3,500	350	n/a	6,500	360	2,100	3,200	8,400	14,800	5,900	51,300
2001	5,500	3,600	390	n/a	6,700	320	1,800	3,100	8,800	16,300	6,700	53,300
2002	5,400	3,400	430	n/a	5,900	320	2,100	3,300	8,300	16,900	6,800	52,700
2003	5,200	4,000	470	n/a	5,300	330	2,400	3,600	8,600	19,800	6,200	55,700
2004	5,100	4,000	490	n/a	3,900	380	2,300	3,600	9,200	20,700	7,100	56,900
% of UK GVA												
2000	0.9	0.5	0.05	n/a	1.0	0.05	0.3	0.5	1.3	2.3	0.9	7.8
2001	0.8	0.5	0.06	n/a	1.0	0.05	0.3	0.5	1.3	2.4	1.0	7.8
2002	0.8	0.5	0.06	n/a	0.8	0.05	0.3	0.5	1.2	2.4	1.0	7.5
2003	0.7	0.5	0.06	n/a	0.7	0.05	0.3	0.5	1.2	2.7	0.9	7.7
2004	0.7	0.5	0.06	n/a	0.5	0.05	0.3	0.5	1.2	2.7	0.9	7.3
% p.a. average growth, 2000 prices												
1997–2004	3	2	7	n/a	n/a	2	0	2	2	9	8	5
Exports (£ millions)												
2000	710	420	2,000	n/a	1,000	n/a	940	300	950	2,500	690	9,500
2001	730	520	1,900	n/a	1,000	390	910	290	830	3,900	910	11,000
2002	890	510	2,300	n/a	1,200	n/a	840	280	790	3,500	1,000	11,300
2003	1,100	580	2,200	n/a	630	n/a	810	240	1,200	3,900	1,000	11,600
2004	1,100	570	2,200	n/a	550	n/a	940	150	1,500	4,700	1,300	13,000

*Total excludes crafts and designer fashion as figures are not available for every year.
Source: http://www.culture.gov.uk
Note: Code as in Table A2.2.2

Table A2.2.4 Geographical distribution of the UK creative industries (% of sample)

London	22
South East England	17
Eastern England	9
South West England	9
West Midlands	7
North West England	8
York & the Humber	7
Scotland	6
East Midlands	5
North East England	3
Northern Ireland	3
Wales	3

Source: UK Innovation Survey, 2005

creative industries totalled £13 billion in 2004, equating 4.3 per cent of all goods and services exported. More than a third (36 per cent) of the total creative industries exports was contributed by the software, computer games & electronic publishing sector.

A2.2.4 The location of the creative industries in the United Kingdom

In the 2005 UK Innovation Survey there is also information on the location of the firms in the creative industries. The data in Table A2.2.4 reveal that 40 per cent of these enterprises are based in London and the south-east.

A2.2.5 Creative employment in the United Kingdom

The occupational composition of the labour force is basically covered by the Standard Occupational Classification (SOC). The SOC is based on two concepts: kind of work and type of skill. Despite recent revisions in 2000, the SOC still provides only a partial coverage of the cultural sector. There are two key reasons for deficiencies in the SOC's 'fitness for purpose' pertaining to the cultural sector.

Firstly, the key purpose and function of the SOC is to identify the competency-defined roles of individuals (termed 'occupations'). Therefore, if one is interested in measuring the economic scale and scope of a series of interrelated economic activities (e.g. an industry or sector), the SOC is the wrong place to start, as the SOC primarily tracks what activities an individual undertakes; it is less concerned with the particular sector or industry in which these activities take place.

There is also the issue of 'non-creative' workers who work within the creative sector. For example, the SOC contains an occupation code for accountants who work within the creative sector. In principle, it is possible to identify these non-creative occupations within the creative sector by cross-referencing occupational codes with SIC codes for the business unit in which the occupation takes place (so-called SIC–SOC mapping, or SIC–SOC matrix). In practice, this analysis produces its own complications. Using SIC codes as the foundation for the measurement of employment is preferable.

Secondly, some new cultural activities are still not identified as 'occupations' within the SOC. For example, there is a set of codes for IT workers, but these do not identify computer games occupations, digital sound and image production, or web designers, even though the numbers employed in such activities are now significant.

Despite these reservations the DCMS list of relevant occupations is reproduced in Table A2.2.5. There are some notable absences in the codes, and many activities consequently remain invisible and uncounted (or rather, bundled up with others, and therefore unidentifiable as creative).

Table A.2.2.6 reproduces the DCMS data on employment in the creative industries/activities based on this occupational classification. The data also include an estimate of jobs in creative occupations in businesses which are classified as being outside these industries, e.g. graphic designers working in a manufacturing firm.

The data shows that in the summer quarter of 2005, creative employment totalled 1.8 million jobs. This comprised just over 1 million jobs in the creative industries and a further 780,000 creative jobs within businesses outside these industries. Total creative employment increased from 1.6 million in 1997 to 1.8 million in 2005, an average growth rate of 2 per cent per annum, compared to 1 per cent for the whole economy over this period. Software, computer games & electronic publishing showed the largest increase in employment between 1997 and 2005 with an average growth rate of 6 per cent per annum. The design sector, including designer fashion, also showed an increase above the overall average for the creative industries over the period (5 per cent per annum).

Higgs et al. (2008), using a different methodology (and based on the Labour Force Survey), estimate overall creative employment in the United Kingdom in 2006 of 1.98 million representing 7.0 per cent of UK employment. This estimate is close to that of the DCMS. Of the total, 1.29 million are estimated to be employees in the creative sector (a little higher than in the DCMS estimates), of whom 0.7 million are creative specialists, and 0.58 million are support workers. There are also 0.7 million creative workers outside the creative sector (slightly lower than the DCMS estimate). It estimated that in 25-year average, growth rates are 3.2 per cent for total creative employment (compared to 0.8 per cent for the UK workforce), 4.3 per cent for employment in the creative sector, and 3.3 per cent for creative occupations.

A2.2.6 International comparisons

One can undertake similar exercises using US occupations data. That data is, however, very detailed. This data indicates that under the employment code 27-0000, encompassing arts, design, entertainment, sports, and media occupations, employment in

Table A2.2.5 Occupations in the creative sector

VISUAL ART
2431 Architects
3411 Artists
3421 Graphic designers
3422 Product, clothing, and related designers
5414 Tailors and dressmakers
5423 Bookbinders and print finishers
5491 Glass and ceramics makers, decorators and finishers
5492 Furniture makers, other craft woodworkers
5495 Goldsmiths, silversmiths, precious stone workers
5499 Hand-craft occupations NEC

AUDIO-VISUAL
1134 Advertising and public relations managers
1136 IT/Communications managers
2131 IT professionals
3415 Musicians
3432 Broadcasting associate professionals
3433 Public relations officers
3434 Photographers and audio-visual equipment operators
5233 Line repairers and cable jointers
5244 TV and video engineers
5494 Musical instrument makers and tuners

PERFORMANCE
3413 Actors, entertainers
3414 Dancers and choreographers
3416 Arts officers, producers, and directors

BOOKS AND PRESS
3412 Authors, writers
3431 Journalists, newspaper, and periodical editors
5421 Originators, compositors, and print preparers
5422 Printers
5423 Bookbinders and finishers
5424 Screen printers

HERITAGE
2451 Librarians
2452 Archivists and curators
3551 Conservation and environmental protection officers
3552 Countryside and park rangers
4135 Library assistants/clerks
5113 Gardeners and groundsmen/groundswomen

2004 was 2.5 million, with a projection of 2.9 million in 2014 representing 1.7 per cent and 1.8 per cent of the total labour force respectively (see www.bls.gov/emp/emptabapp.htm). Clearly this is not a total count of relevant occupations but is indicative of a similar pattern to that in the United Kingdom.

According to Americans for the Arts (www.artsusa.org/CreativeIndustries), using Dunn and Bradstreet data and defining the creative industries by focusing solely on businesses involved in the production or distribution of the arts, as of January 2007

Table A2.2.6 Creative employment (summer quarter), United Kingdom

Year	Adv	Arch	A & A	Crafts	Des	VFP	MVPA	Pub	SC & EP	R & TV	TOTAL
Employment in the creative industries											
2005	89,100	83,100	22,900		3,400	51,000	185,300	173,800	341,600	95,200	1,045,400
Employment in creative occupations in businesses outside the creative industries											
2005	134,300	25,100	–	95,500	112,100	12,800	51,100	79,500	255,200	13,500	779,000
Total creative employment											
1997	201,000	95,800	20,200	95,000	80,700	64,200	226,300	308,500	379,400	97,600	1,568,700
1998	204,200	101,500	19,800	119,800	88,800	64,100	217,800	317,100	426,000	101,500	1,660,700
1999	200,900	101,500	20,800	96,800	93,500	61,900	255,700	317,000	488,600	92,500	1,729,300
2000	206,000	102,600	20,900	111,300	98,500	67,500	224,300	283,900	544,600	109,800	1,769,400
2001	220,500	103,400	20,900	115,100	103,000	75,500	224,600	293,300	567,700	104,100	1,828,100
2002	215,400	102,900	21,400	114,100	115,000	68,900	240,800	286,800	556,700	108,800	1,830,700
2003	213,800	103,100	22,500	108,700	113,200	74,300	245,800	305,200	581,200	110,900	1,878,800
2004	200,000	102,600	22,500	112,900	110,400	65,500	232,300	274,300	593,900	110,600	1,825,000
2005	223,400	108,200	22,900	95,500	115,500	63,800	236,300	253,300	596,800	108,700	1,824,400
Annual growth											
1997–2005	1%	2%	2%	0%	5%	0%	1%	–2%	6%	1%	2%
2004–2005	12%	5%	1%	–15%	5%	–3%	2%	–8%	0%	–2%	0%

Source: DCMS (2006)

there were 2.7 million people working for 546,558 arts-centric businesses (2.0 per cent and 4.2 per cent, respectively, of US employment and businesses).

The difficulties of international comparisons of the size, employment, and activity in the creative industries are discussed in great detail in UNCTAD (2008). The data published therein mainly relates to trade (exports and imports) and shows that of the top-ten world importers of creative products, the United Kingdom is second with 8.04 per cent of the total behind the United States with 27.08 per cent and Germany is third with 6.96 per cent. Amongst the top-ten exporters the United Kingdom is sixth (with 7.61 per cent) behind China (with 18.29 per cent), Italy, Hong Kong, the United States, and Germany. Thus, the United Kingdom is a big player in trade in such products, but by no means the biggest.

A2.2.7 An overview

Although there remain issues relating to the precise accuracy of the figures presented above, the picture is clear. In the United Kingdom (and elsewhere) the creative industries represent a significant proportion of economy-wide businesses, output, employment, exports, and imports. Moreover, creative occupations in the creative industries and elsewhere are a considerable proportion of total employment. In these circumstances, these industries, occupations, activities, and especially the associated innovations merit greater attention than they have traditionally been given. This also implies that innovation in such industries also merits more attention that it has traditionally been given.

3
Aggregate Measures of Soft Innovation

3.1 Introduction

After defining changes of an aesthetic or intellectual nature, with significance indicated by market impact, as soft innovation, the next obvious task is to attempt to generate some measures of the extent of such activity. This and the following two chapters (Chapters 4 and 5) attempt to quantify the amount of soft innovation taking place and, where possible, contrast with the extent of the more commonly measured technological product and process innovations.

In general there is no data that has been collected for the purposes of measuring soft innovation. The OECD (2006) *Oslo Manual* recommends a method by which direct data on marketing innovations, which is considered a part of soft innovation,[1] may be collected but the approach has not yet been employed and thus no data are available (although some may be obtained in the future). It is thus necessary, if soft innovation is to be measured, to use proxy indicators that have been collected for alternative purposes and are thus likely to be less precise.

A number of measures of innovative activity have been employed in economics in the past that generally fall in to two classes – those that

[1] 'To gain an idea of the scope of marketing innovations, enterprises might be asked to estimate the percentage of total turnover that is affected by marketing innovations. Innovation surveys can ask two separate questions concerning marketing innovations. One asks for an estimate of the percentage of turnover due to goods and services with significant improvements in product design or packaging. The second asks for an estimate of the share of turnover affected by new marketing methods in pricing, promotion or placement. Note that questions on share of turnover due to changes in product design should not be combined with questions on share of turnover due to product innovations (i.e. these two questions should be separate), since some new or improved products might be both product and marketing innovations. Nor should questions on new marketing methods in product design be combined with questions on the share of turnover due to other new marketing methods. As with other questions concerning the impact on turnover, enterprises will likely only be able to provide rough estimates at best' (OECD, 2006, pp. 110–111).

measure inputs used in the process of generating innovation (e.g. R&D expenditures) and those that measure outputs of innovative activity (e.g. patent counts; see, e.g., Griliches [1995]). Although it is useful to try and explore both input and output measures for soft innovation, as will be obvious from Chapter 2, it will not be possible to find indicators of soft innovation from the R&D data (as R&D data is collected on the basis of the TPP definition of innovation, which rules out aesthetic improvement as innovation) or from patent counts (because only advances of an industrial nature can be patented), although R&D and patent counts may provide measures of TPP innovation for comparative purposes.[2]

With the other input and output measures that have been employed in economics, one being (changes in) productivity, it has been argued that as innovation occurs better products are produced and more efficiently, so that productivity increases. Unfortunately the reliability of productivity measures depends upon how well the output (and input) measures are 'quality adjusted'. Generally the extent of quality adjustment is either non-existent or built on weak foundations. The most widely used method for quality adjustment is the 'matched models approach', although the most theoretically supported approach involves the use of hedonic methods (see, e.g., Trajtenberg [1990] and Griliches [1990]). In both cases, products are considered mixtures of performance characteristics, and quality is said to improve with increases in the amounts of such characteristics. Unfortunately, partly on conceptual and partly on practical grounds, aesthetic characteristics are rarely incorporated in such approaches, and, as such, soft innovation is unlikely to be properly measured. This is shown by Requena-Silvente and Walker (2006) who illustrate that hedonic price indices that omit model-specific unobservable product attributes are subject to considerable bias. In Griliches' terminology, soft innovations either occur in hard-to-measure sectors or comprise changes that are hard to measure (see Berndt and Hulten [2007]).

At the micro level, a practical approach is to look at individual industries in great detail and isolate for each industry some physical measures of soft innovation. This might be, for example, the number of new books published in publishing sector, the number of new CDs released in the market

---

[2] In considering measures for innovation in the creative industries, Handke (2007), in addition to separating input and output measures also distinguishes between humdrum innovation (which is TPP innovation in the sense used here) and content creation (which is more like soft innovation as defined here). She also emphasizes that content creation cannot be measured through R&D and patents. Her recommendations for measuring content creation are discussed in Chapter 4 in the context of the music industry.

in the music industry, or the number of new films in the movie industry, etc. Weighting particular innovations by market impact can be used to indicate those of greatest significance. This approach is explored in Chapters 4 and 5 in order to look at individual industries/products. However, in order to consider all the industries that undertake soft innovation and all the activities that involve soft innovation, such an approach alone would neither provide a global picture nor enable comparisons across industries or time because of the different types of outputs in different industries and resultant different units of measurement. Instead, macro-analysis requires the use of measures that are not industry-specific nor show particular industry-level biases.

In this chapter, a number of alternative measurement exercises are pursued in order to provide indications of the extent of soft innovation in the economy as a whole. These exercises should be considered as complimentary to, rather than competing with, the micro-level exercises, for each has some advantages and some disadvantages. The micro-level exercises are reported on in Chapters 4 and 5. This chapter explores six different macro indicators that individually and in totality reveal a picture of soft innovation at the macro level. The six indicators[3] are:

- *Innovation survey indicators for creative industries*: There are several problems with using innovation survey indicators in this way, as discussed by Marzal and Esparza (2007), but the data merits some exploration.
- *Measures of innovative outputs and inputs in the creative industries*: This approach looks at the value of the output of (an output measure) and employment in (an input measure) those cultural industry sectors/activities that are considered to generate soft innovations.
- *Measures of inputs to soft innovation outside the creative sector*: As indicators of innovative activity in the creative industries do not extend to activities outside the creative sector, these try to also measure employment generated through soft innovation in the other parts of the economy.
- *Design activity*: The activities that generate soft innovation (in both the creative and other industries) may be called 'design' activities, and thus exploration of data on design and design rights may also give some insight into the extent of soft innovation (both as an input and output measure).

---

[3] Jensen and Webster (2007) have undertaken a useful exercise of comparing different measures of innovation across a given sample of firms and have found that they vary substantially. There are thus advantages in using a wide range of measures. Jensen and Webster (2007) in fact recommend trademarks as superior indicators.

- *Copyright and trademarks*: Although it is not possible to patent aesthetic innovations, they can be trademarked or copyrighted. Counting trademarks and copyrights is thus a useful measurement tool (an output measure) covering the creative and other sectors.
- *The PIMS database:* Finally, the extensive longitudinal PIMS database that has been used for analysing innovation and marketing is explored to see if that offers some possibilities for measuring soft innovation.

3.2 Innovation surveys

Over the last 15 years, across Europe and in other countries a series of innovation surveys (the Community Innovation Surveys, CIS) have been undertaken by National Statistical Offices using very similar questionnaires. These surveys have provided considerable new and insightful data on the innovation process. The questionnaires are built on the definitions to be found in the Oslo and Frascati manuals discussed in the previous chapters.

The data that is currently available in the public domain is from the Fourth Community Innovation Survey covering the 2002–4 period[4], undertaken in 2005, and the results of the 2007 UK Innovation Survey (similar to CIS but not termed as such) are also available. Wilkinson (2007) explores innovation in the creative industries by considering the UK results to the Fourth Community Innovation Survey using three main indicators of innovation.

1. If a firm is engaged in the introduction of new or significantly improved products (goods or services) or processes; is involved in innovation projects not yet complete or abandoned; or incurs expenditure in areas such as internal R&D, training, acquisition of external knowledge, or machinery and equipment linked to innovation activities.
2. If a firm is engaged in organizational innovation.
3. If a high proportion of the firms turnover is due to new or improved products.

It was found that that 78 per cent of firms in the creative industries met the first criterion, a higher proportion than in any of the other broad industry categories identified in the data. Compared to the other industries, firms in the creative industries were also significantly more likely to have carried

---

[4] First results of the 2007 UK Innovation Survey are available (Robson and Haigh, 2008), and although this contains a large sample of firms from the creative industries, the results for these firms are not yet separately available.

out one of the forms of innovation listed above. In the creative industries it was found that, on average, new-to-market products accounted for almost twice as much of industry turnover as for other industries. In addition, 52 per cent of firms were found to have undertaken organizational innovation compared to 40 per cent for firms in other industries.

The survey data (see DTI [2006]) also indicates that the creative industries employ a higher proportion of graduates regardless of geographic location and, on average, have a noticeably higher percentage of science and engineering graduates. The lack of qualified personnel as a barrier to innovation is ranked higher by this sector compared to the other industries. It was generally found that the more innovative the organization, the greater are the perceived barriers to innovation, and the creative enterprises rate most barriers to innovation higher than in other industries. The creative industries also tend to operate on a more national and international level with just under a quarter of their largest markets being regionally/locally based. There appears to be greater regional variation in the percentage of innovation active enterprises with over 75 per cent of creative firms in Yorkshire and Humberside, Northern Ireland, and the south-east having innovation activity. Creative businesses are also more active at protecting their innovations due, in part, to greater levels of originality.

These findings suggest that the creative sector is very innovative, and given that new products in the creative industries have been defined as soft innovation, much of what is being observed may well be soft innovation. Being a survey instrument that is used in many different countries such data may also have the advantage of allowing some international comparisons. It is, however, necessary to provide some health warnings.

1. The data here refers only to the creative sector. It does not include other parts of the economy where soft innovation might also be occurring.
2. The 2005 survey sampled only around two-thirds of the industries which make up the creative sector. The results are thus not complete, although the 2007 Innovation Survey in the UK promises to cover all thirteen industries in the sector.
3. It is not clear what the responses of businesses to questions on turnover due to new or improved products refer to. According to the definitions they should be responding only re TPP innovation. However, the very high numbers would suggest otherwise. For creative industries most product innovation will be soft (and thus non-TPP) innovation and one must suspect it is, at least partly, to this that they are referring. In fact it is

tempting to consider such responses as measures of soft innovation in this industry, but one cannot know whether this is correct.

4. Finally, the questionnaire is based on innovation definitions prior to those in OECD (2006), especially the previously discussed definition of marketing innovation.

Thus, although the data suggests considerable innovative activity in the creative sector and perhaps more than in other sectors, the innovation surveys provide only a partial picture that may well be flawed.

3.3 Output of soft innovation and employment of soft innovators in the creative industries

In Appendix A2.2 (in the previous chapter) a list of the industries in the cultural sector is provided. Each of these industries has been assigned with a function, a number being labelled 'creation' by the DCMS. This may mean that the main function of these industries is to create innovations. In addition, the value of their output should provide a measure of the extent of soft innovation. This is, however, output of soft innovations only in the creative sector and does not measure such innovations in other sectors (except to the extent that such sectors buy-in from the creative sector). For example one would not expect such a measure to capture soft product innovation in the manufacturing sector. In addition, the measure pertains to the home production of soft innovation. Some of this output may be exported and not utilized by the UK economy as a whole. On the other hand, soft innovations may also be imported from overseas and imports are not reflected in this measure.

Despite these limitations the measure has some usefulness as an initial yardstick. The set of industries of which the output is to be measured is listed in Table 3.1.

Table 3.2 provides (on the basis of data from the ONS Annual Business Inquiry [ABI] for 2005) some estimates of gross value added (GVA) for sectors as closely representative of those listed in Table 3.1 as possible. In addition, estimates of employment have been added. Where total employment figures were not provided these have been generated by summing full-time and part-time employees, assuming that a part-time employee equals half a full-time employee.

For purposes of comparison the ABI considers GVA from R&D activities as being valued at £4,740 million and related employment to be 102,000.

Table 3.1 Soft innovators (creation activities) in the cultural sector

74.20/1 Architectural activities

74.87/2 Speciality design activities including fashion, interior, graphics – previously included in 74.87/2 SIC 92

92.31/9 Other artistic & literary creation and interpretation

      Play writing and scenography

72.22 Other software consultancy and supply

74.40 Advertising

74.81/2 Portrait photographic activities – previously other portrait photographic activities

74.81/3 Other specialist photography

74.81/4 Film processing – previously coded in 74.81/9 SIC 92

74.81/9 Photographic activities NEC

92.11/1 Motion picture production on film or video tape

92.11/9 Other motion picture and video production activities

92.20/1 Radio activities

92.20/2 Television activities

92.72/1 Casting activities included previously 92.72 other recreational activities NEC SIC 92

      Screenplay and film development

      Leisure software design/development

      Audio visual research and development

      Activities of literary creation

      Heritage, museum & tourism services

      Design, development of sports programmes & events

63.3 Activities of travel agencies & tour operators

Table 3.2 Innovative output and employment in the creative sector, 2005

Activity	GVA (£ millions)	Employment (thousands)
74.2 Architectural & engineering activities & related technical consultancy	18,844	1373
72.22 Other software consultancy and supply	24,118	352
74.4 Advertising	6,496	89
74.81 Photographic activities	895	28
92.11 Motion picture and video production	1,044	26
92.20 Radio and TV activities	8,009	74
92.31 Artistic and literary creation	1,987	70
Total	61,393	1,012

Source: ONS Annual Business Inquiry, 2005

This latter figure compares with an alternative estimate (see Chapter 2) of total employment on R&D performed in UK business in 2005 of 147,000 (www.statistics.gov.uk/statbase/datasettype.asp?vlnk = 569).

Though this data relates only to the creative sector and not to soft innovation activity in the other sectors, as mentioned earlier, the total GVA in the relevant sectors of £61,393 million represents approximately 5 per cent of GDP. The size of the total GVA (and employment) is obviously mainly a reflection of architectural & engineering activities and related technical consultancy and other software consultancy and supply. Nevertheless, even if these are removed completely from the picture, GVA and employment in the remaining activities still by far exceed the GVA of R&D in the economy as a whole.

The employment figures in Table 3.2 may be inflated by non-creative workers in the innovation producing sectors. Higgs et al. (2006) consider employment in creative activity as made up of three 'modes': specialist workers within a creative profession within a creative sector, workers in a non-creative profession within a creative sector, and workers in a creative occupation outside the creative industries. The creative core then consists of those workers engaged at the pre-creation stage (including preservation, access, collecting, and licensing activities) and the creation stage of the value chain. Their estimate of specialist workers within a creative profession within a creative sector (552,170 in 2001) best corresponds to soft innovation-producing workers. This is still large compared to numbers employed in R&D activity in the whole economy.

Even after making large allowances for data deficiencies the picture would still seem to indicate that the extent of innovation-generating activities directed towards soft innovation just in the creative industries is far greater than that directed towards the more commonly considered R&D activities, not only in that sector but in the economy as a whole, and thus far exceeds resources devoted to the more commonly explored TPP activities.

3.4 Employment of innovators outside the creative industries

This section considers soft innovation production outside the creative sector. This is to be approached in several ways starting here by considering creative employment in what Higgs et al. (2008) categorize as the employment of creative workers in a creative occupation outside the creative industries. The estimate of Higgs et al. (2008) is that the number employed in specialist creative occupations outside the creative industries in 2001 was 645,067, which represents 2.5 per cent of the total workforce. Although this number may also include workers producing functional innovations, it is so much in excess of the 147,000 employed in business R&D in the economy as a whole as to leave plenty of scope for a large number of employees to be involved in soft innovations. This would again seem to indicate that the extent of innovation-generating activities directed towards soft innovation is significant and probably far greater than that directed towards the more commonly considered R&D activities.

3.5 Design

A fourth measure of innovative activity relates to designing. Both input and output measures may be constructed. On the input side the approach is to measure labour and other inputs to design activity. On the output side the approach involves counting registered design rights. The second *Oslo Manual* states that there are two important types of design, and that these are to be treated differently (OECD 2006, p. 41):

Industrial design is an essential part of the TPP innovation process...it is listed...in the same subsection as tooling up, industrial engineering and production start-up, [but] may also be a part of the initial conception of the product or process, i.e. included in research and experimental development, or be required for marketing technologically new or improved products.

Artistic design activities are TPP innovation activities if undertaken on a technologically new or improved product or process. They are not if undertaken for other creative product improvement, for example purely to improve the appearance of the product without any objective change in its performance.

Industrial design expenditures are therefore very close to R&D and may even be included within R&D as an input to generating TPP innovations. However, design expenditures aimed at producing soft innovation, which would be included under the heading of artistic design, would not be considered as contributing to TPP nor be included as part of R&D. Thus, a measure of expenditure on artistic design would (with relatively efficient markets) reflect the (quality-adjusted) level of activity in the production of soft innovations. Although there is no reason why all expenditures on soft innovation should be termed artistic design expenditures, if these could be measured it would go some way to meeting the desired measurement objective. Unfortunately such data is not available.

Table 3.3 Proportion of respondents with different innovation investments, UK, 2005

Intramural R&D	32%
Extramural R&D	12%
Acquisition of machinery, equipment, and software	47%
Acquisition of external knowledge	14%
Training in connection with innovation	42%
Design functions	19%
Marketing related to innovations	25%

Source: UK Innovation Survey 2005 (CIS4)

The available data relates to design activities as a whole and reflects not only soft innovation activities but also TPP activities. In the UK innovation surveys, unlike in most countries that carry out innovation surveys, design expenditure is separated from other investments for innovation. This enables quite a detailed analysis of the role of design and creativity, a lot of work on which has been published in DTI (2005).

Using the CIS 4, design spending is calculated to be about 5 per cent of the total of innovation-directed business spending, a higher share than external knowledge acquisition, but considerably lower than the shares of R&D, capital expenditure, and marketing. Using the fourth UK Community Innovation Survey, Tether (2006) shows, as reproduced in Table 3.3, that, while a larger number of firms recorded R&D and capital expenditure as compared to design expenditure, some 19 per cent recognized an explicit role for design in preparing for or implementing innovations in products or processes.[5] This design investment propensity does not vary significantly across industrial sectors, with a similar percentage of respondents in sectors such as knowledge-intensive services and retail reporting design activity as in manufacturing industries.

In a similar way, DTI (2006) suggests that a recent survey of the design industry for the UK's Design Council (2005) can be used to define a 'design-using' approach to innovation. Also a 'technology-led' mode can be applied to a subset of firms that engage in R&D activity, intramural or extramural, and assign some importance to patents to protect their innovations. They calculate that 34 per cent of firms are technology-led (of which only 9 per cent are design users) and 66 per cent are not (of which 58 per cent are design users).

[5] The CBI (2007) estimate that if market-related innovation work, design- and innovation-related capital expenditure, and training are all included, then average innovation investment in the United Kingdom is about 5 per cent of turnover.

There may, of course, be a substantial overlap between the two sets of firms. The majority of technology-led innovators are also design users, often as a complementary investment to translate R&D results into new and improved products and processes. Tether (2006), finds, for example, that 71 per cent of those firms with specific design activity also have intra-mural R&D, 81 per cent have capital expenditure (CAPEX), 76 per cent spent on training (for innovation), and 63 per cent on marketing. Thus, different innovation-directed business activities tend to be deployed jointly which tends to muddy the waters for measurement. He also finds that the probability of a firm undertaking a design function conditional on other inputs is low, that is, commitment to design seems to follow on other innovation investments, but the inverse is not the case.

Issues of interpretation are involved if any conclusions are to be drawn on the extent of soft innovation using such data but it seems safe to conclude that design-based or design-inclusive modes of innovation play a significant and distinctive role in innovation. The DTI (2006) also con-cludes that complementary investment in technology and design together are consistent with higher levels of final innovation outcomes.

There are also other estimates of design expenditures. The Design Coun-cil (2006) estimates total design employment in the UK in 2003–4 to be 134,000 designers with 51,500 managers and directors. These are spread across 12,450 design consultancies, 47,400 are self-employed or freelance designers, and 77,100 designers in 5,900 businesses. Turnover of design businesses was estimated to be £11.6 billion in 2004/5 encompassing communications, digital and media, interior and exhibition, product and industrial, fashion and textiles, and service design. These totals appear to be about five times the scale of design investment for innovation calculated from the CIS innovation survey.

Other design council data shows the markets for the design industry, including the use of in-house design teams, and is reproduced in Table 3.4. As may be seen the spread is economy-wide but there is some emphasis on service sectors.

Although this data, representing input measures of design activity, is far from definitive, they suggest that there is design activity occurring that is over and above activities counted as R&D, i.e. TPP investment. That activity may be associated with or even prompted by R&D, but as such activities are contributing to the innovation process, these expenditures may well indi-cate soft innovation activities. Such activities occur in every industry but to an extent they vary with the data source being used. It would not, however,

Table 3.4 Design industry – user sectors

Industry	Percentage
Textiles, leather, and clothing	1
Wood and wood products	0
Publishing, printing & paper	3
Chemicals, plastic/rubber products, man-made fibres and fuels	2
Glass, ceramic, and other mineral products	1
Metal products and machinery	2
Furniture, jewellery, and musical instruments	1
Manufacturing – other	4
Wholesale and retail	13
Post and telecommunications	4
Financial services	8
Other business services	13

Source: Design Council (2006)

be a simple exercise from such data on design inputs to extricate a clear picture of the extent and pattern of soft innovation.

As stated earlier there are also output measures of design activity. In the United Kingdom, designs that are artistic and are not to be mass-produced will receive automatic copyright protection. However, copyrights (in the United Kingdom at least) are not registered[6] and thus counting copyrights as a measure of design activity is not realistic (see below). There is, however, also a 'Design Right' in the United Kingdom, which is a free automatic right given when an original design is created, and protects a design for up to 15 years. In addition, there are Registered Designs[7] which give up to 25 years protection to a design. The main advantage of a Registered Design over an Unregistered Design Right is that an Unregistered Design Right can only be used to prevent copying, whereas a Registered Design yields a true monopoly and applies even if an imitator comes up with the same or a similar design independently and without copying. In the United Kingdom, such design protection has been available for almost fifty years. From 2002, the Design Right has been extended so that there are now European Community registered design rights and European Community unregistered design rights (see www.ipo.gov.uk/design/d-applying/d-should/d-should-designright.htm).

Potentially, the number of design registrations can be used as an indicator of innovation. This measure would cover both TPP and soft innovation and thus a measure of soft innovation would reflect the difference

---

[6] Although can be in the United States.
[7] Design patent in the United States.

Soft Innovation: Economics, Product Aesthetics, and the Creative Industries

between numbers of design rights granted and some measure of TPP innovation such as R&D and/or patents granted. A headcount would be simplest but adjustment for quality would be preferred although it is unlikely that there would be enough data to allow this. Unfortunately, data from the UK Fourth Community Innovation Survey (see H M Treasury [2006]) indicates that across all firm sizes only 4 per cent of respondents considered registration of design as an IP protection mechanism of high importance as compared to 11 per cent who considered confidentiality agreements, 5 per cent patents, 16 per cent trademarks, and 6 per cent copyright to be of highest importance. In larger firms with more than 250 employees the figures were higher at 11, 22, 13, 16, and 10 per cent, respectively, but this suggests that design registration data may be a very incomplete indicator of innovation.

Table 3.5 Statistics of applications for community design rights from 2003 to 31 December 2006, European Union.

3-EU UE Country	Total	EU sourced (%)	World sourced (%)
AUSTRIA	5,283	2.98	2.33
BELGIUM	4,329	2.44	1.91
BULGARIA	32	0.02	0.01
CYPRUS	8	0.04	0.03
CZECH REPUBLIC	1,059	0.60	0.47
GERMANY	54,497	30.78	24.00
DENMARK	5,154	2.91	2.27
ESTONIA	48	0.03	0.02
SPAIN	15,287	8.63	6.73
FINLAND	1,874	1.06	0.83
FRANCE	18,665	10.54	8.22
UNITED KINGDOM	16,861	9.52	7.42
GREECE	90	0.05	0.04
HUNGARY	402	0.23	0.18
IRELAND	945	0.53	0.42
ITALY	34,961	19.74	15.39
LITHUANIA	61	0.03	0.03
LUXEMBOURG	502	0.28	0.22
LATVIA	103	0.06	0.05
MALTA	12	0.01	0.01
NETHERLANDS	8,097	4.57	3.57
POLAND	2,285	1.29	1.01
PORTUGAL	1,541	0.87	0.68
ROMANIA	35	0.02	0.02
SWEDEN	4,410	2.49	1.94
SLOVENIA	212	0.12	0.09
SLOVAKIA	258	0.15	0.11
TOTAL	177,081	100.00	77.97

Source: SSC007 – Statistics of Community Designs 2006, rep 1/3, 05/02/2007

In the United Kingdom, Patent Office data (www.ipo.gov.uk/design/
d-applying/d-should/d-should-designright.htm) indicates that registered
designs have fallen from 9,000 in 2002 to less than 4,000 in 2005, suggesting
a considerable decline in such activity. However, it is from 2002 that the
European Design Right was available. Data on European Design Rights can
be found at oami.europa.eu/en/office/stats.htm. European data, of the sort
detailed in Table 3.5, might be used to give some indication of different rates
of (TPP and soft) innovation across countries, but one would be reluctant to,
for example, take the observed German dominance of registration as reflecting greater innovativeness rather than just greater use of the system.

Overall, although data on design activities seem promising for the
measurement of innovation activities in total, and soft innovation activities in particular, the available data is not internally consistent, is difficult
to interpret and also may require some quality adjustment. The general
picture is, however, one of extensive design activity and by implication
extensive soft innovation activity.

3.6 Copyrights and trademarks

Copyrights and trademarks are means by which innovation, and particularly aesthetic innovations, may be protected. Issues of Intellectual Property Rights are discussed in more detail in Chapter 9. A brief introduction
is offered here prior to the discussion of the use of headcounts of copyright
and trademark applications as measures of innovative activity. If used,
such measures may encompass all sectors of the economy and both TPP
and soft innovation.

3.6.1 Copyright

Copyright (see www.ipo.gov.uk/copy.htm) can be obtained for any medium and means that any work copyrighted cannot be reproduced in
another medium without permission. Copyright does not protect ideas,
only the work per se. Copyright does not have to be applied for but is
provided automatically and protected through the courts. Copyrighted
work may have other IPR protection and even several copyrights, e.g. an
album of music may have copyrights for individual songs, sound recordings, logos, etc. The logo may also be registered as a trademark. Copyright
protects: literature including novels, manuals, computer programs, song
lyrics, etc.; drama, including dance and mime; art, including paintings,

engravings, photographs, architecture, maps, and logos; layouts; recordings; and broadcasts of a work.

Copyright is so associated with the creative industries that some authors have defined an almost identical sector called copyright-protected industries. For example, Theeuwes (2004) defines the copyright-based industry as consisting of the following sectors:

1. Press and literature
2. Photography
3. Visual arts and museums
4. Music, theatrical productions, and operas
5. Motion pictures and videos
6. Radio and television
7. Software and databases
8. Multimedia and Internet
9. Research
10. Design, advertising services, and architecture
11. Copyright Collective Management Societies

These sectors match almost completely our definition of the creative sector. Using these definitions, Theeuwes (2004) provides estimates of the size of the copyright-based sector in the Netherlands. In 1998 the value added of the copyright-based sector was 5.5 per cent of the gross domestic product (GDP), an increase over the 1995 value of 5.2 per cent of GDP. In 1989 the percentage of the copyright-based industries stood at 4.3 per cent. In 1998 more than 419,000 persons worked in the copyright-based industry, adding up to roughly 338,000 full-time equivalents. As a percentage of total employment in the Netherlands this amounts to 5.4 and 5.5 per cent respectively. Compared with 1994 the percentage of persons employed remained constant. The picture is very similar to that found in the United Kingdom.

Such data, however, does not measure the extent of copyright per se and thus the extent of soft innovation, but indicates the size of the industries based on it. In fact, given that copyrights do not have to be registered there are many difficulties in collecting copyright count data. Png (2006) considers the issue of quantification of copyright activity. His findings are not optimistic. He states that data on the creation of copyrightable items is scarce. As an alternative he suggests using product launches in copyright industries. For example Png and Wang (2006) look at motion pictures and indicate that in most countries the number of new movies being produced is almost constant over time. The data available on books, music, and video games is discussed in detail in Chapter 4.

Although there is limited data on the extent of copyrighted advances to use as a measure of soft innovation, Mazeh and Rogers (2005) observe that in each decade since the 1970s, the number of copyright legal disputes in the United Kingdom has increased – but one cannot distinguish whether this is as a result of more use of copyright (and thus more soft innovation) or that copyright has become more valuable.

3.6.2 Trademarks

Trademarks (see www.ipo.gov.uk/tm.htm) are instruments that protect corporate identity. Application may be made to register a trademark that is distinctive, not similar or identical to any earlier marks, and not deceptive or contrary to law or morality. The mark may register a name, logo, slogan, domain name, shape, colour, or sound. Renewal in the United Kingdom is carried out every ten years.

Trademarks are registered and may be counted and thus represent a valuable source of data on innovative activity. They represent an output measure of such activity. Although soft innovations cannot be patented, they may be protected by trademarks. But trademarks may also be used to protect TPP innovations and so trademark data does not provide an unadulterated measure of soft innovations. However, trademark counts may in fact be a preferred indicator of the sum of TPP and soft innovations rather than say R&D, because R&D excludes soft innovation. Nevertheless in certain industries, e.g. services in particular, trademark registrations will be a far superior indicator of total innovative activity than the R&D measure because such industries will have much more soft innovation.

Trademark counts have the disadvantage of not distinguishing the significant from the insignificant. Some trademarks will protect widely used innovations whereas others may cover products with very small market shares. In principle one may weight marks by the market share of the product protected, or, copying the practice applied to patent counts, use renewal data to reflect importance. Here, however, analysis concentrates on headcounts rather than extending to introduce such weighting.

Greenhalgh et al. (2001) provide considerable data and analysis on trademarks and the related service marks in the United Kingdom and the United States, and much of what follows is based on that work. The data source of Greenhalgh et al. (2001; Marquesa UK Trade Marks [A] Applications CD-ROM, Search Systems Ltd. [1996]) detailed all trademark applications made in the previous eight years or so along with earlier applications which had not 'died' (been allowed to lapse or abandoned) before the start of the time frame. It encompasses new applications made between 1989 and 1995, but retains a count of the stock of 'live' trademarks at 1989 taken out in earlier years. Trademarks are classified into forty-two classes (economic sectors), of which thirty-four relate to goods and eight relate to services. It is found that:

1. When considering all goods marks versus all service marks, goods marks accounted for 94 per cent of pre-1989 surviving trademarks, for 82 per cent of applications in 1989, and for 77 per cent of applications in 1995; therefore, quite clearly goods classes account for the larger (but declining) percentage of the total marks throughout the period.
2. The rate of growth of applications from 1989 to 1995 was far greater in the service mark classes (98 per cent) than in the goods mark classes (41 per cent). Thus, although goods marks dominated, service marks were becoming more important.
3. Of the five classes enjoying the highest rates of expansion over the whole period, four were service sectors for which registrations grew by more than 100 per cent in two years, namely advertising and business, communication, education and entertainment, and miscellaneous services. Two other service classes, insurance and financial and material treatment also experienced growth of more than 80 per cent between 1989 and 1995, but concentrated in the last two years.
4. The period 1989 to 1995 is best regarded as two smaller sub-periods: 1989 to 1993 and 1994–1995; the first of these sub-periods saw trademark applications fall by 15 per cent. Of the applications across the total forty-two sectors, thirty-seven were less in 1993 than 1989, and only five were greater. All the expansion came in the last two years of the data, which might have been due to changes in registration requirements.
5. Very different time trends are observed for British patent publications, which fell while trademark indicators rose.

In the face of changing registration requirements, the changes in total applications are difficult to interpret. One would not wish to interpret them as a reduction in innovative activity. However, the different patterns in the overall growth of patenting and trademarks may be suggestive of an increasing relative importance over time of soft innovation (which can be trademarked but not patented), relative to TPP innovations (which can be both trademarked and patented). In addition, the growing importance of the service as opposed to goods sectors may also reflect relatively more soft innovation. Although it is not necessary that the service sector will generate mainly soft innovations as opposed to TPP innovations, much of the creative sector, which is a major source of soft innovation, will fall within the remit of the service rather than the goods sector.[8]

Greenhalgh et al. (2001) find that that the pattern observed in the United Kingdom was also seen in the United States for 1989–95, where (although overall rates of growth for both goods and service marks were higher in the United Kingdom), nearly three-quarters of marks were in goods and more than a quarter in services but there was a more rapid growth in service marks in later years. Total application rates for service marks rose rapidly from 1993. The interpretation would seem to be similar for the United Kingdom.

Greenhalgh and Rogers (2005) have extended this earlier work looking at a sample of 2,054 UK firms and UK and EC trademarks and UK and European Patent Office (EPO) patents for the period from 1996 to 2000. They find that:

1. For the whole sample, the proportion of firms which made at least one UK trademark application within any year (average for the five-year period) was 30 per cent and the average number of UK trademarks per firm per year was 4.7.
2. Patenting activity was lower, with 9 per cent of sample firms publishing a UK patent per year and 8 per cent publishing an EPO patent, whilst the number of patents per firm per year was modest: 0.35 UK and 0.77 EPO patents.
3. Around 18 per cent of sample firms reported R&D, the average annual value of this expenditure being £23 million in 2000 prices.
4. The service sectors were particularly active in obtaining trademarks whereas the manufacturing and utilities sectors were active in both obtaining trademarks and patenting.

Given that soft innovation can be trademarked but not patented and that generating soft innovations activity is not counted in the R&D expenditure, whereas TPP innovation can be trademarked, patented, and is included in R&D, these observations indicate that, as the extent of patenting and the proportion of firms carrying out R&D is much lower than the proportion of firms applying for trademarks, the number of firms undertaking soft innovation (perhaps in addition to TPP innovation) is much larger than the number of firms doing TPP innovation alone. Firms seem to apply for almost three times as many trademarks as patents, suggesting

[8] The issue of innovation in services comes close to soft innovation although the boundaries are somewhat different. DTI (2007) provides insights into innovation in services.

Table 3.6 Proportion of firms making an application for IP 1996–2000 by sector

Sector	No. firms	UKTM	ECTM	UKPAT	EPOPAT
1 Agriculture/mining	67	0.19	0.12	0.21	0.12
2 Manufacturing	640	0.67	0.55	0.40	0.35
3 Utilities	26	0.85	0.62	0.50	0.42
4 Construction	89	0.39	0.22	0.22	0.09
5 Finance	191	0.52	0.26	0.05	0.06
6 Real estate	112	0.22	0.12	0.03	0.01
7 Wholesale	181	0.52	0.33	0.12	0.07
8 Retail	132	0.75	0.40	0.08	0.05
9 Hotel/catering	54	0.65	0.35	0.06	0.00
10 Transport/communication	115	0.57	0.43	0.10	0.05
11 Business services	259	0.57	0.43	0.08	0.06
12 Other services	188	0.56	0.37	0.10	0.12

that soft innovation may be two to three times as extensive as TPP innovation. In addition, soft innovation may be relatively more important in services.

Of particular interest are Tables 3.6 and 3.7 taken from Greenhalgh and Rogers (2005), illustrating the sectoral breakdown of trademark and patent registrations. While Table 3.6 provides the number of firms applying for IP protection at least once, Table 3.7 takes account of multiple applications. The tables show that patent applications (either to the UK patent office or to the EPO) are concentrated in manufacturing (40 per cent) and utilities (50 per cent), with most other sectors showing 12 per cent or less applications. It would seem obvious to take this as an indication that TPP innovation is concentrated in these two sectors as compared to the other sectors that undertake little TPP innovation.

Table 3.7 Numbers of new IP assets sought by sector, 1996–2000

Sector	No. firms	UKTM	ECTM	UKPAT	EPOPAT
1 Agriculture/mining	67	235	97	169	44
2 Manufacturing	640	19,931	11,395	2,700	6,467
3 Utilities	26	2,272	461	79	59
4 Construction	89	616	231	92	42
5 Finance	191	4,216	1,675	85	243
6 Real estate	112	530	171	6	1
7 Wholesale	181	1,717	958	74	83
8 Retail	132	7,619	2,263	38	29
9 Hotel/catering	54	1,262	427	5	0
10 Transport/communication	115	4,617	2,028	62	740
11 Business services	259	2,583	1,681	61	33
12 Other services	188	2,779	1,246	222	128

The trademark applications data show that a greater proportion of firms in manufacturing (67 per cent) and utilities (85 per cent) also applied for trademarks which may be taken out for both TPP and soft innovations. As the proportions are higher than for patent applications, this could reflect soft innovation activity over and above TPP activity. However, the other sectors also show extensive trademark activities with, for example, retail showing a greater proportion of firms applying than in manufacturing, and seven sectors (in addition to manufacturing and retail) consisting of more than half the sample firms applying for UK trademarks. The interpretation of this data is once again that although trademarks may reflect both TPP and soft innovation, the patent data shows a low level of TPP innovation in all sectors other than manufacturing and utilities, and as such the joint picture revealed by the patent and trademark data may be interpreted as indicating high levels of soft innovation in a wide selection of sectors.

Analysing the data in Table 3.7, which allows for multiple applications by firms, the picture is similar, although innovative activity in utilities is downplayed here. Total patent applications are dominated by the manufacturing sector with more applications than all the sample firms in other sectors. With trademarks, however, although manufacturing firms submit the largest number of applications, other sectors in total exceed that number. The interpretation is again that TPP innovation is concentrated in manufacturing, but the other sectors are also involved in innovative activities that are likely to be soft innovations rather than TPP innovations.

Trademark data is not perfect and has to be used carefully. It is not easy, for example, to quality adjust the raw data. It would appear however that such data indicates that in the UK and US economies many more firms are undertaking innovative activity than would be judged by looking at, for example, R&D expenditures or patent applications alone. This is in itself an important finding.

It seems valid to draw the finding that, as trademark indicators show so much more innovative activity than R&D and patent indicators, and that only TPP innovations can be patented and count for measuring R&D, a possible measure of soft innovation at a high level of aggregation may be based on the difference between the level of copyright activity and the level of R&D and/or patenting activity. The measured higher level of activity indicated by the trademark data must then reflect extensive soft innovation in the economy in addition to any TPP innovation activity occurring.

3.7 The PIMS database

Opening up the definition of innovation to include non-functional improvements brings the literature on the economics of innovation and that on new product development in the management field closer. The study of new product development in the management and especially marketing fields pays little apparent attention to whether the new product represents a functional or an aesthetic innovation. This literature seeks to explore (see, e.g., Brown and Eisenhardt [1995]) how a product is developed, and whether it succeeds, whatever the origins of the product or its nature. Similarly this literature also explores how firms attempt to build their brand image, and although brand image may just be an aesthetic aura attached to a particular firm's products, this aura is seen as an important product characteristic. Previously the economics literature on innovation could argue that the marketing and other literatures pertaining to new product development were not exclusively concerned with TPP innovation, and therefore such work could be ignored. However, once the definition of innovation is widened, as suggested here, to include aesthetic change, this argument fails.

A particularly useful database that has been used to explore innovation in the management/marketing literature is known as Profit Impact of Market Strategies (PIMS). PIMS is a large-scale study designed to measure the relationship between business actions and business results. The project was initiated and developed at the General Electric Co. from the mid-1960s and expanded on at the Management Science Institute at Harvard in the early 1970s; since 1975 the Strategic Planning Institute has continued development. The PIMS database of business unit performance information contains data on over 3,000 businesses in North America, Europe, and elsewhere. Each business unit is described using over 400 variables, all supplied by the managers of the business units, related in terms of the characteristics of the market in which it operates; the competitive position of the business in that market; and profits, cost structure, capital employed, and productivity. The contents and the history of the PIMS databases are described in greater detail in Buzzell et al. (1987) and Farris and Moore (2004).

A fact of particular interest here, for the study of soft innovation, is that the PIMS database contains information not only on R&D of business units, but also on other measures of innovation including IP gained and in particular the proportion of revenue earned from goods and services less than three years old. As the definitions are not constrained by the OECD

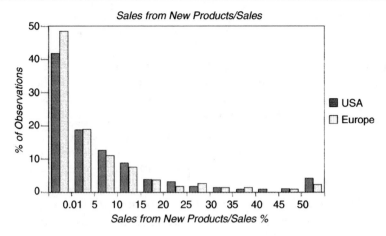

Figure 3.1 Proportion of revenue arising from products and services less than three years old

Source: Clayton and Carroll (1994)

rules (as the data in the CIS is supposed to be), this latter indicator should reflect both TPP and soft innovation. Figure 3.1, taken from Clayton and Carroll (1994), indicates the pattern of innovation revealed by this measure. It clearly shows that almost half of all firms have some sales from new products, far more than might be expected if only TPP innovation were being explored.

The advantage of the PIMS database is not, however, so much in showing the patterns of innovation as much as in the work that has been done on the database showing the impact of innovation and other factors on firm performance. This is discussed further in Chapter 11.

3.8   Conclusions

The aim of this chapter has been to explore the input or the output indicators that can be used to measure the extent of soft innovations at the economy-wide level. The indicators explored include: measures of innovation in the creative industries, taken from the Community Innovation Survey; the output of 'creation activities' and core creative employment in the creative industries; creative employment in non-creative industries; design activities in all industries; copyright and trademark applications in the United Kingdom and Europe; and the PIMS database.

None of the measures are ideal; they all have problems relating to data availability, interpretation, or evaluation, but together they tell a consistent picture.

The CIS data and the design data suggest that soft innovation is extensive throughout the economy and compared to TPP innovation particularly important in the non-manufacturing sectors. There is some suggestion from the CIS data that the rate of (soft) innovation in the creative sector may be faster than in other industrial sectors.

The employment data suggest that the total employment generated through activities that would encompass both soft and TPP innovation inside and outside the creative industries considerably exceeds the estimates of R&D employment in the whole economy by a factor of 7.

It has been suggested that a useful measure of soft innovation, at a high level of aggregation, may be based on the difference between the level of trademark activity and the level of R&D and/or patenting activity. Trademarking has the advantage of being a measure on which time series data is reasonably easily available and which can also indicate patterns by industry. This indicator not only shows extensive soft innovations in most industries, but also suggests that it has been increasing over time.

In totality, therefore, the picture is one which reveals widespread soft innovation, with such activity occurring in most industrial sectors. TPP innovation on the other hand, as reflected in patenting data, tends to be more concentrated in the manufacturing and utilities sectors. The consideration of soft innovation thus not only shows innovation occurring in the creative sector at a significant rate, which TPP indicators do not generally reflect, but also that the patterns of innovation outside the creative sector is more balanced than might have been thought. There is also some suggestion (in the trademark data) that the rate of soft innovation may be speeding up, or at least that the ratio of soft-to-TPP innovations is increasing.

This chapter has used a number of different indicators of soft innovation, some more amenable to data collection and analysis than others. The content above does however show that, at the aggregate or at the industry level, there are soft innovation indicators for which data can be reasonably easily collected over time on an internationally comparative basis. The two obvious indicators are registered trademarks and design rights. This suggests that future macroeconomic research does not have to be confined exclusively to analysis of TPP alone because only indicators of TPP are available (i.e. R&D and patent counts), but may properly be extended to include soft innovation using indicators such as trademark and design right registrations as proxies for soft and TPP innovative activity jointly.

While the main objective of this chapter has been to observe the impact of macro indicators, the next two chapters (Chapters 4 and 5) consider industry-specific indicators of soft innovation to observe, inter alia, how far the above picture is further confirmed. The approaches discussed in this chapter could have been employed in the exercises of Chapters 4 and 5 with little change, but this would show hardly anything new and in any case there is not appropriate data available. Instead, it has been found useful in those chapters to largely follow the advice of Png (2006) and use counts of new product variant launches as a measure of innovation.

4

Soft Innovation in the Creative Industries: Books, Recorded Music, and Video Games

4.1 Introduction

The aim of this and the following chapter is to look at soft innovations in particular products or industries in order to (*a*) further explore the means by which the extent of such innovation may be measured, and (*b*) draw out some patterns regarding the extent, nature, and determinants of such innovation. There is also further interest in how functional or TPP innovation interacts with soft innovation. This chapter considers products that are aesthetic in nature and are representative of the creative sector. Changes in such products are one part of soft innovation. The next chapter considers products that are not part of the creative sector, but nevertheless involve changes that can be identified as soft innovations. In both cases, measures of the extent of innovation will rely to a large extent on counts of new product variants launched in the market, and market success data will be used as an indicator of significance to weight the count data.

The three examples considered in this chapter include:

1. Books, where the main interests lie in new books launched, the lifetime profile of the sales of a book, relative sales of successful and unsuccessful books, and the impact of and on related TPP innovations.
2. Recorded music, where the interests are similar to those for books but in addition there are more aspects related to soft innovations and TPP innovations, especially as music recording and reproduction requires hardware, and the hardware has changed over time.

3. Video games, where the interests are similar to the previous two but now the hardware-specific nature of some software creates a much more complex pattern of innovation and sales.

The latter two cases are examples of markets that are now being called two-sided[1] and are spawning a growing literature of their own (see, e.g., Rochet and Tirole [2006]). The difference between them is that for video games the software is often not compatible between consoles, whereas this is not so for most recorded music. The recent literature in this area has explored pricing in such markets and the extent to which platform variable costs will be passed through to end users in various ways.

4.2 Product variant launches as a measure of the rate of soft innovation

The main measures of soft innovation activity that are employed in this analysis relate to the number of new product variants launched per period.[2] The most basic such measure is a simple headcount of the number of new variants launched. More launches means more innovation. A better measure corrects this for market size by considering the ratio of the number of new variants launched in a period compared to the number of existing variants. However, just taking the number of new variants launched in each period to indicate the rate of innovation may be misleading, for no allowance is being made for what is and what is not a significant new variant. Many variants may be launched, but very few may sell more than a nominal amount. The extent of innovation will thus be better indicated by looking at the sales or market share-weighted numbers of new and existing variants.[3]

A useful sales-weighted measure of innovation can be constructed as $I(t, n, \tau) = s(t, \tau)/S(t, n)$ which for any time t, and for the highest selling n variants, measures the sales (value or number) of those of these variants, $s(t, \tau)$, launched in the period (t, τ) as a proportion of the sales (number or value) of the total highest selling n variants, $S(t, n)$. The greater the sales enjoyed by new as opposed to existing variants, the higher will be the

---

[1] Rochet and Tirole (2006) define a market as two-sided if the platform can affect the volume of transactions by charging more at one side of the market and reducing the price paid by the other by an equal amount. In the video game example the buyer (gamer) buys a game developed by a seller (game publisher) and plays it using the console developed by the platform.

[2] As recommended by Png (2006).

[3] Although sales-weighted measures of innovative activity have the disadvantages that they may reflect diffusion patterns as well as, or instead of, innovation patterns and may classify sleepers (products that take a long time to have market impact, e.g. *the Lord of the Rings*) as non-innovative.

measured rate of innovation. The choice of n will be determined by the desire to be comprehensive, however, as will be seen below, sales often decline rapidly once one moves away from the leading variants and thus n may not need to be too large. The choice of τ will depend upon the speed with which new variants are purchased. This may be chosen differently for different products or countries. This indicator may be derived at the level of the market, or at the level of the firm.[4] When working at the level of the firm the indicator is very close to another common measure of innovative activity – the proportion of sales arising from products launched in some pre-specified recent period. The measure is also unit independent and as such may be compared across different products. Unfortunately it has not been possible to always locate data that would allow the indicator to be calculated.

4.3 Book publishing

4.3.1 Introduction

Printed books have now been in existence for more than 500 years. In that time the means by which they have been written, printed, reprinted, and sold has changed extensively. Such TPP innovation is one characteristic of the book publishing industry. Here, however, the primary interest is soft innovation in the industry. This is considered primarily to be reflected in the number of significant new titles launched in the market, such titles representing new product variants. This section is thus concerned mainly with patterns in the launch or relaunch of titles and their subsequent sales. Conceptually it is considered that new titles are launched and made available to the buying public. Those whose sales exceed the initial print run will be reprinted (or perhaps, recently, made available through an electronic download mechanism). Those whose sales do not meet expectations may remain available but may be taken off the market and in some cases even be pulped. It is assumed that, in the majority of cases, once a title has been acquired the consumer will not buy that title again (although with some books such as the Bible or the Koran this may not be a justified assumption).

---

[4] For an individual firm the measure might reflect the proportion of the sales of 'its own' n best-selling variants that have been launched in a given specified period. Alternatively one might use an indicator such as $I_i(t, n, \tau) = s_i(t, \tau)/S(t, n)$ which for any time t, and for the highest selling n variants, measures the sales (value or number) of those of these variants, $s(t, \tau)$, launched by firm i in the period (τ, t) as a proportion of the sales (number or value) of the total highest selling n variants 'in the market', $S(t, n)$.

Table 4.1 Total value, and volume sales of UK book publishers, 2004/5

	Total	Home	Export
Value sales (£ millions)			
2005	2,768	1,768	1,000
2004	2,660	1,751	909
Unit sales (millions)			
2005	788	459	329
2004	756	468	288

Source: UK Book Publishing Industry Statistics Yearbook 2005, The Publishers Association 2006, http://www. publishers.org.uk

The Publishers Association[5] (www.publishers.org.uk) estimate that there are about 60,000 publishers in the United Kingdom with at least one title in print, but only 2,719 were (big enough to be) registered for VAT. Nielsen Bookscan estimates that there are about 1.6 million titles currently available for sale in the United Kingdom. The UK market and UK exports in 2004 and 2005 are as detailed in Table 4.1, total sales being about £2.8 billion in 2005.

4.3.2 *The number of new titles launched*

The crudest measure of soft innovation is a headcount of the number of new titles published. Whitaker Information Services estimate the total number of new titles and new editions published in the United Kingdom as 206,000 in 2005 and 161,000 in 2004 (see Table 4.2). The data suggests that the number of new titles published each year has been increasing over time and in this crude sense the rate of soft innovation has been increasing.

Internationally, there is similar data on the number of books launched[6] for a number of countries to be found at www.uis.unesco.org/TEMPLATE/ html/Exceltables/culture/Books.xls, which is partly reproduced[7] in Table 4.3. Not too much should be read in to the international comparability of this data, although the time series dimension should be reasonably reliable. In the time series dimension it is clear that in most countries the number of titles published per annum is on an upward trend.

[5] A trade body for the UK industry.

[6] The number of titles refers to non-periodic printed publications (books and pamphlets) published in a particular country and made available to the public. Unless otherwise stated, statistics on titles refer to both first editions and re-editions of books and pamphlets.

[7] The data source also provides data on a much wider set of countries, especially developing countries, that show much lower levels of activity.

Table 4.2 New book titles and editions launched, UK, 1996–2000, by category

Category	1996	1997	1998	1999	2000	2001	2002
Art	2,154	2,213	2,304	2,523	2,788	2,945	2,811
Biography	3,292	3,164	3,180	2,900	3,114	3,456	3,232
Children's books	8,045	8,208	8,497	9,099	10,397	10,784	10,519
Computers	3,515	2,978	3,010	3,886	3,803	3,785	4,381
Economics	4,519	4,305	4,529	4,670	4,726	5,095	5,232
Education	2,170	2,055	2,011	1,838	2,071	2,153	2,742
Engineering	1,854	1,651	1,851	1,706	2,069	2,137	1,951
Fiction	9,209	8,965	9,236	9,800	10,860	13,076	11,810
History	4,348	4,168	4,546	5,193	5,771	5,517	6,385
Law	2,562	2,882	2,554	2,848	2,902	3,579	3,799
Literature	3,107	2,884	2,930	2,936	3,150	3,130	3,270
Management	2,931	3,086	3,221	3,393	3,203	2,903	3,749
Medicine	3,964	4,052	3,842	4,093	4,260	3,465	3,544
Political Science	2,294	2,517	2,532	2,670	2,863	2,953	3,441
Psychology	1,290	1,321	1,329	1,383	1,490	1,452	1,510
Religion	4,331	4,109	4,379	4,595	4,466	4,229	4,641
School textbooks	3,629	3,049	4,141	3,963	4,640	3,808	4,464
Social Sciences	4,068	4,254	4,400	4,495	4,547	4,638	5,134
Social Welfare	2,678	2,497	2,879	2,655	2,652	2,694	2,991
Travel	2,155	2,258	2,802	3,077	3,223	3,535	3,420
SUBTOTAL	72,115	70,616	74,173	77,723	82,995	85,334	89,026
Other categories	29,389	29,413	30,461	32,432	33,420	33,667	36,364
TOTAL	101,504	100,029	104,634	110,155	116,415	119,001	125,390

Note: Figures include new and revised titles
http://www.publishers.org.uk/paweb/paweb.nsf/pubframe!Open)
Source: Whitaker Information Services, http://www.whitaker.co.uk

Table 4.3 Number of new books published, by country, 1995–9

COUNTRY	YEAR	Total
Canada	1995	17,931
	1996	19,900
	1997	21,669
	1998	20,848
	1999	22,941
Czech Republic	1995	8,994
	1996	10,244
	1997	11,519
	1998	11,738
	1999	12,551
Denmark	1995	12,478
	1996	12,352
	1997	13,450
	1998	13,175
	1999	14,455
Finland	1995	13,494
	1996	13,104
	1997	12,717
	1998	12,887

(*Continued*)

Table 4.3 (Continued)

COUNTRY	YEAR	Total
	1999	13,173
France	1995	34,766
	1996	49,123
	1997	45,453
	1998	47,916
	1999	39,083
Germany	1995	74,174
	1996	71,515
	1997	77,889
	1998	78,042
	1999	–
Hungary	1995	9,314
	1996	9,193
	1997	9,343
	1998	11,306
	1999	10,352
Iceland	1995	1,522
	1996	1,527
	1997	1,652
	1998	1,796
	1999	–
India	1995	11,643
	1996	11,903
	1997	12,006
	1998	14,085
	1999	–
Indonesia	1995	–
	1996	4,018
	1997	1,902
	1998	537
	1999	121
Iran, Islamic Republic of	1995	13,031
	1996	15,073
	1997	10,410
	1998	12,020
	1999	14,783
Italy	1995	34,470
	1996	35,236
	1997	36,217
	1998	30,835
	1999	32,365
Norway	1995	7,265
	1996	6,900
	1997	6,220
	1998	5,068
	1999	4,985
Poland	1995	11,925
	1996	14,104
	1997	15,996
	1998	16,462
	1999	19,192
Portugal	1995	–
	1996	7,868
	1997	8,331

(Contined)

Table 4.3 (Continued)

COUNTRY	YEAR	Total
	1998	2,186
	1999	–
Spain	1995	48,467
	1996	46,330
	1997	48,713
	1998	55,774
	1999	59,174
United Kingdom	1995	101,764
	1996	107,263
	1997	106,444
	1998	110,965
	1999	–
United States	1995	62,039
	1996	68,175

Source: www.uis.unesco.org/TEMPLATE/html/Exceltables/culture/Books.xls

In most countries the number of new titles launched each year has been increasing over at least the last decade. This basic indicator of the extent of innovative activity thus suggests an increasing amount of soft innovation in book publishing not only in the United Kingdom but in nearly all other countries.

Such a headcount of new titles, however, is very rudimentary. One step towards refining the measure is to correct for the size of the market which can be done by relating the number of new book launches to the existing stock of titles already in the market. For the United Kingdom this is possible using the data above from Nielsen Bookscan and Whitaker Information Services which indicate 206,000 new titles and a stock of 1.6 million existing titles yielding an estimate of the rate of innovation as approximately 206,000/1,600,000, i.e. 12.8 per cent per annum in 2005. In an economy where growth in labour productivity (a commonly used indicator of the rate of innovation) on average is approximately 2.5 per cent per annum, this is a high rate to observe. However, as stated, taking the number of new titles launched each year to indicate the rate of innovation may be misleading for no allowance is being made for what is and what is not a significant new title. The next step is to consider indicators of significance.

4.3.3 *Significant new titles*

Many new titles are innovations of little economic significance. Only a few are significant. It has been argued in earlier chapters that sales or market share may be used to indicate significance. Using data from the *New York*

Times on fiction book sales, Sorensen (2007) observes a left-hand side skew in the distribution of book sales. Of the 1,217 books for which sales data was observed the top twelve (1 per cent) accounted for 25 per cent of total six-monthly sales and the top forty-three (3.5 per cent) accounted for 50 per cent of sales. The 205 books that made it to the *New York Times* best-seller lists accounted for 84 per cent of annual sales in the sample. This indicates that to encompass the vast majority of sales in the industry, and thus also most significant innovations, one does not have to go far down the sales order. This finding is reinforced by a simple exercise carried out on data related to the sales in the United Kingdom of the top ten selling fiction paperbacks in the week ending 28/04/07 (sourced from *The Times*) which showed that compared to the top-seller for the week (unit sales 40,285), the tenth bestseller had sales of only a quarter (11,930), and thus the sales of titles quickly tail off as one moves down the sales order. Thus, to study significant soft innovations in publishing most new titles may be ignored and the analysis can concentrate upon just the best-sellers.

This is a result confirmed by data on authors' earnings. Kretschmer and Hardwick (2007) argue that writers work in 'winner-takes-all' markets and as a result the distribution of income is highly unequal. The top 10 per cent of professional writers in the United Kingdom earn about 60 per cent of total income (they earn at least £68,200 per annum); the bottom 50 per cent earn about 8 per cent of total income. In their UK sample, 7.2 per cent of professional writers earned £100,000 or more from writing (mean = £188,062). In Germany, the top 10 per cent of professional writers earn about 41 per cent of total income (they earn at least €40,000/£27,600 per annum); the bottom 50 per cent earn about 12 per cent of total income. In their German sample, just 1.7 per cent of professional writers earned £100,000 (€145,000) or more. None of the German writers in the sample earned more than £345,000 (€500,000).

4.3.4 *Significant innovations*

Building upon the idea that only the best-sellers are of significant economic value, soft innovation in book publishing over time can be explored by looking at only best-sellers. Using data for a relatively short recent time span on weekly sales of the top twenty-five best-selling books in the United Kingdom published (print only) in *The Times* books section each Saturday (sourced originally from Nielsen Bookscan), it is possible to illustrate the life cycle of sales for best-selling books in the United Kingdom. Considering just those four books that entered the top twenty-five best-selling lists on 2 February 2008, reveals a cycle as in

Table 4.4 Life cycles of entries to UK twenty-five best-selling books list, 2/2/08, rank and unit sales

Week Book no.		1	2	3	4	5	6	7	8
1	Rank	8	1	4	12	12	22	–	–
	Sales	20,616	28,719	20,968	19,160	15,293	15,456	–	–
2	Rank	16	5	6	13	8	6	21	25*
	Sales	10,835	20,756	19,170	19,076	15,865	23,571	13,895	11,936
3	Rank	21	19	–	–	–	–	–	–
	Sales	10,040	11,030	–	–	–	–	–	–
4	Rank	25	14	16	22	19	18	–	–
	Sales	8,273	14,445	12,840	13,307	12,819	15,088	–	–

*This book re-entered at 16 (14,729) the following week.
Source: *Times*, books section, 2/2/08–22/3/08

Table 4.4. This suggests that sales of books peak early after launch and then gradually fall, at least in terms of rank. This data suggests that sales peak, in most cases, in the second week on the chart (although book two peaked in the sixth week) and that rank is also highest in the second week on the chart.

Using the weekly data from the '*New York Times* Best Seller List' for fiction titles[8] from January 1970 until the present[9] the patterns of sales of the top ten best-selling titles in the United States has been explored. The top ten items from the list were selected in each week, providing ten items for each week of data over thirty-five years. This data has then been grouped into five-year periods for the analysis – 1970–4, 1975–9, 1980–4 . . . 2000–4, resulting in seven time periods from 1970 to date with around 2,600 data points for each time period – i.e. ten entries (i.e. the top ten) × 52 weeks × 5 years. For each five-yearly period, the number of titles that appeared in the top ten and for how many weeks these titles remained there was calculated. The same analysis was undertaken for authors. The main limitations of this data are that (*a*) there are no sales figure data so there is no indication of the order of magnitude between the top items and the lower items and as such, the top-seller is treated the same as the tenth seller, and (*b*) titles that cross two five-year time periods may be underrepresented in both periods, but this is expected to have only minor consequences. The basic data are presented in Table 4.5.

[8] Taman Powell, a Warwick Business School (WBS) doctoral student undertook the majority of the analysis for this section.
[9] The weekly *New York Times* Best Seller List for fiction titles was obtained for the period from January 1970 until the present in PDF format. These files (*c*.2,000 of them) were then converted into straight text files and a programme developed to extract relevant data, and combine this data into a usable format for manipulation in Microsoft Excel.

Table 4.5 *New York Times,* top ten fiction best-sellers, numbers of authors and titles, 1970–2004

	1970–4	1975–9	1980–4	1985–9	1990–4	1995–9	2000–4
Titles – number in top 10	166	159	209	254	298	340	491
Titles – average weeks in top 10	15.7	15.6	12.5	10.2	8.7	7.7	5.3
Authors – number in top 10	120	116	130	146	159	162	215
Authors – average weeks in top 10	21.7	21.4	20.1	17.8	16.4	16.1	12.1

Source: See text

This data indicates that the number of titles that enter the top ten per period has increased significantly since 1970–4 with 166 in the first period and 491 in the later period. It is also clear that the number of weeks that a book spends in the top ten has fallen considerably. Under either metric the data suggests that the rate of innovation as indicated by the number of significant new products launched has increased by about a factor of 3 over thirty years. A similar pattern appears with authors, the number entering the top ten in each five-year period has increased, but the time spent at the top has decreased.

This finding from the *New York Times* data that over time a greater number of titles has been entering the top ten and that the time spent there has reduced considerably suggests that the product life cycle of significant innovations in book publishing as shown above has considerably shortened over the last thirty years.

4.3.5 A market share-based innovation indicator

It was suggested above that an indicator of innovation that measures the proportion of sales that arise from recently launched product variants would be of considerable utility in indicating patterns of significant innovation. Unfortunately, the *New York Times* exercise for the US market, although informative, does not provide a sales-weighted index of innovation because data on neither the quantities sold nor the sales revenue are available. However, the finding that in 2000–4 a title on average spent 5.3 weeks in the top ten is equivalent on average to 19 per cent of sales being from titles new to the top ten each week. Also as the US data has shown that the number of weeks a title spent in the top ten has fallen from 15.7 to 5.3 weeks between 1970 and 2004, this suggests that there have also been significant increases over time in the proportion of sales that result from recently launched product variants – the preferred measure.

Further data has been collected[10] for the United Kingdom from the *Sunday Times* that publishes a top ten paperback fiction best-sellers list each week, which importantly includes an estimate of the number of copies of each title sold that week (the data originates from Nielsen) and the number of weeks for which the title has been in the top ten. Data was available for the period from January 2003 and was collected through to end of December 2007, covering in total 237 weeks. The measure of interest was the proportion of sales that arise from recently launched product variants. A recently launched product variant was defined as a book that had been in the top ten list for less than four weeks. The weekly sales of all books that fulfilled this criterion were summed and then divided by the total sales for the week of all ten books on the weekly best-seller list.[11]

In Figure 4.1 the weekly intertemporal pattern is plotted. The minimum was 0 per cent (where all the books have appeared on the list more than three times) and the maximum was 94 per cent. Although later peaks are higher than earlier peaks a trend is not obvious. However, the average for the five-year period is 45 per cent, whereas the average for 2003 is 46 per cent, for 2004 is 42 per cent, for 2005 is 39 per cent, for 2006 is 43 per cent, and for 2007 is 53 per cent. Since 2005 the trend is clearly upward. Thus, there seems clear evidence (*a*) that the rate of churn is high reflecting a high rate of successful new product introduction and (*b*) that even though over a short period, there is evidence of increasing churn in the UK market for fiction paperbacks reflecting an increasing rate of innovation.

4.3.6 *TPP innovation*

The picture of new title launches and sales patterns in this industry is one of extensive innovation, considerable market churning, and obvious dynamism. Behind this activity there is also considerable TPP innovation that may be one factor driving the observed soft innovation. For example, the introduction of the paperback as opposed to the hardback and now

---

[10] Daine Nicolaou, a WBS doctoral student, undertook this work.

[11] For two weeks every December (2003–2007) there was incomplete data as the newspaper listed the 'Bestsellers' for the whole year (but without how many weeks each book had been on the list or the weekly sales of each book). In addition, towards the end of each year paperback fiction books were not ranked but replaced with children's books. There were also monthly best-sellers lists for April 2005, May 2005, September 2005, June 2006, and August 2007. These were excluded from average calculations. Some books had weekly sales of combined editions. These were included. Almost every month there was one week in which only five books were ranked.

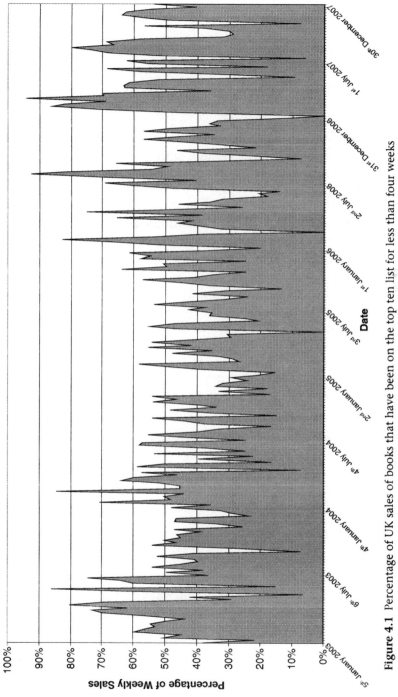

Figure 4.1 Percentage of UK sales of books that have been on the top ten list for less than four weeks

electronic downloads are major TPP innovations that have affected new title launches and product sales (especially through price impacts). In addition, the advent of word processors, the downplaying of the role of copy editors, the introduction of camera-ready copy and the demise of typesetting, and also the general computerization of production, stock control, ordering, printing, and major changes in marketing (e.g. Amazon), etc., all have enabled new books to be more quickly (and perhaps more cheaply) produced, launched, and sold. All such TPP innovations have contributed to the growing dynamism of the product portfolio.

4.3.7 Book publishing: an overview

Overall, the evidence on the book publishing industry indicates extensive and increasing soft innovative activity as shown by an increasing number of significant innovations and more churn in the market as product life cycles shorten. The extant literature on innovation does not appear to offer any examples of where functional innovations come and go at anywhere near the rate exhibited.

This has not occurred in isolation. TPP and soft innovation have interacted, and not only in terms of the former driving the latter, for soft innovation may well drive the sales that provide a derived demand for TPP innovations. The relationship should actually be considered interrelated. In terms of soft innovation, however, the pattern observed is of a high rate of innovativeness with extensive and increasing churn in bestselling authors and titles, that rate probably being beyond what one might expect to find in industries more usually considered as leading innovators.

4.4 Recorded music

4.4.1 Introduction

As with books,[12] recorded music[13] is an industry where a major innovation activity is the launch of new titles, i.e. recordings, in the market. These titles will remain in the market for a while and may or may not sell. Eventually titles that do not sell will be taken off the market. The analysis

---

[12] Ernie Lee, a WBS doctoral student, undertook much of the detailed data collection for this study of recorded music.

[13] The evolution of music and innovation in music prior to recording can be found in Scherer (2006).

of the industry is thus open to similar approaches to the methods applied to books, with soft innovation being reflected in titles launched and the sales of new titles. The main difference, however, is that compared to books, over time, the recorded music industry has experienced several changes in the media through which the music can be played or reproduced and thus in the products embodying the music. These changes in media do of course reflect TPP innovations but such innovations may have also impacted on soft innovations. It is implicitly assumed here that consumers will only buy one copy of any title for a given media but may buy extra copies if extra media are used or the media is replaced.

4.4.2 Media innovations

The main media on which recorded music has been available since the 1970s are vinyl (and a record player) either as long-play (LPs) record albums or singles, tape cassettes (and a cassette player), and from 1983 compact discs (CDs; and a CD player). Tables 4.6 and 4.7 chart[14] the rise and decline of the importance of these different media in the United Kingdom. Currently the advent of music downloads from the Web is considerably changing the marketplace. International Federation of the Phonographic Industry (IFPI)[15] data indicates that worldwide, record companies' digital music sales are estimated to have grown from 5.5 per cent in 2005 to around 10 per cent of industry sales for 2006, nearly doubling in value to approximately US$2 billion (up from $1.1 billion). Single track downloads were estimated to be 795 million in 2006, up 89 per cent from 2005. The number of tracks available online doubled to over 4 million in 2006. This compares to around 150,000 CD albums available in the biggest 'bricks and mortar' music stores. There are nearly 500 online music services available in over forty countries worldwide.[16] Similarly recorded content and new titles may also be available through different media. The main interest here, however, is not in the media per se but in recorded music titles launched for any (or all) of the different media. Such changes may make the statistical picture of

---

[14] Two tables are provided as neither seemed to be extendable to the full period and they measure different things. The main story is however clear. The source of these tables is the British Phonographic Industry (BPI), the UK industry trade body.

[15] IFPI is a trade body that represents the recording industry worldwide, with a membership comprising some 1,400 record companies in 75 countries and affiliated industry associations in 49 countries.

[16] Perhaps surprisingly one result of the digital revolution is that classical music was the fastest-growing music genre in the United States, growing by 23% in 2006, with exceptional digital sales on particular classical titles.

Table 4.6 UK sales* of CDs, LPs, cassettes, and singles† (million)

	LPs	Cassettes	CDs	Singles†
1973	81.0	9.8	–	54.6
1974	89.5	14.0	–	62.7
1975	91.6	16.5	–	56.9
1976	83.8	16.0	–	56.9
1977	81.7	18.5	–	62.1
1978	86.1	20.6	–	88.8
1979	74.5	23.5	–	89.1
1980	67.4	25.2	–	77.9
1981	64.0	28.7	–	77.4
1982	57.8	31.5	–	78.6
1983	54.3	35.8	0.3	74.0
1984	54.1	45.3	0.8	77.0
1985	52.9	55.4	3.1	73.8
1986	52.3	69.6	8.4	67.4
1987	52.2	74.4	18.2	63.4
1988	50.2	80.9	29.2	60.1
1989	37.9	83.0	41.7	61.1
1990	24.7	75.1	50.9	58.9
1991	12.9	66.8	62.8	56.3
1992	6.7	56.4	70.5	52.9
1993	5.0	55.7	92.9	56.3
1994	4.5	56.0	116.4	63.0
1995	3.6	53.4	139.2	70.7
1996	2.4	46.2	159.7	78.3
1997	2.5	36.6	158.8	87.0
1998	2.2	32.2	175.7	79.4
1999	2.3	18.4	176.9	80.1
2000	3.2	11.4	201.6	66.1

*Trade deliveries. †All formats combined (7″, 12″, cassette and CD).

Source: British Phonographic Industry, www.statistics.gov.uk/StatBase/Expodata/Spreadsheets/D6507

Table 4.7 UK retail album sales, by format (units %)

	2000	2001	2002	2003	2004	2005	2006
CD	93.7	97.6	99.0	99.4	99.4	99.6	98.3
LP	0.6	0.5	0.4	0.4	0.3	0.2	0.2
Cassette	5.4	1.8	0.5	0.2	0.1	–	–
Digital*	–	–	–	–	–	–	1.4
Other†	0.3	0.1	–	0.1	0.3	0.2	0.2
Total	100	100	100	100	100	100	100

*Digital represents sales of 9 million albums, April–December 2006.
†Other includes minidisc, DVD audio, DVD video, and albums released as 7″ single box sets.

Source: The Official UK Charts Company, *BPI Statistical Handbook*

the industry unclear, and perhaps not as reliable as it might have been, but the data still reveals a reasonably consistent picture.

4.4.3 *Market size*

IFPI Market Research, April 2007, shows that in the first quarter of 2007, UK album sales (although down) were 32 million units, single track downloads were 11.5 million units, and 980,000 digital albums were sold. For 2006 as a whole, overall album sales declined by 2.5 per cent to 155.1 million units, but in the digital albums' market 2.2 million units were sold between April and December 2006; digital sales comprised 1.4 per cent of the overall album market. UK acts claimed a 61.9 per cent share of best-selling albums in 2006. Per capita album sales were higher in the United Kingdom than anywhere else in the world – with an average of 2.9 albums bought by every man, woman, and child in the country every year. Norway is second at 2.7, with the United States third at 2.6. The singles market grew by 39.7 per cent, fuelled by growth in downloads with digital accounting for 79 per cent of singles sales (this data was sourced from BPI; figures are sales registered 'over the counter', through retail outlets in the United Kingdom, recorded by The Official UK Charts Company. http://www.bpi.co.uk/stats). Although other markets such as Japan, The Netherlands, and Australia showed different temporal patterns (see IFPI), this is clearly a thriving industry.[17]

In the United States the overall retail value of the record industry was $11.5 billion in 2006, a 6.2 per cent decline compared to 2005. There were 615 million CDs shipped,[18] a 12.8 per cent drop from the previous year. Digital music formats again demonstrated growth in 2006, with 586 million digital singles downloaded in 2006, representing a 60 per cent increase, and 28 million albums downloaded, a 103 per cent increase. Revenues from various mobile formats grew 84 per cent to $775 million and subscription service revenues were $206 million, a 38 per cent increase on the previous year. The growth in digital revenues partially compensated for the decline in physical sales.

---

[17] On the supply side Universal maintains its position as the world's biggest recording company, with a 25.5 per cent share of the world market. Sony BMG is next with a 21.5 per cent share followed by EMI at 13.4 per cent and Warner at 11.3 per cent. The independent sector holds steady with a 28.4 per cent global share.

[18] An IFPI term.

4.4.4 *Numbers of new titles*

Although IFPI data suggest a greater number of (new and reissued) album releases, data from the *BPI Statistical Handbook* indicates that in the United Kingdom a total of 33,524 new albums were released in 2006, 31,291 in 2005, and 29,510 in 2004 (see also Table 4.10). Although the number of new titles being launched, as already argued, is a rather rudimentary measure, these figures do suggest that in some absolute sense the amount of soft innovation in this industry is extensive and increasing. However, in order to get a clearer picture it is important to attempt to separate from the 30,000 or more (album) titles being launched each year those that are a success in terms of market share and thus market impact.

4.4.5 *Patterns of success*

The top five best-selling music genres in the United Kingdom are rock, pop, rhythm and blues (R&B), dance, and middle of the road (MOR). Rock's share of album sales in the United Kingdom has been increasing since 2003 (40 per cent in 2006), whilst the share of pop has been decreasing in the same period (24 per cent in 2006). Together, these five genres accounted for 87.6 per cent of total album sales volume in 2006 (2005: 85.7 per cent; 2004: 83.2 per cent).

Using sales as a proxy for market impact, the data in Table 4.8, referring to the best-selling singles in the United Kingdom, is indicative of the fast rate at which sales fall as one moves down the best-selling list. Basically the sales of top singles have been anything from 1.5 to 3.6 times those of the

Table 4.8 Best-selling singles by decade, UK (million)

	Decade					
Rank	1950	1960	1970	1980	1990	2000
1	1.39	1.89	2.05	3.55	4.86	1.79
2	1.24	1.75	1.98	1.891	1.84	1.34
3	1.17	1.52	1.97	1.77	1.78	1.17
4	0.92	1.52	1.79	1.51	1.72	1.17
5	0.88	1.41	1.51	1.43	1.67	1.13
6	0.82	1.40	1.38	1.42	1.54	1.08
7	0.77	1.38	1.30	1.40	1.52	1.08
8	0.74	1.36	1.18	1.36	1.45	1.07
9	0.71	1.21	1.15	1.32	1.40	1.00
10	0.68	1.20	1.14.	1.20	1.35	0.95
1/10	2.04	1.57	1.79	2.96	3.60	1.88

Source: 'Pop is dead? Long live pop', Times 2, pp. 12–13, *Times*, 11 January 2008. Based on data from The Official UK Charts Company (sales up to November 2007, including digital downloads from April 2005)

Table 4.9 Chart album sales volume as a percentage (%) of weekly best-selling album sales volume

Year	Chart position				
	10	20	30	40	50
1997	18	10	7	5	4
1998	28	15	10	6	5
1999	26	16	10	7	6
2000	20	12	8	6	4
2001	24	15	10	8	6
2002	24	16	12	8	7
2003	29	19	13	10	8
2004	30	19	13	10	7
2005	24	16	11	8	6
2006	22	14	9	7	5

Source: Millward Brown data from *BPI Statistical Handbook 2007*

tenth best-sellers. This picture of a sharp decline in sales as one moves down the charts is further reinforced by the data in Table 4.9 which lists sales of albums of different ranks as compared to the sales of the highest selling album. There have been fluctuations over the years but it is obvious that sales soon plunge as one moves down the best-seller lists. The main point is that when measuring significance through sales, significant innovation can be largely observed by looking at the quite small number of best-sellers.

This fact that very few albums are significant innovations in terms of market impact is further shown by UK data on album sales in charts compiled by The Official UK Charts Company and reproduced in Table 4.10. This data indicates that of the 33,524 new albums launched only

Table 4.10 Number of new albums (all genres) released and charting, UK, 1997–2007

Year	New album/titles (units)*	Top 40 debuts (units)†	Top 40 debuts (%)
1997	18,386	n/a	–
1998	17,597	n/a	–
1999	17,865	n/a	–
2000	19,312	n/a	–
2001	21,316	n/a	–
2002	25,048	n/a	–
2003	26,537	n/a	–
2004	29,510	229	0.78%
2005	31,291	236	0.75%
2006	33,524	233	0.70%
2007	n/a	289	–

Source: Millward Brown data from *BPI Statistical Handbook 2007* and *Music Weekly 2004–2006*

Table 4.11 Number of top forty debuts in UK weekly album sales charts

Period	Week	2004	2005	2006	2007
1	1–6	7	20	10	13
2	7–10	13	13	11	15
3	11–14	21	19	27	30
4	15–18	15	16	18	18
5	19–22	19	23	17	32
6	23–26	23	23	25	27
7	27–30	13	12	10	20
8	31–34	7	13	12	11
9	35–38	22	18	22	25
10	39–42	31	28	23	36
11	43–46	38	34	33	36
12	47–52	20	17	25	26
Total		229	236	233	289
Average		19	20	19	24

Source: Compiled from data in *Music Weekly* 2004–2007

233 entered the top forty chart positions in 2006 (with only 236 in 2005 and 229 in 2004). This figure represents 0.7 per cent of new albums released in 2006 (0.75 per cent in 2005 and 0.78 per cent in 2004).

Although it has not been possible to obtain the data necessary to calculate the sales-weighted measure of innovation discussed when looking at books (proportion of sales derived from newly launched products in a given period), it is possible to calculate a related measure that indicates new entry and churn amongst the best-selling titles. The greater the entry and churn, the more significant will be soft innovation. The data in Table 4.11 for the UK shows (as well as strong seasonal patterns) that about nineteen new album titles on average chart each month. This suggests that on average about half the top forty titles will change each month or that there will be complete churn of the top forty on an average in every two months. Alternatively one may see that about 230 (289 in 2007) new albums enter the charts for the first time each year (compared with 30,000 product launches). If there was a complete change of albums in the charts each month, there would be 480 debuts recorded in a year; 230 debuts in a year thus means that almost half the top forty will change on an average each month. The greater number of debuts in 2007 is not however on its own convincing evidence of speeding up.[19]

---

[19] Caves (2000) refers to the work of Petersen and Burger (1975) and Lopes (1992) to present data on the number of records and the number of performers making the weekly US Top Ten and the share of performers who are new, established, or fading stars. This data does suggest that artists' lifetimes at the top are getting shorter with US Top Ten sales by established performers declining.

Table 4.12 Major product classes in the music recording industry

Date of introduction	Product class	Production design hierarchy			Customer design hierarchy	
		Recording media	Recording unit	Playback unit	Early application	Types of music
1880s	Acoustic cylinders	Tin foil wax cylinder	Stylus etches wave form on cylinders	Movement of stylus drives horn	Juke box, home listening	Expansion of folk to classical
1900s	Acoustic discs	Shellac record	Stylus fetches waveform on discs	Different stylus and player	Home listening	Addition of opera
1920s	Electrical recording	Shellac record	Electrical recording from microphones	Movement of stylus driver speakers	Home listening	Addition of jazz
Late 1940s	Vinyl (long playing) LPs	Vinyl record	Move to magnetic tape for editing	Narrower stylus, lighter pickups	Home listening	Initially classical later rock and roll
Late 1950s	Stereo music	Vinyl with lateral and vertical cuts	Continued move to magnetic tape	Stereo players	Home listening	Rock and roll
1960s	Transistor players	Not applicable	Not applicable	Transistor players	Young users tolerated poor sound quality	Rock and roll
Mid-1960s	Magnetic tapes	8-track and cassette	Integrated and separate recording and playback machines		Cars, other portable	Rock and roll
Late 1970s	Digital	Compact discs (CD) and others	Digital recording	CD and other players	Home listening and portable	Addition of disco, rap

Source: Read and Welch (1976); Robertson and Langlois (1992); Langlois and Robertson (1992); Chanan (1995); Millard (1995)

4.4.6 *TPP innovation*

Since the beginning of the recorded music industry in the 1880s there have been many technological changes in products and processes. This has been illustrated to some degree by the changes in formats discussed above. Table 4.12, taken from Funk (2007), lists changes in major product classes over a longer period. The changing nature of the media and recording technology as reflected in product quality, length of recording, ease of selection, etc., all have had impacts on the customer demand for recorded music. However, just as such technological advances stimulated the demands for the music, the soft innovations must have also stimulated demand for the hardware that recorded and reproduced that music. TPP and soft innovations interact and interplay and neither the hardware or software markets would have developed as they have without the innovation in the other.

4.4.7 *Recorded music: an overview*

The overall picture of soft innovation in the music industry is similar to that seen with the book publishing industry. There is very extensive soft innovation as indicated by the data on launch patterns, but many titles fail and only a few are significant in terms of sales. There is also a high rate of churn in the top titles. However, unlike with books, in the data analysed here there is no convincing evidence that this rate of churn recently has been speeding up. It is, however, also an industry where new digital technologies are prominent in their impact and also an industry where there has been much TPP innovation over the last 100 years.

4.5 Video games

4.5.1 *Introduction*

The video games industry[20] is an example similar to recorded music and books industries, whereby the extent of soft innovation can be measured by new variant (title) launches, except that, to a large degree, games are console-specific and cannot be interchanged from one hardware set to

---

[20] Sunila Lobo, a WBS doctoral student, has made a major contribution to this section of the chapter. Throughout, no importance is placed upon the distinction between video games and computer games.

another.[21] Some titles are available on multiple platforms, although Clements and Ohashi (2005) report that this is true for only 17 per cent of the titles in their sample. Converting a game from one system to another requires additional development time and cost, and contractual agreements with platform providers sometimes demand exclusivity to one game system. Over time, the hardware on which the games are played has improved (e.g. PlayStation, PlayStation 2 and PlayStation 3) and with this the games themselves have been revamped, improved, and/or new titles launched. There has also been a growth in games available for PCs as opposed to games consoles. See Green et al. (2007) for a detailed discussion.

The market on the supply side involves the platform developers/suppliers/manufacturers, games developers, and games publishers. Clements and Ohashi (2005) describe how game publishers provide finance for game development, manage relations with hardware providers, and perform packaging and marketing. A software publisher may either develop games in-house or subcontract game development to independent developers. Platform providers also publish some software titles themselves, but these 'first-party' titles comprise a modest share of the software variety available for their own consoles. A new title for Microsoft's Xbox 360 console or Sony's PlayStation 3, both of which have high-definition graphics, can cost as much as $30 million (*The Economist*, 8–14 December 2007, p. 75) to develop. Independent publishers pay a royalty fee to a platform provider for every unit of a game title sold; such software licensing fees may be the primary source of revenue for hardware producers.

4.5.2 *The market*

The video games industry today is dominated by three major games hardware producers, namely Nintendo, Sony, and Microsoft. The three main games platforms are Microsoft's Xbox 360, Nintendo's Wii, and Sony's PlayStation 3 (PS3) (*The Economist*; 8–14 December 2007). These are seventh-generation game consoles. There is usually only a four- to six-year gap between each company's release of the next generation of consoles.

Sega and Atari were the major players (other than Nintendo) and major consumer console players in the 1970s (up until the 1990s for Sega, and until the mid-1980s for Atari), but have lost their dominant hold on the

---

[21] It is implictly assumed that, in general, consumers will at any one time have only one console, but when updating consoles may have to update software.

Table 4.13 Top ten game publishers
in the UK, 2007

1. Electronic Arts
2. THQ
3. Ubisoft
4. Nintendo
5. Microsoft
6. Sony
7. Take-Two
8. Activision
9. Sega
10. Eidos

consumer console market today. Sega was a major console manufacturer between 1989 and 2001, but then chose to leave the consumer console business from January 2001 onwards. In 2006, it was however still in the top ten in the list of games publishers published by ELSPA.[22] The top ten game publishers in 2007 are listed in Table 4.13.

Data from ELSPA shows that in 2006, the UK game industry, had (all-format) sales of game software totalling £1.36 billion (with a further £0.94 billion of revenue attributed to sales of hardware such as consoles[23]). In total 65.1 million units were sold.[24] Console games accounted for 75 per cent of software unit sales and 79 per cent of revenues. In 2006, the best-selling software format was the PlayStation2, which also shipped a total of more than 40 million consoles across Europe. In second place were games for the Nintendo DS, with Sony's PlayStation Portable at number three, followed by the Xbox 360, the Xbox, the Wii, and the GameCube (Nintendo). Sales of PC titles showed increase by 7 per cent in 2006.

According to ELSPA, for weeks 1 through 50 of 2007, the total number of units sold was up 16.6 per cent on 2006 in terms of units and 25.3 per cent in terms of value – £1.518 billion compared with £1.212 billion for weeks 1–50 in 2006.

4.5.3 Number of titles

Clements and Ohashi's (2005) study of US console games developers, 1994–2002, estimates the number of games in the market at 1,234 in

---

[22] The Entertainment & Leisure Software Publishers Association, a British game-industry trade body.

[23] Source: http://news.cnet.co.uk/gamesgear/0,39029682,49286924,00.htm, accessed on 19 December 2007 – article was posted on 15 January 2007 on the site.

[24] Source: http://news.spong.com/article/14502

1994, 1,480 in 1996, 1,494 in 1998, and 1,678 in 2000. This suggests a proportionate increase between 1994 and 2000 of 26 per cent, or approximately 4.5 per cent per annum. ELSPA quote that in the twelve months from January 2004 to end December 2004, 827 computer and video games were published in the United Kingdom (www.elspa.com). Such data suggests that there are large numbers of new games being launched in the market, and although it is a rudimentary measure of the rate of innovation (as has already been argued figures of this kind do not take account of the significance of individual innovations), this in turn suggests extensive innovative activity.

4.5.4 Patterns of success

Although there may be many games in the market at any point in time, and also many new games launched, as with the other two examples (books and music) previously discussed, they enjoy varying patterns of market success. The difference with this example, however, is that the sales patterns for software will reflect the console or hardware ownership patterns and changes therein in addition to software-related factors as is the nature of two-sided markets with different platforms (Armstrong 2006). Thus, if a new console is launched that is very successful, there is likely to be a high demand for software related to that platform rather than other platforms.

Once again it is found that sales decline quite quickly as a game moves down the best-selling chart, and thus sales of a limited number of best-sellers can provide a reasonably reliable indicator of what is happening in the whole market. Although it has not been possible to locate relevant supporting UK sales data (i.e. including number of units sold), some data relating to the Japanese market for the period from 2004 to 2008 has been located at http://forum.pcvsconsole.com/viewthread.php?tid=13452. This data shows that in the week 26 November–2 December 2007, in Japan the best-selling title ('Professor Layton and the Devil's Box') sold 293,897 copies, whereas the tenth best-seller ('Yu-Gi-Oh! World Championship 2008') sold only 34,620 copies.

For the United Kingdom, ELSPA data can be used to look at sales patterns for best-selling games. Most games appear to have short lives. At one extreme 'Dr Kawashima's Brain Training: How Old Is Your Brain?', a Nintendo DS game, has stayed in the top ten sales charts, 1995–2007, for 80 weeks as of 15 December 2007), spreading over two years, with its upgrade version on the top ten weekly charts for twenty-five weeks (the second longest time). In third place in terms of number of weeks, 'Fifa 08' (the latest instalment of Electronic Arts' football video game, released in the third quarter of 2007) had already been on the ELSPA Weekly Charts' Top Ten for twelve weeks as of 15 December 2007. At the other extreme, only four of the top ten games on the ELSPA Weekly Chart – week ending 15 December 2007 – have stayed on the charts for two months or more.

Table 4.14 presents data from ELSPA/Chart Track from 1995 to 2007 (week 50) on the number of weeks for which titles have been at number one in the sales charts. 'Who Wants To Be A Millionaire' was number 1 the most number of weeks between 1995 and week 50 2007 (eighteen non-consecutive weeks), while the rest were mostly only at number one for ten weeks.

Data for the top ten titles that made number one in 2006 are presented in Table 4.15 and for 2007 in Table 4.16. Only 'Fifa 07' reappears from 2006 in the 2007 top ten games. Jointly the tables indicate that between 2006 and 2007, the number of weeks at number one has halved for a top-selling game, to only four weeks from eight weeks. On average a top ten game spent 4.2 weeks at number one in 2006 but only 2.7 weeks in 2007. This compares with eleven weeks on average for the top-selling number one games in the period 1995–2007. The reduction over time in the weeks spent at number one and thus the resultant increase in the number of titles that reach number one indicate a pattern of soft innovation very similar to that already seen with books.

Table 4.14 Entertainment software: weeks at no. 1 from 1995 until week 50, 2007

TITLE	Weeks at no. 1
WHO WANTS TO BE A MILLIONAIRE	18
FIFA SOCCER '96	11
FIFA – ROAD TO THE WORLD CUP 98	11
GRAND THEFT AUTO: VICE CITY	10
NEED FOR SPEED: MOST WANTED	10
TOMB RAIDER	10
NEED FOR SPEED: UNDERGROUND 2	10
FIFA 07	10
MEDAL OF HONOR: FRONTLINE	10
POKEMON YELLOW	10

Source: ELSPA/Chart-Track

Table 4.15 Entertainment software: weeks at no. 1 in 2006, top ten

TITLE	Weeks at no. 1
FIFA 07	8
FIFA WORLD CUP GERMANY 2006	6
GRAND THEFT AUTO: LIBERTY CITY STORIES	5
NEED FOR SPEED: MOST WANTED	5
CARS	5
TOMB RAIDER: LEGEND	3
NEED FOR SPEED: CARBON	3
FIFA STREET 2	3
LEGO STAR WARS II: THE ORIGINAL TRILOGY	2
HITMAN: BLOOD MONEY	2
AVERAGE	4.2

Source: ELSPA/Chart-Track

Table 4.16 Entertainment software: weeks at no. 1 in 2007, top ten

TITLE	Weeks at no.1
SPIDER-MAN 3	4
HARRY POTTER & THE ORDER OF THE PHOENIX	4
TRANSFORMERS: THE GAME	3
LOST PLANET: EXTREME CONDITION	3
FORZA MOTORSPORT 2	3
FIFA 08	2
FIFA 07	2
FINAL FANTASY XII	2
COMMAND & CONQUER 3: TIBERIUM WARS	2
BIOSHOCK	2
AVERAGE	2.7

Source: ELSPA/Chart-Track

4.5.5 *A sales-weighted innovation indicator*

In the cases of books and recorded music it has been argued that, because sales decline quickly as one moves down the list of best-sellers, a useful indicator of the rate of significant innovation is provided by looking at the share of the sales of the top best-selling titles that are attributable to recently launched titles. Although it has not been possible to locate UK sales data to enable calculation of such an index for games, monthly data relating to the Japanese market for the period from November 2004 to mid-2007[25] has been located at http://forum.pcvsconsole.com/view-thread.php?tid=13452, which does enable this exercise to be performed.

---

[25] Data was missing for July and August 2007, and there was only limited data for September, October, and December 2007.

Table 4.17 Proportion of sales of top ten game titles accounted for by titles in the top ten for less than four weeks

Year	Average (%)
2005	81
2006	56
2007	78
Maximum	100
Minimum	20
Mean	70

Source: Derived from data available at http://forum.pcvsconsole.com/viewthread.php?tid=13452

In this exercise[26] a title is defined as new it if has been on the best-sellers list for four weeks or less, and the index is calculated as the proportion of total weekly sales of the top ten titles that meet this criterion. Table 4.17 presents the results which are also presented on a weekly basis in Figure 4.2.

The mean new title share of 70 per cent over the whole period is high and illustrates a rate of innovation similar to that in books in the United Kingdom (where the matching statistic is 45 per cent). This rate does, however, vary on a weekly basis over the time period for which data is available. The data run is probably too short to confirm any direction of movement.

4.5.6 TPP innovation

TPP innovation has already been discussed above. The close relationship between the hardware and the software means that TPP advances in hardware enable the games to be more realistic and perhaps more exciting to the player. At the same time the demand for better games also drives the development in hardware. This is very similar to books and recorded music.

4.5.7 Video games: an overview

The above analysis shows that the games industry is very innovative in soft innovation terms, launching numerous new titles each year. Few, however, succeed. The life cycle of a new successful title is short and from UK data for 2006 and 2007 there is evidence, as with books and

[26] The detailed data collection and estimation has been undertaken by Dania Nicolaou, a WBS doctoral student.

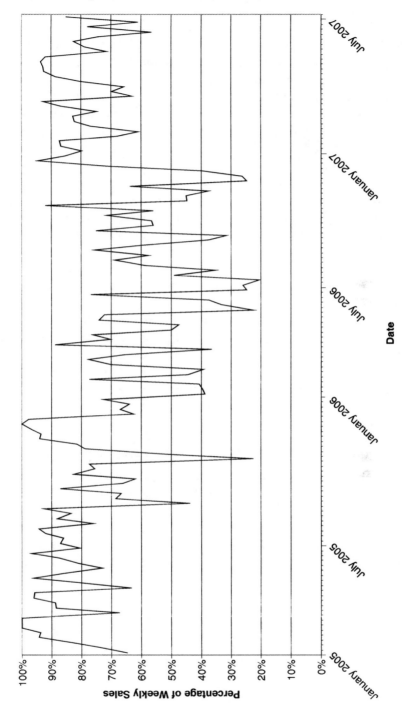

Figure 4.2 Video games: percentage of top ten titles sales attributable to titles on the top ten list for less than four weeks

recorded music, that life cycles are getting even shorter as games seem to hold their ranking (e.g. at number one) for increasingly short periods. In the absence of detailed sales data it was not possible to calculate the sales-weighted innovation measure described above for the United Kingdom. However if only four of the games in the top ten sales were in the top ten for more than two months this suggests that in a year at least 36 titles will have been in the top ten. This is very high and gets close to similar indicators calculated for books. It was however possible to calculate the sales-weighted indicator for Japan for the period from January 2005 to June 2007. This data showed that on average, titles that have been in the listing for four weeks or less (new titles) accounted for 70 per cent of top ten sales. This is a high rate of innovation. However, whether this was increasing over time was not clear from the short data run available.

4.6 Soft innovation in the creative industries: conclusions

This chapter has discussed soft innovation in three product areas (books, recorded music and video games) belonging to the creative industries. The main measures of the rate of innovative activity have involved using industry specific metrics largely building upon data relating to the number of titles (product variants) launched at different points in time. The results illustrated both the extent and nature of soft innovation.

The first observation on soft innovation in these industries is that many new titles are launched each year. This indicates high rates of soft innovation. However, of the new products launched very few succeed (in terms of sales). The most successful products sell in very large quantities but sales quickly decline as the success rank falls.[27] It has been shown that in books and video games, product life cycles are becoming shorter and these markets exhibit greater and greater churn with more and more 'best sellers' each year. These findings are interpreted as indicative of not only high rates of innovation but also increasing rates of significant soft innovation in books and video games but not necessarily in recorded music.

Sales-weighted indicators of innovation have been proposed, with a recommendation for one particular indicator that may be reasonably simply calculated if there is sales data upon the limited number of best-selling titles (and may be applied to the firm or the industry). The preferred

---

[27] For interest, Sedgwick (2002) provides some useful related observations upon the history of blockbusters and also-rans in Hollywood movies.

measure indicates the proportion of the sales in time t of the n best-selling titles that is due to those titles launched in the period t − τ where n and τ may be chosen as appropriate to the case. Calculation of this indicator for books in the United Kingdom and video games in Japan have been undertaken but data upon recorded music sales did not allow calculation in that case. When used, the preferred index showed high rates of soft innovation that were also getting faster in the case of books, although the data was too short in the case of video games for conclusions to be drawn. It has also been possible to confirm high rates of soft innovation using various other indicators, although there is little evidence from these that soft innovation in the recorded music industry is getting faster.

Overall, the three industries studied reflect rates of innovation that are orders of magnitude greater than are common in studies of technological change. Many studies of innovation will talk of technological change at the rate of 2.5 per cent per annum on average in the economy as a whole based upon changes in labour productivity over time. These examples, where there is complete product churn in a couple of months are in a different league. It is, however, difficult to propose direct comparators that would provide evidence of this. The most obvious example of the fastest rates of innovations cited are in terms of price falls for microprocessors (e.g. from an index of 1,000 to an index of 50 over four years from January 1996–January 2000[28]) but this does not directly compare with the number of new product launches. This emphasises even more that if the concept of innovation does not cover soft innovation of the kind analysed here then the dynamic picture of the economy will be considerably biased and perhaps overly pessimistic. In the next chapter we see if the picture extends to soft innovation outside the creative industries.

One lesson from the above analysis for further study of innovation in the creative industries is that although data upon trademarks, design rights etc may be used, it has been found particularly useful to use the (if possible sales weighted) numbers of product variant launches as a measure of the rate of innovation. Although this is demanding in terms of data sourcing the advantages seem to outweigh the costs. Over and above the sources for data that have been used here (where being in the public domain was a key characteristic) there is much data in the private domain that can be acquired (at a price) that might enable further similar analysis for other products.

---

[28] See http: //www.in3.dem.ist.utl.pt/inov2001/files/k_flamm.pps

Although the causes of soft innovation have not been explored in any depth, it is clear from the three examples studied here that there are clear links between soft innovation and TPP innovations. The former affects the sales of the latter and the latter affects both the sales of the former and the ability to deliver new products more quickly, more cheaply and with greater quality improvement. This line will be followed through in chapter 7 when the determination of the supply of innovations is modelled.

5

Soft Innovation Outside the Creative Industries: Food, Pharmaceuticals, and Financial Services

5.1 Introduction

This chapter considers soft innovation in those parts of the economy where innovation is traditionally most studied (i.e. those industries not distinguished as creative) by looking at innovation in three particular industries. As it is important to consider both goods and services the examples include the Food Industry and Pharmaceuticals as representative of goods and Financial Services as representative of services. To some extent, at least, these choice were conditioned by data availability, but the choices are explained further as the chapter proceeds.

The focus of interest is once again on the introduction of new product variants and product innovation. In these industries, however, not all new product variants that are launched will be soft innovations and many may in fact be TPP innovations (they will show changes in functionality). A basic problem with working on soft innovation in these sectors is making a distinction of soft innovations from those that are TPP innovations. Many innovations may in fact show characteristics that reflect both aesthetic and functional change. The imprecision of the line between soft and functional innovations outside the creative sector means that where the line might be drawn requires discussion in each case.

5.2 The food industry

5.2.1 *Introduction*

A food industry is found in all economies and is probably one of the oldest if not the oldest industry in the world.[1] Food producers in the 2007 UK R&D Scoreboard (www.innovation.gov.uk/rd_scoreboard) registered an R&D sales ratio of only 1.4 per cent on average, compared to the all-industry estimate of 1.8 per cent, and thus the industry is not high on the list of industries undertaking TPP innovation. However, there is evidence that soft innovation, as indicated by launch patterns of 'soft' new products and product variants that offer aesthetic rather than functional change, is frequent and widespread in the industry.

Food has both functional and aesthetic characteristics. In developed economies, such as the UK, food is no longer considered to be just a means to avoid dying or to stave off hunger pangs; it is a product that is to be enjoyed for its taste, appearance, smell, etc.

However, there are still functional characteristics that are of importance. For example, most current food-related debate in the UK relates to food and health. This reflects concern arising from, amongst other things, past food scares over the last two decades, including salmonella and e-coli outbreaks, BSE, and foot-and-mouth infection; obesity, particularly in young people; cholesterol levels in the adult population (see, e.g., www.americanheart.org/presenter.jhtml?identifier = 3036361); increasing levels of diabetes (see, e.g., www.cdc.gov/diabetes/statistics/incidence); food allergies and intolerances; the effects of using pesticides on food; and concerns surrounding genetically modified (GM) produce. In the context of breakfast cereals, Mintel (2006) reports that continuous product development between 2000 and 2005 was at least partly due to consumer demand for healthier products. The impact of food on health is perhaps best considered a functional characteristic of food rather than an aesthetic characteristic.

Mintel (2006) also reports that product development was at least partly due to consumer demand for more premium/organic, and more adult-oriented products. Thus, for example, the welfare of third-world growers has been promoted through fair-trade produce and there is now widespread acknowledgement of global warming, which has highlighted the risks involved in transporting food long distances and prompted a demand for local food. Also, in the last ten years, organic food consumption

---

[1] This section relies heavily upon work undertaken by a WBS doctoral student, Diane Skinner.

114

has shifted from the margin to the mainstream. As a result, amongst the important characteristics of food requirement today are perceptions, at least, of whether food is fair trade or not, and whether food is organic or not. These are, arguably, best viewed as aesthetic characteristics of food.

The innovation activity that occurs in the food industry may be vertical or horizontal. Illustrations of the two types helps to set the picture. Vertical product differentiation is often associated with marketing food of the same type through segregation into ranges of differing qualities, for example the differentiation between Tesco's premium 'Finest' range,[2] which is sold at a higher price than the standard equivalent, and, similarly, Tesco's low-priced 'Value' range which is sold more cheaply than the standard equivalent. It has been found that premium product quality shows a statistically significant positive impact on success rate, implying that premium quality can be seen as a means of differentiation that may give the manufacturer a competitive advantage (McNamara et al. 2003, p. 11). Horizontal differentiation can be seen, using Tesco as an example again, in the different food ranges that it offers (as of late 2007): Healthy Living, Free-From, Wholefoods, Tesco Ingredients, Organic, Fairtrade, Low Carbohydrate, 'Fresh in the Capital', Tesco Kids products, and Local.

A particular type of innovation that is observed in this industry is line extensions. The marketing literature documents many types of line extensions, such as novel versus older line, non-branded versus branded, slot-filler versus new-attribute expansions, and co-branded versus self-branded ingredients. Generally such extensions encompass small adaptations of an existing product, normally already available in the market. Line extensions are defined by the American Marketing Association (www.marketingpower.com/mg-dictionary-view2101.php)[3] as:

A new product marketed by an organization that already has at least one other product being sold in that product/market area. Line extensions are usually new flavors, sizes, models, applications, strengths, etc.

Line extension is an activity that can well be encompassed within the definition of soft innovation and thus an activity also worth observing.

---

[2] For the non-UK audience, Tesco is the largest UK supermarket chain.
[3] See also Bennett (1995).

5.2.2 *The market*

Between 2002 and 2006, UK consumer expenditure on food products[4] grew by 15.8 per cent at current prices, to £54.6 billion.[5] The current pattern of production, distribution, and retailing of food in the United Kingdom (and the rest of the world) represents considerable change since the end of the Second World War. Among other trends the more important include: (*a*) farmers have become dependent increasingly upon non-farm inputs such as pesticides and machinery; (*b*) supermarkets using central-ized depots have replaced small independent shops and most food pro-duced for sale is now carried by road over great distances; (*c*) the world has globalized in the sense of more and more extensive trade; (*d*) since the Second World War the British have expanded their eating habits from eating local food only to experimenting with a variety of dishes from overseas, albeit anglicized; (*e*) fast food has become extremely popular (Wimpy began selling burgers in Britain in the 1950s); and (*f*) most of the British population has become more affluent, and consumerism has grown rapidly with more disposable income being available for trying out new foods and restaurants.

Today, the food industry, in at least most developed countries (see Winger and Wall [2006]), is represented by large numbers of producers, often small, but increasingly a small number of large supermarket retailers. There is competition not only for sales between retailers, but competition between food product suppliers to gain access to retail space. Supermarkets in the United States and Europe may carry as many as 40,000 food and beverage stock-keeping units (SKUs) on their shelves, while in Australia and New Zealand the supermarkets have around 12,000 to 25,000 lines on their shelves. These figures may sound high but compared to the numbers of products potentially available are in fact quite small. However, Winger and Wall (2006) cite that, of the average 40,000 SKUs in a US supermarket, an average family gets 80–85 per cent of its needs from just 150 items, a supermarket shopping exercise takes on average twenty-four minutes, and the buyer would scan only 910 SKUs. Only 26 per cent of customers buy a wide variety of foods and brands.

---

[4] Defined to encompass meat and meat products; fish and fish products; fruit and veget-ables; dairy products, eggs, oils, and fats; and bread, cakes, biscuits, and cereals plus a variety of other food items that are not covered elsewhere (excluding sugar and sweet products), alco-holic drinks, and hot and cold beverages (including fruit juices, tea, and coffee).

[5] Source: http://www.researchandmarkets.com/reports/c81040

5.2.3 *Extent of innovation: new product launches*

It has not been possible to locate data on best-selling products for the food industry of the sort that was available for books, recorded music, and computer games that would have enabled a similar study of significant soft innovation as covered in Chapter 4. A variety of other approaches have thus been explored in the attempt to illustrate the extent of soft innovation in this industry. All these approaches primarily build upon observing the pattern of new product variant launches.

The existing literature on new products in the food industry is informative. According to McNamara et al. (2003), thousands of new products (variants) are launched every year. In Germany, for example, 32,478 new products were introduced in the food market in 2000 (Madakom 2001, cited in McNamara et al. 2003). Winger and Wall (2006) cite that in the United States about 18,000 'new' products are offered to the supermarkets each year (typically in Australia and New Zealand, there are between 5,000 and 10,000) and about 10 per cent are chosen to be displayed on the shelves. New introductions to the shelves are almost always linked to the discontinuation of another product.

Winger and Wall (2006) also argue that generally the majority of these products do not offer radical change. Hoban's (1998) review of the evidence on the degree of newness of products introduced in the US food market classifies only 1 in 100 or 200 products as really new. Equity transfer products (products with a strong franchise brand name) or line extensions (the majority of about 75 per cent) were dominant. Siriwong-wilaichat (2001) found that in Thailand between 1996 and 1999 only 9 per cent of new food products launched could be classified as completely new to the market. Watzke and Saguy (2005) in a review article comment that out of 24,543 new products that Ernst & Young and AC Nielsen researched in the United States, only 539 were innovative.

Thus, the literature indicates that there has been, and continues to be considerable launching of new products and variants in this industry. The research also indicates that in a sense many of the innovations are not radically new. However, in the absence of detailed knowledge as to whether this is in a functional or a market impact sense, the implications of this finding for measuring the extent of soft innovation are unclear. That said, the relative importance of line extensions and equity transfer products does suggest that a large proportion of the innovation in the food industry has been soft innovation.

Two particularly illustrative examples of soft innovation in the food industry where change can be observed are chocolate and breakfast cereals. Cadbury (now including Fry's) continues to produce Cadbury Dairy Milk (now 100 years old), Flake, Creme Egg, Picnic, Crunchie, Double Decker, Milk Tray, Fry's Chocolate Cream (launched in 1866), and Turkish Delight (launched in 1914). There are thus some long-established brands. However, *Financial Times* (2007) argues that a new generation of chocolate buyers have become more knowledgeable and demanding during the last ten or fifteen years and are purchasing high-cocoa-percentage bars, as well as 'origin' chocolate from specific parts of the world, and single-estate chocolate at the high end of the chocolate market.

Last year (2006), approximately 170 new organic chocolate products were launched globally and sales of Green & Black's, the UK's largest organic chocolate brand, rose 28 per cent to 36 million pounds (*Financial Times* 2007). In 2005, Cadbury's acquired Green & Black's which has seen sales growth of 40–50 per cent since the acquisition. In 2005, Cadbury Schweppes' sales of Dairy Milk increased by 7 per cent whilst Green & Black's sales increased by 49 per cent. The story of Green & Black's is also an interesting example of horizontal differentiation. Launched as a single high-end product in 1991, the company now offers sixteen different product variants. The launch of such chocolate and the brand proliferation are good examples of soft innovation and typical of what would be missed by concentrating solely upon TPP innovation.

The number of breakfast cereal lines have also expanded massively over the last decade. Today, one complete side of a multiple retailer supermarket aisle tends to be devoted to breakfast cereals. Kellogg's, for example, has expanded its range by providing both new products and variations on existing products and we have counted up to eighteen horizontally differentiated product derivatives currently available for some of Kellogg's most popular cereals. Similarly, the Weetabix range, produced by the Weetabix Food Company, now encompasses seven variations, including three in its a Weetabix Disney range. Quaker Oats is still sold in its original form, together with an organic version, a real fruit version, a maple flavoured 'real fruit and nut' version, and ten derivatives of Oatso Simple muesli. Such line extensions and marketing innovations are all part of soft innovation.

All this suggests that much product innovation in this industry is not of the TPP kind, rather it is soft innovation, catering to people's different tastes and aesthetic preferences rather than offering different functionality.

The literature contains a number of findings regarding the success of new product launches suggesting that most product innovations are failures. For example, McNamara et al. (2003) citing Madakom (2001) state that of 32,478 new products introduced in the German food market in 2000, a large share did not survive beyond the first year. Although there is some evidence that truly innovative products are often more successful for a company (Stewart-Knox & Mitchell 2003), Winger and Wall (2006) report various findings on failure rates from the literature (relating to different places and times) that reinforce the view that most new food products fail. They quote findings from the literature that show failure rates ranging from 48 to 99 per cent.

5.2.4 *Extent of innovation: trademarks*

In the absence of more detailed data on the patterns of product innovations in this industry, some further information may be gained by exploring trademark data. As argued in Chapter 3, trademarks may be counted to measure jointly both soft innovations and TPP innovations. However, in an industry such as this where, it has been argued, there is limited R&D, one might expect that TPP innovations are few in number and thus trademark counts will mainly measure soft innovations. Table 5.1 presents for four countries a count of trademarks registered in the food industry during 2004 and 2005.

Of the total number of trademarks across all industrial sectors registered in 2005, those in the food industry represented 10, 3, 17 and 8 per cent, respectively, for the United Kingdom, the United States, Germany, and Korea, indicating that when soft innovation is taken into account alongside TPP innovations, the food industry may well be one of the more innovative. The interpretation that these marks also indicate soft innovations suggests that there are particularly high levels of soft innovative activity in industries in NICE Class 30 in all four countries. Unfortunately, as the trademark data are available only for two years it is not possible to draw inferences on trend changes in activity over time.

5.2.5 *TPP innovation*

Soft innovation activity in this industry as in other industries may well be, at least partly, dependent upon TPP innovations in production and transportation processes. A lot of product innovation in the food industry will be based upon the imagination of chefs, packaging experts, etc. However,

Table 5.1 Trademark registrations, the food industry

Trademark registrations (2004 and 2005)[6]

Food classes	UNITED KINGDOM		UNITED STATES		GERMANY		REPUBLIC OF KOREA	
	2004	2005	2004	2005	2004	2005	2004	2005
29	1,111	1,090	2,256	2,546	3,456	3,657	2,517	3,215
30	1,444	1,374	3,555	4,134	4,596	4,851	3,139	3,551
31	484	444	1,280	1,342	1,466	1,611	980	1,294
32	814	924	1,157	1,429	2,862	3,161	1,265	1,646
Total (29–32)	3,853	3,833	8,248	9,451	12,380	13,280	7,901	9,706

Key to classes (NICE[7] classification)

Class	Description
29	Meat, fish, poultry, and game; meat extracts; preserved, dried, and cooked fruits and vegetables; jellies, jams, and compotes; eggs, milk and milk products; edible oils, and fats
30	Coffee, tea, cocoa, sugar, rice, tapioca, sago, artificial coffee; flour and preparations made from cereals, bread, pastry and confectionery, ices; honey, treacle; yeast, baking-powder; salt, mustard; vinegar, sauces (condiments); spices; ice
31	Agricultural, horticultural, and forestry products and grains not included in other classes; live animals; fresh fruits and vegetables; seeds, natural plants and flowers; foodstuffs for animals, malt
32	Beers; mineral and aerated waters and other non-alcoholic drinks; fruit drinks and fruit juices; syrups and other preparations for making beverages

new process innovations may also provide or have provided a basis for new products. For example, freeze drying revolutionized the instant coffee market. New knowledge regarding ripening and storing have made the worldwide trade in fruit and vegetables feasible. The growth of large supermarkets would seem at least in part to be based upon the use of IT advances in logistics, electronic funds transfer, refrigeration technology, and plant breeding. The ability to reflect customer demands in new products would also appear in part to be related to changes in methods of data capture reflecting customer expenditure patterns. Thus, although it may well be that soft innovation is widespread, that innovation could be built upon technological process innovation.

[6] Data taken from WIPO website http://www.wipo.int/ipstats/en/statistics/marks/, accessed on 17/12/07.

[7] The NICE Classification consists of a classification of goods and services for the purposes of registering trademarks and service marks and is based on a multilateral treaty administered by WIPO called the Nice Agreement Concerning the International Classification of Goods and Services for the Purposes of the Registration of Marks.

5.2.6 *The food industry: an overview*

Judging innovativeness in the food industry solely on the basis of R&D expenditure, which mainly reflects TPP innovation, would not provide a true picture of an industry that is continually launching new product variants on the market and changing products on offer to meet consumer desires and needs. The actual pattern may be better reflected in the trademark statistics, which, in conjunction with the literature on new product launch patterns, suggest: (*a*) that product innovation is extensive in the food industry; and (*b*) that many of the innovations may be soft in nature. To some degree such soft innovation may be based upon technological innovations.

However, most new products fail and thus the extent of significant innovation may be much less than the total launch numbers would suggest. In approximate terms, using the Winger and Wall (2006) numbers cited above, a US supermarket would carry about 40,000 SKUs and replace about 1,800 of these per annum, i.e. at the rate of 4.5 per cent per annum. However, of these new products Winger and Wall (2006) also cite evidence that only 42 per cent (756) appear to be still 'alive' after thirty-nine weeks. Using the thirty-nine-weeks' life as an indicator of innovation significance suggests that the rate of significant product launch is 1.9 per cent per annum. This is still extensive, but is of course far less than any estimates seen in the three creative industries studied.

5.3 Pharmaceuticals

5.3.1 *Introduction*

The pharmaceuticals industry[8] is always considered to be amongst the most TPP active of industries as measured by its R&D expenditure and patents registered. The 2007 R&D Scoreboard (www.innovation.gov.uk/rd_scoreboard/) reports R&D spending of £47 billion in 2006 in the UK industry (compared with £2.5 billion in the food industry). The industry is considered here precisely for that reason, for even with such apparently extensive TPP innovation it is still possible to identify much soft innovation.

The nature of soft innovation in pharmaceuticals merits some initial discussion. Recalling that soft innovation relates to aesthetics rather than

---

[8] Much of the work on this section of the report has been undertaken by a WBS doctoral student, Sotiris Rompas.

functionality and will also encompass marketing innovation as defined above, some examples of soft innovation become immediately apparent. For example, a quick casual glance at the over-the-counter painkiller shelves in the supermarkets will reveal that there are many variants of particular pharmaceuticals. For example, one may obtain plain aspirin tablets, capsules, or caplets. There is soluble aspirin and children's aspirin and low dose and high dose aspirins. There is branded aspirin (Anadin) or the generic. There is aspirin mixed with other painkillers. The variety is large if not endless. Such variety may be considered to be a clear example of past soft innovation. Even if one does not fully agree with this reasoning, many products on the markets are differentiated at least partly if not wholly by aesthetic rather than functional characteristics. Secondly, as discussed above, line extensions may be considered as soft innovations. In this industry (Hong et al. 2005), line extensions can be a new formulation of an existing product or a new modification of an existing molecular entity.

A third area meriting consideration is the launching of new products that are generic versions of existing drugs. A generic drug is a bioequivalent product of the original. Two drugs are considered pharmaceutical equivalents (bioequivalents) when: (*a*) they contain the same active ingredients; (*b*) they are of the same dosage form and route of administration; and (*c*) they are identical in strength and concentration. Although the functionality of the generic is essentially the same at the therapeutic level,[9] generic versions of original products can differ along several dimensions: (*a*) shape; (*b*) release mechanism; (*c*) labelling; (*d*) scoring;[10] and (*e*) recipients.[11] If the launch of generics is considered soft innovation, these dimensions (plus brand image) could serve as the categorizations by which the new products differ.

This argument is contentious. It is usually argued that a generic product is an imitation and not an innovation. This is correct if one is measuring innovation by functionality. However, soft innovation is not about functionality but aesthetics, with its significance measured or judged by market impact. A generic product will differ from the original in some way,

---

[9] Interestingly, the generic may be a functional innovation locally, i.e. for the producer (a product with different functionality to ones previously produced) but a soft innovation for the market. This chapter takes the market perspective.

[10] A score is a debossed line running across the planar surface of the tablet that can be used to facilitate the breaking of the tablet into fractions when less than a full tablet is required for a dose.

[11] An excipient is an inactive substance used as a carrier for the active ingredients of a medication.

even if only in terms of product name, brand (or no brand), or packaging. These are aesthetic differences (or indicators of marketing innovation). However, one might expect the market impact of the generic in terms of sales compared to the original to be large[12] (because one expects it to be priced low relative to the original) and thus, in terms of the current metric, a generic product as an aesthetic innovation may be considered important.

5.3.2 The market

Datamonitor (2004)[13] indicates that in 2003 the global pharmaceuticals market grew by 7.5 per cent to a value of $462.3 billion, and forecasted a value of $647.9 billion in 2008, an increase of 40.1 per cent since 2003. Cardiovascular drugs make up the largest sector, accounting for 19.5 per cent of the market's value. The US market dominates global pharmaceuticals sales, generating 47 per cent of the revenue. The global biotechnology industry grew by 13.7 per cent in 2003 to reach a value of $102 billion. In 2008 the global biotechnology industry was forecasted to have a value of $162 billion, an increase of 58.8 per cent since 2003. Product sales remain the dominant revenue source for the global biotechnology industry. In 2003, two-thirds of industry revenue came from product sales. North America continued to dominate with nearly 48 per cent of the global biotech industry revenue coming from this region. Amgen maintained its position at the top of the global biotechnology industry, accounting for over 8 per cent of the global industry revenues (Datamonitor 2004). The supply side of the industry is made up of a limited number of large multinational companies.

5.3.3 Extent of innovation, new product launches

Following the previous examples, an analysis of product launch patterns is a useful means to obtain some measures of soft innovation. Roberts (1999) takes a market-based approach to innovation in pharmaceuticals and explores product innovations according to year of introduction, annual

---

[12] Kanavos et al. (2008) provide some detail on off-patent drugs, but argue that despite recent emphasis upon generics there is little knowledge on the mechanisms driving generic competition, the impact of regulation upon generic competition, and the extent to which generics deliver savings.

[13] The Datamonitor report was obtained freely through EBSCOhost and Business Source Premier (*www.ebscohost.com*).

product sales, therapeutic market membership, and total therapeutic market sales in the United States for the period from 1977 to 1993, using data supplied by Intercontinental Medical Statistics America (IMS). The products may be TPP innovations or soft innovations in the sense defined here. To keep the analysis manageable, Roberts (1999) only considers products with sales in excess of $1 million in any one year in the sample period. He finds that 4,914 new products launched in the study period meet his sampling criterion, of which 1,070 are attributable to forty-two companies that for at least one year are in the top forty by sales. Roberts quotes Ali (1994) that in general roughly 10 per cent of all new products introduced to the market may be considered new to the world. Thus, if as an extreme 'new to the world' is taken to mean that they offer different functionality, this still allows that of the 4,914 products launched some 90 per cent may be candidates to be counted as soft innovation.

In a related exercise Roberts looks at the market share of new products in their year of innovation. For this exercise he restricts the analysis to the sample of 1,070 products launched by companies in the top forty by sales. Noting that the 90th percentile of initial market shares in this data set is 15.6 per cent, a 15.6 per cent initial market share is used to separate 'innovative' from 'less innovative' products (this is similar to the concept of market significance used here). These 'innovative' products have annual average sales (over all years) of $71.7 million, roughly six times the $12.1 million for the remaining products. Overall, Roberts, work indicates that, as found above (*a*) there are many innovations being introduced of which at least some may be 'soft innovations', but (*b*) that only small numbers of these have significant market impact.

Hong et al. (2005) provide some insight to line extensions in pharmaceuticals. A line extension is defined in this study of US pharmaceuticals as another product that a company introduces within the same market as its existing product, being either a new formulation or a new molecular entity within the same Hierarchical Ingredient Code (HIC) drug category. However, if the new formulation is a tablet or a capsule of an existing product, it is not defined as a line extension. The market definition is based on a therapeutic categorical system of three-digit HICs which classify drugs into distinct categories such as anti-hypertensive drugs and non-steroidal anti-inflammatory drugs. The study explores orally administered, non-antibiotic, single-pharmaceutical ingredient brand name drugs.

A set of twenty-seven brand-name prescription drugs that lost patent protection between 1987 and 1992 were selected for study. Of those, nine lost their patents in 1987, five in 1988, three in 1989, and ten between 1990 and 1992. All the brand-name drugs except for one were indicated for chronic diseases. Overall, product extension was observed in eight of the twenty-seven brand-name drugs, some with more than one extension. Of nine extensions, four had their formulation modified. All the formulation modifications involved extended-release or delayed-release dosage forms. In other words, soft innovation as indicated by line extension was widespread.

Prasnikar and Skerlj (2006) study generic pharmaceutical companies that are manufacturers and also have a R&D department in central and eastern Europe. Out of a total of 972 projects/products identified, 34 projects were at the pre-launch stage in 2002. Of these 6 per cent were line extensions and 59 per cent were existing products being offered to new markets. Only 35 per cent were new products with improved functionality. Again the indication is that, numerically at least, soft innovation is widespread.

5.3.4 *Extent of innovation, FDA review types*

Another potential indicator of soft innovation comes from a headcount of the number of drugs submitted in the United States to the Food and Drug Administration (FDA) for the different types of review each year.[14] There are three types of reviews: Original New Drug Applications (ONDA), Abbreviated New Drug Applications (ANDA), and Supplemental New Drug Applications (SNDA). ONDA encompasses application for approval for new chemical entities, and as such will primarily indicate TPP innovation.

ANDA encompasses applications for generic versions of patented ethical (prescription) drugs. More specifically, an ANDA contains data that, when submitted to the FDA's Center for Drug Evaluation and Research, Office of Generic Drugs, provides for the review and ultimate approval of a generic drug product. Generic drug applications are called 'abbreviated' because they are generally not required to include pre-clinical (animal) and clinical (human) data to establish safety and effectiveness. Instead, a generic applicant company must scientifically demonstrate that its product is bioequivalent (i.e. performs in the same manner as the original drug). Once approved, an applicant may manufacture and market the generic drug product. It has been argued above that new generics may be considered soft innovation.

---

[14] This sort of information does not appear to be available for the United Kingdom, but as pharmaceuticals is a world market this does not seem important.

The FDA defines SNDA as changes to drugs or their labels after they have been approved. Similarly, to change a label, market a new dosage or strength of a drug, or change the way it manufactures a drug, a company must submit a supplemental new drug application (SNDA). SNDAs may capture particular aspects of soft innovation such as line extensions, packaging, and labelling.

Data from the Drugs@FDA database,[15] for the eleven-month period ending November 2007, indicates approval of 71 ONDAs, 421 ANDAs, and 1,013 SNDAs. The size of the latter two categories relative to the former suggests that there may well be extensive soft innovation in this industry.

Tables 5.2 and 5.3 provide more details on ONDA and SNDA applications. The first point to note is the very low numbers of new molecular entities being approved: only fifteen of 71 ONDA drug approvals fall into this category. New formulation is dominant. Labelling revision is by far the dominant category in the SNDA list, with packaging change coming in a very poor second. All this suggests that in terms of numbers, innovations in the pharmaceutical industry are much more likely to be at the soft rather than functional end of the spectrum. If not purely aesthetic, new product variants may also differ partly on aesthetic and partly on functional grounds. This data indicates that there may well be large numbers of soft innovations in the pharmaceutical industry. However, as in all sectors, market share data is required if the significance of soft innovation is to be assessed. Table 5.4 provides data on the shares of generic medicines in Europe.[16] Although there are considerable differences across countries, this data clearly indicates that generics have an important market impact and thus that at least some past soft innovations have been significant on these terms. The data also show that in most countries the importance of generics is increasing.

5.3.5 *TPP innovation*

Much of the above discussion has already encompassed TPP innovation, but two points are worth making regarding the connection of soft and TPP innovation. The first is that, as elsewhere, soft innovation in this industry may be dependent on TPP innovation. However this is an industry that makes significant use of patents to protect Intellectual Property (IP), as patents are considered most effective. It is also an industry facing considerable

---

[15] www.fda.gov/cder/drugsatfda/datafiles/
[16] Source: Simeons and De Costar (2006).

Table 5.2 ONDA drug approvals, January–November 2007

Chemical types	Number
New molecular entity	15
New ester, new salt, or other non-covalent derivative	2
New formulation	26
New combination	4
New manufacturer	13
New indication	9
Drug already marketed	–
OTC switch	2
Total	71

Table 5.3 SNDA drugs approvals, January–November 2007

Approval type	Number
Accelerated approval	3
Control supplement	28
Efficacy supplement	28
Formulation revision	33
Labelling revision	754
Manufacturing change	15
New dosage regimen	18
New Indication	31
Administration	1
OTC labelling	3
Package change	34
Patient population altered	23
Supplement	42
Total	1,013

Table 5.4 Market shares of generic medicines in Europe (%)

	By value			By volume		
Year	1994	1999	2004	1994	1999	2004
Country						
Denmark	39.3	30.3	29.7	61.3	59.0	69.7
Netherlands	8.5	12.0	17.7	19.9	33.0	44.3
Poland	66.1	59.2	60.5	90.8	84.3	84.7
UK	8.6	11.8	20.1	–	–	–
Austria	5.5	5.7	8.8	9.2	11.0	15.8
Belgium	0.8	1.2	4.8	2.2	3.1	8.0
France	0.9	1.2	6.6	1.8	2.2	10.4
Italy	0.9	0.7	2.5	1.4	1.2	4.5
Portugal	0.5	0.5	8.6	0.8	0.9	7.2
Spain	1.7	1.9	5.0	2.0	2.5	8.1

regulation. In the circumstances, soft innovation (especially the introduction of generic variants) may often lag much behind TPP innovation. Although product variants may be put on the market and appeal through differences in taste, appearance, packaging, etc., the Intellectual Property Rights (IPR) regime may delay the process considerably. Moreover (although not in the United States), in many countries the health sector is not a free market. The behaviour of the main (state sector) buyers may be very different from the behaviour of individual consumers. The performance of the market may thus differ considerably from what would be expected in a free competitive market.

5.3.6 *Pharmaceuticals: an overview*

The pharmaceutical industry was chosen as an object of study because this industry is one where TPP innovation is usually considered to be particularly strong, R&D is high (in total and as a percentage of sales), and patents are widely used. Even so, the indicators presented here suggest that there is much more innovative activity taking place that would not be considered (at least wholly) to be within the definition of TPP innovation. Whether it be repackaging, line extensions, new generic products, changes in delivery methods, or many other similar phenomena, there are many changes that are encompassed within the definition of soft innovation. Arguably there is sufficient evidence to suggest that soft innovation is even more widespread than TPP innovation in this industry. It has also been shown that, in common with other industries, only a small proportion of innovations are market successes and thus only a small proportion of the soft innovations can – using the framework adopted in this volume – be considered significant innovations.

5.4 Financial services

5.4.1 *Introduction*

Financial services has been chosen as the final example partly because this is a service sector, but also because the example is not one that would immediately seem a fruitful area in which to find soft innovations. Financial innovation can be defined as the act of creating and then popularizing new financial instruments as well as new financial technologies, institutions, and markets. Financial innovations differ from the other innovations discussed in this chapter for they are in many ways less obvious and more hidden. An informative discussion of certain aspects of innovation within banking can be found in Appendix C of NESTA (2007).

5.4.2 Soft innovation and TPP innovation

If a new financial service involved R&D activity, it would be included as part of TPP innovation. As soft innovations are non-functional innovations and are not measured in R&D activity, it is useful to list examples of what activities in banking and insurance *are* considered by the *Frascati Manual* to be included in R&D (OECD 2002, p. 50) and thus are not soft innovations. The list encompasses:

- Mathematical research relating to financial risk analysis
- Development of risk models for credit policy
- Experimental development of new software for home banking
- Development of techniques for investigating consumer behaviour for the purpose of creating new types of accounts and banking services
- Research to identify new risks or new characteristics of risk that are required to be taken into consideration in insurance contracts
- Research on social phenomena with an impact on new types of insurance (health, retirement, etc.), such as on insurance cover for non-smokers
- R&D related to electronic banking and insurance, Internet-related services, and e-commerce applications
- R&D related to new or significantly improved financial services (new concepts for accounts, loans, insurance, and saving instruments)

If, on the other hand, innovation is the result of 'financial design', adaptation, a me-too process, or the application of existing general banking knowledge, then the product would not be so counted and could represent a soft innovation.

5.4.3 Patterns of soft innovation

It has however proved difficult to isolate soft innovations in this industry and to obtain data on such innovations. Some innovations (e.g. new options products or futures and derivative contracts) have been considered as candidates but although these may be considered as soft from one side of the market, they may not necessarily be considered so from the other. Tufano (2003) has surveyed the literature on financial innovations and states:

I asked my research assistant to compile a complete list of security innovations so that I could update an estimate from the mid-80s that showed that 20 per cent of all new security issues used an 'innovative' structure. . . . He provided me with a list of 1,836 unique 'security codes' used from the early 1980s through early 2001, each purporting to be a different type of security. Some of the securities listed were nearly-identical products offered by banks trying to differentiate their wares from those of their competitors. Others represented evolutionary improvements on earlier products. Perhaps a few were truly novel. Nevertheless, the length of the list represents a 'normal' pattern of financial innovation, where a security is created, but then modified (and improved) slightly by each successive bank that offers it to its clients.

This immediately indicates that although there are many innovations to be found in this sector, the normal pattern is one where only a few are truly functionally novel, TPP innovations, and most represent only modifications and slight improvements to existing products, where various banks are 'trying to differentiate their wares'. These might be considered as soft innovation.

5.4.4 *Soft innovation: credit cards*

A particular illustrative example of soft innovation in financial services is credit cards[17] in the UK market. A credit card may be used repeatedly to borrow money or buy products and services on credit. These were first used in the 1920s in the United States. Bank of America created the BankAmericard in 1958, a product which eventually evolved into the Visa system.[18] MasterCard came in to being in 1966 when a group of credit-issuing banks established MasterCharge. In 1966 Barclaycard in the United Kingdom launched the first credit card outside of the United States.

Credit cards have become an increasingly popular form of payment. Bank of England Statistics[19] (series LPMVWAY) indicate that as of 31 January 2008 the amount outstanding of monetary financial institutions sterling net credit card lending to individuals was £46,069 million.

Over time many new credit cards have been launched, each bank basically having its own version or versions and with differentiation between products being largely limited to branding. This is one form of soft innovation. Another type of soft innovation is that individual banks have gone extensively into line extensions. To exemplify, Table 5.5 lists the major

---

[17] Much of the further work in this section is based upon the research of a WBS doctoral student, Ye Zhou, specially undertaken for this project.

[18] Rysman (2007) provides a recent study of card usage.

[19] www.bankofengland.co.uk/statistics/index.htm

Table 5.5 Barclays credit cards (December 2007)

Card names	Features
Platinum Credit Card with Balance Transfer	0% interest on balance transfers for 14 months from account opening; 0% interest on purchases for 3 months from account opening; 14.9% APR
Flexi-Rate® Credit Card	0% interest on balance transfers for 10 months; 0% interest on purchases for 10 months from account opening; the more you repay the lower your interest rate will be and could be as low as 9.9%; 14.9% APR
Platinum Credit Card with Long Term Balance Transfer	5.9% p.a. on balance transfers for the life of the balance; 0% interest on purchases for 10 months from account opening; 14.9% APR
Platinum Credit Card with Cashback	0% interest on balance transfers for 12 months from account opening; 2% cash back on supermarket and petrol (up to £15 per month); 0.5% cash back on all other spending (up to £15 per month); 14.9% APR
OnePulse Credit Card	0% interest on purchases for 6 months from account opening; in-built Oyster card for the easiest way to travel around London; go cashless with OneTouch payments a new and quick way to pay for purchases of £10 and under; 14.9% APR
Breathe Credit Card	The card that donates 50% of net profits to projects that tackle climate change; 0% interest on balance transfers for 12 months from account opening; 5.9% purchase rate on public transport (excludes transport for London); 14.9% APR
Simplicity Credit Card	A small rate that stays small; the offer of a lifetime; 6.8% p.a. on every purchase and every balance transfer you make; 6.8% APR
Initial Credit Card	With a credit limit of up to £2,000 to get you off to a good start; 27.9% APR
Football Credit Card	0% interest on football season tickets (over £250); 0% interest on balance transfers for 12 months from account opening; earn reward points at selected retailers to swap for football merchandise; Win Barclays Premier League match tickets and get ongoing access to exclusive football offers; 14.9% APR
Charity Credit Card	0% interest on purchases for 6 months from account opening; 0% interest on balance transfers for 6 months from account opening; £5 donated to charity when you first use your card, plus ongoing donations; 14.9% APR
Student Credit Card	Up to 20% off on student essentials from Argos; no over limit fees; 14.9% APR
Graduate Credit Card	0% interest on balance transfers for 9 months; receive a return flight to selected European destinations; a credit limit of up to £4,000; 16.9% APR

Barclaycard variants on the UK market as of December 2007.[20] The different Barclaycards show little functional difference. From the viewpoint of interest rates on balance transfers, except for the Platinum Credit Card with Long-Term Balance Transfer at 5.9 per cent per annum, almost all Barclaycards had 0 per cent interest on balance transfers. From the perspective of annual percentage rate (APR), other than the Simplicity Credit Card, Initial Credit Card, and Graduate Credit Card having 6.8 per cent APR, 27.9 per

---

[20] See http://www.barclaycard.co.uk

cent APR, and 16.9 per cent APR, respectively, all the other Barclaycards had the same 14.9 per cent APR. However, as reflected by their names, different credit cards have their own special features to appeal to particular audiences. For example, the OnePulse Credit Card has an in-built Oyster card for an easy way to travel around London. The Football Credit Card charges 0 per cent interest on football season tickets (over £250). The Student Credit Card gives up to 20 per cent off on student essentials from Argos. Given the limited functional differences, these different credit cards do not represent TPP innovations but rather, soft innovations, in the credit card market. No data on their market shares is available to enable assessment of their market significance.

5.4.5 *TPP innovation*

Some of the soft innovations in the financial services industry may be the result of 'supply-side' TPP advances. For example, advances in IT have supported sophisticated pooling schemes that are observed in securitization. IT and improvements in telecommunications (and more recently the Internet) has also facilitated a number of innovations (not all successful), including new methods of underwriting securities, new methods of assembling portfolios of stocks, new markets for securities, and new means of executing security transactions. Also new 'intellectual technologies', i.e. derivative pricing models, are credited with stimulating the growth and popularization of a variety of new contracts. Without the ideas developed by Black, Scholes, Merton, and many others, many developments in derivative products would probably never have occurred.[21] The basic point is that soft innovations do not occur in isolation. As argued elsewhere, soft innovation and TPP innovation interact.

5.4.6 *Financial innovation: an overview*

The OECD definition of what constitutes R&D, and thus TPP innovation in the financial services sector, enables some clarification of what a soft innovation is in the financial services sector. Data limitations however make detailed analysis difficult. The innovation pattern observed is of a sector that is innovatively very active with an apparently continuous supply of new product variants which often functionally differ little from

---

[21] Post the credit crunch there may be mixed views as to whether this would have been a desirable outcome.

what was previously available. New product variants may well be tailored to meet customer preferences without representing any particular functional advance. Soft innovations such as line extensions and branding are to be found much like in other industries used here as examples. Thus, even in a sector that might not originally be thought of as a home for soft innovation, such activity is present.

5.5 Soft innovation outside the creative sector: an overview

It is more difficult to isolate and measure soft innovation outside the creative sector than in the creative sector. In this chapter, however, using a variety of different indicators, many associated with exploring the rate of launch of new product variants, it has been shown in three very different industries – food, pharmaceuticals, and financial services – that there is considerable evidence to indicate that soft innovation, i.e. innovation of an aesthetic rather than functional nature, is widespread. Some of that innovation may be of a horizontally differentiated kind, while some may be of a vertically differentiated kind. It is argued that line extensions and new generic products, as well as marketing innovations, may be considered as part of such innovation, and some new product variants may offer a mix of both aesthetic and functional innovation.

The three industries explored were chosen (*a*) to represent both goods (food and pharmaceuticals) and services (financial services); (*b*) because they were considered either traditionally innovative (pharmaceuticals) or non-innovative (food); and (*c*) much studied (pharmaceuticals) or little studied (financial services) industries. In each case it was shown that the industries were similar in revealing considerable soft innovation that standard metrics of innovation usually ignore. It may well be, therefore, that standard metrics considerably downplay the amount of innovation in such industries. This is similar to the finding in Chapter 3 that when trademarks were counted alongside patents and R&D, there was a considerable change in the overall picture of innovative activity observed.

The rates of innovation observed here were not in the same class as seen in the creative industries studied in Chapter 4 in that, as far as the data would allow a conclusion to be drawn, the rates of new product variant launch were much less. It was however the case, as seen in the food industry, that, as also seen in the creative sector, of the product innovations launched, very few succeeded. Therefore not all of the soft innovations observed were significant.

In empirical analyses of innovation in industries such as these, it would appear that R&D and patent counts will miss soft innovations. Preferred measures might therefore include trademark counts or new product variant launch counts that will encompass both soft and TPP innovations.

Although the task here was not to explain the causes of soft innovation, just as in the creative sector, TPP may provide some 'supply-side' explanation for the extent and timing of some soft innovations. For example, in financial services advances in IT and improvements in telecommunications (and more recently the Internet) may have facilitated a number of innovations; TPP innovations in pharmaceuticals may well provide opportunities for new line extensions and soft innovation; and new food technologies may have also allowed further soft innovation. These ideas are pursued in Chapter 7.

This chapter closes a part of the book that has been designed to introduce, define, and flesh out the concept of soft innovation and then to provide some indicators by which it can be measured and by using such indicators provide some estimates of its extent. At the end of this part the concept is clear, several measures and proxies for quantification have been provided, and also some data has been explored. It has been shown that soft innovation is extensive and that the inclusion of soft innovation as an aspect of innovation provides quite a different pattern of overall innovative activity in the economy. The next section of the book addresses the theory relating to the determination of such innovation.

Part II

The Economic Analysis of Soft Innovation

6

The Economic Analysis of TPP Innovation as a Foundation for the Analysis of Soft Innovation

6.1 Introduction

There is a considerable literature in economics dealing with the analysis of innovation (see, e.g., Stoneman [1995]), with the majority of that literature concerned with the traditionally studied technological product and process (TPP) innovation (although within this literature process innovation is more studied than product innovation). The purpose of this chapter is to look, in a general way, at the extent to which the decisions to generate and launch soft innovations and the (intertemporal) demand patterns for such innovations can be analysed in a way similar to this mainstream literature on TPP innovations and thereby provide a platform for later chapters that consider more detailed modelling of soft innovation activity. The classic work of Pavitt (2000) on taxonomy of innovation tells us that there is considerable heterogeneity in (TPP) innovation patterns in any economy suggesting that it may well be possible to ride on the back of the TPP literature to also analyse soft innovation.

Although economics is a very broad field of study and has a wide range of different approaches which have been used to explore innovative activity (see, e.g., Dosi et al. [1988]), neoclassical is by far the largest school of economics, and it is the neoclassical literature that is considered here.[1] The principal foundations of the neoclassical approach are that firms and consumers are rational, with firms pursuing profits and consumers

---

[1] Interestingly Goettler and Shachar (2001) in exploring competition in the television industry in the United States find that firms' observed strategies and behaviours are generally confirmed to be as predicted by such modelling (they are Nash equilibrating) and only depart from the equilibrium because firms may use rules of thumb or suffer bounded rationality.

maximizing utility, that utility functions and production functions exhibit the required convexity (i.e. declining marginal utility and marginal productivities with appropriate scale economies), and that markets clear.

6.2 Some models of TPP innovation

Much of the standard literature exploring the economics of innovation and technological change is based on modelling frameworks, the purpose of which is to explain (or understand) the determinants of expenditure by firms on the development of new products and processes. Such expenditure is usually implicitly assumed to be incurred on R&D. This chapter starts by considering two such models in the marginal tradition. Because the economics of innovation has also enjoyed a major contribution from game theory, the section then proceeds by illustrating the nature of the game theoretic approach and the contribution that it makes to the issues under consideration.

In recent years there has been a revival of interest in the process of creative destruction first introduced to the literature by a Schumpeter (1950). This is therefore considered next. This is followed by a discussion of two particular aspects of innovation modelling: (*a*) the treatment of time, stocks, and flows; and (*b*) uncertainty, prior to the consideration of market failure, which is the main foundation of approaches to the consideration of policy in the TPP literature.

6.2.1 *Standard approaches to the modelling of product and process innovation*

As an example of the approach commonly used in the main-line technology literature, consider the following simple model related to the firm's decisions on investments in the development of process innovations (which by definition reduce costs of production). Assume that (*a*) the firm i faces a demand curve for its product, such that demand is q_i at price p_i, given supply of q_j from rival firms; (*b*) the unit costs of production are c_i; and (*c*) c_i is determined by the firms' own expenditure on technology development, R_i, i.e., R&D, such that $c_i = c(R_i)$ and $c'_i < 0$. The firm makes profits Π_i given by

$$\Pi_i = q_i p_i(q_i, q_j) - c(R_i)q_i - R_i \tag{6.1}$$

which it maximizes by the choice of q_i and R_i. At the profit maximum two conditions hold.

$$-q_i dc(R_i)/dR_i - 1 = 0 \tag{6.2}$$

and

$$p_i(q_i,q_j) + q_i(\delta p_i/\delta q_i + \delta p_i/\delta q_j \cdot dq_j/dq_i) - c(R_i) = 0 \tag{6.3}$$

The first condition states that, to maximize profit, at the margin R_i will be such that the marginal reduction in production costs induced will equal the marginal cost of generating that reduction. The second condition states that marginal revenue equals marginal cost. The two conditions jointly determine R_i, unit costs of production, and output and profits of the firm.

Taking the argument further, marginal revenue obviously depends upon the reactions of rival firms to changes in the output of firm i (dq_j/dq_i) and the elasticities of demand in the market (due to $\delta p_i/\delta q_i$ and $\delta p_i/\delta q_j$). Defining η as the firm's own price elasticity of demand taking into account both the market elasticity and the reactions of rivals, the first order conditions yield that

$$p_i(q_i,q_j)(1 + 1/\eta) = c(R_i) \tag{6.4}$$

Defining η_{CR} as the negative of the elasticity of unit costs with respect to R, then after substitution

$$R_i/p_i.q_i = \eta_{CR}(1 + 1/\eta) \tag{6.5}$$

and the ratio of the firm's R&D expenditure to sales depends upon the elasticity of costs with respect to R_i and the elasticity of demand with respect to its own price. Much of the extant literature discusses the main determinants of these two crucial parameters. In particular it has addressed how the demand elasticity varies with market structure, especially the number and concentration of sellers, and whether, as a result, competition or monopoly encourages R_i and thus innovation (Cohen 1995).

Results for an individual firm can be extended to the level of the industry. A result of particular interest is that if there is free entry to the industry, then market structure and the expenditure (of firms and industries) on developing new process technologies are co-determined and neither causes the other (see Dasgupta and Stiglitz [1994]).

Models of this kind may also be used in the analysis of product instead of process innovations, although product innovations have been less studied in economics. The main change to be made is that innovation is then assumed to impact on the demand for the firm's product rather than upon its unit costs of production. A simple variant of the model assumes that the firm faces a demand curve for its product, such that demand q_i is a function of its own price p_i; the output of rival firms q_j; and own expenditure on new product development, R_i, i.e. R&D. These expenditures improve the quality or desirability of the firm's product. The unit costs of production, c_i, are assumed fixed and given. The profit of the firm is then given by

$$\Pi_i = q_i p_i(q_i, q_j, R_i) - c_i q_i - R_i. \tag{6.6}$$

The firm chooses q_i and R_i to maximize profits, and at the profit maximum two conditions hold

$$q_i(\delta p_i / \delta R_i) = 1 \tag{6.7}$$

and

$$p_i + q_i(\delta p_i / \delta q_i + \delta p_i / \delta q_j . dq_j / dq_i) - c_i = 0 \tag{6.8}$$

i.e.

$$p_i(q_i, q_j)(1 + 1/\eta) = c_i \tag{6.9}$$

The first condition requires that the marginal increase in revenue from the last unit of expenditure on R equals the cost of that expenditure (which in turn equals 1). The second condition again requires that marginal revenue equals marginal cost. Jointly the conditions determine expenditure on new product development and thus the product 'quality', the output of the firm, total costs, total revenue, and profits.

Defining η_{PR} as the elasticity of own price with respect to R, the first order conditions yield that

$$R_i / p_i q_i = \eta_{PR}. \tag{6.10}$$

Thus the expenditure on new product development as a proportion of sales depends upon the elasticity of product price related to R. This is a deceptively simple expression, for the η_{PR} term incorporates, inter alia, both the impact of R on own price and the impact of the reaction of rivals on this price.

The essence of these two models is that firms spend on developing new process or product technologies in order to pursue profits. This expenditure is usually identified as, and incurred on, R&D. It is generally assumed that greater expenditure leads to improved technology, often with some declining marginal productivity in product development further assumed. The models are frequently employed primarily to look at the impact of different market structures (e.g. competition or monopoly) on techno-logical innovation.

In the literature on new growth theory (Jones 1999), a rather more dynamic approach built around the concept of an intertemporal ideas production relationship has been taken to consider how the output of new product and process technologies relate to the expenditures on this activity. This allows that the stock of technology/designs/knowledge/ideas grows over time at a rate determined by the resources devoted to their production but the relationship is intermediated by the existing stock of designs. For example, it may be assumed, that if $A(t)$ is the stock of ideas and $R(t)$ are resources devoted to R&D in time t, then

$$\mathrm{d}\log A(t)/\mathrm{d}t = \gamma A(t)^{\alpha}.R(t)^{\beta} \qquad (6.11)$$

where the γ, α, and β are parameters. The parameter α allows for declines or increases in the productivity of knowledge production as knowledge expands (known as 'standing on shoulders' effect). Note that in general there is little discussion in the literature as to what goes on in firms that might generate such results as these above.

6.2.2 A game theoretic approach

Most of the more recent literature analysing TPP innovation and especially product and process development expenditures relies upon game theor-etic arguments (see, e.g. Beath, Katsoulacos, and Ulph [1995] for an early survey). In such approaches the incentive to innovate is provided by the difference between profit earned when the firm innovates and rivals do not, compared to the profit earned when rivals innovate and the firm does not. This approach provides a reminder that, when considering innov-ation, the counterfactual scenario for the firm will, because rivals do not tend to stand still, rarely be the status quo. Generally, for a process innov-ation, the profits of a firm not innovating when others do innovate will be less than profits prior to such innovation, and, as such, to use the status quo as counterfactual would be misleading.

Most of the game theoretic literature, especially as it relates to R&D, assumes the existence of a patent system. The rationale for a patent system is discussed in Chapter 11, but in the models, the patent system is con-sidered as a means by which one firm may monopolize a new technology.

It is generally assumed that the first firm to make a discovery will be able to patent that discovery and will have exclusive charge of the intellectual property (IP) embodied therein (although the patent system also provides that others will be able to know what the knowledge is that is being patented). This has led to the development of models in which R&D is seen as a race, with the result that the winner takes all.

In these racing models it is generally assumed that faster innovation is costlier. As the winner takes all, by trying to be the first to the winning post competing firms will tend to use up in the race all the rents from innovation. This has led to some results indicating that firms may innovate faster than is desirable (also known as common pool problems). There is also a literature on whether in repeated races there will always be the same winner (increasing dominance) or whether there is leapfrogging (e.g. Vickers [1986]). It may be noted that in such models market structure is endogenous.

6.2.3 Creative destruction

When innovation takes place, often the innovator is a new organization and with this innovation may replace an existing supplier. For example, a better lawnmower may cause the demand for the inferior model and its manufacturer to disappear. Similarly, through casual empiricism, one may see how the development of flat screen televisions has decimated the industry supplying cathode ray tubes. Such effects caused Schumpeter to describe innovation as a process of creative destruction – the creation of the new destroys the old.

An important implication of the process of creative destruction is how this impacts on the gains to be made from innovation. Consider a (monopolist) market incumbent and a challenger, either of whom may develop new technology. Assume the incumbent makes gross annual profit with the current technology of Π, which in the absence of innovation will continue in perpetuity, yielding a present value of the income steam Π/r, where r is the discount rate. Assume that whichever firm introduces the new technology will win the whole market (i.e. there is complete creative destruction) and the new technology will enable that firm to make annual profits of Π^* ($\Pi^* > \Pi$) with a present value Π^*/r.

If the incumbent introduces the new technology, then its gross annual profits will increase to Π^* with a present value Π^*/r. It might thus be thought that the incentive to the incumbent to innovate is the increase in profits or producer surplus with a present value $\Pi^*/r - \Pi/r$. However, if a challenger introduces the new technology instead and drives the incumbent out of the market, the incumbent will make zero profits (whereas the entrant will make gross profits of Π^* with a present value Π^*/r). This implies that with free entry and creative destruction (a) the incentive to the new entrant to innovate is Π^*/r; (b) the incentive to the incumbent to innovate is not the increase in producer surplus ($\Pi^*/r - \Pi/r$), but rather the difference between the profits when it retains its incumbency with new technology (Π^*/r) and that which it gets when the challenger takes over (zero), i.e. the incentive is also Π^*/r; (c) the incentive to innovate to both the incumbent and a new entrant may be greater than the social gain (the gain in producer surplus) that it generates.

This argument does need moderating to take into account that, in a world with creative destruction, there is always the possibility that at some future date the profits of an innovator may be reduced to zero due to new innovation, thus profit gains do not exist in perpetuity. The more probable the events of replacement, the lower are the expected private gains to innovation. However, the important principle is that with creative destruction the gains from innovation may fall on different economic actors than the losses (Aghion and Howitt 1997). As an example one may look at Petrin (2002) where, among other matters, the impact of the introduction of the minivan to the US auto market impacted on the demand for other vehicles.

6.2.4 Time, stocks, and flows

The above discussion is very atemporal, but much of the economics of innovation, for obvious reasons, concerns time. The consideration of time also introduces matters of stocks and flows.

Some products can be stored (capital goods) and generally will only be purchased infrequently. Thus, for example, a consumer durable once purchased will yield its service over a considerable period of time, and it may be many years before it is replaced. On the other hand some products cannot be stored for long periods and thus may be purchased by individuals in frequently. An example would be perishable food products. Defining $X(t)$ as the number of units of a product sold in time t, $S(t)$ the stock of the product held by consumers at the end of time period t, and δ the proportion of the stock that is lost or destroyed or disappears in each time period, then, $S(t) = (1 - \delta) S(t - 1) + X(t)$. For a non-storable product $\delta = 1$.

If buyers only ever acquire one unit of the product and if there is a total number of potential buyers (at any price) N, then the maximum demand for a non-storable product is of course N in each time period. For a storable product at time t, the maximum sales will be $N - S(t)$ which will be declining over time (if δ is not too large) as sales are made in each period. If δ is small, for a particular product or product variant, it may be that suppliers of storable products will experience markets where flow demand is shrinking over time as the number of owners of the product increases. In order to maintain sales it will be essential for the supplier to continually supply new products or variants to the market. For example, as the potential of one marketed consumer durable is exhausted, replacement products or variants will be required to maintain sales and profits. In certain sectors, therefore, a continuous supply of new products or product variants is in fact the basis for the continued existence of supplying firms.

Most of the economics found in standard textbooks is concerned with non-storable products where demand arises anew in each period (or the analysis is completely atemporal, which is in effect the same). It is not common to find in textbooks discussions of products of which individuals will only buy one in their lifetime and there is no repeat purchasing (in fact market satiation is often ruled out by assumption). Within the literature in the economics of TPP innovation it is, however, more common to approach such issues. This literature is often found under the headings of the economics of diffusion and may refer to either the purchase of new process technologies by firms or the purchase of new durables by households.

To exemplify, consider a new consumer durable of which buyers are only likely to ever buy one unit in a lifetime. How the purchases of this product will be spread over time and the resulting intertemporal pattern of ownership will depend upon both the demand and supply sides of the market. On the demand side, in time t, each potential buyer who has not already purchased the new durable must decide whether to purchase at time t or to wait until time $t + 1$ or later. Similarly on the producer side the seller must decide whether to produce (and sell if inventory possibilities are ignored) at time t or to wait until time $t + 1$ or later. These decisions are generally determined by two effects, labelled profit and arbitrage effects (see Ireland and Stoneman [1986]). The seller must decide in each time period whether a sale will not only be profitable, but also whether it might not be more profitable to sell at a later date. There might, for example, be some advantage in waiting if the prices of raw materials are going to fall in the future or if production technology is going to improve making production cheaper. The buyer, on the other hand, has to decide not only whether at current prices a utility gain can be made, but also whether by waiting a greater gain could be made because of lower prices or improved quality. In other words the demand for storable products may be affected by future expected changes in prices and the cost of production.

The literature on technological diffusion (see Stoneman [2002]) also considers other factors that affect the diffusion of TPP innovations. These include information spreading, learning effects, stock effects (more users reduce the gain from adoption), and order effects (early users get greater benefits over the lifetime of the technology) with roles for network externalities and competition between different standards. Perhaps, not surprisingly, this literature rarely considers the demand for non-capital, i.e. non-storable, products (although see Battisti and Stoneman [2000]).

6.2.5 Uncertainty

With the introduction of time into economic analysis it is essential to come to grips with the issue of uncertainty. Time implies that today's decisions depend upon prospective future outcomes which cannot be known with certainty, and thus all decisions are taken in the face of some uncertainty. Mainline economics has tried various approaches to deal with this.

Although a considerable field of study in itself, which it is not possible to fully survey here, some particularly relevant issues can be highlighted. Much of the literature in economics assumes that decision makers are risk neutral (i.e. they do not love or hate risk) and as a result seek to maximize the expected value of the pay-offs to their decisions. In such approaches, it is assumed that the probabilities of the occurrence of certain events are known. As an example, let us assume that there are two potential outcomes from an action, termed A and B, with probabilities of occurrence p and $(1 - p)$, having respective pay-offs π_A and π_B (be it utility or profits). The pay-off π to the risk-neutral decision maker is then determined by the weighted sum of the pay-offs where the weights are the probability of occurrence, i.e. $\pi = p\,\pi_A + (1 - p)\,\pi_B$. In making decisions on actions in a risk-neutral model such expected pay-offs to different actions will be compared.

Alternatively risk aversion might be introduced by assuming that decision makers do not like risk but do like returns and are willing to trade one for another. Thus, for example, a drug company may have the choice of (a) attempting to take the very risky route of producing a blockbuster with large potential returns or (b) a safer route offering fewer returns and less risk or (c) a combination of the two. The models argue that the company will trade off risk against potential return in choosing the route to follow. Stoneman (1981) uses such an approach to model technology adoption in the firm.

A third approach to decision making under uncertainty is the options approach. This essentially states that in the face of uncertainty, decisions that involve commitment may be postponed while further information is sought, or that, to avoid uncertainty, decisions may be made in small steps, each of which generates new information which may justify termination before full expenditures are incurred. If circumstances prove discouraging at any stage, the project can be terminated without the loss being total (Dixit and Pindyck 1994). Typical examples are that investment in new capital goods may be postponed until market information is clearer or that expenditure on an R&D project may be frequently reviewed in case project termination is desirable.

6.2.6 Market failure

Most of the literature in economics on TPP innovation has a normative purpose, the objective being to explore whether, unaided, free markets will generate a rate of innovation (both in terms of the generation and use of new products and processes) that is welfare optimal. If not then market failure is said to exist. If market failure is predicted, whether government policy intervention is desirable, and of what form, is then also considered.

Basic market failure arises when the value of the private incentives provided by the market to the economic sector differ from the social value of the action to be undertaken and thus goods and services are valued imperfectly by the market. If the private incentives are below the social value of the action, then in some area too little will be done. If the private incentive is greater than the social value of action, then in some area too much will be done. Classic examples of such market failures are (a) public goods (e.g. national defence) where the provider by supplying himself or herself also provides others but cannot get a reward for that provision; (b) increasing returns to scale where a producer may not be able to appropriate the benefits of lower costs that are generated by his or her production; (c) externalities in general where one actor's behaviour impacts on the benefits of others without charge or return; and (d) missing markets, especially insurance markets, so that there is no chance of trade.

The TPP literature, starting with Arrow (1962), has argued that market failures are endemic to the process of innovation. The main line of argument is that the innovation process is concerned with the generation and exploitation of information, and information markets are especially subject to failure. Although this argument has been expressed in many ways, currently the argument is made in terms of two crucial characteristics of a piece of information. The first is whether the relevant information or knowledge is rivalrous, i.e. whether one user having it prevents others from having it or affects the return to be obtained from it by the user.[2] The second is whether the information is excludable, i.e. whether one owner/user can exclude others from ownership or use.[3] If a good is non-excludable, then the initial owner/user will be unable to obtain the full social benefit of that good; if it is also rivalrous this suggests market failure. However, if the good is non-rivalrous the excludability does not matter.

The classic example of market failure in the TPP literature is where a firm, at some cost, develops a new process technology that will reduce the firm's costs and increase its profits. It would also lead to a reduction in product price. The social benefit generated by the firm's actions is the increase in the firm's profits plus the increase in consumer surplus. The firm will generally be unable to capture the increased consumer surplus and thus the incentives to develop the technology may be less than the social gains. In addition if the firm is not able to realize the increased profits because other firms copy its innovation (and due to competition reduce its profits to zero), this will reinforce the failure and the incentive to innovate will be even lower. These market failures will generate levels of innovation that are too low.

To overcome copying and the reduction in the incentives to innovate, there has been, for many years, government intervention through a number of different institutional arrangements which have been put in place to provide inventors with Intellectual Property Rights (IPR) so that they may be rewarded for any knowledge generated. For TPP innovations one usually analyses patent grants but trademarks, copyrights, and design rights fall within the same class of protective instruments.

However, IPR may not always be the complete solution. In game theoretic racing models, where firms compete for the IPR, the literature has

---

[2] It is often argued that information is non-rivalrous in that one's ownership of a piece of information is not affected by another's ownership of that information. However, in terms of value, exclusiveness may be very important.

[3] Public goods tend to be non-excludable.

shown that in some cases the winner-takes-all nature of the conflict causes players to over-invest in new technology rather than under-invest (see above).

The TPP literature has isolated many further reasons why the market for innovations may fail in addition to those briefly mentioned above. Included within these would be issues relating to uncertainty, the non-market nature of many buyers (e.g. the National Health Service), learning by doing or using, network externalities, etc. This is not, however, the place to explore these issues further.

6.3 Soft innovations: a special case?

6.3.1 *Introduction*

Having provided a brief overview of some approaches to analysing technological innovation, this section considers the extent to which such approaches can be extended to also encompass the analysis of soft innovation. In order to do this there is some value in first further discussing the nature of soft innovations. It has been argued above that soft innovation primarily consists of two main activities, namely the launch of new aesthetic products in the creative sector and aesthetic changes to products in other sectors. It has also been emphasized that soft innovation may often involve the introduction of new products that are horizontally or vertically differentiated from those already on the market.

A useful distinction is between consumer products, i.e. products where the demand arises from households (and perhaps government) at home and overseas and producer products, where demand arises from producers (including perhaps government) at home and overseas. That producer demand is also important as a source of demand for aesthetic innovation is indicated by the findings of Higgs et al. (2008) who show that the demand for products from the creative sector is also significant outside the creative sector. It might be thought that producer demand would differ in its nature from consumer demand and be less concerned with aesthetics. However, observation of the style and display of office blocks in the world's major cities indicates that aesthetics are also an important aspect of producer demand as well as consumer demand patterns.

Some soft innovations may be produced in very small quantities, with at the limit perhaps only one unit being produced. Thus, a piece of art may be a one-off (although of course it is possible that there may also be prints of which many copies are made) or a statue (but even this may be reproduced and sold). Many architectural outputs are one-off, specific to client and site (but as a quick overview of housing estates across the country will show, this is not always the case). Customized motor vehicles may be one-offs as may be garden landscaping. Some soft innovations of the performance type may be one-offs, such as large pop concerts, although a theatre production or a stage play (though possibly varying night-to-night) is often designed to be presented in many performances. Where products are one-offs or produced in very small numbers each unit produced is then an innovation, and the production process is also the innovation generation process.

Some of the limited quantity soft innovations may be storable or durable, while others may not be. A piece of art (mostly non-performance art) will generally be durable. However, a stage performance or a pop concert or an orchestral performance will not be durable as such, although recordings of the performance may be durable. In fact live performances are an extreme example of a non-storable product.

With such one-off non-storable products not only will the production process also be the innovation generation process, but the demand for the product (or the consumption process) is also a direct demand for the innovation, although the market will be one in which supply of the product variant or innovation (but not all such products) is limited and fixed. In such cases the pay-off to the innovation generation process will depend upon the costs of (producing) generating the product/innovation and the sum for which it can be sold.

On the other hand, some soft innovations may be produced to be sold in large quantities. Thus, a new pop song will represent a soft innovation but one which, it is hoped by the artists and producers, will be widely reproduced with many copies sold on CDs or the other media on which it is available. Most aesthetic innovation outside the creative sector will tend to be of this kind, so that it is hoped, for example, that a car with an improved exhaust note will sell more. In such cases innovations will tend to be embodied in products, e.g. a CD, a DVD, or a vehicle, and the production process involved is the making of that product. The innovation generation process will involve separate activities, for example the composing of new music, the designing of the car, the writing of new software, or the making of a new film, and generally the innovation generation process will differ from the production process. Such soft innovations will tend to be storable in the medium in which they are incorporated.

The demand for such innovations is a derived demand (derived from the demand for the product in which the innovation is incorporated), and the pay-off of such innovation generation will depend upon the costs of development and the sums (or extra sums) for which the medium can be sold. Of course the product in which the soft innovation is incorporated or presented may be a producer good as opposed to a consumer good.

Two particular characteristics that are not exclusive to soft innovations but may be more common than with TPP innovations are:

1. To be enjoyed, many soft innovations require related/or compatible hardware, e.g. games consoles, CD players, TV sets, where hardware is of little stand-alone value.

2. Many soft innovations are incorporated in durables and purchased only once (e.g. a book or a pre-recorded DVD), but they tend to be cheap (at least relative to hardware costs) and many differentiated product variants may eventually be purchased.

Some of the analytical approaches and concepts raised above in the TPP context can be simply transferred to the soft innovation context without argument. For example, the principle of creative destruction will be just as relevant to a new Beethoven recording causing demand for a previous version to disappear as to the new lawnmower example. Similarly if the innovations, or the goods in which they are incorporated or presented are storable, then buyers and sellers may undertake intertemporal arbitrage to determine the best time to buy and sell, whereas if the products are not storable (e.g. in the case of a theatrical production or a pop concert), then the possibilities of intertemporal arbitrage in the market on both the supply and demand side are very limited. Thus time, stocks, and flows are as relevant in the soft innovation context as in the TPP context. Similarly, uncertainty is as relevant a factor in the analysis of soft innovation as TPP innovation. The risk return trade off will be just as relevant to investments in aesthetic innovations as to a pharmaceutical company developing a new drug.

Despite the similarities, not everything is the same for soft innovation as for TPP innovations. The following sections thus explore in more detail those areas where the shift from TPP innovation to soft innovation may merit some reconsideration of the modelling.

6.3.2 The demand for soft innovations

As stated above, the demand for some soft innovations may be the final demand for one-off products (such as bespoke architectural services), where production and innovation coincide. On the other hand, soft innovation may involve placing in the market a new product or new product variant embodying a soft innovation that may sell in great numbers. The demand may be either consumer or producer demand and may also arise from government.

In many ways, the demand for soft product innovations where production and innovation coincide can be modelled in a similar way to the more frequently modelled TPP innovations. Thus, for example, modelling the demand for architectural services may be little different from modelling the demand for TPP in services such as new transport solutions, organizational innovations, new medical services, and IT solutions to data storage and retrieval, etc. It would seem reasonable that such soft innovation products face a standard demand curve where the amount of the product/innovation demanded (due to buyers utility or profit maximization) is a function of price, income, or investment (depending on whether it is a consumer or producer good) and other standard factors.

This category of innovations may also be considered to include soft product innovations that are one-offs, e.g. a piece of art. In essence this is not a problem, but if, as it may be with a piece of art that potential buyers are not market players (museums) or are driven by motives other than personal utility gains, then the demand for such products may not be as usually modelled. However, the potential impact on economic welfare of one-off innovations of this kind, being one-off, may well be small. Thus, even if one were not able to fully capture this situation, it is unlikely to make any overall analysis misleading.

When looking at soft innovations in products that will be purchased in larger quantities, the demand for soft innovations may be derived from the demand for the products in which they are incorporated. The demand may be either consumer or producer demand and may also arise from government. This will also have similarities to the demand for TPP innovations. If the innovation is embodied in a consumer good, then the demand for that good, and thus the demand for the innovation, can be modelled as deriving from consumers maximizing utility (derived from the functional and aesthetic characters of the goods consumed) subject to income constraints. Utility is increased if either more goods of a given characteristic are consumed or the goods consumed have more or improved functional and aesthetic character. Demand will be related to (changes in) product characteristics, income, and prices. The demand for soft innovations incorporated in producer goods can be considered in similar ways. The difference, however, is that instead of maximizing utilities, demand is determined by the producers' desires to maximize profits (for the private sector and as appropriate for the non-market sector). In principle, nevertheless, this does not have any new major implications.

The important point about soft innovations, however, is that many new products and variants will reflect either vertical or horizontal product differentiation. Neither of these concepts has played a significant role in the existing TPP-orientated economic literature. Some literature on product differentiation, built on in later chapters, would indicate that as soft innovation primarily impacts on the aesthetic characteristics of product variants, the actual demand for a product variant incorporating an innovation will depend upon the extent to which its aesthetics differs from that of other products/variants, the extent to which that aesthetic difference appeals to buyers (reflecting horizontal and vertical differentiation), its price, the price of other products/variants in the market, and also standard control factors such as disposable income.

One might, for example, characterize the demand for a product variant incorporating a soft innovation, q_i, as a function of the number of other variants on the market, n, the characteristics of those products as represented by the vector z_j, the price of those products as represented by the vector $\mathbf{p_j}$, the own price p_i and the vector of own characteristics z_i, i.e.

$$q_i, = q_i(n, z_j, \mathbf{p_j}, p_i, z_i) \tag{6.12}$$

where z_j and z_i incorporate, inter alia, different aesthetic characteristics.

Where this differs from an analysis of TPP innovation is that TPP analysis concentrates upon those characteristics in z_j and z_i that are often clear to define and measure and have agreed scales. Thus, functional characteristics may encompass, for example, speed, where faster is better, or size, where bigger (or smaller) is better, etc. The study of soft innovation extends to aesthetic characteristics which are much less easy to measure. If colour is a characteristic,[4] it is not possible to argue that there exists a scale of colour such that white is a shade of black, or that green is more or less yellow than is blue (in empirical analysis one could, however, define as determinants of demand a number of different 1/0 variables that take a value 1 if the product is a certain colour and 0 otherwise). Similarly it is not possible to define continuous variables to measure smell, touch, appearance, etc. Thus, aesthetic characteristics, although conceptually similar to functional characteristics, will be much more difficult to

---

[4] In case this is thought to be a facetious example, the success of pink mobile phones was phenomenal.

operationalize as arguments in a demand function. In the limit, it may be necessary to include a product- or variant-specific effect in the demand function for a soft innovation that picks up all such aesthetic character-istics of the product and to then accept that the impact of individual aesthetic differences on demand cannot be measured.

6.3.3 *The supply of soft innovations*

A basic principle of the standard economic approach to TPP innovation is that the supply of innovations will be driven by economic incentives (profits or producer surpluses) resulting from the innovation. This section first addresses whether this can also be argued with soft innovation. Of course with both soft and TPP innovation, if the decision-making unit is outside the market (see, e.g., NESTA [2006]), then the profit motive may be much weaker or non-existent. Thus, for example, as hospitals, educational establishments, or museums are not really profit-seeking units, one may not really expect their behaviour to be profit-driven. However, this work is mainly interested in firms in the market sector, where it is a standard assumption of the neoclassical approach to the analysis of TPP innovation that the profit motive is dominant.

The counter argument is that art and the artistic muse do not react to money, and thus much of the so-called soft innovation will not be driven by profit incentives. Therefore art is for art's sake and paying Michelangelo more would not have improved the Sistine chapel. Of course one must have some sympathy with this argument. As an author and as an academic I know that the ideas I generate do not relate to the amount I am being paid per hour. On the other hand I do know that if I have a heavier teaching load, I will do less (although not necessarily worse) research. The quality of the Sistine chapel may not have improved with more resources, but without the desire and financial support of the Pope the Sistine chapel ceiling would probably not have been created at all.

The 'art for art's sake' model is probably perhaps best suited to the lone artist's view of innovation, i.e. one artist working alone and being able to choose what to work on and how to do it. But most soft innovation is not the work of lone artists. Either the lone artist needs materials and financial support while creating, and that support may well react to commercial possibilities or, alternatively, the artist must work as part of a team (e.g. in opera or theatre) and other members of the team may seek financial recompense (see Caves [2000]).

In fact, even if it were to be accepted that the aesthetic muse does not react to money or profit incentives, many more ideas are generated than exploited. The generation of ideas is a relatively cheap process but getting those ideas to market is the expensive part – with TPP innovation it is often argued that the ratio of initial idea, development, and launch costs for innovations is 1:10:100 (see, e.g., Horne [1991]). At some stage in the innovation process, therefore, there will often be a selection process with some ideas being developed further, and of those developed, some being taken forward to the market. This suggests that even if the muse does not react to profit potential in generating ideas, the profit motive may still play a role in making choices as to what ideas reach the market or the speed at which the ideas from the muse are developed and brought to the market.

The view taken here is that, although there may be some merit in the art for art's sake model, in general and in most cases of relevance here, the standard neoclassical economic approach that does not distinguish any differences in motives between the producers of aesthetic and non-aesthetic innovations is appropriate. Thus it does not matter whether one is talking about movie production, record production, fashion design, car manufacture, or the manufacture of electrical products; it is assumed that the dominant drive is the profit motive. This is not to say that the process will not be stochastic, it may well be, but in one form or another profit is being sought.

Taking the neoclassical approach, on the whole, therefore, the rate at which new soft innovations are developed, what is developed, the speed of development, the pricing of soft innovations, even the removal of other soft products from the market will all be determined to some degree at least by profit-seeking motives. This leads to predictions that, given other profit drivers, if the pay-off to aesthetic innovation increases, then expenditure on and output of such innovations will increase. Similarly, if the production of aesthetic innovations becomes cheaper (e.g. as a result of IT), their output will also increase.[5] One might, by pursuing similar arguments, also gain some insight into what sort of aesthetic changes the incentives will encourage, how such innovations will diffuse, and how the profit generated by diffusion will affect the development.

Given the profit motive, the production of soft innovations and how this production process might be represented can be considered. As shown

---

[5] It is worth noting that TPP innovations may affect the basic cost (and feasibility) of developing soft innovations. The soft innovations production process may thus build upon a TPP platform.

above the approaches commonly assumed in the economics of TPP innovation are usually quite simple. In the absence of uncertainty it is generally assumed that as the amount spent on the innovation process by the firm increases then either (*a*) the new process or product developed will have a greater functionality saving more inputs (if a process) or generating greater demand (if a product innovation); or (*b*) enable a given new product or process to be developed more quickly. It is also further assumed that there is declining marginal productivity in this innovation process and thus as the amount spent on R&D increases, the functional gain derived from an extra pound of expenditure declines, and/or the faster the process of development, the greater is the cost of reducing it further. The elasticity of innovative output with respect to input is commonly an important parameter in the determination of model outcomes. A variation is the new growth theory approach which suggests that growth in the number of innovations arising for a given resource spent on development will depend to some degree on the number already made. If uncertainty is allowed for, such standard approaches would consider either that (*a*) the expected value of the discovery increases with the R&D expenditure but at a decreasing rate; or (*b*) the probability of making a discovery in a time period increases with the R&D expended in that period, but at a declining rate.

Although Ginsburg and Throsby (2006) and Caves (2000) provide some fascinating insight as to the economics of what is happening inside the black box summarized by the soft innovation production process, the main interest here is whether what has been done for TPP innovations can be transferred to the analysis of soft innovation. The stance adopted here is that to some degree it can be transferred, but the modelling should not be carried over thoughtlessly to the modelling of soft innovations. Particularly the product differentiation nature of some soft innovations must be held in mind. Relevant points include:

1. It does not seem particularly contentious to argue that the greater the number of day-to-day design improvements generated, the more will be the resources devoted to design. Similarly there would be little argument if it were argued that the number of activities undertaken, such as product branding, marketing and brand identification, differentiation, image building, etc., all of which fall under the aesthetic heading, result in more output in the face of greater resource input.

2. As a general principle it would seem reasonable to assume with soft innovation, as with TPP innovation, that the time taken for development

will decrease with the resources employed, but perhaps at a decreasing rate. Thus, the time needed to make a film or to make a new CD or to develop a pharmaceutical variant will be the shorter, the greater the resources employed in this activity. Of course the relationship between inputs and outputs, as with TPP activity, may be stochastic, so it might be better to consider that expectations of the speed of innovation decreases with resources employed or alternatively that the probability of making a particular discovery decreases with the amount of resources employed, just as with TPP.

3. Taking a Jones (1999) type of approach to soft innovation would allow new music, art, theatre, etc. to build on experience gained from previous activity of this kind (standing on the shoulders of giants). It may also suggest that production of a product with new aesthetics may be cheaper if more such products have already been developed. It could also allow for the exhaustion of ideas in that the more designs already available the fewer are left to discover. These do not seem unreasonable characteristics.

4. Finally, however, one cannot necessarily assume that if the amount spent on the soft innovation process by the firm increases, then the resultant soft innovation will (even in a probabilistic sense) be in greater demand. The argument is that many soft innovations are horizontally differentiated with respect to existing products and increasing the expenditure does not necessarily increase the number of consumers to whom it appeals, e.g. the amount spent on developing a product of a different colour/smell/touch does not affect the numbers who want to buy that colour/smell/touch. Similarly it would also seem that one cannot rank or order different colours/smells/touch in terms of more or less innovation and thus suggest or debate whether the expenditures needed to develop them are producing more or less.

In total, pursuing a similar approach to that found in the analysis of TPP innovations which posits a relationship between the numbers of soft innovations made (or the speed of producing soft innovations) with resources employed (and/or the stock of discoveries to date) does not seem contentious. However, in the light of product differentiation considerations, there are reservations to applying TPP models to the generation of soft innovations. In fact one is on the safest grounds if one looks very sceptically on any approach that relates the quality or demand for a soft innovation to the resources employed in its generation.

6.3.4 *Market failures and soft innovation*

Accepting that soft innovation is driven by profit incentives opens up the door to accessing whether the TPP literature on market failures in innovation (and the rationalization of policy intervention on their basis) can be extended to soft innovation.

Market failure arguments relating to whether products are rivalrous or not and excludable or not relate just as much to soft innovation as to TPP innovation. Designs, logos, shape, smell, and touch are all rivalrous in that these are the tools of competition. Moreover they may all be copied and are thus non-excludable without government (institutional) intervention. In fact the argument may be even stronger than for TPP innovations as many of the soft innovations have characteristics that are most conducive to market failure. They are expensive to produce but cheap to reproduce. This discourages original innovation but encourages copying (legal or not). The incentives encourage fake products (trainers); pirated DVDs, CDs, and videos; and illegal downloading and copying.

Similarly market failure arguments relating to public goods, externalities, and other such phenomena as discussed in the TPP literature will also apply to soft innovations. The welfare implications of creative destruction may also be just as relevant. For example, a new music reproduction format may lead to a loss of value in a music collection in a different format, and this ought to be counted in any summation of welfare gains and losses.

As argued above, the extension to soft innovation brings the analysis of product differentiation to the fore. This field has its own literature (e.g. Dixit and Stiglitz 1977) on whether free markets produce too much variety (with horizontal differentiation) or promote or hinder quality improvement (with vertical differentiation). These literatures thus come in to play when considering welfare issues relating to soft innovation.

6.4 Conclusion

This chapter has explored the extent to which some of the basic foundations of the literature on TPP innovations can be applied to the study of soft innovation. It has been argued that certain basic assumptions, e.g. the profit motive, can be carried over and that certain issues such as uncertainty and creative destruction are equally important in the two different contexts. On the other hand it has been argued that the standard TPP approach cannot be applied to soft innovation thoughtlessly. A full analysis of soft innovation requires at least some customization of standard models. A particular aspect of soft innovation is the product differentiation perspective, and this requires some different approaches to the modelling of the demand and supply of soft innovations as well as to welfare issues. In fact, in earlier literature there has only been a limited application of product differentiation models in the analysis of innovation, especially models of horizontal innovation (perhaps because such differentiation is excluded by OECD definition as innovation).Using such models here provides a much-needed integration.

The chapters that follow consider in greater depth the various topics relevant to the analysis of soft innovation, building on the foundations provided here. Chapter 7 considers the supply of soft innovations, followed by Chapter 8 on the demand for such innovations. This is followed by chapters looking at supplier strategy (largely concerned with uncertainty) and appropriability through IPR.

7
The Supply of Soft Innovations

7.1 Introduction

In Chapters 2 to 5 some patterns of soft innovation have been explored using examples from different industries. It has been shown that in terms of new product variant launch patterns and the purchases of such products there is innovation occurring, in some cases at a very fast rate. The rates, however, differ across products and industries both in terms of extent and nature. In the light of such examples, this and the following two chapters (Chapters 8 and 9) present attempts to model the process of generation and diffusion of soft innovations in a market economy. More specifically the purpose is to gain some insight into what determines the expenditure on developing soft innovations; the number of existing and new product variants in the market; changes in that number, the life and death, or churn of soft product variants; and the resultant welfare outcomes. Issues related to copying and/ or piracy are not however considered in these chapters but are instead considered in Chapter 10 along with IPR. Issues relating to uncertainty are similarly postponed until Chapter 9, which is largely concerned with the issue of product variant launch strategy under uncertainty.

What is actually seen occurring in the market results from the inter- action of supply and demand, but for presentational purposes there are some advantages in considering these separately. It is a matter of choice as to whether one considers demand first or supply first. We will consider supply in this chapter and demand in the next.

It is not the intent of this work to enter into the very detailed world of micromanagement issues (Caves [2000] is particularly good on that), but rather to consider the issues of investment and timing, with and without uncertainty, in the tradition of previous literatures in neoclassical eco- nomics that have been applied to TPP innovation. Chapter 6 discussed the extent to which the existing literature on TPP innovation can be applied to soft innovation and concluded that although there are possibilities, the transposition cannot be undertaken thoughtlessly.

Distinctions were made in the previous chapters (*a*) between producer and consumer products (this chapter concentrates on the latter but the essence of the models does transfer); and (*b*) between storable (durable) and non-storable products (this distinction is also important here). It was also pointed out above that in some industries products are made in very limited quantities, whereas in other industries they are produced in large quantities. Prior to considering the latter, it is worth first considering the former, apparently simpler, case where innovation and production correspond directly. This refers to situations where every product is custom built or designed to purpose, and thus every product to some degree is an innovation. Examples would be architectural designs and advertising campaigns. The lone artist may also be considered to be in a similar position. In industries such as these if actors are economically rational one might expect the market outcome to be close to that shown in the textbooks for any product, and thus the greater the supply of innovations, higher is demand; the lower the cost of creating innovations, the more competitive is the industry. The outcome may differ from the welfare optimum as result of a number of different market failures such as scale economies, reputation effects, monopoly power, and barriers to entry.[1] This is all very traditional.

For the non-bespoke sectors this chapter proceeds by first considering horizontally differentiated and then vertically differentiated innovation.[2] It was argued above that the product-differentiated nature of most soft innovation is an important characteristic that has to be catered for, but is not generally considered, in the TPP literature. This and the following chapters thus emphasize modelling in the product differentiation tradition at the expense of the more traditional modelling. Tirole (1988) is an excellent source for previous literature on product differentiation. The use of the product differentiation approach is of course not totally unique. Prior examples of this approach applied to creative products include Zhang (2002) on music, Chisholm et al. (2006) on film, and Berry and Waldfogel (2001) on radio.

Surprisingly, however, the traditional literature on product differentiation is largely atemporal. It, thus, has to be specifically interpreted if it is to provide insight into innovation and changes over time in the number

---

[1] It might also be that a number of the products so produced are information goods. The market failure problems associated with such products are discussed in Chapter 10.

[2] There are combined models, see, for example, Acharya and Ziesemer (1996), but the extra complexity is not merited here.

and nature of soft products in the market. There are two main ways that this can be done. The first is to consider changes that reflect an equilibrating process whereby, for example, the number of variants approach a (given) equilibrium number. The second is to consider a process whereby, for example, at any moment in time, the actual number of products in the market equals the equilibrium number, but the equilibrium number is changing over time. Observation of changes in the extent of product variety at any point in time could not, of itself, distinguish which process is dominant.

Throughout this chapter the terms product, product variant, media, hardware, and software will be used as already defined above. The product–product variant distinction is of particular importance for the models are concerned not only with the demand for a particular variant, but the sum of the demand for all variants. Clearly the demand for the product is the sum of the demand for all variants, but this does not necessarily mean that product demand is simply and linearly related to the number of variants on the market, for a new variant may take the market from an existing variant without impacting on the overall product demand.

In the final sections of this and the next three chapters the implications of the presented models of soft innovation are highlighted and placed in the context of, and if necessary contrasted with, the implications, in the soft innovation context, of findings from the traditional literature. The purpose, therefore, is to concentrate in this work on developing different modelling approaches where soft-innovation-specific analysis is required, but in drawing together the complete picture to also take account of TPP results where relevant.

7.2 Horizontal product differentiation

Horizontal product differentiation has been defined above as a situation where if two product variants are offered on the market at the same price, some buyers would prefer one and other buyers the other. Key issues in the analysis of markets for horizontally differentiated products concern how many product variants will be on the market, where they may be located, how these outcomes may change over time, and which are the driving forces in this process. In the subsections that follow a simple model of non-storable products under monopoly is first considered, followed by an exposition of the highly influential Dixit and Stiglitz (1977) model allowing for competing suppliers. This is then followed by an analysis of durable products, the joint hardware and software case, and the consideration of location in product space.

7.2.1 Non-durable products, monopoly supply

This section considers a simple framework to illustrate the modelling of demand in markets with horizontally differentiated products and then proceeds to consider, in the face of such demand, profit-maximizing supplier decisions on the number and character of product variants to be launched in that market, and the expenditures to be incurred on the product variant development process. This is then extended to provide some insight into soft innovation.

Assume initially that the product under consideration is non-durable, and thus if a variant is purchased in one time period it will depreciate to 0 within that period. Examples of soft innovations that may fit in to such a category could include certain food products, e.g. ice creams and ready-cooked meals, theatrical performances, or cinema trips. For simplicity also assume (a) that if a buyer purchases a product variant in a period he or she will only buy one unit of that variant and no further units of it or other variants in that period; (b) that there are M potential buyers/consumers in the market; (c) that the income of each consumer j ($j = 1 \ldots M$) is $I_j(t)$ in time t; and (d) individual utility functions are separable in money and the utility derived from the differentiated product.

Assume further (a) that the utility function of consumers is such that for consumer j the preferred, ideal, or best variant of the product in terms of the utility pay-off, variant z_j, yields consumer j utility k_j from the consumption of one unit; (b) that the cost of purchasing variant z_j in time t is $P^*_j(t)$; and (c) the utility derived by consumer j from the consumption of this unit is given in Equation (7.1)

$$U_j(k_j, I_j, t) = I_j(t) - P^*_j(t) + k_j. \tag{7.1}$$

If consumer j buys one unit in time t of a product variant with characteristics x, then it is assumed that he or she will realize utility in that period as in Equation (7.2)

$$U_j(x, I_j, t) = I_j(t) - P_x(t) + k_j - f_j(d(x, z_j)) \tag{7.2}$$

where $P_x(t)$ is the price of product x in time t, $d(x, z_j)$ is the (Euclidean) distance in the product space between the variant with characteristics

x and the variant with characteristics z_j, and f_j translates this difference into a utility loss. The distribution of $k_j - f_j(d(x, z_j))$, which we write as $F(j)$, is indicative of the concentration or dispersion of consumer tastes.

If variant x is the only product variant in the market, the utility gained by consumer j from purchasing this variant x, relative to not purchasing at all will be given by

$$U_j(I_j, x_j, t) - U_j(I_j, 0, t) = k_j - f_j(d(x, z_j)) - P_x(t) \qquad (7.3)$$

and consumer j will demand a unit of x in time t iff Equation (7.4) holds

$$k_j - f_j(d(x, z_j)) - P_x(t) \geq 0. \qquad (7.4)$$

From Equation (7.4) one may observe that the probability that consumer j will demand variant x and thus, as this is the only variant, the product itself, will decline as $P_x(t)$ increases and as $k_j - f_j(d(x, z_j))$ decreases, i.e. as the inherent utility contribution of the product class declines (k_j) or as the marketed variant specification differs further from the ideal.

To generate the overall demand for the product, defined as $X(t)$, from Equation (7.4) and the definition of $F(j)$, it is clear that $X(t)$ is given by Equation (7.5)

$$X(t) = M(1 - F(P_x(t))). \qquad (7.5)$$

It is immediately clear that overall demand for the product (and in this case the single variant) is affected by the number of consumers, distribution of consumer tastes, variant specification, and product price. If the total production costs for the product variant are $C(t)$ one may also immediately write the profits of the supplier in time t, $\Pi(t)$, as in Equation (7.6)

$$\Pi(t) = P_x(t).M(1 - F(P_x(t))) - C(t). \qquad (7.6)$$

A profit maximizing supplier of the single product variant would equate marginal cost and marginal revenue. This is the condition that will hold at the equilibrium and determine product characteristics and price. Thus, ceteris paribus, the lower the production cost per unit of output, the lower will be the variant price, the greater will be sales, and also the more distant will be the ideal specification of the marginal purchaser from the specification of the variant x in the market.

In order to address innovation in this context it is necessary to consider changes over time in the number and types of products offered to the market. In this simple model there is little to say about approaching an equilibrium over time, but factors that would lead to changes in the equilibrium itself include the possibility that, through either process innovation as a result of R&D[3] and/or the buying of new process technology, unit costs of production of the single variant may be reduced and consumer acquisition of the product will increase with demand extending to consumers to whom the product variant suits less and less. It is also possible that changes in the pattern of tastes over time and/or changes in the costs of developing different variants may cause the supplier to wish to change the specification of the product variant and withdraw the old and launch a new variant. However, one cannot fully analyse the real essence of soft innovation if the analysis is restricted to a monopolist offering only a single variant. It is thus necessary to also address if the monopoly supplier has an incentive to introduce further product variants in the market.

The incentives to proliferate variants arise because the monopolist might be able to capture the marginal buyers more cheaply by offering an additional product with characteristics more suited to their preferences instead of by charging lower prices. To model these incentives, assume that if another product variant, y, is made available, then consumers buy either one unit of x, one of y, or no units, but do not buy both x and y. If the consumer j acquires variant y, he or she will realize utility from consumption given by Equation (7.7)

$$U_j(y, I_j, t) = I_j(t) - P_y(t) + k_j - f_j(d(y, z_j)) \qquad (7.7)$$

where $P_y(t)$ is the price of variant y. There are three different actions available to the consumer with different utility pay-offs relative to the no-purchase scenario:

1. Buy neither x or y: utility gain is 0
2. Buy x: utility gain is $k_j - f_j(d(x, z_j)) - P_x(t)$
3. Buy y: utility gain is $k_j - f_j(d(y, z_j)) - P_y(t)$

and variant y will be purchased by consumer j iff Equation (7.8) holds.

$$k_j - f_j(d(y, z_j)) - P_y(t) > k_j - f_j(d(x, z_j)) - P_x(t) \geq 0 \qquad (7.8)$$

---

[3] Within this framework, spending on R&D (or new technology acquisition) will extend to the point where, at the margin, the resultant profit increase generated equals the cost of the R&D undertaken.

which illustrates that at the same prices if the product is going to be bought the consumer will buy that variant closer to meeting his or her own preferred specification (which is a property of horizontal differentiation).

The change in the pattern of demand that results from the launch of a new product arises from changes in the behaviour of two groups of consumers: those who would not have bought x but will now buy y; and those who would have bought x but will now buy y. Ceteris paribus, the total number of buyers is affected only by the numbers in the first category. For consumer j to be in the first category, i.e. to not have bought x but to now buy y it is required that (7.9) holds

$$k_j - f_j(d(y, z_j)) - P_y(t) \geq 0 \geq k_j - f_j(d(x, z_j)) - P_x(t). \tag{7.9}$$

If this condition is satisfied for at least one consumer, then the addition of an extra variant will increase product demand (over both variants) and sales. This condition is more likely to be satisfied the lower $P_y(t)$ is and the lower $f_j(d(y, z_j))$ is, i.e. the closer is the specification of y to the consumer's ideal specification. To complete the picture, assuming that $k_j - f_j(d(y, z_j))$ is distributed across the M consumers as $F'(j)$, and that $f_j(d(y, z_j)) - f_j(d(x, z_j))$ is distributed across the M potential consumers as $DF(j)$, then overall demand for variant y is given by

$$Y(t) = M(1 - F(P_y(t)))(1 - DF(P_y(t) - P_x(t))). \tag{7.10}$$

For a monopolist supplier of both variants x and y, although the new variant may take some market from the existing variant, there may still be an incentive to increase the number of product variants in the market because revenue may be increased as (*a*) more customers are served; and (*b*) customers are charged higher prices as products more adequately meet their preferences. These revenue increases are offset by (*a*) possible higher unit cost of production and (*b*) the required expenditure on launching new variants. For the former it is possible that the cost of production increases, or decreases, with the number of variants in the market, which will impact negatively (positively) on the number of product variants launched. For the latter, the more costly it is to launch new variants, the smaller will be the number of variants launched in the market.

It is however by no means obvious, as discussed in Chapter 6, how the costs of development of new variants should be modelled. When discussing the costs of developing new technology a simple starting point is to hypothesize that the generation of a new variant will require expenditures on labour and materials and the application of new or existing knowledge with perhaps a splash of originality. As has already been argued above, however, with soft innovation, in the absence of a means by which one may judge what is better and by how much, it is difficult to specify a relationship that relates the extent of advance to resources employed in generating the advance. Alternatively another approach in the literature relates future discoveries to prior discoveries. There would then be issues as to whether there are 'standing upon shoulders effects' whereby later developments can build upon earlier ones, and thus get cheaper as they proceed, or whether the cheap discoveries are made first, with later discoveries being more expensive. It is also sometimes argued that some development lines become exhausted and too expensive and new trajectories are developed which re-base the cost of development.

Although to develop soft innovations is costly and expenditure on development will generate soft innovations, it is necessary to be careful when trying to relate the two to each other. In such circumstances, as the points of relevance can be made without commitment to a specific cost of development specification, it is here left open.

One may expect that over some range of the parameters at least, the monopolist will have an incentive to have more than one product variant in the market. The limit to this process will be the point at which the firm's expenditure on developing and launching new variants no longer exceeds the extra revenues so generated, i.e. the marginal cost of proliferation equals the marginal gross profit gain from proliferation. The number so generated might be called an equilibrium number of variants.

Addressing innovation per se more explicitly requires an intertemporal stance, which looks at the determination of the equilibrium number of product variants in the market at a point in time. It is possible that this equilibrium may take some time to establish and at any point in time the number of product variants in the market may or may not be at such equilibrium. If the number at a point in time is below the equilibrium, one may observe expenditure on developing innovations and innovation per se as new variants are launched to take the market to its equilibrium position. Such expenditures on the development and launching of new variants may be considered as expenditure on product innovation. If these new products have functional differences to existing products, this expenditure would be considered as part of R&D. If, however, the differences are aesthetic, then the expenditure will not be so termed, but will be expenditure on developing soft innovation. Such expenditure will thus be driven (*a*) by the profit gains derived from extra variants serving more customers, and from customers being charged higher prices as variants more adequately meet customer preferences; and (*b*) the cost function for developing the new variants.

This is not, however, the only driver of changes in the (number of) variants in the market. It is possible that there will be changes in cost and demand parameters over time that will lead to the introduction of further new product variants that either replace existing variants or add extra variants. Three particular arguments are important. First, R&D expenditure on, or the external acquisition of, new process technologies may affect the unit production costs of the product. This change will have impact on the ideal numbers of product variants and thus also the optimal expenditure on soft innovation (this is exactly the approach taken by Lin and Saggi (2002) in a different context[4]). Second, it could be that over time advances in process technologies (e.g. computer-aided design) could reduce the costs of developing new product variants. This is likely to stimulate the launch of new variants and expenditure of developing new variants (see, e.g., Stoneman [1990]). Finally, the pattern of consumer tastes may change over time (see, e.g., the food industry in Chapter 5) which could encourage the developing and launching of different variants. In such situations, soft innovation and expenditure thereon are the result of the market equilibrium changing over time.

This simple case thus illustrates that with a monopoly supplier the extent of variety in the market depends on the spread of consumer preferences, costs of production and its determinants, and the costs of developing new varieties. If equilibrium takes an extensive period to be established, the market might reveal changes in the number of product variants over time with associated product development costs. The equilibrium may itself also change over time. For example, R&D on process innovation (and the external acquisition of new technologies) may affect unit costs of production and the incentives to launch new product variants. Underlying changes in consumer tastes may also affect the incentives to spend on soft innovation and to launch more and/or different products. Such activities will be again reflected in product development expenditure, the amount of which will depend on the profits to the launch of new product variants and the costs of undertaking such soft innovation.

---

[4] They find that (*a*) process R&D investments increase with the degree of product differentiation, and firms invest more in product R&D when they can do process R&D than when they cannot; (*b*) Bertrand firms have a stronger incentive for product R&D whereas Cournot firms invest more in process R&D; and (*c*) cooperation in product R&D promotes both types of R&D relative to competition, whereas cooperation in both types of R&D discourages R&D relative to cooperation in just product R&D.

The last issue to be addressed in this subsection is whether the supply of new product variants is stimulated by potential entry. The two relevant lines of argument are first that potential entry will encourage an incumbent monopolist to charge lower prices, which may increase the returns from greater product proliferation and thus encourage more product variety. Secondly, if a potential entrant is thinking of entry on the basis of a new product variant, then it does not have to take account of the impact on the sales of its existing variants (as does the incumbent) as there are none. This might be taken to indicate that potential entrants have greater incentive to launch new variants and thus potential entry will encourage proliferation.

However, as argued in the previous chapter, using creative destruction arguments, the incumbent has the same incentives as the potential entrant once the correct counterfactual is specified. Thus, the potential entrant does not have more incentive than the incumbent, but both the incumbent and potential entrant have more incentive than what the incumbent has when there is no potential entry. The implication is that potential entry will encourage soft innovation and the launching of new product variants. Thus, if the number of potential entrants changes over time (perhaps through changes in technology of the spreading of knowledge or capabilities), then soft innovation as measured by variant proliferation will be stimulated. In the next subsection an oligopolistic market is addressed.

7.2.2 The Dixit–Stiglitz model

The monopoly model discussed in the previous subsection had the advantages of introducing approaches and concepts while also being informative as to outcomes and causes. It is, however, necessary to get away from the monopoly assumption and to consider more appropriate scenarios. One approach to the issues at hand that has been particularly influential in the economics literature was introduced by Dixit and Stiglitz (1977). In this approach there are many different suppliers and the market scenario is one of monopolistic competition. Once again however the model is atemporal and thus some interpretation is required if innovation is to be discussed. In addition the product is considered non-storable, but consumers are allowed to buy more than one unit. The model will thus again apply to examples such as food products, some pharmaceuticals, and attending a musical concert.

Consider a situation where potential product variants in a particular sector are good substitutes for each other but poor substitutes for other goods or services in the economy (labelled with a 0 subscript). Let the potential range of the product variants be $i = 1, 2, 3 \ldots$ with an amount $X_i(t)$ of good i being produced in the time period t. Order the variants such that $i = 1 \ldots N$ are produced and those that are $i > N$ are not produced. Products are equally distributed across product spaces as are consumer preferences, and any additional products added to the market do not disturb this distribution. U is defined as a multiple of a representative consumer's utility, then utility generated by total consumption is assumed to be

$$U(t) = U(X_0(t), V(X_1(t), X_2(t), X_3(t) \ldots))$$

which is assumed for simplicity to take the special form,

$$U(t) = U(X_0(t), \{\Sigma_i X_i(t)^\rho\}^{1/\rho}) \tag{7.11}$$

where $0 < \rho < 1$.

U(t) is maximized subject to the budget constraint that

$$X_0(t) + \Sigma_i p_i(t) X_i(t) = I \tag{7.12}$$

where p_i is the price of variant i and I is income in terms of a numeraire, which is to be set to unity. The utility function basically allows that all product variants are horizontally differentiated. Consumers can be buying different variants or each individually diversifying.

Each product variant is assumed to be produced by only one firm and thus the number of suppliers equals the number of product variants. Each firm is assumed to maximize profits assuming all other prices held constant. Each firm has common marginal costs of production $c(t)$ but must bear fixed costs, $a(t)$, to be in the market. At the profit maximum, for each firm, marginal revenue equals marginal costs and thus

$$p_i(t) (1 - \beta/(1 + \beta)) = c(t) \tag{7.13}$$

where $\beta/(1 + \beta)$ is the inverse of the own price elasticity of demand (with all other prices assumed constant). The marginal firm in the market (N) will make zero profits and thus for this firm

$$(p_N(t) - c(t)) X_N(t) = a(t) \tag{7.14}$$

However, as all firms are symmetrical, $p_i(t) = p_N(t)$ for all i, which will also equal the market equilibrium price $p_e(t)$ and thus $(p_i(t) - c(t)) X_i(t) = a(t)$

for all i. Dixit and Stiglitz (1977) then show that the equilibrium number of firms/product variants $N_e(t)$ is given by

$$s(p_e(t)N_e(t)^{-\beta})/p_e(t)N_e(t) = a(t)/\beta c(t) \qquad (7.15)$$

where $s(p_e(t)N_e(t)^{-\beta})/p_e(t)N_e(t)$ is a function that decreases in N for each fixed p. Each active firm will produce output of $a(t)/\beta c(t)$.

One may thus see that the equilibrium number of firms and variants in the market ($N(t)$), is a function of the elasticity of demand, the marginal costs of production, and the level of fixed costs. In one sense, expenditure on generating soft innovation is the expenditure on developing each product variant in this equilibrium multiplied by the number of variants upon the market, i.e. is given by $N_e(t)a(t)$. Then, for example, for a given $a(t)$, the lower the $c(t)$, the greater will be $N_e(t)$, and thus the greater will be expenditure on soft innovation, $N_e(t)a(t)$. Similarly, if β is reduced, $N_e(t)a(t)$ will increase.

Such an approach indicates that at the equilibrium the number of product variants to be expected in the market depends upon launch cost, fixed costs, marginal production costs, market structure, the price elasticity of demand, and consumer preferences. It is worth emphasizing, however, that the logic of the story is that at any moment in time, given a differentiated product market, there is a number of product variants that can be profitably launched in that market (and also the same number of suppliers). It is not profitable to exceed that number, but if the number is not met then more launches may be profitable.

From an innovation viewpoint, changes in the number of product variants on offer (and thus expenditure in their development) could reflect the process of a time-intensive approach path towards a given equilibrium with the number of variants in the market reflecting an equilibrating process filling gaps in the overall number of product variants on offer.

More interestingly, however, the equilibrium could be changing over time. For example it is possible that through R&D on process innovation or by acquiring new technology that $c(t)$ reduces over time (this reduction will be at a rate that equalizes the marginal cost of the reduction in production costs and the profit gain derived from there). If $c(t)$ is reduced over time, then one would expect to observe $N_e(t)$ increasing over time and more expenditure on generating soft innovation. Alternatively it could be that through technological advance the cost of launching new products in the market, $a(t)$, declines over time. As $a(t)$ declines the number of variants in the market will increase. Whether this means that $N_e(t)a(t)$

will increase or decrease depends on the elasticity of launch costs related to N. In addition, fixed costs, market structure, the price elasticity of demand, and consumer preferences may all also change over time, inducing either the replacement of variants or the introduction of more (or fewer) variants with associated development costs.

Although this model is very informative, like all models it tells only part of the story. A major part of that story here is that each product variant is produced by a different firm. Thus, the market impact of changes in the behaviour of each firm is spread across all firms in the market which are assumed to be numerous. It is, of course, possible to consider alternative scenarios. One possibility is a market that will only support a small number of firms/variants. In that case changes in own prices and/or the launch of new variants may have significant impacts upon the revenue of other firms and retaliation of some kind may be expected. In such cases the assumption that the firm may ignore the reaction of others to its own decisions would be inappropriate and the reactions may well act as a disincentive to put new products on the market.

Despite this, a particular advantage of the Dixit and Stiglitz (1977) framework is that it has been used to explore the welfare optimality of the outcome in markets with product variety. In particular, Dixit and Stiglitz (1977) consider whether the market that they have modelled provides too great or too little incentive to generate variety (horizontal differentiation). Their findings are mixed:

In the central case of a constant elasticity utility function, the market solution was constrained Pareto optimal, regardless of the value of that elasticity (and thus the implied elasticity of the demand functions). With variable elasticities, the bias could go either way, and the direction of the bias depended not on how the elasticity of demand changed but on how the elasticity of utility changed. We suggested that there was some presumption that the market solution would be characterised by too few firms in the monopolistically competitive sector. With asymmetric demand and cost conditions we also observed a bias against commodities with inelastic demands and high costs. The general principle behind these results is that a market solution considers profit at the appropriate margin, while a social optimum takes into account the consumer's surplus. However, applications of this principle come to depend on details of cost and demand functions. (p. 308)

The key finding is that 'there was some presumption that the market solution would be characterised by too few firms in the monopolistically competitive sector'. This finding could provide a rationale for government intervention on the grounds that the free market generates too little variety and thus too little soft innovation. On a more dynamic level, and much more recently, Fantino (2008) shows that in a horizontally differentiated market framework, where firms can invest in R&D (our soft innovation process) to modify the level of differentiation of their products, increasing their specialization and their market power, firms under-invest in R&D, because they do not internalize the effects of their research effort on the overall level of substitutability of the other varieties and on the profits of the other firms. Thus, there is also wider support for the view that there may be insufficient variety in such markets.

Despite providing considerable insight into the issue of product variety in a market, when there is an endogenous number of suppliers the above approach may be only useful for certain types of goods. It was presented as a way to look at markets where goods are non-storable or non-durable or of frequent purchase, e.g. chocolate bars and biscuits. It may be less appropriate in other markets. Such markets are thus considered below.

7.2.3 *Single-purchase durable products*

This section looks at the incentives to horizontally innovate when the product is a durable and only one variant will ever be purchased. In a soft innovation context examples might include the purchase of landscape gardening services (or perhaps the purchase of a garden fountain), house redecoration, or purchase of a business suit. The key to the model is that the consumer is assumed to enter the market in each period until a variant is purchased after which the consumer buys no further variants. The main issues in such a market are: (*a*) how will the purchase decision/dates be affected by the extent of variety offered; (*b*) what are the benefits to the suppliers of offering greater variety; and (*c*) what variety will be produced by the market and is it likely to be welfare optimal? The market described is very much like that considered by Ireland and Stoneman (1986) and thus the model follows the approach found there.[5]

Assume (*a*) that consumers can be ranked in terms of the benefit that they will get from acquiring a long-lived product according to an index X; and (*b*) that the annual benefit from having a technology is $g(X, N)$ where N is the number of product variants in the market. By construction, $g_x < 0$; by assumption, product variety enables a consumer to more closely match his or her requirements so $g_N > 0$. For an internal maximum assume

---

[5] See also Stoneman (1990).

that $g_{NN} < 0$. If consumers only ever buy one variant, then total product sales in time t will equal the rank of the marginal consumer in time t, $X(t)$.

Assume initially that N is a constant over time and that the selling prices of all variants are the same, equalling $p(t)$ in time t. Further assume that, although the price may change over time, buyers are assumed myopic (for simplicity) and thus do not engage in intertemporal arbitrage. Following Ireland and Stoneman (1986) the demand for the product will be determined by

$$g(X(t), N) = rp(t) \tag{7.16}$$

where r is the discount rate.

Consider first that there is only one supplier. If that supplier is facing unit production costs $c(t)$ in time t, assumed to decline over time[6], at rate $Dc(t)$, for a given N, the intertemporal profit maximizing sales path will involve prices being set such that

$$g(X(t), N) = rc(t) - Dc(t) \tag{7.17}$$

and for a given N, on the equilibrium path $X(t)$ will satisfy

$$g(X(t), N) = rp(t) = rc(t) - Dc(t). \tag{7.18}$$

Models of this kind predict that (for a given N) the price of the product will decline over time (until production costs stop falling at which point the market closes), with the consumers being served as time goes on obtaining less and less gross benefit.

A monopolist's decision on the extent of product variety reduces to the choice of N. An increase in N will cause buyers to be willing to pay a higher price at a given date of purchase. If the unit productions costs (over time as well as at a point in time) are not affected this will generate higher gross profits because the product can either be sold at a higher price or if desired at an earlier date. These effects provide a positive incentive to the monopolist to increase variety. However, there may be costs of variety proliferation. New variants have to be developed, launched, and marketed and variety will thus only increase to the point where the marginal profit gain from increased variety equals the marginal cost of proliferation. Overall

---

[6] Note that in this framework if the costs of supply are not falling, then, ceteris paribus, sales will only occur in the first period after which the market will close.

development expenditure on generating soft innovations will, as in the models above, depend upon the elasticity of the supply of variety.

This model is already more dynamic than earlier models considered and for example predicts that for a given N the price of the product will fall over time and that one can predict an equilibrium value for the fixed N. It is of course possible that the monopolist may prefer to vary the extent of variety over the lifetime of the product if the costs of developing new varieties is declining over time or consumer responses to new varieties are changing over time. Just as models of this kind predict that the price of the product (on average) declines over time, it would seem logical to argue that a monopolist may wish to increase product variety over time, developing new product variants to meet the preferences of 'more distant' consumers. Expenditure on developing soft innovations will then depend upon the dispersion of consumer tastes.

Ireland and Stoneman (1986) argue that in a model such as this, a monopoly supplier facing (price) myopic buyers will produce a welfare optimal product acquisition path. One might extend this to argue that a monopoly producer facing a variety of myopic buyers would also produce the welfare optimal path of product variety. However, they also argue that if buyers have some foresight with regard to falling prices, then the time path will no longer be welfare optimal, rather it will involve acquisition at too slow a rate. One might argue also that it will produce too small an incentive to increase product variety.

Although not formally analysed, there is a further aspect to the welfare story in this model when there is more than one supplier. It is well known that in markets such as this, where one firm's sale or the sale of one variant takes a customer permanently out of the market for all other firms, that one may well find common pool effects. In the current context this would imply that either (*a*) in the face of competition, a firm will want to develop and launch a variant before its rivals do so; or (*b*) a firm will want to have more variants in the market to head off its rivals. Both effects will encourage variant proliferation and or speed up the launch of new variants in the market.

Such a development process might be modelled as a situation where a variant takes a shorter period of time to develop if development expenditures are greater. In essence if one defines τ as the time to development, and R as resources deployed, then

$$\tau = h(R) \tag{7.19}$$

with $h_R < 0$ and $h_{RR} > 0$. The latter condition implies that halving the period of development more than doubles the cost. If these conditions hold one might expect that as the competition speeds the launch of new varieties, then the expenditure on soft innovation will also increase more than proportionately. This would also imply, following the literature, that a competitive market may offer incentives to soft innovate and variant proliferation that are excessive from a welfare point of view.[7]

7.2.4 Durable products with repeat purchase

The previous section considered durable products with a choice of variety but where the product is bought only once. This section considers products that are still durable but are repeatedly purchased, although each purchase is of a different variant. Examples are books, DVD, and CDs. In such cases the consumer will probably buy many titles, but as the product is storable will not purchase a given title a second time and any later purchases will be of different titles. For such products the consumer enters the market in every period but will never repurchase the same variant.

Assume initially that there is only one product variant in the market, that the variant has an infinite life, and that there is only one supplier. Let the value of purchase to buyers of that variant, as above, be $g(X)$ with X as an index of preference and $X(t)$ as an indicator of the number of buyers to time t. Thus in time t, if $X(t)$ units have been sold, the next buyer will value the variant at $g(X(t))$. Assume myopia[8] and thus the Xth buyer will buy at the first time when $g(X(t)) = rp(t)$ where $p(t)$ is the price of the variant in time t. Demand and sales in time t, $q(t) = DX(t)$ will then equal

$$q(t) = r.Dp(t)/g_{x(t)} \tag{7.20}$$

where r is the interest rate/discount rate and $g_{x(t)} < 0$. It should be noted that if price does not fall in time t, i.e. $Dp(t) = 0$, then there are no sales, i.e. with a single variant, all those who value the product higher than its price

---

[7] Although it is possible to generate a scenario in which the launch of a new variant by a firm would increase the prices at which all variants (from other firms) are sold (for all variants would more closely match individual consumer preferences). In this scenario the firm launching the new variant will bear all the costs but the benefits will be shared by all firms. The costs are internalized by the firms but the benefits are not. In such a case, a competitive market will deter product variety, relative to a monopolized market where all costs and benefits are internalized.

[8] The whole exercise can be performed with other assumptions and different results. See Ireland and Stoneman (1986).

in time t buy that variant by time t, but after that date further sales depend upon reductions in price.

Assume that there is a monopoly supplier facing unit production costs $c(t)$ in time t, assumed to decline over time at rate $Dc(t)$. That supplier will then price as

$$p(t) = c(t) - Dc(t)/r \tag{7.21}$$

and

$$Dp(t) = Dc(t) - D^2c(t)/r \tag{7.22}$$

i.e. prices will fall over time as the costs of supplying the variant fall over time. As prices fall the sales extend to consumers for whom the variant is less preferred.

The profit of the supplier in time t (before any fixed costs) is given by

$$\Pi(t) = q(t)(p(t) - c(t)) = (Dc(t) - D^2c(t))(-Dc(t))/rg_{x(t)} \tag{7.23}$$

and the product will make a contribution to fixed costs up until the point where price equals marginal cost which occurs when the cost of producing the product/variant no longer declines (where $Dc(t) = 0$). One may thus consider that at the time of launch (time 0) the product is sold until the marginal buyer is paying a price that exceeds marginal cost by an amount equal to $-Dc(0)/r$. As the costs of production fall, further sales will take place at lower and lower prices, appealing to buyers who have less and less preference for the variant until costs fail to fall any further, after which the product will no longer be available. For the example of books, therefore, one might expect that when first launched, the price of a title will tend to be high because readers are not willing to wait, but later buyers will be paying less.

As variants age, their potential sales will decline because there is no repeat purchase of variants. Once one has bought a CD of *The Three Tenors* one is unlikely to buy it again. For the producer, this also implies that if old variants have already been purchased, without new varieties there would be no sales. On the other hand, market saturation of one variant may stimulate demands for new variants as consumers seek new music, new films, or new titles.

The incentives to launch new product variants will depend upon the expected accumulated discounted profits over the lifetime of a variant relative to the costs of launch. As in the previous model, these in turn will depend upon the impact of variant proliferation on (*a*) the costs of production, (*b*) costs of product development, and (*c*) sales revenue. The impact of new variants on a supplier's sales revenues will depend, inter alia, on whether the variants compete with each other. Such competition may take several forms, e.g. contemporaneous competition – one book competes for purchase with another book at the same time, or historic competition – a previous purchase may impact (positively or negatively) on a current purchase (e.g. by creating a following for particular authors). The greater such competition, the less is the incentive to a monopolist to launch new variants because new variants reduce revenue from other variants.

However, in addition, as earlier variants age, the sales of these existing variants will be getting smaller, which will free up production capacity and create gaps in consumer demands that will encourage the launching of new product variants. The market has its own in-built dynamic in that saturation of the market for older variants provides an incentive to produce new variants.[9] For a monopolist, therefore, ageing of the existing product varieties would encourage investment in the new development of soft innovations.

In a market with many suppliers the impact on the revenue from existing variants of launching new products may fall on the products of other suppliers and thus not be internalized. This might imply an oversupply of variety. However, the reactions of rivals to the launching of new variants (either in terms of further launches or in terms of pricing) may act to counter such effects.

The implications of this analysis for innovation are already to some degree built in. It is predicted, for example, that the ageing of a variety provides an endogenous incentive for new product variants to be launched over time. In addition, as the costs of production and product development change over time, the equilibrium number of variants in the market will change. For the product that most closely fits the characteristics assumed here, book publishing, it was shown above that (*a*) there are large numbers of new title launches each year of which only a few succeed; (*b*) that the number of launches have been increasing over time; (*c*) best-sellers have turned over more quickly as time has proceeded; and (*d*) there is a growing long tail. Although uncertainty may be part of the explanation for these patterns (see Chapter 9), changes in the costs of production and product

---

[9] One may note that the supply of new variants is not generated by the fact that they are better, only that they are different.

development, as has already been argued, could, as the theory has now shown, also have had some role to play in generating this pattern.

7.2.5 Hardware and software

With many soft innovations, both hardware and software are required to deliver the service flow, e.g. computer games, DVDs, and CDs. The demand for soft innovations and the pay-offs from such innovation will thus depend on the number of owners of the appropriate hardware. In this section we discuss briefly how this will impact on the supply of soft innovations.

Putting aside issues of hardware compatibility, one might expect that the equilibrium number of software products in the market will be determined in a way that is quite similar to the previous model where the determinants of the number of varieties include consumer tastes and their dispersion, the costs of producing software, the costs of developing software, and the ageing of the existing software stock. The equilibrium may involve falling prices for software over time. Innovation in the industry may have some internal dynamic through the effect of the ageing of the existing software stock but may also result from changes in production costs, development costs, and/or preferences.

The hardware side is, however, also important. One route by which this works out is that hardware may improve, which encourages software (soft) innovation. This is considered under vertical differentiation and alternative media in Section 7.3.4. Setting aside such changes, the hardware aspect that matters is that if there are more software variants in the market this will not only increase the sales of software to existing owners of hardware, but also encourage more of the population to acquire the hardware[10] and thus become software buyers. As a result of greater variety, therefore, software producers' revenues may increase because of both sales of the new varieties and increased sales of old varieties as the number of hardware owners increases. Hardware producers will also gain from the increased sales of hardware. This yields a number of possibilities for market failure whereby social and private incentives to put new product varieties on the market differ.

Increased sales revenue (after allowing for increased costs) provides the incentive to spend on soft innovation and such expenditure will continue

---

[10] The demand for hardware will depend upon the software available, in that when choosing whether to buy hardware the consumer will take account of the total service flow available which will depend on (expected) software availability and prices.

until the expected return equals the marginal cost of development. However, the externality to software demand that arises indirectly from inducing extra hardware sales benefits all suppliers of software and not just the software developer of a new piece of software.[11] This suggests that there will be suboptimal investment in such soft innovation. In addition, any extra profit from hardware sales induced by extra variety will tend to go to the hardware producer, again providing too low an incentive to the software producer, unless there is some collaboration between hardware and software suppliers.

Software may also be hardware-specific, for example different software for games consoles is usually console-specific, and the additional supply of a new game for a Nintendo console will have no benefits for an owner of a Sony PlayStation. The demand for a hardware variant may well depend upon (expected) software availability and prices and the pay-off to developing further software depends upon the number of owners of that variant of hardware. Such situations have led to a growing literature that considers whether such markets will generate a dominant standard, or whether there would continue to be many different standards on the market, and also whether any standards established will be the best available. This work (see, e.g., Arthur [1989]) concludes that in many cases a non-welfare optimal standard will be established.

7.2.6 Location in product space

Thus far, product variety has been discussed without approaching the issue of where in product space a firm might locate any new variety. This has, however, been an issue in the literature for many years.[12] The classic argument is attributed to Hotelling (1929), who argues that there is a tendency for products to be close in product space. The argument is as follows.

Consider a market (ice cream sellers on a beach is a classic example) where buyers bear two costs – the price of the product and the costs of travel to the supplier (or divergence from optimal preference). A buyer will purchase one unit of the product if the utility gain from purchase (assumed the same for all buyers), U, exceeds price (same for all purchasers) p, plus travel costs (differing across purchasers) D_i, i.e. iff $U \geq p + D_i$. The

[11] Although if different hardware are incompatible, this effect may be limited.
[12] An interesting creative product application is undertaken by Goettler and Shachar (2001) related to network TV programmes.

travel costs depend upon where the seller of ice creams is located (on the beach), so that they will be low for customers located nearby and high for distant customers. Assume that the customers are evenly located. It is argued that a single seller will locate in the middle of the beach for this will maximize the number of buyers, for a given price, for whom $U \geq p + D_i$, or alternatively, enable the buyer to charge the highest price to a given number of buyers. Locating to the left of centre may eventually (if the beach is of fixed length) cause the loss of customers to the right because of higher travel costs, with no gains of customers on the left and vice versa.

The interesting issue now arises as to where a second seller will locate. It is assumed in this story that the first seller may relocate if necessary once the second has located. It is assumed that each customer, if buying, will frequent the closest seller. The predicted outcome is that the two sellers will locate next to each other at the centre of the beach, with one enjoying sales on the left-hand side and the other on the right-hand side and having half the market each. Why? It is sometimes thought that the two sellers will locate one-quarter of the length of the beach from each end (also minimizing travel costs). If this choice was made, one seller could increase sales by moving towards the centre and gaining sales from his rival where they compete, but without losing sales where they do not compete. This will cause the other seller to do the same and thus move to the centre as well.

This argument is used to support the view that although there may be many product variants they will all be similar, for example one observes that supermarkets locate close to each other or that all designs are similar. A prediction, therefore, would be that soft innovations will be close to variants already in the market. It is not clear, however, that the above results apply for more than two product variants. There is also an alternative story (Salop 1979).

Assume that instead of a beach the buyers of ice cream are equally distributed on the banks of a lake around which they must walk to the ice cream seller. A single seller may locate anywhere on the circumference of the lake without any effect on sales. Two sellers may locate next to each other, one servicing the left-hand arc of the lake and the other servicing the right. If this was done, then the most distant customer would have to travel half the circumference of the lake (and back) to buy an ice cream. Alternatively if the buyers were to locate opposite each other, each again servicing half of the circumference, the most distant buyers would only have to walk a quarter of the circumference and back. The sellers would thus be able to charge higher prices or sell more ice cream if they are located opposite each other rather than next to each other. In other words the result has changed completely from the Hotelling example. Thus, the Hotelling result does not necessarily extend to different preference mappings and there are no necessary predictions that soft innovations will always ape existing variants.

These two simple stories suggest that although product variants may group in preference space, this is not a necessary outcome. One might argue further as well that if preferences instead of being evenly spread across the population are in fact more unevenly distributed, then the incentives will be to encourage innovations servicing the thicker parts of the market with a smaller number servicing the thinner (e.g. pop music recordings versus classical music recordings). Furthermore, if the production costs or fixed costs vary with the aspects of product space being serviced, and/or if there are scale economies (or diseconomies) of production, one might expect these to also affect the soft innovations launched in the market. Seim (2006) explores product location choice in the video rentals industry through a simulated theoretical model and illustrates the incentives for spatial differentiation. He shows that the number of competitors increases almost linearly with firm size but that expansion of characteristics space and dispersion of consumer preferences induce little additional entry.

An alternative factor that may influence location in product space is the costs and/or benefits of clustering. If clustering in product or geographical space has positive externalities, then one might expect products to be closely located. If not then dispersion is more likely. Pandit et al. explore clustering in the British Broadcasting and Financial Services industries and show that there are advantages from clustering in these two industries that match similar findings for newer high-tech industries. Kennedy (2002) has also observed that in prime-time television programming in the United States networks imitate each other when introducing new programmes and that on an average imitative introductions underperform differentiated introductions. The results are considered to be consistent with herd behaviour.

From an innovation perspective, one might expect changes over time in product locations if the equilibrium takes time to establish or if the equilibrium is changing over time. In the latter case the changes are likely to reflect changes in the distribution of consumer tastes (if tastes change and product development costs are not excessive, then some existing products may be taken off the market and new products may enter), growth in potential entry, a reduction in fixed costs or reduced development and production costs, and any clustering externalities.

7.2.7 *Horizontal product differentiation, an overview*

The subsections above have explored several different approaches to modelling the supply of horizontally differentiated product variants to the market and the resultant expenditures on generating innovations, with special reference to scenarios that are found within industries that experience soft innovation. Scenarios encompassing durable and non-durable products, single purchase and multiple purchase, single product markets, and hardware and software markets have been explored. A crucial issue as to how different factors will affect the expenditure on developing soft innovation is the elasticity of supply of such innovations to development expenditure. However, it is not possible to state a priori what this might be.

Of the factors discussed as encouraging more variety it is clear that if the number of suppliers is predetermined, then more suppliers means more variety. However, if there is free entry then the number of suppliers is endogenous. It has also been argued that lower production costs encourage higher product sales and more variety and lower costs of developing new variants also encourages more variety.

Innovation as reflected in the number of new varieties placed upon the market in a period may reflect a time-intensive approach to a predetermined equilibrium, but consideration of changes in the equilibrium over time seems a more fruitful approach. Then innovation may reflect expenditure of R&D on process innovation or the buying in of new technology (which may be determined endogenously) which through an impact on production costs will encourage more variety and the launching of new variants. In addition, if R&D and new technology reduce the costs of generating new variants, the number of new variants may again increase over time. This link between TPP innovation and soft innovation so indicated is an important point to note.

In addition, new product launches may be induced by changes in consumer tastes and for some products, endogenously by the market for older variants becoming saturated or exhausted. Some literature suggests that variants will be grouped in product space, while other literature suggests otherwise, but changes in the distribution of consumer tastes (ameliorated by launch costs) may also lead to new variants being launched (and old variants retired).

Even without considering issues relating to copying which are postponed until Chapter 10, there is little agreement in the literature as to whether the free market provides excess incentives to horizontal product variety. Although Dixit and Stiglitz (1977) suggest not, there is the potential for scale economies, common pool effects, and creative destruction effects to generate excess incentives, and thus the issue is not resolved. The outcome may well be situation-specific. The literature also does not suggest that, unaided, the market will always choose the optimal degree of standardization or the optimal standards.

7.3 Vertical product differentiation

7.3.1 Introduction

If two product variants are vertically differentiated, then at a common price all consumers prefer the same one to the other. A simple model of vertical product differentiation concerns the demand for products that come at different agreed quality levels. A useful example is aircraft travel where there may be economy class, club class, and first class, with an agreed quality ordering (and of course different prices). If creative or non-functional products are vertically differentiated, then they must also show an agreed quality ordering. For example an amateur dramatics theatrical performance will be of lesser quality than a West End performance, a meal in one's local pub will be of lesser quality than in a three Michelin-starred restaurant, some perfumes are of higher standard than others, and some fabrics feel better than others. Classic literature references are to Shaked and Sutton (1982, 1983).

Vertical product innovation will involve the introduction of a new product that is agreed by the market to be of different quality to existing products. The quality may be higher, and, as discussed in earlier chapters, this is probably the scenario that the authors of the *Oslo Manual* had in mind. However, a lower quality product might also be introduced and such an introduction is considered here to also be an innovation. The lower quality product would of course also require a lower price if it were to sell.

To consider incentives to (soft) innovate in a vertically differentiated market the subsection below first considers a simple modelling framework. This is followed by a discussion of incentives to produce variety and then consideration of alternative media.

7.3.2 A basic model

At a point in time t (with t subscripts subsumed) assume a population of size M, identical in tastes but differing in incomes I, which are assumed to be uniformly distributed such that the density function equals m on $[a,b]$ where $a > 0$ and $a < b$ and 0 otherwise. There is a consumer product available as a single variant that can be purchased at price p and if purchased the consumer j will obtain utility ul_j. Only one unit is purchased in a time period. Consumers are assumed myopic and the product is thus purchased by consumer j iff $ul_j \geq p$, or alternatively if $I_j \geq I^c = p/u$, where I^c is a threshold level of income above which the consumer purchases the product. Given the density function of income this generates the demand (X) for the product/variant

$$X = m(b - I^c) = m(b - (p/u)) \text{ for } X < M \qquad (7.24)$$

and $X = 0$ if $I^c \geq b$; $X = M$ if $I^c < a$.

The first issue concerns the level of quality that will be chosen for the variant. Assume a monopoly supplier. That supplier's decisions will at least partly depend on the costs of producing quality. It has been argued above that in the soft innovation case it is not obvious that one can directly relate product quality to the expenditure on the development of that product. However, given that that argument mainly referred to horizontal differentiation and here it is vertical differentiation that is being discussed, it is assumed that the costs of generating quality (be it design or R&D costs) written as R, are such that

$$R = Au^\delta \qquad (7.25)$$

where A and δ are positive parameters. Assume also that unit production costs (c) are such that higher quality variants costs more to produce and thus

$$c = vu \qquad (7.26)$$

where v is a parameter.

The profits of the firm are thus given by

$$\Pi = (p - vu)(m(b - (p/u))) - Au^\delta \qquad (7.27)$$

$$= mp(b + v) - mp^2/u - mbvu) - Au^\delta.$$

Taking derivatives with respect to p yields

$$m(b + v) - 2mp/u = 0 \tag{7.28}$$

i.e. at the profit maximum the price p^* is given by

$$p^* = u(b + v)/2. \tag{7.29}$$

Substituting into the profit function yields

$$\Pi = (u(b + v)/2 - vu))(m(b - (b + v)/2) - Au^\delta \tag{7.30}$$

and differentiating with respect to u yields that

$$m(b - v)/2 = \delta Au^{\delta - 1} \tag{7.31}$$

or that the optimal quality choice, u^*, is given by

$$u^* = [m(b - v)/2\delta A]^{1/(\delta - 1)} \tag{7.32}$$

Expenditure upon developing quality is then given by

$$R = A(u^*)^\delta \tag{7.33}$$

This result indicates that the chosen quality of the marketed product will be the greater is the lower A (i.e. the costs of R&D/design), the greater is m, i.e. the density of buyers at any particular quality, positively related to b the highest income level, and negatively related to v which indicates how unit costs increase with quality. Expenditure on developing the product increases with quality but may be increasing or decreasing in A.

Innovation in terms of the launch of new product varieties may occur in the market (putting aside the approach to equilibrium argument) if R&D or adoption of new technology causes production costs to fall so that v is reduced. It can be seen from Equations (7.29)–(7.33) that any new equilibrium will then involve a new product variant of higher quality (and lower price) and thus presumably a new variant replacing the old. If changes in underlying technology cause reductions in A (the costs of R&D/design), then again there will be an incentive to launch a new product of higher quality. Whether R will also increase depends upon δ.

A dynamic version of this modelling framework has been used by Stoneman (1989) to explore how quality will develop over time if each buyer will only ever buy one unit in a lifetime and the monopoly supplier has to decide upon the time profile of quality to maximize own discounted profits. It is shown that if production costs and the costs of R&D also fall over time, then quality will be increased over time up to the point in time where R&D costs stop falling. Price will also fall until production costs stop falling. It is further argued that allowing for replacement demand speeds the rate of quality improvement.

7.3.3 Product variety

The single good case is a simple one. Are there, however, any incentives for (vertical) product variety? Sutton (1986) argues that this depends on the nature of technology and tastes, specifically the relationship between consumers' willingness to pay for quality improvements and the increase in unit variable cost associated with such improvements.

Assume all consumers have identical tastes but different incomes and a consumer with income I derives utility $u(I - p)$ from consuming one unit of a product of quality level u, at price p, while if he does not buy the product at all his utility is represented by $u_0 I$. A number of goods of various quality levels, $u_n > u_{n-1} > \ldots > u_1 > u_0$, are offered on the market at prices $p_n > p_{n-1} > \ldots > p_1 > 0$, respectively. For each variant assume, without prejudice to the underlying market structure of the supplying industry, that $p = c(u)$ where $c(u)$ is the unit variable cost incurred in producing a product of quality u. Sutton (1986) shows that consumers will, if $c(u)$ increases steeply enough with u, partition themselves by income, in such a way that brands of successively higher quality are purchased by consumers in successively higher income bands, reflecting the fact that the utility function has the property that a consumer's willingness to pay for quality improvements is an increasing function of income.

The outcome will be that in the absence of fixed costs of product diversity, there will be a number of products in the market, each serving a different part of the income spectrum. Fixed costs relating to product variation will determine the extent to which groups of consumers are serviced by a product as opposed to individual consumers.[13] In a market with vertical product differentiation, therefore, there may well be a variety of products of differing quality in the market at any one time sourced from one or more suppliers. The number of varieties will be such that the last product launched is just profitable and a further launch would not be profitable.

---

[13] Although Elliott (2004) argues that in the face of uncertainty but informative advertising there may not be significant vertical differentiation.

Innovation in terms of new products may occur over time as external factors lead to changes in either the profit maximizing number or quality of products in the market. These changes might be, for example, changes in consumer income affecting demands for quality, changes in production costs through TPP innovation, and/or changes in the costs of designing or generating new products, all of which will have an impact on potential product quality or potential changes in product characteristics. These will be the drivers of product innovation in the market.

There is a literature relating to the impact of the number of suppliers on the extent of vertical variety. For example Greenstein and Ramey (1988) explore the effect of market structure on the returns from process innovation with vertically differentiated products and find that competition and monopoly in the old product market provide identical returns to innovation when (a) the monopolist is protected from new product entry; and (b) innovation is non-drastic, in the sense that the monopolist supplies positive quantities of both old and new products. If the monopolist can be threatened with entry, monopoly provides strictly greater incentives to innovate. As in Sutton (1986) it would however be more desirable to consider the supply industry structure as endogenous. Sutton (1986) argues that supply industry market structure is endogenous and determined by fixed costs. Even if the supply industry market structure is endogenous it is still useful to ask about the impact of potential entry.

Lutz (1996) explores the impact of potential entry on the market outcome and concludes that with identical quality-dependent costs as the potential entrant the incumbent will always deter entry if possible (which is when fixed costs are high). If entry is deterred, quality will be set at a level lower than the optimal quality set if entry were accommodated. If entry is not blockaded, quality will be set at a level strictly lower than the optimal quality set under monopoly. Noh and Moschini (2006) also analyse the potential entry of a new product into a vertically differentiated market. They find that entry-quality decisions and the entry-deterrence strategies are related to the fixed cost necessary for entry and to the degree of consumers' taste for quality. Welfare is not necessarily improved when entry is encouraged rather than deterred. Reisinger (2004) analyses a model of vertical product differentiation with one incumbent and one entrant firm. It is shown that if firms can produce only one quality level, this can be lower than in monopoly if qualities are strategic complements. If firms can produce a quality range and practice non-linear pricing, welfare in case of entry deterrence is higher than in monopoly because the incumbent enlarges its product line. If entry is accommodated, consumer rent increases but the consequences on welfare are ambiguous.

These results suggest that potential entry may well impact upon quality and variety. The impact on welfare is not, however, unambiguous. They also suggest that over time product innovation may well reflect the entry of new suppliers on to the market.

7.3.4 Alternative media

Prior to the end of this section it seemed appropriate to talk of competition between media and the related topic of hardware and software, continuing the discussion started under horizontal innovation. Much of the work on product differentiation conceptualizes a rather narrowly defined product where, in the words of Dixit and Stiglitz (1977), variants are good substitutes for each other but poor substitutes for other goods and services, e.g. ice cream. In the soft innovation context there may not be this neat separation. Thus, for example, a similar service may be offered by alternative products, e.g. taste buds may be sated by chocolate or fruit, or for an example of particular interest, similar services may be supplied by different media, e.g. news may be obtained from radio or newspapers. Similarly, at a moment in time there may be competition between different media supplying a similar service as in the case of radio and newspapers, but over time the number of competing media may increase, e.g. in TV programme reproduction the media have extended from VCRs to recordable DVDs and PVRs.

In principle this aspect makes very little difference to the arguments above except where the use of new media requires the acquisition of both new hardware and software. If software for one medium is not playable on another, then the costs of transferring from one medium to another will be much higher. The higher the switching costs, the more limited may be competition between the media.

When a new medium arrives on the market (e.g. record players preceded CDs, which preceded downloading or MP3 players), the new will often, with its associated software, provide a vertically differentiated improvement upon the old. However, as the new media appears in a market where a previous medium was dominant, a switch of medium requires investment in new hardware and new software, but in the face of past investment in software in another medium. For the new to succeed in the market its quality and price must overcome the drag of past investments in software.

However, the cost of supplying software for a new medium may be quite low, given that masters previously supplied in one format now just have to be reworked in a different format and re-supplied. The new format may provide suppliers with a 'second bite of the cherry'. New media may thus encourage the relaunch of old product variety in a new format.

The appearance of the new, however, may impose some welfare costs on consumers in that new software stocks would be required (my vinyl cannot be played on my CD player, although my CDs can be played on my DVD player), and the existing software stock will be devalued. Such effects are considered again in the next chapter.

7.3.5 Vertical soft innovation: an overview

Innovation instead of being horizontal may be vertical, and despite the implicit assumptions in the OECD guidelines, the new product may offer either higher or lower quality. As quality improves for given price or price falls for a given quality, demand for the product increases. Innovation, i.e. new product launches, as with horizontal differentiation, may result either from a move towards an equilibrium or a shift of the equilibrium. The latter seems to be of greatest interest. It has, thus, been argued that process R&D and/ or process innovation will affect the costs of production and product launch and thereby the number of products launched upon the market. Soft innovation will therefore be closely tied to TPP innovation. Changes in incomes and tastes of consumers will also matter in that if they change over time then so may the ideal product specifications and this may lead to new variants being launched and existing variants being withdrawn.[14] There is some support for the view that more actual and potential suppliers stimulate product quality, and thus product innovation may reflect changes in these factors. However, it is probably best if market structure is considered endogenous. There are some extra issues to consider when hardware and software are jointly required to produce service flows, and also when there are different media producing a similar service. There is no strong evidence in either direction as to how entry

---

[14] Siebert (2003) analyses the optimal provision of goods in a market characterized by vertical product differentiation and duopoly. He finds that an innovator will always withdraw its own existing product from the market in order to reduce price competition and to avoid cannibalizing its new product demand. In contrast to horizontally differentiated markets, firms are better off not to offer a range or interval of product qualities in vertically differentiated markets. Hence, firms fare better, despite offering a smaller variety of goods.

(and market structure) impact upon welfare nor whether free markets will produce optimal variety.

7.4 Conclusions

Following arguments presented above, this chapter has concentrated on an approach to analysing the determinants of the rate of soft innovation that stresses the product differentiating nature of such innovation. The standard TPP-orientated literature in the determination of R&D and innovation emphasizes the importance of market structures (if exogenous), the elasticity of product demand and the elasticity of costs with respect to R&D as prime determinants of expenditure on R&D and thus the rate of product or process improvement over time. The equivalents of such factors may also play a role in the determination of the rate of soft innovation. The results of the analysis of models of horizontal and vertical product differentiation suggest that the number of new soft variants of products being launched, the number of product variants in the market at any one time, their location in product space, prices, quality, and expenditure on new product development will reflect the state of, and changes in, the nature of competition, fixed costs, demand elasticities, the distribution of consumer preferences, the costs of development, market structure, and many other factors.

The different scenarios and different games assumed in the literature make general predictions rather difficult except to the extent that it is expected that expenditure on soft innovations will extend to the point where the marginal gross pay-off equals the marginal cost of further innovation. Innovative activity at this point, however, is determined by many factors.

In addition to such positive issues, this chapter has also explored normative issues. In the TPP literature the major consideration is whether expenditure on R&D will be welfare optimal. Here the main concern has been whether in a free market there will be too much or too little incentive to variety from a welfare point of view and, thus, whether there is a need for policy intervention. For these purposes issues relating to copying have been set aside (but are to be discussed in Chapter 10). Even so, the different models have different normative predictions. In some scenarios expenditure on developing variety may be too low. In others it may be too great. The literature on TPP innovation indicates that one should also take into account considerations such as common pool issues, monopoly power, and creative destruction. One can only infer that on the optimality issue there is no general finding to be carried forward. In fact, Lancaster's (1990) survey is still surprisingly definitive. This finds that:

The fundamental structure of all optimal variety problems, for the individual firm as well as society, is the interplay of two elements in the economy – the existence of a gain from variety and the existence of scale economies of some kind. If there are no economies of scale associated with individual product variants (in distribution as well as in production), then it is optimal to custom produce to everyone's chosen specification. If there is no gain from variety and there are scale economies, then it is clearly optimal to produce only a single variant if those economies are unlimited, or only such variety as uses scale economies to the limit (all products at minimum average cost output). Most cases involve a balance of some variety against some scale economies, the solution depending on the preference properties of consumers, the scale properties in production and distribution, and the way in which the social welfare criterion is derived from individual preferences. Different criteria and assumptions can lead to quite different conclusions.

In addition to issues relating to copying, another factor that has largely been ignored in this chapter is uncertainty. This is not because it is irrelevant but rather because it is addressed in more detail in Chapter 9 (on diffusion).

In addition to the actual findings, this chapter illustrates how models designed for exploring product differentiation can usefully be used for analysing innovations in differentiated markets (such analysis could also be applied to TPP innovation as well as soft innovation). In particular the application of models of horizontal differentiation and reduction in vertical product quality are rare. It seems that this is a useful extension to the literature in that usually product differentiation and innovations are separately analysed, whereas it is clear that there are useful modelling commonalities that can be profitably exploited.

8

The Diffusion of Soft Innovations

8.1 Introduction

This chapter is concerned with the diffusion of soft innovations. Through the interaction of supply and demand, the outcome of a diffusion process is the intertemporal purchasing or ownership pattern of a new product (or variant) or process. The previous chapter concentrated upon the supply of soft innovations in the light of presumed demand patterns with the demand side played down. This chapter concentrates upon the nature of intertemporal demand for soft innovations in the light of supply-side factors but with those factors played down.

The chapter is concerned with both kinds of soft innovation, i.e. innovation in aesthetic or creative products and also innovation in the aesthetics of functional products. The prime purpose of the chapter is to provide understanding and insight into (*a*) the intertemporal demand pattern for products that experience soft innovation; (*b*) the intertemporal demand pattern for new variants encompassing soft innovation; and (*c*) the interaction between these two. To date diffusion analysis has rarely been used to look at innovations in differentiated product[1] markets, i.e. the patterns and determinants of the diffusion of new product variants, but has primarily been used to look at generic technologies, e.g. robots or televisions or washing machines. The extension to product variants is an important part of analysing soft innovations, but being something new is potentially ground breaking. Although the main purpose is positive analysis, there is also the intention to attempt to derive some normative implications upon which policy may be built, this being discussed at the end of the chapter.

An important finding from the existing TPP-based literature is that new technologies when put upon the market take time to diffuse. The lifetime

[1] See Tirole (1988) for details of horizontal and vertical product differentiation.

sale will not be instantaneous.[2] Typically the literature indicates that ownership of a new technology tends to follow an S-shaped curve over time, with the proportion of owners starting low then growing at an increasing rate until after a point of inflexion at which the rate of growth, although still positive, declines, with ownership approaching an asymptote (see Stoneman [2002]; Geroski [2000]). This pattern is generally revealed when one looks at individual households, firms, or groups such as industries, nations, or even internationally (see Stoneman and Battisti [2009]). The product life cycle is an alternative way to look at this diffusion pattern. A typical product life cycle starts with limited but fast growth in sales, with the rate of growth after some point of inflexion declining as an asymptote of ownership is approached. The product life cycle reflects sales, which for a durable, non-depreciating good is equivalent to the first difference in total ownership, and thus the intertemporal sales pattern is just the first difference of the diffusion pattern. It is thus expected that by using diffusion analysis it will be possible to also provide some insight into the life cycle of soft innovations.

Examples of diffusion patterns for soft innovations have been produced in Chapters 4 and 5. For example, the product life cycle of best-selling books was shown. Also illustrated was the rise and fall of different music reproduction media (LPs, tape cassettes, CDs, etc.). The development of the market for video games was discussed, as were changes in the demand patterns for certain foods, the development of credit card markets, and also innovation in pharmaceuticals. These examples are cited not just to ground what is discussed here, but also to indicate that markets differ and thus approaches to explaining diffusion in those markets differ. Thus, for example, the determinants of the diffusion (product life cycle) of a new book title may differ from the diffusion of a new music recording because the latter requires compatible hardware. Similarly a video game may experience a different diffusion pattern from a music recording because the game is console-specific. The nature of products thus must be taken in to account.

Within the confines of the existing literature, a common representation of the S-shaped diffusion pattern is the logistic diffusion curve which may be written in continuous time as

$$m(t) = M/(1 + \exp(-\alpha - \beta t)) \qquad (8.1)$$

---

[2] This tends to rule out the specific analysis of bespoke markets from a diffusion viewpoint, for in such markets each product is unique.

where, once diffusion is complete M units of a new product will have been sold and at any point in time $m(t)$ have already been sold. α is a constant of integration locating the curve on the time axis, and β is known as the speed of diffusion and determines how fast the asymptote (M) is actually reached. The logistic curve illustrates an increasing rate of growth of ownership up to 0.5 M (a result special to this particular curve) after which growth slows but remains positive up to M. Prime questions relate to the determinants of the sigmoid shape itself, α, β, and M.

There is now an extensive and growing literature that looks at the diffusion of innovations. In economics (see Stoneman [2002]) that literature is biased towards the adoption and spreading of process innovations across firms whereas in marketing there is a much greater emphasis on new products (see, e.g., the classic paper by Bass [1969]). There may be more balance in the sociology literature between products and processes (see, e.g., Rogers [2003]). The different disciplines also differently emphasize different factors in the diffusion process. The sociology literature emphasizes that different individuals will have different levels of willingness to take risks and to lead and that the most adventurous will be earliest adopters. Marketing, on the other hand, tends to build on psychological approaches to consumer behaviour; emphasizes the role of information spreading in the diffusion process; and seeks to explore how firm strategies with respect to advertising, pricing, and the use of other marketing tools may influence the adoption pattern. The economics literature that is of main concern here has also considered differences between potential buyers and information spreading as factors important to the diffusion process but has been more explicit as to how these play a role through their impact on the utility or profit gains that arise from the use of new technologies.

Approaches in the economics literature to diffusion fall in to two main classes – disequilibrium and equilibrium approaches. The first of these considers diffusion as a process that once started has its own dynamic leading to completion of the process at a rate at each point in time proportional to the distance still to be travelled. The process is self-propagating. Such diffusion processes are considered to either be driven by information spreading (e.g. the epidemic approach found in Mansfield [1963a, 1963b, 1968]) or by profit reinvestment (e.g. Metcalfe 1988). Some of the recent game theoretic signalling literature (see, e.g., Choi [1997]) queries the whole representation of information acquisition as a passive process. In conjunction with the lack of any decision theoretic foundations, although still talked of, the disequilibrium approach has been somewhat put aside in favour of equilibrium models.

Equilibrium models essentially argue that the usage or ownership of new technology at different points in time will reflect the gains in profit or utility to be derived from purchase relative to the cost of acquisition (and in some models the expected changes in the cost of acquisition). The gains are then related to the number of other users through, for example, rank, order, or stock effects (see Karshenas and Stoneman [1993, 1995]). Allowing marginal gains to equal marginal costs of acquisition yields a solution for the equilibrium number of users at any time. Diffusion proceeds over time as the technology improves, the costs of acquisition fall, or the characteristics of the buyers change. Diffusion is not self-propagating. In such equilibrium models (and even in some of the disequilibrium models) the factors that influence the diffusion process such as prices, product qualities, or number of suppliers may also be considered as endogenous to the diffusion process. Models such as these provide a much stronger theoretical foundation for the diffusion process as a result of rational decision making by economic agents. They may also provide insight into the differences between early and late adopters. The equilibrium literature has also addressed network and other externalities, and standards and compatibility, although as yet the new literatures on two-sided markets (Rochet and Tirole 2006) have not made a great impact.

In what follows we briefly discuss the epidemic or disequilibrium approach before moving to consider diffusion with horizontal product innovation using the preferred equilibrium approaches, first for non-durable products, then durable products, and subsequently products requiring both hardware and software inputs. This is followed by a discussion on diffusion with vertical product innovation and diffusion of alternative media. Throughout, issues relating to risk and uncertainty are played down for the sake of simplicity. These are considered more fully in Chapter 9.

8.2 The epidemic approach

The epidemic approach has played a considerable role in the diffusion literature, especially in marketing, but, for reasons to be detailed, the approach is given only limited attention here. A common, basic version of the model applies to products that are durable but of which any buyer will only ever buy one unit. It is often considered that the approach is particularly useful for analysing products subject to fads or fashions. Thus, in terms of creative products, the approach might be applied to, for example, a high-priced fashion item, say, a pair of cowboy boots or a leather jacket.

Assume initially (*a*) that there is only one variant in the market; (*b*) that once diffusion is complete *M* units of the new product/variant will have been sold; (*c*) that at any point in time *m*(*t*) have already been sold; and (*d*) in time *t* the probability of any of the (*M* − *m*(*t*)) non-owners buying a unit is positively related to the probability of meeting an existing owner,[3] which is determined by (*m*(*t*)/*M*) as β(*m*(*t*)/*M*) where β is a positive parameter, then

$$m(t) - m(t-1) = \beta(m(t)/M)(M - m(t))\qquad(8.2)$$

which may be written in continuous time as

$$m(t) = M/(1 + \exp(-\alpha - \beta t))\qquad(8.3)$$

which is the logistic diffusion curve discussed above.

This model generates a diffusion process that is self-propagating, which once started will carry on until the asymptote is reached. The crucial assumption generating this result is that the probability of purchase increases with usage. This is often put down either to information spreading affecting knowledge of existence or performance (Bass 1969) and/or reducing the risk of ownership (Mansfield 1968). Literature has suggested that for technologies that yield the greater gains (in utility or profits), diffusion will start earlier, be faster, and also have higher asymptotes (Mansfield 1963*b*; Griliches 1957).

The fact that current usage may encourage further usage because of information spreading or risk-reducing externalities may well be a significant insight and reflect an important factor affecting the adoption of new technologies (e.g. word-of-mouth recommendations could affect demand for a new book title or video game). However, the way in which learning is modelled in this approach and also the way that uncertainty reduction is assumed to have an effect are primitive and may be misleading. Thus, for example, buyers act as passive recipients and not seekers of information. Information just comes to them. Alternatively, information is assumed to reduce the buyers' views of the risk attached to the technology, whereas it might increase that risk. Davies (1979) also criticizes the implicit assumptions about the homogeneous nature of the population, with each member being identical to the others. In essence, although it is not difficult to see that such an approach could be applied to aesthetic products and soft

---

[3] It is because of the importance of interpersonal contact that this approach is likened to the spreading of infections, i.e. epidemics.

innovations, there are too many open questions for it to stand as a complete explanation of the diffusion process (even for fashion goods as suggested).

Extending the epidemic model beyond the confines of the assumptions employed here is also difficult. In particular, it is not clear how and where in this approach one might take account of the existence or introduction of new product variants. Moreover, given the lack of any decision theoretic base, there seems little guide as to what would be the best way to rationalize any approach actually taken. In all, the decision theoretic models appear to hold better prospects for detailed analysis.

8.3 The diffusion of soft innovations in horizontally differentiated markets

8.3.1 *A simple decision theoretic approach*

This section considers a simple model, introduced in Chapter 7, of a market with horizontally differentiated product variants. It is assumed that the product is non-durable and thus if a variant is purchased in one time period, it will depreciate away to 0 within that period. The product may be aesthetic or functional, although if it is the latter, the variants are considered to differ in terms of aesthetic characteristics in line with the concept of soft innovation. Examples include pre-prepared and restaurant meals, cigars, theatrical productions, Beaujolais nouveau, cheaper clothing, etc.

To simplify the analysis it is also assumed that (*a*) a consumer will at most buy one unit of the product in a period, thus purchasing one unit of any variant reduces the demand for all other variants by that consumer in that period to 0; (*b*) individual utility functions are assumed separable in money and utility derived from the differentiated product; and (*c*) potential buyers know of the product and its performance characteristics.

Let there be M potential buyers/consumers in a market, the income of each consumer j ($j = 1 \ldots M$) being $I_j(t)$ in time t. Assume that for consumer j the ideal or best variant of the product in terms of the utility pay-off is variant z_j, which will yield consumer j utility k_j from the acquisition of one unit. If instead of variant z_j the consumer buys one unit in time t with characteristics x, the consumer will then realize overall utility of $U_j(x, I_j, t) = I_j(t) - P_x(t) + k_j - f_j(d(x, z_j))$ in that period, where $P_x(t)$ is the price of product x in time t, $d(x, z_j)$ is the (Euclidean) distance in the product space between variant characteristics x and variant characteristics z_j, and f_j translates this difference into a utility loss. It is assumed that $k_j - f_j(d(x, z_j))$ is distributed over the M potential consumers according to $F(j)$.

If there is only one product variant in the market (variant x), the utility gained by consumer j from purchasing the variant x relative to not purchasing at all will be given by

$$U_j(I_j, x, t) - U_j(I_j, 0, t) = k_j - f_j(d(x, z_j)) - P_x(t) \qquad (8.4)$$

and consumer j will purchase a unit of x in time t iff

$$k_j - f_j(d(x, z_j)) - P_x(t) > 0. \qquad (8.5)$$

To generate the number of buyers in time t (equal to the number of units sold in time t) $X(t)$, it is clear that $X(t) = M(1 - F(P_x(t)))$. It is then immediately obvious that total sales are affected by consumer preferences and incomes and suppliers' choices of prices and variant specification.

The factors that in this context that may generate a diffusion pattern, whereby sales of the product follow an S-shaped curve as detailed above, or at least increase over time include:

1. Reductions in the price of the product/variant $P_x(t)$. Any reduction in price will increase the utility gain to buyers who were previously on the margin of purchase. As the price falls, the distribution over the N potential consumers $F(j)$ is mapped out. One may note that differences between buyers and non-buyers at a point in time, and early and late buyers over time, will largely reflect $k_j - f_j(d(x, z_j))$, i.e. the difference between the inherent utility contribution of the product class and how the marketed variant specification differs from the ideal. For early adopters this will be small and for later adopters it will be large. As price falls, those for whom it is large also become buyers. If the rate at which price falls and the distribution of buyers are appropriate, the mapping of $F(j)$ may generate the often observed S-shaped curve. It should be noted, however, that price is an endogenous variable that will be set by the interaction of the supply and demand sides as discussed in the previous chapter.

2. An alternative driver of diffusion is that the single variant in the market could change in terms of performance characteristics. One possibility is that the variant experiences vertical improvement, a case we consider later. Alternatively it might be that the product experiences changes in horizontal characteristics to appeal to a thicker part of the market.

Although possible, the introduction of new horizontal variants is more interesting and discussed immediately below.

3. Finally, consumer preferences may change and so the distribution $F(j)$ will change over time. This could also result in a different pattern of sales over time.

Of more interest here, and quite rarely considered, is the impact of placing other horizontally differentiated product variants in the market (see Stoneman [1990]). The perspective is that the product is either in the creative sector and thus such new variants represent soft innovation, or the product is functional when these variants are considered here to differ in terms of soft characteristics. If in addition to variant x, variant y is also made available, consumers will buy either one unit of x, one of y, or no units at all. It was shown in the previous chapter that a consumer will realize utility $U_j(y, Y_j, t) = Y_j(t) - P_y(t) + k_j - f_j(d(y, z_j))$ from the purchase of y where $P_y(t)$ is the price of variant y. It was then shown that variant y will be purchased by consumer j iff

$$k_j - f_j(d(y, z_j)) - P_y(t) > k_j - f_j(d(x, z_j)) - P_x(t) > 0 \qquad (8.6)$$

and, assuming that $k_j - f_j(d(x, z_j)) - P_x(t)$ is not affected by variant y also being on the market, any change in the pattern of demand for the product relative to the single variant scenario will reflect the change in behaviour of two types of consumers: those who did not previously buy x but will now buy y; and those who previously did buy x but will now buy y. The demand for variant y thus is made up of two parts, those who previously were not buyers plus those who are switchers that previously bought x. As can be seen from Equation (8.6) the sales of variant y (ceteris paribus) will increase as its price $P_y(t)$ decreases, and that customers with preferences closer to the specification of variant y are more likely to buy variant y. The introduction of variant y is more likely to reduce the demand for variant x, the lower is $P_y(t)/P_x(t)$; customers with preferences closer to y than x are more likely to switch. The sales of x and y, and thus their diffusion, will develop over time as prices change and or as further new variants are put on the market.

Overall unit product sales are affected by the number of variants in the market only if there are consumers who did not previously buy x but will now buy y. For consumer j to be in this first category it is required that

$$k_j - f_j(d(y, z_j)) - P_y(t) > 0 > k_j - f_j(d(x, z_j)) - P_x(t). \qquad (8.7)$$

If this condition is satisfied for at least one consumer, then the addition of an extra variant will have increased product demand and sales, i.e. to have stimulated diffusion. By implication the lower is $P_y(t)$, the greater is the extra number of buyers of the product induced by the entry of the new variant (although it should be noted however that this price is endogenous). In addition, the closer is the specification of variant y to the preferences of consumers not being served by variant x the more will product diffusion extend. However, it is not necessarily going to be optimal for a supplier to choose that variant specification – a specification closer to x may offer a thicker market with more potential buyers (see the discussion in the previous chapter).

Although this is a very simple exercise and ignores many potential factors, it illustrates that in a model of horizontal product differentiation that includes no explicit improvements or changes in product functionality, the rate at which product variants diffuse and the rate at which the product per se diffuses, may be significantly affected by soft innovation increasing the number of product variants in the market.

8.3.2 Durable products

Of the examples of soft innovations discussed in earlier chapters, some emphasis was placed upon products that were durable with many variants available. Buyers may buy only one copy of any particular variant but may acquire copies of many different variants either at a point in time or over time. Obvious products to be considered under this heading are books, CDs, and DVDs. This section considers diffusion in such markets.

For greatest simplicity it is assumed that there are only two time periods, today (period 0) and tomorrow (period 1). Initially it is further assumed that only one product variant (x) is available, which is durable and can be purchased in either period 0 at prices $P_x(0)$ or in period 1 at (actual in time 1 and expected in time 0) prices $P_x(1)$. The performance of x and the utility contribution in period 1 is the same whether the product is bought in period 0 or 1, although the service flow is only enjoyed if the product is owned. The utility enjoyed from ownership in a period of ownership is as in the previous model. Income of consumer j is I_j in both periods and the discount factor (one divided by one plus the discount rate) is ρ.

The consumer may buy variant x either in period 0, or in period 1, or not at all, yielding utilities respectively of:

Buy in period 0: $I_j(1 + \rho) + (k_j - f_j(d(x, z_j))(1 + \rho) - P_x(0)$
Buy in period 1: $I_j(1 + \rho) + (k_j - f_j(d(x, z_j)) - P_x(1))\rho$
Do not buy: $\quad I_j(1 + \rho)$

For the sake of the argument and considerable simplicity, allow that not buying at all is an inferior option. Consumer j will then buy the variant in period 0 if that yields the greatest gain and in time period 1 if that yields the greatest gain. Thus the consumer will:

Buy in period 0 if $(k_j - f_j(d(x, z_j))(1 + \rho) - P_x(0) > (k_j - f_j(d(x, z_j)) - P_x(1))\rho$
Buy in period 1 if $(k_j - f_j(d(x, z_j))(1 + \rho) - P_x(0) < (k_j - f_j(d(x, z_j)) - P_x(1))\rho$

To buy in period 0 requires that $(k_j - f_j(d(x, z_j)) > P_x(0) - \rho P_x(1)$, i.e. the utility gain from having x in period 1 is greater than the potential gain from delaying purchase and buying in period 1 at the price $P_x(1)$ rather than $P_x(0)$. Clearly, assuming that $k_j - f_j(d(x, z_j))$ is positive, then purchasers will only delay if the price is expected to fall over time. The greater is $k_j - f_j(d(x, z_j))$, the less likely is delay. Allowing that $k_j - f_j(d(x, z_j))$ is distributed over the N potential consumers according to $F(j)$, then

$$X(0) = N(1 - F(P_x(0) - \rho P_x(1)))\qquad(8.8)$$

and

$$X(1) = N - X(0).\qquad(8.9)$$

Although in reality the picture will be complicated by information spreading issues and other such factors, the prediction of this story is that, in the absence of expected reductions in the price $(P_x(0) - \rho P_x(1))$, the sales of the single variant will be concentrated early in the life of the variant with more limited, if any, sales later. Later sales would be induced only by expected and actual lower future prices. In fact if prices do not change over time, all sales will be at the early date because of discounting. Whether sales are shifted over time will depend on (expected) intertemporal price differences which in turn will be dependent upon costs and competition in the industry supplying the product.

To extend the analysis, consider that an extra product variant is (and it is known at time 0 will be) available in period 1 as well as the original variant. For example it is known that in the future there will be more Rolling Stones CDs available or new book titles will be launched. Also assume that the characters of these products are known and that the utility gain to having y (x) is independent of whether x (y) is owned or not. The prices of y in period 1 is written as $P_y(1)$.

There are five choices open to the consumer (assuming doing nothing in both periods, i.e. not buying x or y, is an inferior option[4]) with associated discounted utility gains as follows.

1. Buy x in period 0 and nothing in period 1:

$$(k_j \ - \ f_j(d(x, z_j))(1 \ + \ \rho) \ - \ P_x(0)$$

2. Buy x in period 0 and y in period 1:

$$(k_j \ - \ f_j(d(x, z_j))(1 \ + \ \rho) \ - \ P_x(0) \ + \ (k_j \ - \ f_j(d(y, z_j))(\rho) \ - \ \rho P_y(1)$$

3. Buy nothing in period 0 and x in period 1

$$(k_j \ - \ f_j(d(x, z_j))(\rho) \ - \ \rho P_x(1)$$

4. Buy nothing in period 0 and y in period 1

$$(k_j \ - \ f_j(d(y, z_j))(\rho) \ - \ \rho P_y(1)$$

5. Buy nothing in period 0 and x and y in period 1

$$(k_j \ - \ f_j(d(x, z_j))(\rho) \ - \ \rho P_x(1) \ + \ (k_j \ - \ f_j(d(y, z_j))(\rho) \ - \ \rho P_y(1)$$

The consumer maximizing utility will buy x in period 0 if

$$(k_j - f_j(d(x, z_j)) > P_x(0) - \rho P_y(1) \tag{8.10}$$

otherwise he or she will buy x in time period 1, i.e. if

$$(k_j - f_j(d(x, z_j)) < P_x(0) - \rho P_x(1) \tag{8.11}$$

The consumer will buy y (in period 1) if

$$(k_j - f_j(d(y, z_j)) > P_y(1) \tag{8.12}$$

The structure of the model is such that the demand pattern for x is the same whether or not the new variant is put on the market, as long as prices are not affected by the new variant being launched. Similarly the demand for the new variant is unaffected by the presence of the old variant if prices are not affected. (Whether prices are affected could depend upon supplier

---

[4] It is possible to modify the argument to allow instead that the net benefits of ownership decline as income reduces. In such a case early buyers will have higher incomes and late buyers will have low income, but also as price falls over time the threshold income above which purchase takes place will reduce and thus diffusion over time will reflect the income distribution.

costs.) Increases in ownership of the two variants will each depend upon the intertemporal pattern of prices.

More interestingly however, the introduction of the new variant y in period 1 may increase total product sales. If $G(j)$ is the distribution of $k_j - f_j(d(y, z_j))$ over j, total sales of x and y in period 2 relative to when only variant x was available will be greater by an amount $N(1 - G(P_y(1)))$. Thus, in the absence of new differentiated variants being put on the market, the demand for the product would only be maintained by falling prices for the original variant but would eventually fall away to 0 when diffusion would terminate. The continued existence of the industry results from the continuous launching of new product variants maintaining demand for the product, i.e. soft innovation is the sine qua non of the industry.

8.3.3 Hardware and software

This section explores the diffusion of products that involve both hardware and software in the generation of the service flow. Initially an example such as recorded music in a particular medium (e.g. CDs, tapes, or vinyl) is considered where software from all suppliers is compatible with the hardware. In such a case the demand for, and diffusion of, soft innovations will depend upon the number of owners of the hardware but also on the software available with the number of potential buyers of hardware determined endogenously.

Consider the hardware acquisition decision of a consumer who has not previously acquired the technology. For the purposes of this exercise consider initially that all consumers are completely myopic and take no account of costs and benefits beyond the decision period t (for ease of exposition, t subscripts are implicit where obvious). Assume that consumer j with income I_j can become a hardware owner at price P_h, but will only generate utility from this hardware if software is also purchased. All hardware and software are compatible. The consumer's utility from purchasing x_j units of software is given as $U_j(x_j, i_j)$ where i_j is expenditure on all other goods. Assume that $U_{j1}' > 0$, $U_{j1}'' < 0$; $U_{j2}' > 0$, $U_{j2}'' < 0$; and also that U_{j1}' is increasing in N, the number of different software products in the market, reflecting results from above. Let the average price of software be P per unit, then $i_j = I_j - Px_j - P_h$.

A utility maximizing hardware owner will choose the number of units of software to acquire by maximizing $U_j(x_j, y_j)$ subject to $i_j = I_j - P x_j - P_h$ yielding, at the point where $U_{j1}' = P$, a value x_j^* and thus expenditure on software of Px_j^*. At this point a hardware owner will obtain utility $U_j(x_j^*,$

$I_j - Px_j^* - P_h$). Note that x_j^* will increase as P decreases. Note also that as $U_{j1}' > 0$ is increasing in N, the greater the product variety, the greater will be the number of units of software purchased by a hardware owner. Should the consumer choose not to acquire the hardware and thus obviously not buy software, his utility will be given by $U_j(0, I_j)$.

Assume that there is total population of size M, and potential buyers can be ranked by the value of $U_j(x_j^*, I_j - Px_j^* - P_h) - U_j(0, I_j)$, then the marginal hardware buyer will be that consumer for whom Equation (8.13) holds

$$U_j(x_j^*, I_j - Px_j^* - P_h) = U_j(0, Y_j). \tag{8.13}$$

From Equation (8.13), given that $U_{j1}' > 0, U_{j1}'' < 0; U_{j2}' > 0, U_{j2}'' < 0$ and that U_{j1}' is increasing in N, it can immediately be seen (a) that the lower the P_h, the more hardware owners there will be, because a price reduction will increase residual income of a hardware owner, enable overall utility to be higher for such an owner than previously, and thus encourage further ownership; (b) a reduction in the price of software P will have the same effect of increasing hardware demand, with some of the extra residual income being spent on more software; and (c) an increase in total software availability will increase the utility of hardware owners even if they do not buy more software (which we predict they will) and therefore encourage hardware ownership.

Writing

$$U_j(x_j^*, Y_j - Px_j^* - P_h) - U_j(0, Y_j) = H_j(Y_j, P, P_h, N) \tag{8.14}$$

the number of hardware owners will be given by the number in the population M multiplied by the proportion of the population for whom $U_j(x_j^*, I_j - Px_j^* - P_h) - U_j(0, I_j) > 0$. Define the distribution of $U_j(x_j^*, I_j - Px_j^* - P_h) - U_j(0, Y_j)$ over the population as $H(j)$, then the number of owners m is given by

$$m = N(1 - H(0)), \tag{8.15}$$

where $H(0)$ is declining in P, P_h, and M.

The model above tells a clear story: the diffusion of hardware is determined by the income of potential buyers, its own price, the number of software variants available, and software prices. Note that an increase in the number of software variants impacts on the overall software market because (a) it increases the sales of software to existing owners of hardware;

and (*b*) also encourages more of the population to acquire the hardware and thus become software buyers.[5]

This framework has been presented in a rather timeless way, but it is not difficult to see how the approach can generate an intertemporal diffusion pattern. First, reductions in the cost of producing hardware may generate reduction in its price and further purchases of hardware. This will increase the demand for software. Secondly, over time the number of software titles available may increase and this will increase both the demand for hardware and, directly or indirectly, the demand for software. Finally, the price of software may fall over time with the same effect as increasing the number of titles available. With changes in the number of software titles available being an indicator of soft innovation, it may be seen from this analysis that soft innovation and functional innovation interact in the demand process.

The previous example, indicative of the recorded music case, is special in that all software and hardware are compatible. This would be relevant also to DVDs and VCRs. However, for some products this is not the case. Thus, for example, different software for games consoles is usually console-specific. The consumer, therefore, faces two decisions when deciding whether to adopt a technology. The first is whether to acquire a technology at all, and the second is which 'standard' to acquire. The term 'standard' is used here to link into a related literature that has considerable normative overtones (see below).

In the relevant literature it is generally argued that the benefit to an owner of a particular hardware standard depends upon the software available for that standard. However, the supply of software for that standard depends upon the potential return to the writing of that software which will depend on the number of owners of that hardware standard. In reality it is really expectations that matter. It is the hardware owner's expectations of software availability that matter and the software suppliers' expectation of hardware numbers that also matters.

There is the potential here for strong network externalities. If many buyers acquire a particular standard, then there is an incentive for more software to be developed, which will reinforce the demand for that standard. The optimality of a single consumer's decision upon the standard will thus depend upon whether it is the same as others choose.

Choi (1997) analyses such a situation. In her approach she looks at the interaction between information externalities (as per the epidemic model) and network externalities in an environment of consumer uncertainty.

---

[5] Also, but not covered here, more variants may mean more competition to any particular software provider.

She considers irreversible investments in a technology that is available in two formats, A and B. The net benefits for an individual choosing technology A(B) are $\alpha(\beta) + \upsilon n$ where n is the number of people choosing the same format. Prior to first investment in a format the benefits or pay-offs to that format, α and β, are not known with certainty, but once used by one potential adopter the true value of the pay-off is known. Prior to first use α and β are assumed independently distributed and have continuous and positive density on support $(0, \infty)$.

For the sake of argument put aside the network externalities for a moment. The first buyer of the new technology must choose one format. Let this be technology A. The purchase will reveal to everyone the true returns to technology A. The second buyer will then also have to choose between A and B. The comparison is a simple one. If $E(\beta)$ is the expected value of the net benefits of B, the second buyer will choose format B if $E(\beta) > \alpha$ and technology A if the reverse is true. If the second buyer chooses technology A, then the true value of the benefit of technology B will not be revealed. The third buyer will thus have no more information than the second. But as the third buyer is the same as the second, he or she will also choose A and thus the true value of the benefit of B will never be revealed. All buyers will choose A. If, on the other hand, the second buyer chooses B, then the true benefit of B will be revealed and all future buyers may see whether $\alpha > \beta$ or $\alpha < \beta$ and make the correct technology choice in future periods. Clearly the market will only reveal the true benefits of both technologies if the first two users make different technology choices.

When network externalities are included in the story there is an extra force to take into account. If the first user chooses technology A, then the second user will know the inherent return to that technology. The choice facing this second user is A or B. If B is chosen and found to be superior to A, then the true returns to B are known and since they are greater than A all future adopters will choose B. Having chosen B the second adopter will thus get the greatest possible pay-off. However, if B is chosen and is revealed to be inferior, all future adopters will know this and will then choose A. The returns to A will then increase as network effects kick in. The buyers that chose B will thus suffer much lower relative returns than just $\alpha - \beta$ because the returns to A will be $\alpha + \upsilon n$ and the returns to B will be just β. In making the decision on whether to buy A or B the second buyer is thus trying to avoid being stranded with an inferior technology.

In such a scenario the launch of many variants of the hardware may slow diffusion of that hardware by (*a*) confusing consumers as to which variant will be dominant eventually and thus have good software supply and (b) dispersing software suppliers' efforts so that less variety is available for each platform.

In terms of soft innovation, the arguments are that (a) the availability of soft innovations for different standards will impact upon the outcome of any competition between standards, (b) the success of demand for different soft innovations will be related to hardware ownership patterns, and (c) the overall demand for the technology (hardware and software) may reduce in the face of uncertainty with respect to standards.

8.4 The diffusion of soft innovations in vertically differentiated markets

8.4.1 Non-durables

With vertical product differentiation, if two product variants are on the market, then all consumers agree on the quality ordering of the variants, e.g. first class rail travel is of higher quality than standard class, a Michelin-starred restaurant is preferred to McDonald's, and haute couture offers higher quality than high street chains (classic references are Sutton [1986] and Shaked and Sutton [1982]). The analysis of diffusion within such contexts concerns changes (over time) in the sales of the product and different variants of the product.

Consider again the simple model of vertical product differentiation, presented earlier in the previous chapter. There is a population of potential consumers j of size M, identical in tastes but differing in income I_j, which is assumed to be uniformly distributed such that the density function equals m on $[a,b]$ where $a > 0$ and $a < b$, and 0 otherwise. There is a consumer product available initially as a single variant that can be purchased at price p, and if purchased the consumer j will obtain utility uI_j. Only one unit is purchased in a time period and the product is non-durable.

The product is purchased by consumer j iff $uI_j \geq p$, or alternatively if $I_j \geq I^c = p/u$, where I^c is a threshold level of income above which the consumer purchases the product. Given the density function of income this generates the total demand (X) for the product/variant

$$X = m(b - I^c) = M(b - (p/u)) \text{ for } X < N \qquad (8.16)$$

and

$$X = 0 \text{ if } I^c \geq b, I^c < a, \qquad (8.17)$$

207

i.e. the product is purchased if income exceeds a critical level p/u. The demand for the product will increase if the price falls, the quality u increases, or the incomes of potential consumers increase.

Diffusion, that is increases in the demand for the product over time, could arise from changes in consumer incomes over time and/or reductions in prices and increases in quality of the variant. The latter two will be dependent upon the costs and development activities of product suppliers as well as the nature of competition in the supply industry.

Of more interest here is the impact of the introduction of another variant in the market (in this context a soft innovation). The impact of the introduction of another variant will obviously depend on the quality and price of that variant. One possibility is that the new variant is of similar quality to the original variant but is offered at a lower price. For example, recently some airlines introduced planes carrying only business class passengers and hope to gain trade by offering lower prices than existing suppliers (all have since closed). Although the existing supplier might react by also reducing prices, and thus the final impact of the market shares of variants is not clear, the introduction of the new variant will directly and indirectly increase the overall demand for the product.

A second possibility is that the new variant offers higher quality at the same price as the previous variant. In many ways this is the sort of change that we think the OECD had in mind when it discusses technological product innovation. This would be equivalent to airlines offering sleeper seats without increasing the price. Again one might expect either the specification of the existing variant to be improved or its price to be reduced and thus one cannot predict the outcome in terms of variant shares, but overall one would expect some extension of purchase and further product diffusion.

A third possibility is that the new variant offers lower quality, but it is priced in a way to make it preferred to the existing higher quality variant at its higher price. This is the budget airline strategy, where service quality is reduced but price is also reduced but proportionately by more. The OECD definition of technological product innovation seems to rule out such a possibility. As the nature of competitive response will determine the market share of the variants, one can say little definite about these, however once again the launch of the new product variant will increase overall product demand.[6]

---

[6] There is a limit to this process, in each case once the critical value of income is less than ($Y^c < a$), the number of buyers equals the whole population.

In summary, although the impact upon the diffusion path of introducing a new (soft) variant will depend upon prices, quality levels, rivals' reactions, and market structures, etc., which are to be determined endogenously within the supply side, it is clear that one might expect the new variant to partly replace the old, but not completely, and also stimulate overall demand for the product. Once again, therefore, such innovation may stimulate demand and diffusion of both creative and functional products (see also Stoneman [1989]).

8.4.2 *Alternative media*

In Section 8.4 the diffusion of products requiring joint hardware and software inputs was considered. This encompassed, for example, the market for recorded music available on CDs. This section is related to the introduction of innovations that have a similar purpose but require new investments in hardware and software. Examples in the case of recorded music are the shift from vinyl to tape or from tape to CDs (see Stoneman [1991], for an earlier analysis of a failed technology, digital audio tapes [DAT]). The shift from VCRs to DVDs is an example in the video industry. We label such innovation as the introduction of new media.

The competition between media is in principle little different than the competition between hardware variants with incompatible software. There are three main characteristics to consider. Firstly, to generate the service flow both hardware and software are required and the software is generally not compatible across media. Thus vinyl cannot be played on a CD player (although CDs can be played on a DVD player). Secondly, the hardware and software are durable. Thirdly, the different media tend to arrive in the market at different times – record players preceded CDs, which preceded downloading or MP3 players. This has two main implications: (*a*) the new and old media tend to be vertically rather than horizontally differentiated, with it being agreed by (nearly) all consumers that the new offers enhanced performance compared to the old, which is why they are considered here rather than above and (*b*) the new media tend to appear in a market where a previous medium was dominant, and a switch of medium requires investment in new hardware and new software, but in the face of past investment in another medium.

To model the diffusion of new media products it is necessary to consider whether the new medium will be additional to, or a replacement for, the old medium, i.e. when a CD player is bought will all the vinyl equipment be discarded? The results of the model are emphasized if it is assumed that the new makes the old completely obsolete, and thus the modelling proceeds in this way, but in reality this may not be so.

Adapting the earlier model, assume that for consumer j with income I_j owning a prior technology with a past software investment of y_j the utility gained from this hardware is $U_j(y_j, I_j)$. For this consumer to switch to a new medium requires hardware costs of P_h, and with a price P per unit, optimal software purchases of x_j^* and thus software costs of Px_j^*. Residual income is then $I_j - Px_j^* - P_h$ and utility is given by $U_j(x_j^*, I_j - Px_j^* - P_h)$. On the assumption that with the new medium in place the utility derived from the old medium is 0, the utility of the marginal consumer to switch to the new medium will be

$$U_j(x_j^*, I_j - Px_j^* - P_h) = U_j(y_j, I_j). \qquad (8.18)$$

This formulation suggests, from Equation (8.18), that the lower the new media hardware and software prices, the higher the incomes, and the greater the quality of the new media, the greater will be the demand for the new media. Earlier analysis would also indicate that the utility of the consumer will be increasing in the number of software variants on the market and thus as the supply of software variants for the new media increases, so hardware and software demand will increase. In terms of diffusion, the new media will replace the old as hardware and software prices fall, incomes rise, quality of the medium improves, and software variant availability increases. These will, however, be partly determined endogenously by supply–demand interaction. Finally, early buyers of the new media are likely to have lower stocks of software for the prior technology, higher incomes, and greater preference for the product class.

8.5 An overview

This chapter has addressed the demand for, and diffusion of, soft innovations. Diffusion is related to how innovations spread across their potential market. In the case of soft innovations this means how a product and also product variants spread. Of course the two are interrelated and one issue addressed is how the diffusion of the latter impacts upon the diffusion of the former. If every new variant replaced an old variant, then product and variant diffusion would be identical. It has been suggested, however, that, although more in some markets than others, the addition of a new variant is not always at the expense of complete removal of an older variant, although that is not ruled out.

It has been argued that there are some basic issues that will have an impact on the diffusion process. These include information on whether the product/variant is stand-alone, if the service requires hardware and software inputs, whether there is competition from previous media, and whether the product is durable. It is also clear from above that the nature of competition in the market will have an impact upon the diffusion pattern. Whether the new variants are horizontally or vertically differentiated also matters. Finally, it has been emphasized that many of the important drivers of the diffusion process are endogenously determined in the interaction between the demand and supply sides.

Overall, the results indicate that for stand-alone non-durable products, be they aesthetic or functional, soft innovation increasing the number of product variants in the market over time will increase the overall demand for the product as will reductions over time in prices, improvements in average quality, and higher incomes. It would be expected that consumers with higher incomes and those who particularly like the variants in the market will buy first. Later buyers may be induced to buy due to lower prices and different variants, and this will extend product diffusion. However, the supply of different variants and lower prices will be dependent upon supplier behaviour.

For durable free-standing soft innovations the expectations of future changes in price and quality or variety will also matter. Current sales may also depend upon past sales (e.g. as with books) as particular varieties will not be purchased more than once. In this case, continuing product demand will be heavily dependent upon a continuous stream of new variants, the supply of which will again depend upon the supply side and how it interprets the incentives to this. For joint hardware and software products the extent of compatibility between software and platforms also matters.

For vertically differentiated producers it was shown that changes over time in the price quality ratio (again endogenous) was a prime determinant of diffusion. Generally diffusion proceeds as price falls, quality improves, or incomes increase. An 'alternative media' scenario was also discussed, it being argued that stocks of software for previous media will act as a drag on diffusion of new media, but the greater the performance improvement of the new media as compared to the old and the more software available on that new media, the faster will be diffusion.

In the examples addressed in Chapters 4 and 5 above there were some examples where there was speeding up of the rate of churn of successful products with associated changes in the product life cycles. Without detailed analysis of each case it is not possible to be definitive about why this has come about. From the above, however, some issues for discussion include changes in the speed of the spread of information, lower prices on launch, slower expected price reductions, changes in consumer incomes, and changes in the rate of new product introduction.

8.6 Normative issues

In addition to the positive aspects of this study it is useful to explore whether there are any normative implications of the diffusion analysis. In essence the question is whether a free market will generate a diffusion path that is too fast or too slow from a welfare point of view and thus whether intervention is desirable. To some degree this overlaps with the discussion of normative issues regarding the supply side in the previous chapter but there are also separate issues. In fact, although it is quite common to discuss normative issue regarding R&D and the generation of new technologies, the diffusion side is much less often discussed (although see Stoneman and Diederen [1994]). As a result there is little literature on the welfare aspect of diffusion (especially in the sorts of models discussed above).

In the general literature on diffusion it is commonly presumed that diffusion should be as fast as possible although very rarely is that argument based on logical reasoning. Such an argument can soon be dismissed both for soft innovations and other innovations. The grounds for this are, for example: (*a*) if diffusion is fast, buyers may miss out on future improvements in durable products or future reductions in prices that may have been beneficial; (*b*) from a social point of view, if products are becoming cheaper to produce society may benefit from waiting; and (*c*) early adoption may encourage replacement of the existing technology too soon.

More important than any of these, however, is that potential buyers of new technology do differ from each other in terms, at least, of incomes and tastes. Thus one buyer's preferences do not necessarily match those of other buyers. Early users of a technology will be those that have seen that the technology can yield a utility gain and have thus adopted it. This does not necessarily mean that such gains are available to non-users of different characteristics. Non-users may be so because the technology does not yield them a utility gain. To justify intervention and to stimulate further usage on the grounds that past adopters have gained from a new technology is not sufficient in itself, because the observation does not of itself indicate that further adopters of differing characteristics can also get a positive return from adoption. If non-users for whom usage does not yield a utility gain are to be encouraged to adopt new technology, there must be a further argument that the prices underlying the utility calculation do not reflect social costs and benefits.

Whether the prices that underlie the diffusion process do carry correct information about social costs and benefits is explored in Ireland and Stoneman (1986), who look at a model of new process diffusion across firms where buyers are of differing characteristics (see David and Olsen [1986] for an alternative approach in a similar frame).[7] They show that if the supply sector is monopolized, then its pricing will generate diffusion that is welfare-optimal if the buyers have myopic price expectations, but a path involving diffusion that is slower than is welfare optimal if buyers have perfect foresight. If the supply sector is competitive, then diffusion would be welfare optimizing under perfect foresight but too fast under myopia. The need for intervention in both inter- and intra-firm diffusion processes in a world where differences across buyers are important is thus a matter of the structure of the supply industry (which can be observed) and the nature of firms' technological expectations (which cannot be observed).[8]

The classic rationale[9] for policy intervention on the grounds of market failure is the existence of externalities. Laffont (1988) defines an externality as

the indirect effect of a consumption activity or a production activity on the consumption set of a consumer, the utility function of a consumer or the production function of a producer. By indirect we mean that the effect concerns an agent other than the one exerting this economic activity and that this effect does not work through the price system.

The definition rules out effects that work through the price system, but includes externalities not intermediated by the market. The presence of externalities transmitted outside the market system provides an unambiguous

---

[7] These models essentially endogenize the unit cost of the technology.

[8] Interestingly, if intervention is desired the main policy instruments to be employed would be subsidies (or taxes) for particular classes of users. However, if the supply industry is monopolized, then the monopolist may appropriate that subsidy through changes in its intertemporal pricing schedule, making appropriate policy design doubly difficult.

[9] See Kaivanto (2004).

signal of incomplete private appropriation of the costs and or benefits of an individual's actions. If one consumer's behaviour causes an unappropriated benefit to another individual by, for example, improving the other individual's knowledge base, then the true social benefits of the first action are not gained by the decision maker and there will be under-investment in the new technology. The diffusion path will be suboptimal. Learning effects and some network externalities will fall under this heading.

Although it was argued above that the epidemic model was not very informative, the general principle that information is important and its spread may be an important part of the diffusion process, are relevant points to hold in mind when discussing market failure. Two particular examples are relevant. If the ownership of a technology by an early buyer provides information to other potential buyers (about existence or risk), then the action of the early buyer generates a positive externality. As the early buyer cannot internalize the value of that externality, then some early buyers may be deterred from buying when it would be socially desirable for them to do so.[10] A second example is that if advertising stimulates innovation (as commonly argued in the Bass [1969] model), then unless the full benefits of the advertising can be appropriated by the advertiser there will be insufficient incentive to advertise, too little advertising, and diffusion will be too slow from a welfare viewpoint. In general if there is more than one supplier in the market, each offering differentiated variants, there is almost bound to be some spillover of product-specific effects even from variant-specific advertising and thus too little incentive to advertise (see, e.g., Barroso [2007]).

A further externality concerns standards (see David and Greenstein [1990]). Technologies with joint hardware and software inputs have already been discussed above. With such technologies there may be standards incompatibilities and standards wars in which the dominant standard will be established. A recent example is the adoption of the Blue-Ray standard for high definition (HD) DVDs. Two relevant earlier examples include:

1. When video recorders first appeared in the market, there were three basic types – VHS, BETA, and Video 2000. This is a technology for which the greater the number of users of a format, the greater the supply of software (films) for that format. However, the software was not compatible across the formats.

---

[10] Unless a monopolist supplier can internalize the benefit to itself and stimulate demand with lower prices.

2. In the personal computer markets the two main formats were IBM clones (or PCs) and Apple machines. Full benefit of a computer can only emerge when software is available. However, to a large degree PC software cannot be run on Apple machines and vice versa.

These and other examples illustrate that such technologies often exhibit network externalities that are format (or model) specific and which, as a result, play a major role in standards wars. The purchaser of a new technology may only get the full benefits if other buyers choose the same format or standard. If a buyer chooses a format that others do not choose then his or her benefits from adoption may be much less. The bases of the models that are analysed in this area are that there are two competing formats of a technology, say A and B. The benefits to an individual or firm from purchasing format A and format B are $\alpha + \delta_A x_A$ and $\beta + \delta_B x_B$ respectively where α and β are the inherent benefits of each format (and may differ across potential buyers) and x_A and x_B are the number of users of technology A and B respectively. As benefits increase with the number of users there are network externalities that are specific to the owners of that specific format.

In such a framework, Arthur (1989) has shown that if the potential buyers of the technology fall into two groups, some with an inherent preference for variant A of the technology and others with an inherent preference for variant B, and these buyers arrive at the market in a random order, then as long as the network externalities are positive (*a*) eventually one format will become dominant and be the industry standard and (*b*) one cannot predict in advance which standard will become dominant. In fact the determination of the dominant format depends to some degree at least on chance and thus history matters, i.e. there is path dependency. If there is a run of arrivals at the early stage who inherently prefer technology B, then technology B is likely to build up network externalities encouraging even those who inherently prefer A to choose B. Alternatively if there is an early run of buyers who prefer A then A might become dominant. As arrivals at the market are random one cannot predict the eventual outcome. Crucially these results indicate that unaided, if the market establishes a dominant standard, that standard will not necessarily be the best, for with another standard dominant total benefits may have been higher.

Further developments of the Arthur (1989) framework that allow buyers to be more forward looking and also allow firms to manipulate the market through the sponsorship of particular technologies have also been modelled, but the basic principles are still similar (see, e.g., Katz and Shapiro [1985] and Saloner and Shephard [1995]). In the Choi (1997) model detailed above, the uncertainty about the new technology, combined with the information externality that a firm's use of the technology would generate, leads to excess inertia in the decisions regarding whether to use the new. One might note that this is a very different story to how information externalities drive diffusion in epidemic models. There the emphasis is on the fact that information externalities encourage further use. Here, that is not disputed, it is just that as the information externality may place the buyer providing the information at a relative disadvantage, he or she will be reluctant to undertake the investment that would generate the externality. Further developing the model, Choi (1997) shows that the effects being considered will create an inefficient delay in the adoption of technology. She calls such effects 'Penguin effects' whereby each user is reluctant to move first as long as there is a possibility that his or her choice might make him or her a technological orphan.

The insight thus provided in this discussion is that, in general, the existence of alternative incompatible formats of a technology appearing in the market simultaneously, especially in the presence of network externalities and with uncertainties as to the actual benefits of the different formats, can lead buyers in a market to delay adoption while the standards are established through the behaviour of others. It may even be that if all wait for others to act, then the diffusion will never start. It is also quite possible that the final standard established may not be the best format. The latter effects may even reduce the final or asymptotic use of the technology.

In addition to the above there may also be other market failures in the economy that would affect the optimality of the diffusion path generated by the market. For example there may be monopoly power in factor markets. It might also be that the whole national system of innovation in the economy needs improvements to, for example, training and education, capital markets, taxation regimes, or corporate governance. Such ideas will be picked up in Chapter 12.

8.7 Conclusion

Following on the study of the generation of soft innovations in Chapter 7, here the diffusion of soft innovations has been explored. There is an existing diffusion literature (e.g. the classic information-based disequilibrium epidemic approach) that looks at TPP diffusion, but very little of that picks up the issue of product differentiation that has been emphasized here as a part of soft innovation. Most of this chapter has concentrated upon the diffusion path of new product variants and their impact on the diffusion of other product variants and the product per se, primarily in the context of equilibrium models.

It has been shown that, in general, the introduction of new horizontal product variants can stimulate the demand for a product as a whole, although such introductions may also reduce the demand for existing variants. With vertically differentiated innovations it has been shown that the introduction of new vertically differentiated products at the right price can extend ownership of a new technology and that even lower quality (but proportionately lower-priced innovation) variants (a type of innovation ignored by OECD innovations) may also have this effect.

Looking at some special types of products, it has been argued that for some soft products (e.g. books) early sales of a title may be large and quickly exhaust a market (especially if no price reductions are expected) and a continuous flow of new titles will be required to maintain that market. Other types of technologies involving hardware and software were also considered and the interaction between soft innovation and the demand for hardware was emphasized. In addition the influence of hardware innovation on the demand for soft innovations was also noted. Issues of standards and compatibilities were addressed in this context and are also relevant to changes in formats. The issue of network externalities thus raised was considered important.

It was emphasized throughout that demand (i.e. diffusion) and supply interact. The market outcome is thus the result of the combination of supply forces and demand forces. This is particularly relevant when welfare optimality is discussed. The discussion of that issue, drawing on both the general literature and the soft innovations considered here, went beyond the usual statement that fastest is best to consider information spreading as an externality and also the welfare implications of network externalities. It was argued that market failure might well exist in the diffusion process for soft innovations.

The models used in this chapter are not particularly special in that diffusion models involving differentiated products have been explored in the past. Vertical product differentiation models are an obvious way to explore the diffusion of product innovations. Horizontal differentiation models are perhaps not so obvious. However, although used, such models do not have a dominant role in the literature. Their use here may help illustrate the advantages of such models. They could also quite usefully be employed in analysing TPP innovation.

Although uncertainty did figure to a limited degree in the above discussion, in this chapter as in Chapter 7 this aspect has been downplayed. In Chapter 9 the issue is addressed more explicitly.

9

Soft Innovation and Uncertainty: Variant Proliferation, Insurance Markets, and Finance

9.1 Introduction

This chapter is primarily about uncertainty and its impact on the soft innovation process. Uncertainty is an important aspect of all innovation processes and merits such separate and individual attention. In Chapters 7 and 8 uncertainty has been downplayed in order to highlight other issues. Although in Chapter 8 uncertainty in the context of standard setting and the related issue of expectations on future prices and qualities were considered as impacting upon the diffusion or demand for innovations, in Chapter 7 the impact of uncertainty on the development and launch of new soft innovations was not considered at all. This chapter is thus primarily concerned with uncertainty and the development and launching of new soft products and product variants. The interest is partly with positivistic modelling under uncertainty, but there is also a requirement to draw out normative issues. These mainly concern issues of insurance markets and finance for innovation and are addressed at the end of the chapter.

A particularly noticeable characteristic of some industries that engage in soft innovation is the very large number of innovations, usually different product variants, that are launched in any time period (of which very few succeed). In the case of books and recorded music up to 100,000 new titles may be published in any year of which only a hundred or more may succeed in market terms. A similar pattern was seen in the food industry. Of course in other industries there may be far fewer new variants, e.g. in cars. In this chapter we explore the issue of soft innovation and product variant proliferation by considering the pros and cons of two (example) polar strategies that a firm undertaking soft innovation may pursue. The first strategy is to launch a large number of variants (letting a thousand flowers bloom), with each allowed to find its own position in the market in the hope that a small number will succeed (as in books). The second, nurturing strategy, is to launch a smaller number of selected variants supported by advertising and other promotional activities in an attempt to improve their success rates (the car example). Before considering the role of uncertainty in the strategy choice, however, it is useful to consider other factors that also have an impact on the numbers of soft innovations a firm may put on the market. To some extent these arguments overlap those already presented in other chapters above regarding optimum product diversity, but they are brought together here and are presented in a less formal way.

As with most economic questions the determinants of a market outcome can usually be reduced to a consideration of supply-(cost) side factors and demand-side factors. Thus it is with factors that impact upon proliferation. On the supply side, factors that matter are as follows:

1. Fixed costs of production: Higher fixed costs of supplying a product variant on the market will discourage proliferation. The higher the fixed costs attached to producing a variant, the fewer variants a profit maximizing firm would prefer to have in generating its sales revenue. In addition, if the fixed costs exhibit scale economies this will encourage proliferation (Sutton 1986; Dixit and Stiglitz 1977).

2. Development and launch costs: The cheaper it is to develop new variants, the more that will be placed in the market. If the development costs are high (compare, e.g., a new movie versus a new book), then total costs will be high, even if the product fails, which will discourage proliferation. Alternatively, high sales revenues are necessary to cover development costs if those costs are high. It has also been shown above that reductions in development costs will encourage proliferation, but diseconomies of scale in product development may discourage proliferation (see Chapter 7).

3. Royalties: A variant of the previous argument relates to how developers are recompensed. With books, music, or games, authors, musicians, or games writers may be recompensed through royalty contracts. In these cases (in the absence of an advance) the publisher, record label, etc. faces almost zero (fixed) development costs for any variant and this will encourage product variants to proliferate (Caves 2000).

4. Art for art's sake: In the situation where authors, etc. are repaid through royalty contracts why do the authors write or the musicians play when

there is often little chance of success? It may be that they are not profit seeking. If profit is not a motivation, then proliferation will be greater (the art for art's sake argument considered above). In some cases authors may even pay to have a title published. It may also be that there is considerable excess supply of launchable material which encourages proliferation (Caves 2000).

5. Supply externalities. If there are positive externalities between variants, this will encourage a firm (although not necessarily the market) to launch more titles. Externalities may be on the demand or cost side but on the cost side such externalities may, for example, reduce the costs of marketing and advertising per variant as the number of variants launched increases; in addition there may be learning by doing and learning by using externalities in producing new variants encouraging proliferation (Arrow 1962; Mukoyama 2006).

On the demand side there is a similar list of factors that will encourage proliferation:

6. Product lifetime. As the market for old variants dries up, through saturation, in many cases the supplier will cease to exist if new variants are not marketed. The nature of some products may thus encourage further proliferation (see Chapters 7 and 8).

7. Fan bases. Recording artists, film producers, authors, and actors may all develop followings and fan bases that may represent an externality from one product variant to another. That externality will encourage further variant launches and proliferation. The principle is similar to brand extensions (see Antonelli [1997]).

8. Full market exploitation: In some markets one product variant may generate a demand for a related variant. For example, success of a recording artist might encourage previous record labels to reissue previous unsuccessful recordings. Similarly, certain types of books may encourage the launching of others in a similar genre. In such circumstances it may be the case that a firm may launch extra product variants to fully capitalize upon the 'goodwill' created in the market. Fully exploiting a market will mean variant proliferation. It may be likened again to brand extensions. See, for example, Shine et al. (2007) and Bayus and Putsis. (1999).

9. Copying: Similarly, in the face of competition a firm may proliferate product variants and fill up product space in order to prevent copying by others and the subsequent loss of profits (see Takeyama [1994] and Caulkins et al. [2007]).

10. Market stealing. If a market has many suppliers, the launch of another variant, if successful, will be at the expense of the market shares of others rather than the launching firm, whereas if there are few suppliers then it is more probable that own market share will be affected. This suggests that competition encourages proliferation (Connor 1981).

11. Test marketing. Finally, proliferation might actually be a logical reaction to a market in which output may be quickly increased. In such a scenario, a firm may cheaply put small numbers of a variant in the market and, if the variant succeeds, quickly increase production to meet demand (Bradley 2007). If so, many more variants would be launched in a sort of test marketing exercise than if it were difficult to increase output.

Although the list is long and the impact of the factors on the launch of product variants is high, few of the factors in this list relate closely to uncertainty. It is thus uncertainty that the next section considers.

9.2 Uncertainty and variant proliferation

In a discussion of decision making in the cultural industries, Caves (2000) proposes the view that, to a large degree, the state of knowledge is such that 'nobody knows', basically to be interpreted as that in these industries and with soft innovations one can not, in advance, say which innovations/products/varieties are going to be a success and which are going to be failures. In fact if it were to be possible to forecast success, only successes would be launched, all failures would be still born.

For any product or variant there will be an ex ante probability of success, less than 1, which may well vary with the nature of the product and the way that it is marketed and encouraged in the market. In general there will be no product or variant that can be guaranteed to succeed. The ex ante probability of success will be important in decisions regarding whether a particular product will be launched and therefore by implication such probabilities will also impact upon the numbers of products to be launched.

This section explores a variety of models to analyse how uncertainty and product or variant proliferation may interact. The models are relatively standard and may be found in many intermediate texts (e.g. Besanko and Braeutigam [2008]). The analysis starts with models where suppliers of new variants to the market are risk-neutral before consideration of risk-averse actors. The former concentrates on expected returns while the latter emphasizes the risk reduction effects of variant portfolios. A timing model of the real options variety is then considered as an alternative way to approach the issues. An overview is then provided.

9.2.1 Risk neutrality

If players are risk-neutral then they neither like nor dislike risk. Such players are interested only in the expected return from their investments (net of costs). Assume that firm i is able to launch different product variants in the market, but total launch costs, C_i, increase with the number of variants launched, N_i, according to

$$C_i = C(N_i), \quad C'(N_i) > 0. \tag{9.1}$$

Without being specific as to whether the variants are horizontal or vertically differentiated (horizontal is probably closest) imagine that the launch of a new variant is rather like buying a lottery ticket where there is a jackpot to be won if the launch is successful. To make the model simple assume that there can only be one successful variant (there is only one prize) with the prize being of value Π, although other firms could simultaneously launch a similar variant in which case the prize has to be shared. Each variant launched has a probability of winning the prize equal to ρ. As a firm launches more variants the probability of success increases with the number of variants N_i such that firm i has probability[1] of winning the prize $\rho_i = \rho N_i$.

As the prize may have to be shared if a rival should also launch a matching variety to that which wins the prize, the prize expected by any firm i, Π_i, will be declining in N_j the number of variants launched by rivals according to $\Pi_i = \Pi(N_j)$ where $d\Pi/dN_j$ is negative. The expected payoff, V_i, to firm i is thus given by

$$V_i = \rho N_i \Pi(N_j) - C(N_i). \tag{9.2}$$

Assuming N_j is independent of N_i, a firm maximizing V_i will choose N_i such that

$$\rho . \Pi(N_j) = C'(N_i). \tag{9.3}$$

Given the assumption that $C'(N_i) \geq 0$, i.e. total launch costs increase with the number of varieties launched, this may be solved for N_i. For a specific example let

---

[1] We assume that N_i is such that $\rho_i = \rho N_i$ is always less than unity for all i.

$$C'(N_i) = cN_i \qquad (9.4)$$

so that

$$p.\Pi(N_j) - cN_i \qquad (9.5)$$

then at the maximum of V_i, $Ni = Ni^*$, where N_i^* is given by Equation (9.6)

$$N_i^* = p.\Pi(N_j)/c. \qquad (9.6)$$

This immediately confirms certain results generated in Chapter 7, for example the greater the prize, the more varieties will the firm wish to launch, but the greater the cost of launch, the fewer varieties the firm will launch. Such findings can be simply interpreted to imply that (a) the larger the market size or the greater the profit from a successful launch, the more variants that will be put on the market; and (b) as the cost of launching new variants falls, perhaps through TPP innovation, the more variants will be launched. This simple model also indicates that the more varieties launched by rivals, the fewer varieties the firm will launch, perhaps to be taken as an indicator of competitive effects, but the total number of varieties put on the market by the firm and its rivals jointly ($N_i + N_j$) as N_j increases is dependent on the size of reactions to rivals' product launches.

The other result that is clear from Equation (9.7) is that the greater the probability of success of any variant, the more variants the firm will launch, with $dN_i^*/d\,p = \Pi(N_j)/c > 0$ (recalling that pN_i is restricted to less than unity). Although it is not strictly or formally correct, this could be said to indicate that less uncertainty, in the sense of more optimism regarding potential success (higher p) encourages the launch of more new product variants.

To include promotional activities, maintain the assumption that that the prize to a single winner is still Π, but now allow that the probability of a variant k winning the prize is p_k, and p_k is a positive function of promotional expenditures on variant k. Such promotional expenditures may be precisely defined as advertising and other marketing expenditures, but it is just as feasible to consider them to be extra costs associated with a more extensive development processes. Unless the firm is able to determine ex ante that the chances of some k winning the prize will increase more with promotion than other k, the firm will have promotional expenditure that is the same for all product variants. This is rather like a book publisher distributing free catalogues of its titles. Developing this approach, let the promotional expenditure on each variant launched by firm i be a_i, then ρ_k is determined by Equation (9.7)

$$\rho_k = \rho_k(a_i) \tag{9.7}$$

which is the same for all k and written as $\rho(a_i)$. For firm i launching N_i variants the probability of winning the prize, ρ_i, will then be given by

$$\rho_i = N_i\rho(a_i). \tag{9.8}$$

and the firm's total promotional expenditure, A_i, will be given by Equation (9.9)

$$A_i = N_i.a_i. \tag{9.9}$$

As the prize may have to be shared if rivals also launch a variety that is a success, the prize expected by any firm i, Π_i, is also assumed to be declining in N_j the number of variants launched by rivals and A_j, the expenditure of rivals on promotional expenditure according to

$$rmPi_i = \Pi(N_j, A_j) \quad d\Pi/dN_j \le 0 \text{ and } d\Pi/dA_j \le 0. \tag{9.10}$$

The total costs of launching N variants is again assumed related to the number of variants launched such that total launch costs, excluding promotional costs are

$$C_i = C(N_i) \tag{9.11}$$

The expected pay-off to firm i, V_i, is then given by

$$V_i = N_i\rho(a_i)\Pi(N_j, A_j) - C(N_i) - a_iN_i. \tag{9.12}$$

The firm has two choice variables, N_i, the number of variants to launch and a_i, the amount to spend promoting each product variant. The first-order conditions for a profit maximum, using * to indicate the optimum, yield that

$$\rho'(a_i^*) = 1/\Pi(N_j, A_j) \tag{9.13}$$

and

$$N_i^* = [\rho(a_i^*)/\rho'(a_i^*) - a_i^*]/c_i. \tag{9.14}$$

It is standard to assume that $\rho(a_i)$ will be increasing in a_i but at a declining rate and thus $\rho'(a_i) > 0$ and $\rho''(a_i) < 0$. Specifically allow that

$$p(a_i) = \gamma a_i^{\eta} \tag{9.15}$$

where η is the elasticity of the probability of winning with respect to promotional expenditures. $p'(a_i)$ is then given by $\eta\gamma\, a_i^{\eta-1}$, which to be positive requires that $\eta > 0$, and $p''(a_i) = (\eta - 1)\eta\gamma\, a_i^{\eta-2}$, which to be negative requires $\eta < 1$. After substitution Equation (9.13) becomes Equation (9.16)

$$\eta\gamma\, a_i^{*\eta-1} = 1/\Pi(N_j, A_j) \tag{9.16}$$

or Equation (9.17)

$$a_i^* = (1/(\Pi(N_j, A_j).\eta\gamma))^{1/(\eta-1)}. \tag{9.17}$$

Equation (9.17) indicates that optimal promotional expenditure per variety, a_i^*, given the expenditure of rivals on new variants and promotion (assumed invariant), will equalize the potential gains in expected winnings to the expected cost of their generation through promotion.

Equation (9.17) also suggests, given $0 < \eta < 1$, that (a) larger prizes would mean more promotional expenditure per variety; (b) a given prize increment will produce smaller increments in promotional expenditure per variety as such expenditure increases; and (c) more launches by rivals and more promotional expenditure by rivals (assumed invariant with respect to own promotion expenditure) deter own promotional expenditure per variety.

After substitution from Equation (9.15) the second first-order condition Equation (9.14) can be written as (9.18).

$$N_i^* = (a_i^*/c_i)[(1/\eta) - 1)] \tag{9.18}$$

From Equation (9.18), given $\eta < 1$: (a) as launch costs c_i increase, the number of variants launched decreases; (b) the number of variants launched increases with η; and (c) the number of variants on the market increases with a_i^*, but this relationship is not causal because both the number of variants and the promotional expenditures per variant are determined endogenously.

From Equation (9.18) total promotional expenditures (on all variants), $N_i^*a_i^*$, will increase with a_i^*. Using Equation (9.17) one may see that if rivals increase their promotion expenditures A_j, this will reduce a_i^* which will reduce $N_i^*a_i^*$. Thus, rivals' promotion in this framework leads to reductions in own promotion (but without further conditions one cannot say whether $N_i^* a_i^* + A_j$ increases or declines). The key finding in this framework is, however, that, although not causally, the number of variants launched and the promotional expenditure on each variant by the firm (ceteris paribus) are positively related. One would thus not expect to observe some firms with high numbers of variants and low promotion expenditures and others with a low number of variants with high promotion expenditures. Promotional expenditures and the number of variants launched are de facto complements and not substitutes.

In order to derive these results it was assumed that firms were not able to determine ex ante which of their own product variants had the greatest chances of winning the prize or the chances of which variant would be most increased by promotional activity. This does not seem a particularly realistic assumption (e.g. publishers, record companies, and food producers are always choosing varieties on the basis of expected success) and there are some advantages from its relaxation. It is thus assumed that, although still probabilistic, the firm is able to select some product variants as more likely to win the prize than others. Assume that the firm can order the variants by their probability of winning the prize and that the firm will launch first those with the highest probability of success. The overall probability of the firm winning, ρ_i, is the sum of the individual probabilities of each individual variant winning, and thus if N_i is the number of variants launched

$$\rho_i = \rho(N_i) \tag{9.19}$$

where $\rho'(N_i)$ is positive but now declining in N_i (i.e. $\rho''(N_i)$ is negative).

In the absence of promotional activity, with the value of the prize given by Π, and the costs of launching new variants being $C(N_i)$, with $C'(N_i) > 0$, the value of the firm, to be maximized by the choice of N_i, is given by Equation (9.20)

$$V_i = \rho(N_i)\Pi(N_j) - C(N_i). \tag{9.20}$$

The first-order condition for the determination of the number of varieties launched is given by Equation (9.21)

$$\rho'(N_i^*).\Pi(N_j) = C'(N_i). \tag{9.21}$$

From Equation (9.21) it can be seen that (a) the number of products launched will be positive; (b) the more costs of launch increase with N (the larger is $C'(N_i)$), the smaller will be N_i^*; and (c) the smaller the prize, the smaller will be N_i^*. These now appear standard results for this type of model. More interestingly, however, if $\rho'(N_i)$ is less for a given N, then N_i^* will be less. Thus, the lower the prospects of an extra variant winning, the smaller will be the number of variants launched. This is quite as one would expect. If firms can order variants in terms of their market prospects and launch the most promising first, when the probability of winning increases only slightly with the number of launches the number of variants launched will be low. One might even characterize markets by the rate at which the number of launches impacts upon the probability of winning the prize – in markets where this is small the optimal strategy will involve the launch of few variants and in markets where this is high the strategy will involve launching many variants.

To add promotional activities to this framework, assume that the probability of a brand being a success can be increased with promotional spending. Rather than formally solve the problem of which brand(s) the firm will promote, assume instead that the more varieties over which promotional spending is spread, the lower will be the probability of any of the firm's brands winning the prize, i.e. assume that the overall chance of firm i winning is given by

$$\rho_i = \rho(A_i, N_i) \tag{9.22}$$

where $\rho'_1 > 0$, $\rho''_1 < 0$, $\rho'_2 > 0$, $\rho''_2 < 0$, and $\rho''_{12} = \rho''_{21} < 0$. The value of the firm is given by

$$V_i = \rho(A_i, N_i)\Pi(A_j, N_j) - C(N_i) - A_i \tag{9.23}$$

where A_j is the promotional expenditure of rivals. A_j and N_j are assumed invariant to the behaviour of firm i.

The first-order conditions for the maximum are Equations (9.24) and (9.25)

$$\rho'_1(A_i^*, N_i^*)\, \Pi(A_j, N_j) - 1 = 0 \tag{9.24}$$

and

$$\rho'_2(A_i^*, N_i^*)\Pi(A_j, N_j) - C'(N_i^*) = 0. \tag{9.25}$$

Substitution yields Equation (9.26)

$$\rho'_1(A_i^*, N_i^*)/\rho'_2(A_i^*, N_i^*) = 1/C'(N_i^*). \tag{9.26}$$

By assumption, $\rho'_1 > 0$, $\rho'_2 > 0$ and $C'(N_i^*) > 0$, thus, from Equation (9.26), it is to be expected that A_i^* and N_i^* will be positive. For simplicity assume that $C'(N_i^*) = c_i a$ constant then, taking the differential yields Equation (9.27)

$$\rho''_{11} dA_i^* + \rho''_{12} dN_i^* = (\rho''_{21} dA_i^* + \rho''_{22} dN_i^*)/c_i. \tag{9.27}$$

Thus

$$dA_i^*/dN_i^* = (-\rho''_{12} + \rho''_{22}/c_i)/(\rho''_{11} - \rho''_{21}/c_i). \tag{9.28}$$

The sign of dA_i^*/dN_i^* depends upon the signs of the two bracketed terms. If the two terms have opposite signs, then dA_i^*/dN_i^* will be negative, whereas if they have the same sign, it will be positive. The two terms are such that the first will be positive iff $\rho''_{22}/\rho''_{12} > c_i$ and the second if $c_i > \rho''_{21}/\rho''_{11}$. There seems no reason to rule out any possibility and as such dA_i^*/dN_i^* may be positive or negative.[2]

It is thus possible to have a situation where $dA_i^*/dN_i^* < 0$. In this case a reduction in the number of varieties launched is associated with an increase in promotional expenditure in total and per variant on average, and rather than allowing a number of varieties to exist in the market, a preferred strategy is to nurture the new variants. However, this is a little misleading. This is not a causal relationship, it is an association that exists at equilibrium. Whether this is the pattern at equilibrium, depends upon the costs of launch and how the chances of winning respond to promotional expenditures, the numbers of products launched and the cross-elasticities.

9.2.2 Spreading risks

The model(s) in the previous section assumed that firms investing in new variants were risk-neutral and thus their behaviour was driven purely by the pursuit of expected returns. It was possible to isolate some conditions based on the underlying parameters of cost functions and the demand curve that differentiated between situations in which it was optimal for the firm to (a) pursue a variant proliferation strategy; and (b) limit product proliferation and undertake more variant nurturing. However, to assume

---

[2] If as in the previous model it were assumed that it was not possible to select the variant to be promoted, then it would be that $\rho''_{12} = \rho''_{21} = 0$ and given $\rho''_{11} < 0$ and $\rho''_{22} < 0$ promotional expenditures and number of variants launched would be positively, although not causally, related.

risk neutrality as a means of modelling decision making under uncertainty seems, to some degree at least, to avoid the essence of uncertainty. This section therefore moves away from the assumption of risk neutrality and considers a world of risk-aversion where economic actors do not like risk. In particular it is assumed that economic actors like returns but not the risks associated with them.

Most literature in the field has argued that risks may be reduced by portfolio diversification (Brealey and Myers 2003). This section explores whether such a rationale can be used to justify letting a thousand flowers bloom, i.e. the launch of many variants instead of nurturing a limited number. The modelling framework used is known as a means variance model (Markowitz 1987), which although now somewhat dated, deals with the essence of the issues without too much complication.

Consider the simplest case where the returns to firm i (although i subscripts are dropped as unnecessary) from any variant k put on the market can be characterized by a distribution with mean and variance of μ_k and σ_k^2 respectively. The mean and variance of the firm's portfolio of variants launched is defined by μ and σ^2. The overall mean return to the firm's portfolio is given by Equation (9.29)

$$\mu = \left(\sum_{k=1}^{N}\mu_k\right)/N. \tag{9.29}$$

For simplicity, and also to focus on the risk element, it is assumed that any variant that is successful will win the same prize, and thus μ_k is the same for all k. Then μ is a constant independent of N, the number of variants launched on the market. Also for the sake of simplicity, assume that there are, at any time, sufficient total number of variants put upon the market by the firm that the covariances of the returns between any variants launched are 0. The overall variance of the returns to the firm's portfolio σ^2, will then be given by Equation (9.30)

$$\sigma^2 = \left(\sum_{k=1}^{N}\sigma_k^2\right)/N^2. \tag{9.30}$$

Equation (9.30) shows that as N increases so the overall variance reduces (as a thought exercise consider the case where σ_k^2 is the same for all variants at σ^{2*}, then as N increases σ_k^2 will take the value of σ^{2*}/N, which is declining with N). This illustrates that risk can be reduced by holding a mixed portfolio and provides a rationale for variety proliferation. Further assume that by choice of a variant portfolio the firm maximizes utility given by Equation (9.31).

$$U = a\mu - 0.5b\sigma^2 - C(N) \tag{9.31}$$

where $C(N)$ is launch costs, increasing in N. Positive launch costs can provide the limits to proliferation in this model in that proliferation will only extend until the utility gain from any induced risk reduction equals the utility lost from the extra fixed costs.

In general some product variants will attract more risk than others. On the basis (given the same mean return) that those variants with the lowest σ_k^2 will be undertaken in preference to those with a higher σ_k^2, σ_k^2 will be increasing as N increases. This suggests that the risk of the whole portfolio σ^2 may increase or decrease with N depending on whether the portfolio risk-spreading effect or the movement to more risky projects is dominant. It is assumed here that $d\sigma^2/dN \le 0$ but $d^2\sigma^2/dN^2 \ge 0$.

At the maximum the optimal N, N^* will be chosen according to the first-order condition Equation (9.32):

$$-(d\sigma^2/dN)/(dC/dN) = 2b. \tag{9.32}$$

Given $d\sigma^2/dN$ is negative and dC/dN is positive, N^* will be positive. Confirming earlier results the greater is dC/dN, the cost of launching a new variant, the fewer variants that will be launched. With respect to risk and uncertainty (a) the faster risk reduces as N increases, the more variants that will be launched; and (b) the less risk-averse the firm (the smaller is b), the more variants will be launched.

These results suggest that in some circumstances when (a) launch costs are low, (b) there are many projects with not very risky returns, and (c) the firm is not particularly risk-averse, it will be an optimal strategy to let a number of variants to be launched and promoted. In other cases only a few variants may be put in the market by any one firm. This still, however, leaves open the issue of promotional activity.

The previous section addressed a scenario when the firm undertook promotional activity to stimulate the chances of winning the prize, but it was argued that the more variants over which the promotional activity was spread, the less effective that activity would be at the margin. This enabled the identification of situations where letting numerous variants to be launched was the best strategy and other situations where restricting launches and nurturing a few product variants was the best strategy. Similar arguments can be used in the current context.

If it is assumed that the promotional activity does not affect mean returns but instead impacts upon the variance of the returns, and if the impact of promotional spending on the overall variance of the portfolio is very sensitive to the number of variants launched, then this will tend to generate some situations where nurturing a few product variants will be the best strategy as it most effectively reduces risk attached to the portfolio. However, if the impact of promotional spending upon the overall variance of the firm's portfolio of varieties changes little with the number of varieties launched, then pursuing the 'numerous variants in the market' strategy may be preferable.

9.2.3 *Learning and real options*

The biggest recent breakthrough in the literature on decision making under uncertainty has been the introduction of real options approaches. Although surveyed in several places, the volume by Dixit and Pindyck (1994) is still the prime source of material. The key to these models of decision making is that when deciding upon an irreversible course of action under uncertainty the decision maker always has the option to postpone his or her decision until a later date and does not have to decide today. That postponement should yield extra information that has to be offset against any potential losses from not acting, but while those losses are less than the potential gain from waiting so the decision maker should wait.

An entrepreneur considering the introduction of new soft innovations or product variants thus has the choice of deciding to proceed, to stop completely, or to wait. The third choice is important and, ceteris paribus, if waiting provides more information, then it is a desirable choice. Within the context of the issues discussed in this book there are several questions that could be approached in the framework of a real options approach to decision making under uncertainty. One issue addresses the incentives to undertake search in order to be better informed on whether to launch a new product. Another concerns whether to launch products, in order to learn about the market from its reaction to those products. A third concerns reputational effects and how they might be built up over time and exploited. All are possible lines of enquiry.

These are not, however, directly the topics discussed here. Instead, here the issue is, when will a firm launch a new product variety? Thus, rather than exploring how many varieties will a firm launch, this section explores the firm's choices as to whether to launch immediately or to wait. This illustrates another aspect of decision making under uncertainty but also will inform the proliferation debate, for if the factors that influence launch dates lead to clustering of launches in time, then it will appear that firms are proliferating variety.

The model most frequently used to illustrate the real options approach (Dixit and Pindyck 1994, pp. 136–44) assumes that the cost of launching a variant is c with the pay-off V where V evolves over time according to a Brownian motion process whereby

$$dV = \alpha V dt + \sigma V dz \tag{9.33}$$

where dz is the increment of a Weiner process and α and σ are constants such that the change in log V over time is normally distributed with mean $(\alpha - 0.5\sigma^2)t$ and variance $\sigma^2 t$.

Dixit and Pindyck (1994) show that the firm will invest in the project when $V \geq V^*$ where

$$V^* = c \cdot (\beta/(\beta - 1)) \tag{9.34}$$

and where β is

$$\beta = 0.5 - \alpha/\sigma^2 + ([\alpha/\sigma^2 - 0.5]^2 + 2r/\sigma^2)^{0.5} > 1 \tag{9.35}$$

where r is the interest rate/discount rate. This illustrates that the new product will not be launched at the first date when $V^* = c$, but rather at some other time when $V^* > c$, the higher requirement on V^* reflecting the option value that has to be discarded when a commitment is made to launch the variant.

Dixit and Pindyck (1994) show that β decreases as σ increases (i.e. as uncertainty increases) and as the discount rate, r, increases and α (the mean return) decreases. As β decreases, so $(\beta/(\beta - 1))$ increases and the larger is the wedge between V^* and c. Thus more uncertainty, a higher discount rate, and a lower mean return all increase the size of the wedge.

In terms of launching new product variants one may argue that those variants that have the highest mean return and/or offer the most certain returns have lower barriers to overcome before they are launched and as such are more likely to be launched in any period. On the other hand, more risky variants (or products with lower mean returns) are less likely to be launched. In addition, variants that are costly to launch are less likely, ceteris paribus, to be launched in any period. Comparing firms, one might also argue that firms that are optimistic regarding returns, and see fewer risks and lower costs of launching variants will also tend to launch more products than other firms.

The stochastic nature of this model does not allow one to solve for the optimal launch date, only for the conditions that have to be met for the launch to take place. One may, however, consider that if launch costs are low in a period, more variants will be launched in that period.

Moreover, if there is a reduction in the future expected interest and discount rates, then that will also encourage earlier product variant launches. As these factors may impact upon all potential variants, this could produce a bunching of variant launches in time. Similarly if there is a wave of optimism in the economy (or a particular success in a product type that can be copied) leading to a higher expected mean return, this will have similar effects. Some changes (say a technological change) that reduce the costs of launching variants could also have a similar impact.

Is it possible by building on these results to say anything informative about promotional activity? It is possible that promotional activity might reduce risk and promote sales. More promotion might thus encourage more and earlier launches. It is, however, difficult to see why a nurturing strategy might be optimally based upon the reasons detailed in this framework.

9.2.4 Uncertainty and variant proliferation: an overview

This section has had two main objectives. The first was to illustrate how uncertainty may impact as a relevant factor in decision making with respect to the rate of soft innovation. This has been done by considering three different modelling frameworks that are commonly used in the literature for analysing decision making under uncertainty. The first approach assumed risk neutrality with decision makers maximizing expected returns, the second allowed for risk aversion and considered how portfolio effects reduce risk, while the third approach (while still assuming risk aversion) is built on a real options approach.

The second objective was to explore why, in many cases, firms in industries that generate soft innovations launch so many new varieties, the greater number of which fail. This has been considered in terms of when launching a large number of variants strategy would be preferred to a nurturing strategy where only a few nurtured variants are launched. It was clear that the basis of the choice had to lie in the uncertain nature of the market. One relevant factor was the cost of launching varieties. In each model the cheaper it was to launch a new variety, ceteris paribus, the more that would be launched. In addition the bigger the prize to be won, when successful, the more varieties that would be launched. Beyond that it was also found that:

1. In a model with risk neutrality, varieties would be launched until the marginal expected gain from winning the prize equalled the cost of the launch. This would generally encourage variety proliferation unless

(*a*) promotional activity also increases the probability of winning the prize, and (*b*) the effectiveness of promotional activity declined with the number of product variants launched.

2. In a means variance model, firms would launch a large number of varieties in order to reduce risk. Once again this would encourage proliferation unless promotional expenditures increased the mean return or reduced the variance of returns and the effectiveness of such activity declined with the number of variants on the market.

3. In the real options approach the proliferation issue concerned whether a firm would launch a number of new variants at the same time. It was shown that the firm's beliefs as to discount rates, market buoyancy, and launch costs impacted on launch decisions for all varieties in the same way, and thus varieties would tend to be launched at the same time. No reason for nurturing was found in this framework.

Overall, therefore, that a huge number of books, computer games, CDs, DVDs, new foods, new drugs, and new financial products are put in the market is not irrational. It may well be a rational reaction to the uncertain environment. This does not mean however that in certain industries where launch costs are much higher (e.g. motor manufacture, consumer electronics) it is not also rational for firms to limit the number of varieties that they launch and to nurture them in the market.

It has thus been shown not only that uncertainty is a relevant factor in the soft innovation process, but also that the nature of the outcome in relevant markets will reflect the extent and nature of that uncertainty. This, however, immediately leads to another question. In markets with uncertainty will there be any market failure in the innovation process that will lead to insufficient or excessive soft innovation? That issue is considered in the next section.

9.3 Uncertainty and market failure

9.3.1 *Introduction*

The above analysis of decision making under uncertainty has generated a number of conclusions with respect to when different launch strategies are optimal. It would appear, however, that the introduction of uncertainty does not per se have any specific implications as to whether the preferred strategies are likely to be welfare suboptimal or not in terms of excessive product proliferation or soft innovation. Previous conclusions drawn above in this area will thus tend to hold.

This does not, however, mean that there are no welfare implications that arise from the presence of uncertainty. In fact there are the two major market failure issues to which uncertainty gives rise which relate respectively to (*a*) possible missing markets and (*b*) failure in the market for finance for innovation. The issues are not peculiar to soft innovation and have been well rehearsed in the literature with respect to TPP innovation. However, as the policy recommendations to which they give rise have largely been confined to expenditures on TPP innovation rather than soft innovation, the arguments merit discussion at some length here. It is natural, given the discussions above, to pursue a line of argument that says that if such market failures are a rationale for public support to TPP innovation, and as such failures may also exist with soft innovation, it is reasonable to also provide public support to innovation that encompasses aesthetic advances of both a horizontal and vertically differentiating kind.

9.3.2 *Insurance*

The first issue to address is the issue of missing markets. In a market with uncertainty those who face risk may be unwilling carriers and if forced to carry such risk, they may prefer to avoid undertaking an action. Thus, for example, there may be economic actors who are very creative and perhaps potentially very impressive innovators, but who are very risk-averse and may not innovate. However, if there are markets that allow the risk to be shifted (at a price) to another party, then a potential flow of innovation may be forthcoming. Such risk shifting is a function of insurance markets.

Arrow (1962) argued that economies may not offer a complete set of insurance markets and some risks cannot be insured against. Innovation is one activity where risks may be difficult to insure against which could lead to market failure and may validate government intervention. The three main reasons why the private sector may not provide insurance coverage and insurance markets may be absent (see a standard text such as Besanko and Braeutigam [2008]) are that (*a*) risks are highly correlated, (*b*) adverse selection problems exist, and (*c*) there are moral hazard problems. The first of these is characterized by a situation where the losses being insured against are positively correlated with each other (e.g. the losses may be cyclical) and private insurers may be unable to pool risk and thus will not offer cover. The adverse selection scenario occurs when policyholders differ in their loss probabilities, but insurance companies cannot distinguish high-risk individuals from low-risk ones. As a consequence, many low-risk individuals may purchase little or no insurance coverage (because the presence of the high risks drives up the insurance premiums) thus potentially raising the overall riskiness of the insurance portfolio. Moral hazard occurs when the actions of the insured can affect the magnitude or the probability of a loss, but the insurance company cannot directly monitor the policyholders' actions. The optimal insurance contract will be a partial coverage contract, which provides the insured with some incentive to reduce expected losses, but that does not expose the insured to large financial penalty if a loss occurs.

It is commonly argued that in some cases government intervention or social insurance may solve the no-market problem. For example, because government has a greater capacity to borrow than even the largest private insurance company, and thus can cope with cyclicality in the returns, the pooling problem could be overcome by government-backed policies. The adverse selection problem might be solved by compulsory social insurance programs, although full coverage policies will generally make low-risk individuals worse off and benefit high-risk individuals, and it is unlikely that innovators would welcome compulsion. Moral hazard does not provide a strong rationale for government intervention. There may thus be some argument for government intervention in the innovation process on such grounds, but the arguments are not overwhelming.

9.3.3 *Finance for innovation*

All innovation, be it soft or functional, has the character of an investment, i.e. funds are expended in advance of product launch and are returned only if the product is successful. A necessary requirement of such activity is thus funding of the investment. This funding may cover R&D costs, launch costs, design costs, rehearsal costs, royalty advances, architectural fees, and many similar expenditures. The funds for such activity may be generated from two main sources, one being internal to the innovating firm (or the innovator's own funds), the other being external (such as bank borrowing, equity, loans, trade credit, etc.). A basic difference between internal and external funds is that, in the presence of uncertainty, the use of external funds shifts some of the risk of the investment to the funder (partly of course at the cost of a higher required repayment).

The risk-shifting properties of external financing raise the same problems with respect to the availability of external finance as with respect to the provision of insurance cover for risky projects of which moral hazard and adverse selection have been concentrated upon. There is now a literature that addresses whether financial factors constrain firms' investment activity that basically builds upon these two issues.

Stiglitz and Weiss (1981) consider a firm to be credit rationed if it does not get as much credit as it wants although it is willing to meet the conditions set by the lender on equivalent credit contracts. According to Hall (2002) a financial constraint is said to exist when, even if there are no externalities involved in the firm's investment activity, there is a wedge (perhaps even a large wedge) between the rate of return required by an entrepreneur investing his or her own funds and that required by external investors. In essence therefore, a firm is considered credit or financially constrained if it cannot raise external funding at the market price or, in order to raise external funding, it has to pay over the market price.

It is unnecessary to repeat the full theoretical grounding for propositions relating to the existence of financial constraints. This can be found elsewhere, including in Bond et al. (2003) and Hubbard (1998), and in the innovation context in Goodacre and Tonks (1995). The main foundations of the theory are based on asymmetric information between firms and the suppliers of finance with associated moral hazard and adverse selection problems. It is, however, commonly argued that, in particular, small firms in high-tech industries may be more prone to financial constraints because they offer riskier investments, greater information asymmetry, shorter track records, less collateral, and assets that are less realizable.

Recent empirical literature, for example Carpenter and Petersen (2002*b*), Basu and Guariglia (2002), and Bond et al. (2003), has addressed the proposition that many dimensions of firm behaviour and performance may be affected by financial and/or liquidity constraints by exploring whether the firm's investment in plant and machinery is particularly sensitive to cash flow on the grounds that a changed availability of internal funds would not much affect investment if external funds were not constrained. Aghion et al. (2007), using international data, find that financial constraints are particularly important to small firms and in industries that rely on external finance. A more limited literature, surveyed by Hall (2002), in a similar way looks at the impact of financial constraints on R&D expenditure as an indicator of innovation. Her findings suggest that:

1. There are financial constraints to investment and innovation in Europe (e.g. Canepa and Stoneman [2003]).

2. Small firms are more likely to be financially constrained in their innovative activity (e.g. Carpenter and Petersen [2002a]).

3. Firms (especially small and start-up firms) in R&D-intensive industries face a higher, pooling equilibrium cost of capital (e.g. Westhead and Storey [1997]).

4. The evidence for a financing gap for large and established firms is harder to establish (e.g. Bond et al. [1999]).

Canepa and Stoneman (2007) use an alternative approach based upon replies to the second and third UK Community Innovation Surveys. Analysis of the CIS2 data (individual returns for UK firms, 1994–6) indicates that (correcting for firm size) there is evidence that a firm in a high-tech sector has more chance of experiencing a greater impact from financial constraints than a firm in a low-tech sector.

Further results using the CIS2 data also provide clear evidence that once one has corrected for industrial sector, then small firms experience greater risks of experiencing an impact from financial constraints than do large firms. The CIS3 data set (individual returns for UK firms, 1998–2000) confirms these results. Overall, one may thus conclude that, in the UK at least, financial factors do have an impact upon innovative activity. Further support for this view from the diffusion side can be found in Canepa and Stoneman (2005). That impact is more severe in higher-tech sectors and for smaller firms. There is no reason why such arguments should be limited to TPP innovations and not also be relevant to soft innovation.

9.4 Conclusions

Uncertainty is a fundamental part of the innovation process. The costs of product development and launch are incurred upfront but profits will only flow if the product is successful in the market and can generate revenues greater than the production and development costs. The revenues, however, cannot be known with certainty in advance. This is so for all technologies be they soft or of the TPP kind. In the case of soft innovations, however, one may observe in certain markets that the number of new product variants being put in, or available through, the market at each moment in time may be much larger than at the TPP end of the spectrum. Recorded music and book publishing are the obvious examples.

There may be many reasons for such a pattern being observed with some soft innovations, but this chapter has explored whether it is related to uncertainty and especially the link between market uncertainty and the potential to select and nurture new product variants. The interim summary of the positive results has already shown that uncertainty is a relevant factor in the soft innovation process and that the nature of the outcome in relevant markets will reflect the extent and nature of that uncertainty. It has also been shown that in an uncertain environment variant proliferation may (or may not, depending upon the situation) be a preferred strategy in the face of the potential to use promotional activities to increase the chances of a new variant being successful. Once again such analysis could be applied to the launch of new TPP products but such applications are limited. For TPP innovations, however, there are no such obvious examples of the extent of proliferation that has been found with some soft innovations.

The positive modelling did not appear to lead to any new normative implications. In the latter part of the chapter it was shown, however, that under uncertainty, issues of missing insurance markets and financial constraints may well limit the extent of innovative activity to a level that is welfare suboptimal. This result is widely recognized in the literature on TPP innovation. It was thus suggested that there may be grounds for government intervention in terms of supporting insurance markets in order to fill missing markets, or providing finance for innovation in high-tech small and medium-sized enterprises (SMEs) (see, in the creative industry context, Fathom [2007]). The main point however is that these arguments do not just relate to OECD-defined R&D, they also encompass expenditures on soft innovation, i.e. the development and launching of new varieties of aesthetic products and new aesthetically changed products in functional markets. This is a lesson that does not seem to be reflected in current policy (see Chapter 12).

10

Soft Innovation, Intellectual Property Rights, Competition, and Welfare

10.1 Introduction

The discussion of soft innovation above has largely proceeded without discussion of unauthorised copying, plagiarism, or other such breaches of intellectual property rights (IPR). Ignoring IPR problems in this way has enabled concentration on other issues, despite the fact that the breach of such rights, based on Arrow's paper (1962), was considered for many years the foundation of much of the literature relating to innovation and market failure (alongside the missing market and uncertainty issues discussed in the previous chapters). In addition, with the advent of digitalization, the spread of the Internet, and the availability of various new storage and reproduction media, the problems of unauthorized, and usually free, copying of materials has become an issue of major concern.[1] In this chapter IPR issues are therefore at the centre of attention.

Such a discussion is essential if the nature of, and problems associated with, soft innovation is to be understood. However, at first sight it might seem that soft innovation has no particular characteristics that would make any such discussion distinct relative to a TPP-orientated approach. Such a view would be misleading. The primary difference is that, as has already been argued above and will be discussed further below, soft innovations, to a large degree, cannot be patented. Instead other IPR mechanisms have to be used if such protection is desired. Such

[1] For example, a recent study by Rob and Waldfogel (2007) observes with respect to movie consumption amongst a sample of US undergraduates that unpaid first consumption reduces paid consumption by about 1 unit. Unpaid second consumption has a smaller effect of 0.20 units. In their sample, unpaid consumption made up 5.2% of all movie viewing and reduced paid consumption in their sample by 3.5%.

other mechanisms may have similar fundamental rationales but they operate differently and protect different product characteristics. The distinctive character of this chapter thus comes from a greater emphasis on these other IPR institutions.[2]

The literature on IPR is now quite enormous, and so is not surveyed in detail here. A good source is the American Bar Association (2007). Instead three main interrelated strands are explored, although the treatment of each is not meant to represent an exhaustive literary survey. The first strand concerns whether or when non-market institutions will be required to strengthen IPR and what form the institutional arrangement might take; the second relates to the effectiveness of such institutions in improving the innovative process and in particular whether they improve economic welfare; the third concerns the impact of different product market structures (e.g. monopoly versus competition) on innovation in markets with institutional support to IPR.

One of the major conceptual advances made by Arrow was to propose that innovation should be considered as similar to knowledge and/or information. Arrow's view was that as knowledge is expensive to produce but cheap to reproduce, in the absence of property rights,[3] it will tend to be undersupplied in a free market. Simply exemplified, in a soft innovation context, unauthorized free downloads of music will deter further title launches. Since Arrow's ground-breaking paper, this argument has been expressed in many ways. Currently it is usually presented as whether or not a product (or variant) will be undersupplied depends upon the extent of rivalry and excludability for that product.

Rivalry is related to whether the ownership of a product by others impacts either a little or a lot upon an owner's enjoyment of, or return to, ownership. For example defence services (non-rivalrous), once established for a nation, can be enjoyed by one and all with no deterioration. On the other hand most consumer products will be rivalrous in that physically one consumer's use of such a product prevents its use by another. In a physical sense information tends to be non-rivalrous in that one person having a

---

[2] The stance taken here mostly reflects the UK institutions where non-industrial and soft innovations cannot be patented. In the United States however there are design patents. In general terms, a 'utility patent' protects the way an article is used and works (35 U.S.C. 101), while a 'design patent' protects the way an article looks (35 U.S.C. 171). Both design and utility patents may be obtained on an article if invention resides both in its utility and ornamental appearance. A utility patent has a term of 20 years (if renewal fees are paid) whereas a design patent has a term of 14 years without renewal fees. The design patents match UK and European design rights.

[3] A useful review of this appropriability issue is to be found in Winter (2006).

piece of information does not prevent others from also having it; however, economically, information may be rivalrous because the value of a piece of information may decline as others acquire it. A useful distinction is between rivalrous in consumption and in production. A piece of music may be non-rivalrous in consumption, that is my enjoying it does not affect your enjoying it; however, if one company were to compete with another in offering music concerts, then this may well affect their individual returns.

The extent to which a product is excludable reflects whether it is easy or difficult for a product owner or supplier to limit or control ownership by others. Thus, defence services are non-excludable. Private, non-durable consumer goods are excludable. If a product or service is non-excludable, then the provider will be unable to obtain the social benefit derived from his or her provision of that product or service, suggesting market failure with under provision. If information or innovation is not excludable, then there will be less investment in information provision. If a product is non-rivalrous, excludability does not matter. If it is rivalrous, excludability does matter.

Innovation as information or knowledge is generally rivalrous in production but does not, without special institutional arrangements, offer complete excludability. It is rivalrous because, for example, the returns to an innovating firm will depend upon whether the innovation is copied (as a result of which an innovator might face competition and lower returns). The degree of excludability depends upon the innovation itself and other factors. Excludability can be produced through, for example (see Geroski [1995]) secrecy, information sharing arrangements, control of strategic resources, specialized knowledge, threats, and learning by doing.

The four main institutional arrangements that exist in most countries in order to reinforce IPR[4] are (*a*) patents which protect the technical and functional aspects of products and processes; (*b*) copyright which protects material such as literature, art, music, sound recordings, films, and broadcasts; (*c*) design rights (or design patents) which protect the appearance or visual appeal of products; and (*d*) trademarks which protect signs that can distinguish the goods and services of one trader from those of another. Each has its own particular modus operandi which will be explained as the chapter proceeds.

Pitkethly (2007) reports the results of a survey of IPR awareness and use in 1,700 UK firms in 2006. Firms were asked to indicate the importance to their business of various methods of protecting innovations, both formal and

---

[4] The institutional detail in this chapter is largely taken, and can be updated, from the UK Patent Office website www.ipo.gov.uk

Table 10.1 Percentage of respondents rating method of protecting innovations as 'essential'

No. Employees	0–9	10–49	50–249	250 +	10–249	10 +	Total
1. Patents	13.2	13.1	10.5	18.4	12.7	12.9	13.2
2. Trademarks	12.8	14.8	20.6	32.8	15.7	16.3	13.2
3. Copyright	22.5	16.3	16.5	20.5	16.3	16.4	21.9
4. Registered designs	10.1	11.0	6.5	9.2	10.3	10.2	10.1
5. Confidentiality agreements	26.6	29.6	29.7	40.9	29.6	30.0	26.9
6. Secrecy	18.9	21.5	18.0	33.4	21.0	21.4	19.2
7. Complexity of design	7.3	5.3	5.9	9.1	5.4	5.5	7.2
8. Lead-time over competitors	14.3	18.2	17.4	21.2	18.1	18.2	14.8

Source: Pitkethly (2007)

strategic, ranging from unimportant to essential. The percentage of respondents rating different mechanisms as essential is reported in Table 10.1.

As can be seen, the non-formal protective mechanisms (that determine excludability in the free market) are perceived to be at least as, if not more, effective means of protection than patents and some other IPR[5] mechanisms. Of the formal IPR mechanisms, copyright is considered by the most to be important, and design rights by the fewest, while patents and trademarks rank equally in the middle. Even so, the proportions considering the formal IPR arrangements as essential are not large. Pitkethly (2007) reports that these data correlate well ($R^2 = 0.75$) with the findings of the UK Innovation Survey 2005, and are broadly similar to findings regarding the relative effectiveness of IPRs, lead-time, and secrecy by Levin et al. (1987).

In Table 10.2 preliminary findings from the UK Innovation Survey 2007 are presented. These show lower levels of importance imputed by firms than those reported by Pitkethly (2007). Copyrights and trademarks are more often rated important than patents and design rights. Further information on the use of institutional IPR is available for the 27 EU countries. It is estimated, based on the CIS 2004, that for firms using any of the four main protection mechanisms, the most commonly used was to register a trademark (about one-third of the sample); patent application and registered industrial designs were used to a similar extent, by 28 per cent of firms each, while the least used protection method, by 11 per cent of users, was copyright, a rather different pattern to that found in the United

---

[5] Eurostat reports that actual usage in the UK, for 2000, was 12.7% of firms applied for a patent, 32.9% registered a trademark, 22.7% registered an industrial design, and 31.1% claimed copyright (Source: Eurostat – Community Innovation Statistics from CIS 3, epp. eurostat.ec.europa.eu/pls/portal/url).

Table 10.2 Percentage of respondents rating method of protecting innovations as of high importance

No. Employees	10–250	250 +	Total
1. Patents	6	15	6
2. Trademarks	8	19	8
3. Copyright	8	14	8
4. Registered designs	5	14	6
5. Confidentiality agreements	12	26	13
6. Secrecy	8	17	9
7. Complexity of design	4	9	5
8. Lead-time over competitors	10	17	10

Source: Robson and Haigh (2008)

Kingdom (source: Eurostat – Community Innovation Statistics from CIS 3, epp.eurostat.ec.europa.eu/pls/portal/url).

It is not, however, obvious that non-institutional arrangements are necessarily to be preferred to alternative institutional arrangements that might be put in place to encourage excludability. A basic and important difference between institutional and non-institutional arrangements for the protection of intellectual property (IP) is that the former usually require, whereas the latter do not necessarily require (especially if the mechanism is secrecy), that the knowledge being protected is made known to the world. Thus, for example, to obtain a patent an inventor has to make the knowledge for which the patent is sought known to the world in the patent application which is accessible to all. This requirement to make the knowledge available yields two important social benefits: (*a*) it prevents resources being wasted in rediscovering that which has already been discovered; and (*b*) it redefines the knowledge baseline for any future research in the field, enabling what are called 'standing-upon-shoulders' effects. These social benefits are not available if protection is obtained through secrecy.

The rest of this chapter begins by looking at the operation of the patent system. Although patents may not be very relevant to soft innovations, much of the relevant IPR literature has been created for this particular instrument and this it is a good place to start. The chapter then moves to discuss copyrights, design rights, and trademarks. For each institutional arrangement the sections will first explore the form of the arrangement, then effectiveness, and when relevant, the impact of different product market structures (e.g. monopoly versus competition) upon innovation in markets with such institutional arrangements. The findings on the three cross-cutting themes are summarized in the concluding section of the chapter.

10.2 The patent system

A patent protects new inventions and covers how things work, what they do, how they do it, what they are made of, and how they are made. It gives the owner the right to prevent others from making, using, importing, or selling the invention without permission. To be granted a patent an invention must be new; involve an inventive step that is not obvious to someone with knowledge and experience in the subject; be capable of being made or used in some kind of industry; not be a scientific or mathematical discovery, theory, or method; not be a literary, dramatic, musical, or artistic work, a way of performing a mental act, playing a game, or doing business; not be the presentation of information or certain type of computer programs; should not involve an animal or plant variety; not pertain to a method of medical treatment or diagnosis; or be against public policy or morality. Most, if not all, soft innovations will fall outside these restrictions and therefore may not be patentable.

Patents may however be directly relevant to the amount of soft innovation if the production of generics, as in pharmaceuticals, is considered a soft innovation. It was argued in Chapter 4 that as generics do not differ from the original except in terms of characteristics that are not functional, the launch of new generics might be considered as soft innovations. They might of course also be considered imitations. The purpose of the patent systems (and other IPR instruments) is of course to prevent copying or the production of generics. It might thus be argued that patents, although not applying to soft innovations per se, may slow them down by preventing imitation of functional advances.

Once granted a patent, the holder has the right to (not unfairly) determine access to the knowledge embodied in the patent and charge licence fees for use of that knowledge. If granted, the patent must be renewed every year after the fifth year and may then provide up to twenty years' protection. If the holder becomes aware that his or her rights are being infringed, recourse is to the courts with the possibility of terminating the infringements and receipt of damages.

Within the European Union, firms may apply for either national or European patents, with the latter providing community-wide protection, while the former provide only national protection. Table 10.3 provides information on national applications for European patents in 2005. There were 128,679 applications in total, the greatest number of applications coming from the United States (32,738), followed by Germany (23,789), and Japan (21,461). Of the EU countries, France followed Germany with 8,034, the

Table 10.3 Patent applications, EU, 2005

Origin	Total	
Austria	1,053	0.82%
Belgium	1,658	1.29%
Bulgaria	11	0.01%
Switzerland	5,027	3.91%
Cyprus	35	0.03%
Czech Republic	73	0.06%
Germany	23,789	18.49%
Denmark	1,174	0.91%
Estonia	3	0.00%
Spain	972	0.76%
Finland	1,514	1.18%
France	8,034	6.24%
United Kingdom	4,649	3.61%
Hellas	67	0.05%
Hungary	81	0.06%
Ireland	311	0.24%
Iceland	28	0.02%
Italy	4,199	3.26%
Lithuania	152	0.12%
Latvia	1	0.00%
Luxemburg	181	0.14%
Latvia	7	0.01%
Monaco	15	0.01%
Netherlands	7,799	6.06%
Poland	111	0.09%
Portugal	41	0.03%
Romania	8	0.01%
Sweden	2,486	1.93%
Slovenia	87	0.07%
Slovakia	16	0.01%
Turkey	68	0.05%
EPC	63,650	49.46%
Japan	21,461	16.68%
USA	32,738	25.44%
Other	10,830	8.42%
non EPC	65,029	50.54%
Total	128,679	100.0%

Source: www.delury.ec.europa.eu/contenidos/index.php?Id)

Netherlands was third with nearly 7,800, while the United Kingdom only put in 4,649 applications.

In Table 10.4 are listed the companies that most frequently applied for patents to the European Patent Office (EPO) in 2005. The top twenty-five applicants represent about 18 per cent of the patent applications filed. On average, 69 per cent of the applicants at the EPO are granted one patent per year, 1 per cent of the applicants receive more than fifty patent grants per year (www.delury.ec.europa.eu/contenidos/index.php?Id).

Table 10.4 Top applicants at the EPO in 2005

Rank	Company	Count	Share (%)
1	Koninklijke Philips Electronics	4,173	3.2
2	Siemens Aktiengesellschaft	1,548	1.2
3	Matsushita Electric Industrial Co., Ltd	1,194	0.9
4	Sony Corporation	964	0.7
5	Robert Bosch GmbH	845	0.7
6	Nokia Corporation	683	0.5
7	Fujitsu Limited	672	0.5
8	BASF Aktiengesellschaft	669	0.5
9	Microsoft Corporation	645	0.5
10	Samsung Electronics Co., Ltd	617	0.5
11	Philips Intellectual Property & Standards GmpH	571	0.4
12	3M Innovative Properties Co.	507	0.4
13	International Business Machines Corporation	491	0.4
14	Thomson Licensing	479	0.4
15	General Electric Company	462	0.4
16	L'Oréal SA	448	0.3
17	Canon Kabushiki Kaisha	437	0.3
18	DSM IP Assets BV	390	0.3
19	Delphi Technologies, Inc.	388	0.3
20	LG Electronics Inc.	385	0.3
21	Seiko Epson Corporation	383	0.3
22	Daimlerchrysler ag	367	0.3
23	The Procter & Gamble Company	356	0.3
24	Research in Motion Limited	353	0.3
25	NEC Corporation	342	0.3

Source: www.delury.ec.europa.eu/contenidos/index.php?ld)

To initiate exploration of the economic foundations of the patent system, the obvious place to start is with the simple model proposed by Arrow (1962). This model is often presented as related to process innovation, but soft innovation is largely product innovation and thus a version concentrating on product innovation is instead presented. Assume that an inventor develops a technology that enables a new (vertically differentiated) product to be produced and launched in the market. That product is a drastic innovation such that any prior offering to the market will no longer be offered.[6] For the new product, as drawn in Figure 10.1, there is a linear demand curve, AU, and associated marginal revenue curve, AV. Output is Q and price P. Production costs per unit of output are such that marginal cost (MC) equals average costs (AC) equals c. The gross social welfare (i.e. before taking account of any losses from the previous technology) generated by the new technology is equal to the sum of consumer

---

[6] This requires that the demand curve for the old product in the presence of the new product priced at marginal revenue (the monopoly price) is such that even priced at marginal cost demand will be zero.

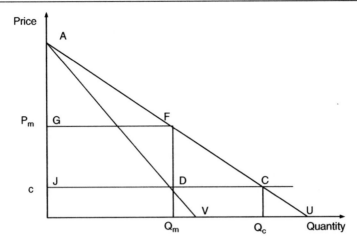

Figure 10.1 Incentives to innovation

and producer surplus (profits). This sum would be maximized if price were equal to marginal cost, when output $Q = Qc$ and the welfare contribution will be the triangle ACJ. The 'static' social benefit from an innovation will thus be maximized when the goods are sold at marginal cost. This welfare argument could be used to justify free downloads or unrestricted copying. However, if price does equal marginal costs of production, then all the welfare gain is received by consumers, and therefore producer surplus (profits) and thus the incentive to innovate are zero, and there will be 'dynamic' inefficiency.

If the new technology is excludable, then the inventor will have monopoly power over the knowledge required to supply the new product. With such monopoly power the inventor will price such that marginal revenue equals marginal cost, price will equal $P_m > c$ and output will be $Q_m < Q_c$. Consumer surplus will be given by the triangle AFG, producer surplus by the area GFJD, and the area FDC is known as the monopoly welfare loss. Note that compared to the static welfare optimum profits are now positive but consumer welfare and overall welfare are reduced. The exclusivity enables the inventor to make supernormal profits. Even with excludability, not all the social benefit pay-offs can be appropriated by the owner of the technology (e.g. there is still a gain in consumer surplus) and as such in a given period the private benefit (producer surplus) will be less than the social benefit, and the private benefit realized by the innovator is less than the potential social benefit of the technology (ACJ).

If the new technology is not excludable, then one may expect other firms to copy the innovator and also supply the product to the market (or what is effectively the same thing, to copy or imitate without payment). As the number of suppliers increases, the price will fall and output will increase. As this happens the profit of the innovator will decline (the innovation is rivalrous) until, at the limit, price equals marginal cost, profits are zero, and the static welfare optimum is reached. Excludability thus allows the originator or owner of an innovation to make profits from the innovation. In its absence the private pay-off to the owner of the new technology may tend towards zero due to copying or freeriding. Such profits provide the incentive to innovate and if there are no profits to be earned there will be no incentive to innovate. However, the provision of these incentives incurs a cost which is the monopoly welfare loss that results from exercising excludability.

In the absence of excludability, the granting of a patent, theoretically, enables the owner of the patent grant to (not unfairly) determine access to the knowledge embodied in the patent and charge licence fees for use of that knowledge for a period equal to the length of life of the patent. After a patent has expired, one expects the free market solution to rule (without excludability, yielding the welfare optimum annually). If the knowledge is not excludable, the best strategy for the patent holder is to charge a royalty on each unit of the new product sold (by imitators) equal to $P_m - c$, at which royalty rate the annual income of the patent holder will be maximized and equal to monopoly profits. This will of course produce the outcome to be found in an excludable market.

Patents are thus a means by which many of the 'externalities' arising from R&D may be market intermediated, and a return by the patent holder can be made for inventive efforts. There is, however, a cost which is the monopoly welfare loss that derives from the monopoly power granted. This cost arises because policies that provide property rights in knowledge to the inventor enable that inventor to receive a return on investment through mark-ups of price over costs which distort sales downward from the optimum level that would occur if the good were sold at marginal cost.[7]

The issue of patents is further complicated in that when a patent application is made, the applicant specifies the body of knowledge over which exclusivity is claimed, and that claim may be broad or narrow. This

---

[7] Although under certain restricted circumstance if the seller can perfectly price discriminate that seller can appropriate the whole (maximal) social surplus.

'breadth' may or may not be agreed to by the patent examiner; however, as the patent examiner will never add to an application it is the innovator who will determine the maximum width of the patent. The wider the patent, the harder it is for potential entrants to enter into the patentees market, but the greater is the possibility of legal challenge to the patent. The patent holder's choice must trade off these two aspects. This is not an issue we wish to cover in great depth because patents are not that relevant to soft innovations, but Yiannaka and Fulton (2006) address it in a model of vertical product innovation. The Yiannaka and Fulton study shows that it is not always optimal for a patentee to go for maximal breadth. The patentee will, however, seek maximum breadth if he or she cannot deter entry and the entrant finds it not optimal to infringe the patent. If the entrant's R&D costs are low and the effect of breadth on patent validity is small, infringement by the entrant is generally not optimal, and thus in such circumstances maximum breadth will be sought. Interestingly, when entry cannot be deterred, the choice of a narrower patent breadth can lead to an entrant choosing a product that results in greater product differentiation compared to a situation where a broad patent is chosen.

The literature in general takes the theoretical stance that, to some degree at least, the patent system has the potential to overcome problems of appropriability or excludability. There are, however, some counter-arguments suggesting that it is not a perfect instrument for doing so. Dasgupta and Stiglitz (1980) have argued that IPR that have the characteristics of patents, where the first one to discover wins the patent, may lead to racing and overinvestment in R&D. They stress that 'patent races' may lead to overinvestment in R&D because of common pool issues or through duplication and repetition (stepping on toes) as well as other game theoretic possibilities. In his contribution to Dasgupta and Stoneman (1987), Dasgupta makes the observation that from a normative perspective each inventor or innovator 'wants to be the winner whereas society does not care who wins', and thus such races or competitions imply overinvestment from a social point of view. Such effects may counteract previously discussed forces that implied underinvestment in R&D (although reducing patent life, see below, may redress this, see Dixit [1988]).

The second argument as to why patents may over-incentivise inventors is based on exploration of the Schumpeterian concept of creative destruction. Building upon the work of Aghion and Howitt (1992) and Grossman and Helpman (1991), it is argued in recent literature (Jones and Williams 2000) that through creative destruction innovation may lead to a redistribution of rents from past innovators to current. Redistribution per se yields no social gain and as such the private pay-off to innovation may exceed the social pay-off.

Jones and Williams (2000) have attempted to estimate the impact of the creative destruction and other effects on R&D. They consider that if the appropriability problem were eliminated, then R&D would increase by 140 per cent. Surprisingly there are very few estimates in the literature of the creative destruction effect. This could be because the effects do not tend to appear until the technologies are used and the study of R&D does not tend to go into the study of use. However, Stoneman and Kwon (1996), using UK data, estimate the impact of technology adoption on firm profits where the profits are calculated as profits without the new technology plus the profit gain from the new technology. They also show that the profits of the non-users do decline as usage of new technology by others extends.[8] Jones and Williams (2000) have estimated that the creative destruction effect stimulates R&D by only 25 per cent. Creative destruction may therefore have some role to play in stimulating the generation and use of new technology, but is outweighed by the appropriability effects. In the terms of Jones and Williams (2000), it is thus unlikely that creative destruction can lead to a redistribution of rents from past innovators to current such that the private pay-off to innovation will exceed the social pay-off.

A third line of relevant comment concerns the observation that innovations are not one-off phenomena. It was argued above that one benefit of patents was that the procedures require the inventor to make his knowledge available to the world. This may generate a 'standing-on-shoulders' effect, whereby present knowledge provides a base for further advances. However, as such benefits cannot be appropriated by the original inventor even with a patent, this might imply that the patent system provides insufficient incentive to innovate. It has also been argued to the contrary that patents, rather than stimulating further innovation, are harmful as they stifle such innovation. This line is argued by Donoghue et al. (1998) and especially by Besen and Maskin (2000). There is also another literature that considers whether with sequential patents there will be increasing dominance or leapfrogging in the market (e.g. Vickers 1986).

In addition to all these different factors the impact of the patent system will depend on the number of years for which a patent is granted. The choice of optimal patent life is a matter of trading off the incentive to the inventor against the accumulation of monopoly welfare losses that are

---

[8] Also that though new technology yields a profit gain, that gain declines as usage extends.

incurred while the patent is in place. From Nordhaus (1969) a literature has grown that attempts to indicate what this optimal patent life will be, taking account of the different arguments already presented on creative destruction, common pool problems, patent breadth, and perhaps standing-on-shoulders (favouring shorter lives) versus potential entry, and shortfalls between private and social returns (favouring longer lives). A very good summary can be found in American Bar Association (2007). A paper particularly relevant here is by Veall (1992) that looks at optimal patent life for horizontal product innovations as modelled by Dixit and Stiglitz (1977). Veall (1992) argues that his results can also be carried over to the trademark context. Assuming Cournot behaviour on the part of firms, it is shown that the optimal patent life is finite. This optimal life will be smaller the greater are the firms' fixed costs, the more substitutable are variants, the lower is industry output, the higher are development costs for each variant, and the higher is the social discount rate. Yiannaka and Fulton (2006) extend the results to a context where breadth is endogenous. Cornelli and Schankerman (1996), however, argue that there is no one optimal length of patent life. The optimum life is situation-specific. Some industries or technologies may need longer than others (the only practical reflection of this is that pharmaceuticals may be extended longer than other patents). Some may not need patents at all. However, if there are no patents or short patents, then alternative forms of IPR protection (such as secrecy) may be more common, and these also have their downsides. It is thus almost impossible currently to advise on optimal patent life.

The theory thus suggests that, in principle, given the correct life, patents can be a useful tool that by providing excludability stimulate innovation; however there is a cost in terms of monopoly welfare loss. This then leads one to ask whether, in reality, patents work. There are a number of ways to explore this issue. The data in Tables 10.1 and 10.2 indicates that patents are only important to a small proportion of innovating firms. It has often been noted that patents are considered to be of considerable importance to pharmaceutical firms (see American Bar Association [2007]). A second approach is to verify whether actual patent lives (either because of non-payment of renewal fees or obsolescence) are long or short. Mansfield (1985) reports that in some industries patent lives are as short as four years. Levin et al. (1987) argue that most patents are duplicated in five years. Pakes (1986) reports that only 7 per cent of French and 11 per cent of German patents go to full term. On the other hand, Landes and Posner (2003), using patent renewal data, indicate that in the United States (where a patent has a twenty-year statutory term provided the patentee pays maintenance fees at 3.5, 7.5, and 11.5 years after the patent has been issued) a patent had an average economic life of about 16.6 years and that about 30 per cent of patents lasted the full twenty-year term. Although such approaches tell us (although not clearly) that patents are important to some degree in generating private returns, they do not indicate whether the private returns generated for the innovators are greater or less than the monopoly welfare loss that society incurs and thus whether patents are socially desirable.

Denicolo (2007) proposes a simple theory that innovators are overcompensated by patents if the profit ratio exceeds the elasticity of supply of innovations (which he suggests is in the range of 0.5–0.7). As even a profit ratio of 0.3 is optimistic, it is unlikely that the patent system as currently structured overcompensates.

Gowers (2006), in reviewing the IPR system in the United Kingdom, suggests that the system works reasonably well although some improvements could be made. In particular he raises issues relating to the patentability of software but concludes that this does not appear to have had a significant negative effect on industry innovation. There are also issues surrounding the expense of gaining patent protection, and, in particular, high translation costs and professional fees for patent agents in Europe and internationally. In addition, the speed of the patent award process at both the US Patent and Trademark Office (USPTO) and the EPO is slowed by large backlogs that impose delays of up to three years on applications. This is not a problem for many industries, but in the high-tech and Internet sectors where business cycles are comparatively short, a long grant time can impose the cost of uncertainty on competitors as to whether a particular invention is proprietary or not.

Citing the literature, Gowers (2006) argues that patents tend to prevent rivals copying proprietary technology only where there are a very small number of patents per product, for example in pharmaceuticals. He also cites evidence that shows that in simple technologies, 28 per cent of firms use patents as a trading strategy to licence a technology, while 46 per cent use patents to fence off an area to competitors and provide more intellectual 'space' to innovate. Sixty-five per cent of firms in complex technologies use patents as a trading strategy to licence a technology (while only 12 per cent use patents as a fence).

Finally, Gowers (2006) argues that a key aspect of enforcing rights is the existence of credible legal sanctions. However, costs can be prohibitive, particularly for small firms. A firm challenging a patent in the United

Kingdom is expected to pay £750,000 for a simple case, largely due to the costs of the adversarial system. Liability for the other side could double this to £1.5 million. The high cost of litigation means that most cases settle out of court. In the United States, which has even higher costs, only 1.5 per cent of all patents are ever litigated, and only 0.1 per cent of all patents are litigated to trial.

The final issue was again addressed here in Arrow (1962) and relates to whether, with patents, monopoly or competition is most conducive to innovation. This reflects a hypothesis first proposed by Schumpeter that market power stimulates innovation. The Arrow conclusion, however, was that competition stimulates innovation. The reasoning is simple. When an innovator sells a new technology to suppliers in a competitive market, that innovator may force monopoly prices on to the market and thus gain monopoly rents. This would not be possible if selling to a monopoly market and thus competition provides greater incentive to innovate. There is a huge literature assessing the validity of such arguments on theoretical and empirical grounds (e.g. Cohen [1995]). Here we make just two points of relevance. The first is, as we have argued above (in Chapter 6), that in the presence of creative destruction the Arrow argument no longer holds and that what matters is contestability in the market. Contestability encourages innovation (see Stoneman [2005]). The second point, which was also made above, is that market structure and innovation expenditures are not necessarily causally related, and may be jointly determined, in which case to study the impact of market structure on innovation is misguided.

10.3 Copyrights

Copyright is an IP right which relates to the expression of an idea, not the idea itself, nor any process by which that idea is embodied in a physical artefact. Many soft innovations can be copyrighted. The UK International Patent Office (IPO) illustrates the copyright principle by citing the example that anyone can write a story based on the idea of a boy-wizard, but they cannot copy text or illustrations (without permission) from other books about the same subject. This is in contrast to the patent system where the idea itself is protected and owned for a period by the patent holder. Copyright protects sound recordings; films; broadcasts; and original artistic, musical, dramatic, and literary works, including, for example, photographs, sculptures, web sites, computer programs, plays, books, videos, databases, maps, and logos. But it does not protect the names, designs, or functions of the items themselves. Moral rights, for example the right to be named as the author, are associated with certain copyright works.

Whereas patents do not cover soft innovations, copyright is particularly applicable to new products in the creative industry and also soft innovation in the non-creative sector. Many soft innovations fall into the category of being expensive to produce and cheap to reproduce and rivalrous in production, the situation in which excludability is of greatest importance to generating incentives to innovate. Current examples include the unauthorized downloading of music and films from the Internet or copying from others' originals, the result of which is that the return to the producer is considerably reduced.

It is not necessary to formally apply or pay for copyright in the United Kingdom.[9] It is an automatic right. The copyright commences as soon as the work is 'fixed', i.e. written down, recorded, or stored (in a computer memory), and in the United Kingdom is established once the copyright symbol (©) is attached to the work with the creator's name along with a date. However, as all copyrights are not registered in the United Kingdom, it is particularly difficult to obtain numbers of copyrights claimed. The owner of the copyright has the right to license or sell it, or otherwise transfer the copyright to someone else.

Copyrights in literary, musical, artistic, and dramatic work in the United Kingdom last for the creator's lifetime plus seventy years (basically the same as in the European Union and in the United States). For films it is seventy years after the death of the last of the directors, score composers, and dialogue or screenplay authors; and for TV and radio programmes it is fifty years from the first broadcast. Sound recording copyright lasts for fifty years. A publisher's right which covers the typographical layout of published editions like books or newspapers (how it is presented on the page) lasts for twenty-five years from creation. These lives (which are under review) are considerably longer than the terms of even extended patent rights.

One reason for the relatively long life of copyrights relative to patents and the non-necessity to apply for registration is provided by Hurt and Schuchman (1966).[10] Primarily discussing books and publishing they propose that one of the arguments in favour of copyrights is based on the rights of the

---

[9] Although this is not the case in all countries. It is the same in the United States but there copyright registration is also available as a legal formality intended to make a public record of the basic facts of a particular copyright. However, registration is not a condition of copyright protection.

[10] Hurt and Schuchman define a copyright as a grant of the aid of state coercion to the creators of certain 'intellectual products' to prevent for a period of years the 'copying' of these products.

creator of the protected object or on the obligation of society towards him or her. In particular it is argued that copyright should exist because:

1. An author has an inherent property right to his or her writings, which is merely recognized by the award of copyright. Hurt and Schuchman (1966) discuss how the validity of this argument depends upon the contested views of what is property.

2. Copyrights may be defended by treating an author's works not as objects, the benefits of which should accrue to the author, but rather as extensions of the personality of the author and subject to protection as such. This theory plays an important role in both the theoretical justification and actual content of the French, German, and Swiss copyright systems. The emphasis of this conception of copyright is on the author's privacy and reputation rather than his commercial interests, and as a consequence under French law the rights granted are virtually inalienable and in some cases perpetual. The three most important are (*a*) the paternity right – the right to be identified as the creator of his works and be protected from plagiarism; (*b*) the integrity right – the right to protection against alteration or deformation of one's work, and the right to make changes in it; (*c*) the publication right – the right not to publish at all. It is not difficult to see that these arguments extend beyond books to films, music, objects of art, etc.

As valid as such arguments may be, for current purposes they are here put aside[11] and instead the rest of this section concentrates on the validity of copyright as an economic mechanism to encourage creativity. It is interesting, however, that even in 2004 Samuelson (2004) can argue that:

As interesting and provocative as the literature on the economics of copyright is, even its most ardent fans would have to admit that economics has rarely played a significant role in the copyright law and policymaking process. (p. 6)

The advantages of copyrights can be viewed using very much the same tools as used in the discussion of patents. As with all IPR mechanisms,

---

[11] It is interesting that in its report to the New Media and the Creative Industries, the House of Commons Culture Media and Sport Select Committee, the House of Commons (2007) express the following opinion upon the Gowers (2006) review of intellectual property: 'Gowers' analysis was thorough and in economic terms may be correct. It gives the impression, however, of having been conducted entirely on economic grounds. We strongly believe that copyright represents a moral right of a creator to choose to retain ownership and control of their own intellectual property. We have not heard a convincing reason why a composer and his or her heirs should benefit from a term of copyright which extends for lifetime and beyond, but a performer should not.'

copyright involves a trade-off between providing an incentive to the producer or innovator but at the cost of a monopoly welfare loss. It may well be that at the welfare optimum, given low reproductions costs, music, video, game downloads should be (all but) free, however if they are free there are no incentives to produce new music, films, or games. The excludability provided by copyrights requires that a price has to be paid for the products and that price rewards the innovator for his or her creative efforts.

Compared to the arguments relating to patents, the case for copyrights has some variations. The first is that, as copyrights do not (everywhere) have to be registered, there is no necessary standing-on-shoulders effect from the copyright system per se. However, it was not clear that the standing-on-shoulders effect is always welfare improving nor that 'the expression of an idea not the idea itself' will necessarily create a platform for further creation. Secondly it is unlikely that protecting the expression of an idea will generate common pool effects in the way that patents do, even though this is a possibility. Finally it does not seem that there is an issue of the breadth of copyright if it is only the expression that is to be protected.

A basic problem with copyright is that the enforcement is in the hands of the owner. Many owners will be individual artists, authors, or perhaps academics for whom the costs of enforcement are too great. Even if the copyright is sold for a fixed sum or on the basis of a royalty to an organization such as a publishing house or a record company, it may be difficult for the owner of the copyright to obtain a merited financial reward. Recent advances in TPP technologies which allow easier copying through downloading from the Web have meant that the enforcement of copyright has become more difficult. Although remedies have been considered, such downloading, it has been argued, has had deleterious effects upon new product launches (see, e.g., www.bpi.co.uk/news/stats/news_content_file_768.shtml). Gowers (2006) cites that by the first quarter of 2006, 1 billion iTunes files and 50 million iPods had been sold, equating to twenty iTunes per iPod.

An obvious difference between copyrights and patents is in the period of protection. In an informative survey of the economics of copyrights Lindsay (2002) argues on the basis of the literature, much as was done re patents above, that

the optimal limits of copyright protection involve complex trade-offs between the benefits and costs of copyright protection. In other words, the objective of the copyright system is not to establish a balance between the interests of copyright owners and users, but to balance the benefits of copyright protection against the costs of the copyright system, including the costs of establishing and enforcing property rights in copyright material. In this sense, the objective of copyright policy is no different from the objective of systems of property rights in tangible material. Although there are good economic explanations for many of the existing legal limits on copyright protection, there is no basis for assuming that the current limits are optimal. There is even less basis for assuming that the limits should be immutable. Given the complexity of balancing the benefits and the costs of copyright protection, it is unlikely that the legislature has sufficient information to establish optimal balances. (p. 111)

Landes and Posner (2003) calculate that roughly 80 per cent of registered copyrights in the United States were not renewed in the 1910 to 2000 period suggesting that, for the expected future, economic benefits from a renewal term were not worth the cost of renewal. In turn, this implies that the average economic life of a copyright was about fourteen years, which is considerably shorter than the statutory term. This suggests that copyright owners generally were not seeking a longer term and thus a longer term may not be desirable.

Within copyrighted works, music had a lower depreciation rate and a longer life than literary (including both books and periodicals) and artistic works. This may be understandable because music is more easily adaptable to changes in taste and context than other works. Png (2006) surveys related literature but with a plea for more future research is no more definitive in his conclusions as to the impact of copyright protection than other writers.

The data in Tables 10.1 and 10.2 implies that although copyright may be important to generating creativity, the area of application is limited to about 10 to 20 per cent of firms. The Gowers (2006) review of copyright in the United Kingdom suggests that copyright suffers from a lack of public legitimacy with little guilt or sanction associated with infringement. While criminal and civil legal sanctions against copyright infringement are tough, infringement is extremely common. The fact that the letter of the law is rarely enforced only adds to the public sense of illegitimacy surrounding copyright law. This is attributed to the fact that enforcement through the civil courts is costly, and cases are difficult to prove. He also notes that a large amount of content protected by copyright is not commercially available:

[T]he existence of such a large volume of old work protected but unavailable (estimates of up to 98 per cent of published work under copyright) means that a great amount of intellectual capital is wasted. Firms and individuals are unable to restore, rework or revive these 'orphan' works to create new commercial and creative capital. (p. 39)

Overall therefore, despite its objectives, the copyright system may have some considerable failings as a protection mechanism and thus as a means by which society can best support the generation of soft innovations.

10.4 Design rights

Design rights apply to intellectual property in the physical appearance of a product and are not concerned with the function or operation of that product. This IP right is not concerned with how the item works but concentrates on the appearance resulting from the features of the product or the way it looks. Design rights emphasize the appearance resulting from the features of physical products or the way they look, whereas patents mainly encompass how an item works, and copyright covers non-physical products such as sound recordings; films; broadcasts; and original artistic, musical, dramatic, and literary works. Contributory features to a product's appearance include lines, contours, colours, shape, texture, and material. Design rights will apply to soft innovations.

In the United Kingdom there are several types of design protection available:

Registered design offers protection throughout the United Kingdom. The protection lasts initially for five years and can be renewed every five years for up to twenty-five years. Application must be made for this IP right, a fee has to be paid, and it is not an automatic right.

Registered community design (RCD) offers like protection in all of the EU member states. This protection can be renewed every five years up to twenty-five years. In the period 2003–2007 approximately 273,000 designs have been registered and published. Following its 2003 launch, the total number of designs registered in the United Kingdom has fallen from 9,000 in 2002 to less than 4,000 in 2005.

UK design right is an automatic right which does not need to be applied for, and prevents others from copying a design but it covers only the three-dimensional (3D) aspects of the item and does not protect the surface decoration of the product or any two-dimensional (2D) pattern such as a wallpaper or carpet design. UK design right lasts for up to fifteen years from creating the design.

Unregistered community design right is also an automatic right for which one does not need to apply and offers protection from copying the design on any item.

Protection lasts for three years after the design has been made available to the public and covers all EU countries.

To qualify for any of these rights, the design must be new and individual[12] in character, which means that the overall impression the design gives the informed user must be different from any previous designs. A design cannot be registered if it is more than twelve months since the design was first publicly disclosed; the design is dictated only by how the product works; the design includes parts of complicated products that cannot be seen in normal use (e.g. vehicle engine spare parts or the parts inside a computer); it is offensive; or it involves certain national emblems and protected flags. A registered design provides the right to sell or licence someone else to use it.[13]

Although there are design rights separate from patents in the United Kingdom and European Union, in the United States there are design patents. These are very similar to US utility patents with similar governing law except that design patents last fourteen years from the date a patent is granted, not twenty years from the date that an application is filed. In Japan there is protection for fifteen years from registration and in Canada ten years. In none of these countries is there protection without registration.

In a static welfare optimum, designs would be freely available but this creates no incentive to generate designs. Design rights, as with other IPR instruments, stimulate creativity through rewarding the designer by granting monopoly power over a design, enabling the generation of a return but at the cost of some monopoly welfare loss. Design rights would appear to be particularly relevant to the protection of soft innovations, especially in the non-aesthetic sector (although it may also be relevant in the aesthetic sector). Their main function would appear to be to limit the copying by other producers of successful products. In doing so they would reinforce product differentiation activities. As the design of successful products cannot be protected by secrecy there may be perhaps more problems in protection in this area than with advances covered by patents. By their nature, designs will not be naturally excludable in a market and thus IPR protection may be of considerable importance in providing excludability.

Design rights are in some ways closer to patents than to copyrights in that they protect ideas (incorporated in a design) as opposed to the

---

[12] In assessing individual character, the degree of freedom of the designer is taken into account.
[13] Examples of protected designs may be found by looking at www.ipo.gov.uk/design/d-applying/d-should/d-should-designright.

expression of an idea. Like patents, design rights do not allow a designer to appropriate the standing-on-shoulders benefits, but there may be no such benefits. Designs may also cause creative destruction relative to previous designs but it is difficult to see that there will be common pool effects relating to design rights. Brought together all such issues will impact upon the optimal life of a design right, but we know of no work, separate from that on optimal patent life discussed above, that tries to separately determine the optimal life of a design right or design patent.

As to whether design rights are effective, the data in Tables 10.1 and 10.2 shows that there is some demand for such rights. The Gowers (2006) review cites the performance, reputation, and export performance of the UK design industry as evidence that they are. This, however, is circumstantial. On the other hand, he also notes that the legal mechanisms to enforce design rights are complex. The uncertainty of the law and the limitations of passing off mean that small designers cannot afford to take the risks associated with legal action and, accordingly, competitors have no economic incentive to seek permission before using the design. Overall there is little strong empirical evidence to show that design rights are effective or that their life is optimal. The implication is that soft innovation, once again, may not be optimally protected.

10.5 Trademarks

A trademark is a sign which can distinguish a firm's goods and services (a service mark being the same as a trademark except that it identifies and distinguishes the source of a service rather than a good) from those of other traders. A sign includes, for example, words, logos, pictures, or a combination of these. Note that whereas patents require novelty and copyright requires originality, the counterpart for a trademark is distinctiveness. The trademark can be used as a marketing tool so that customers can recognize a particular supplier of goods or services through branding. A trademark can also be sold, leased, or licensed for use to another trader.

Whereas patents are not available for aesthetic innovations, such innovations may be trademarked. For example a rock group[14] can trademark its name; a product with a particular aesthetic can be trademarked, e.g. the iPod; and particular products may also be trademarked, e.g. Mars bars and

---

[14] Although the legal protection of personality rights is a confused issue in English Law. See the discussion in Kolah (2002, pp. 83–95).

Crunchie bars. A non-aesthetic product may be both patented and trade-marked and perhaps even have a design right protection as well. An aesthetic product may carry a copyright, a trademark, and perhaps also a design right. If brand extensions are to be considered as soft innovations, then trademarks may also be directly relevant here.

A registered mark confers the right of use of that mark on the goods and services in the classes for which it is registered, and the legal right to take action against anyone who uses the mark or a similar mark on the same or similar goods and services to those that are set out in the registration. To be registerable, the trademark must be distinctive for the goods and services (for which application is made), and not the same as (or similar to) any earlier marks on the register for the same (or similar) goods or services.

A trademark does not have to be registered. An unregistered trademark provides certain rights under common law and the owner can use the ™ symbol. However, it is easier to enforce rights if the mark is registered and use the ® symbol to indicate that it is registered. In the United Kingdom, application for registration is made to the Trade Marks Registry of the Patent Office. There is a need to pay a renewal fee every ten years. European protection through a Community Trade Mark application is made at the Office for Harmonisation of the Internal Market. As with other IPR instruments it is necessary for the owner to themselves police his or her rights through the courts.

Figure 10.2 shows the total number of Trademark Registrations in five Trademark Offices from 1883 to 2005 (source: WIPO). The growing use of trade marks is obvious.

It is commonly argued (see, e.g., Besen and Raskind [1991]) that trademark protection differs from patents, design rights, and copyrights in that trademarks did not originate as an incentive for innovation or creativity. Instead their origin is usually associated with the medieval guild practice of affixing an identifying mark to a goblet or a similar product. Accordingly, the initial purpose of trademark protection was to make it illegal to pass off the goods of another artisan as those of a guild member. This echoes current concerns with fake designer goods such as trainers and watches.

Ramello and Silva (2006) radically argue that trademarks were

originally connected with the problem of information asymmetries and the need to provide information for assisting exchanges so as to avert the market failure brought about by adverse selection. However, this information-conveying function is also accompanied by a differentiation effect, arising from the power of persuasion that

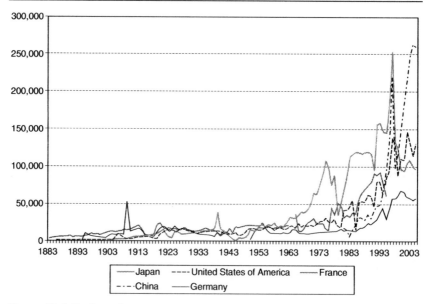

Figure 10.2 Trademark registrations

signs can exert on individuals. The exploitation of differentiation has given rise to the practice of branding, which ties markets and consumption to the realms of meaning and experience. Branding is so all-pervasive in today's economy as to have somehow transfigured it, so that the role of persuasion is now pre-eminent.

Overall, therefore, the process of the mutation of trademark into brand has generated a kind of market for signs and meanings, characterized by a multiplicity of attributes and economic effects that the economic theory has not yet fully understood. (pp. 937–8)

Barnes (2006) argues that

trademark law was not designed to elevate discourse or disseminate knowledge the way copyright law does or lead to life enhancing innovation, as patent law does. Trademarks do not enrich the public domain, that collection of useful ideas and uses of ideas that are the basic tools for promoting progress in science and the useful arts. Trademark law is the poor relation of the intellectual property world, not really 'intellectual' at all.

He goes on to argue that copyrights, patents, and design rights are premised upon public goods arguments related to rivalry and excludability, but the theoretical base for trademarks relies wholly upon private and not public returns. He further argues that because trademark owners contribute to the store of information available for all people to use, their efforts are more similar to the efforts of authors and inventors than is generally recognized. Trademarks have non-rivalrous uses, primarily in the sense that many consumers may use them without interfering with one another's use. In these uses, trademarks have the characteristics of public goods. They can thus be justified on similar grounds.

Over time, trademarks have evolved as a form of indirect protection of the consumer by insuring that purchasing decisions are based on marks that properly identify the product and its source. The value of the trademark is enhanced both by the quality of the product and the public familiarity with it. A trademark may impose costs of advertising and establishing a reputation on a prospective entrant to a market. However, trademark protection may dampen competition by limiting the ability of competitors to copy a successful mark or packaging design, even though these features are not protected by copyright or patent. Trademarks thus provide an economic incentive to certain types of behaviour, especially orderly marketing, by identifying products and their sources and may also help overcome some public goods problems. They do however have associated costs.

The aspect of trademarks concentrated upon here is that they differ from the other IP rights in that not only does the right protect IP, but also enables the accumulation and storage of goodwill, brand awareness, and other similar intangible assets of a firm, perhaps generated in several markets and over many products, and enables those intangibles to be used or exploited in the selling of products in other markets or at future dates. It thus provides a means by which such intangible assets may be transferred over time. This raises the possibility that trademarks enable, at least to some degree, for firms to internalize the standing-on-shoulders effect that copyrights, patents, and design rights cannot.

The standing-on-shoulders effect is where one inventor's discoveries may provide the foundation for discoveries by others, and to the extent that the original inventor receives no reward for this then there will be underinvestment in invention and discovery. If a discovery is trademarked as well as patented, then the trademark may well give an inventor at least partial advantage in appropriating future returns from similar innovations and thus internalize the benefits of standing on shoulders. Thus, for example, Apple computers built a reputation for non-standard, often preferred computer products that they were able to exploit in later and varied products. The Virgin brand has been applied to record shops, airlines, financial services, broadcasting, telecommunications, etc., all exploiting a common pool of goodwill and brand awareness.

265

In the absence of trademark protection these possibilities would not exist and as such the possibilities of transferring reputations for quality and innovativeness across products and time would be limited and the returns to establishing a reputation for quality through innovation would be much less. This is not to say that all the benefits of trademarks are positive. As with other IPR mechanisms the provision of excludability and/or monopoly rights can come at the cost of competition and thus higher prices and loss of welfare. There is a trade off between the static welfare loss and the dynamic benefits.

We have very little information on whether the life of trademarks is long enough or too long. Landes and Posner (2003) find that in the United States the average economic life of a trademark is around 15.5 years which is close to the full term and might suggest that increases in the term may stimulate innovation. However, it does not necessarily mean that the balance between private pay-off and social cost is correct.

In the light of this, a relevant question is whether trademarks work in stimulating innovation. The data in Tables 10.1 and 10.2 show that they are one of the more popular IPR mechanisms. Greenhalgh and Rogers (2007) investigate whether applications for trademarks are suggestive of product innovation improving the profitability and productivity of firms. Data on both trade (and service) marks sought through the UK Patent Office (UKTM) and the European Community Office for Harmonisation of the Internal Market (CTM) was used. They find that stock market values (Tobin's q) are positively associated with R&D and trademark activity by firms. Larger differences are found between firms with and without trademarks for services than for manufacturing. They also find bigger differences in Tobin's q when the services firms apply for Community marks, rather than just applying for UK marks. Even so, the marginal returns to extra trademarks per firm were diminishing quite rapidly over the sample period. They also find that firms that trademark have significantly higher value added than non-trade markers (by between 10 per cent and 30 per cent across all firms). Their interpretation is that trademark activity proxies a range of other, unobservable, firm-level characteristics including innovation that raise productivity and product unit values. Finally they find that in the short run, greater IP activity by other firms in the industry reduces the value added of the firm, but this same competitive pressure has later benefits through productivity growth and this is reflected in higher stock market value.

Gowers' (2006) review concludes that although trademarks are affordable they can take between six and nine months to be granted and currently there is no 'fast-track' route available for firms that require protection more quickly in order to start building up their brand. Evidence to his review raised concerns that copycat packaging (especially from supermarkets) threatened successful brands and was unfair competition, and that the hurdle of 'consumer confusion' required to prove trademark infringement was too difficult to prove in court. He finds that there are in fact large problems with the counterfeiting of trademarks. Similar issues exist in relation to trademark enforcement with copyright, namely the fact that the police have many competing priorities and that litigation is costly.

Overall it appears that trademarks are welcomed by some firms and can yield positive private pay-offs, but there may be enforcement problems. It is not clear that the current system correctly balances private benefit and social cost. However, being available to soft innovations, they may be a valuable institutional tool.

10.6 Conclusions

This chapter has theoretically and empirically explored the justification and operation of four different institutional IPR mechanisms within the soft innovation context. Three of the mechanisms – copyrights, design rights (or design patents), and trademarks – are particularly applicable to soft innovation (as well as TPP innovations) but the fourth, patents, are not applicable to soft innovations. The rationale for a patent system was, however, a useful place to start in terms of evaluating the desirability of such mechanisms.

Each IPR mechanism has a different emphasis. Copyright which is particularly applicable to books, music, films, etc. (aesthetic products) protects expression of an idea, whereas patents protect the idea itself. Protection of an expression may be much less valuable than protection of an idea. Copyrights do, however, tend to have a much longer life than patents. This seems to be based upon the view that copyrights reflect 'an author's works not as objects the benefits of which should accrue to the author, but rather as extensions of the personality of the author and subject to protection as such'.

Design rights are similar to patents but extend to the aesthetic characteristics of a product. In fact in several parts of the world these are called design patents. However, design rights or patents do not require an advance in knowledge. They reflect 3D aesthetic differences between products, and as such are an important IPR mechanism for soft innovation.

Trademarks are different again. There is an argument in the literature as to whether trademarks are an IPR mechanism as are the other three. It is argued here that they are similar but the important point about trademarks is not just that they can be applied to soft innovations but they also allow some amelioration of the standing-on-shoulders problem and as such can be of particular relevance when used in conjunction with other protective mechanisms.

The four mechanisms are not regarded widely to be of prime importance as a means to protect IP. In some circumstances there are other non-institutional means by which such property may be protected, e.g. secrecy and/or lead-time. However in cases where there is no excludability, the different mechanisms do offer some protection. It might even be that in certain circumstances the institutional mechanisms (from a social point of view) are to be preferred to market mechanisms because of the information that they reveal. All IPR mechanism work by providing a stimulus to creativity and innovation by the inventor through monopoly rights that may be exploited to yield a return. The cost, however, is that the use of the monopoly power means a cost to society equal to the monopoly welfare loss. The latter static inefficiency has to be traded off against the gain in dynamic efficiency.

The trade off between social cost and private return is not a simple one (an argument also well made by Towse in the concluding part of Towse [2004]), and issues that have merited consideration include: (*a*) the standing-on-shoulders effect whereby, because institutional IPR mechanisms require revealing technological knowledge, one inventor's discoveries may provide the foundation for discoveries by others and, to the extent that this happens and the original inventor receives no reward for this, there may be underinvestment in invention and discovery; (*b*) the mechanisms are of the winner-takes-all type which leads to common pool problems and although they may stimulate innovation they may stimulate it too much because of rent seeking; and (*c*) creative destruction arguments, which have been more extensively pursued in the new growth theory field, and argue that, when a new technology is introduced, part of the return to the innovator comes from a reduced return to the incumbent, and as society is not concerned with such allocative issues, the mechanisms may provide an over incentive to innovate.

Although such issues, as well as aspects of the breadth of protection, have been addressed in the literature relating to the optimal life for IP, the picture on a theoretical level is by no means clear. On the empirical level there is some evidence that institutional protection does stimulate innovation, but there seems little that relates this to the social costs incurred. Much of the literature, however, concentrates on TPP innovations and patents. In the soft innovation context there is only a limited literature. Given that patents are not available to soft innovation, the discussion necessarily centres more upon the advantages and disadvantages of the other IPR institutions. It has been argued that though these institutions have similar characteristics to patents in their modus operandi, and may offer some protection as desired, they are not, however, always best suited to their tasks.

The recent review of the IPR system in the United Kingdom, Gowers (2006), has looked at the operation of the system and generally gives it a clean bill of health. The common problem of the different mechanisms is however that enforcement is in the hands of the holder of the IPR and enforcement can be prohibitively expensive. The extent of protection offered may thus be limited. The Department for Culture Media and Sports, in reaction to Gowers (2006), set up a Creative Industries Forum on Intellectual Property in 2008 to take matters further in the creative industry (soft innovation) context.

Finally, Arrow (1962) initiated a discussion as to whether, under a patent system (and by implication other IPR institutions), monopoly or competitive product market structures were most conducive to innovation. This is an issue that has also been addressed in earlier chapters. It was argued here however that either (*a*) the question is irrelevant in that market structure and soft innovation are determined simultaneously and neither is causal to the other; or (*b*) that due to creative destruction, it is contestability of the market that matters and not the existing structure. Taking this further, from a creative destruction perspective, monopoly per se does not deter further soft innovation, only a lack of contestability does so. For the purposes of innovation policy, therefore, governments do not need to control monopolies. As long as the market is contestable the economy will, given appropriate IPR mechanisms, generate its own incentives to further carry out soft innovation and the eradication of any incumbent's monopoly.

Anti-trust policy, the main thrust of which is to prevent abuses of dominant positions that eradicate contestability (e.g. entry barriers), would seem to be the appropriate policy stance. From this perspective, market power is the means by which the return that induces the innovation is generated and it is thus desirable. What is not desirable is that current market power should be used to prevent further innovation by limiting market contestability. Policy should worry less about current market positions and concentrate instead on ensuring contestability. However, although contestability yields a greater incentive to innovate, whether it will generate the social optimum will depend upon the nature of competition in the invention-producing industry as well as, inter alia, the particular characteristics of the IPR schema in place. This applies to soft and TPP innovation equally.

Part III

Impacts and Implications

11

The Impact of Soft Innovation upon Firm Performance

11.1 Objectives

This final part of this book addresses two main issues. The first is the impact of soft innovation on firm performance. That is undertaken here. The second is to address government policy in the light of what has come before, which is undertaken in Chapter 12. The part and the book close with concluding Chapter 13.

The objective of this chapter is to explore whether the undertaking of soft innovation by firms impacts upon firm performance or, more precisely, what is the return to investment in soft innovations? The logic for doing so is that there is a considerable literature on the impact of TPP innovations on firm performance that has been influential in persuading academics, commentators, and policymakers that such innovation is the key to economic growth and prosperity. Measuring the impact of soft innovation may then enable such innovation to take its merited position beside TPP innovation.

It should be noted immediately that some innovations may succeed and some may fail. In this chapter both the returns to soft innovations that are particularly successful (which are likely to be the significant innovations in terms defined above) as well as returns to soft innovation in general (which matches in with much of the prior literature on the impact of TPP innovation) are addressed. The soft innovations considered may be horizontal or vertical, and no presumptions are made on this count. The impacts of most concern at the level of the firm are on productivity and profitability, although aspects of performance such as market share, value added, equity values, or total sales may also be useful indicators. At higher levels of aggregation there may also be concerns with market impact (allowing for spillovers to other firms) and economic welfare.

In the sections that follow approaches that have previously been used in economics to look at the impact of TPP (and organizational innovations) on firm performance are detailed in order to explore methods, with critical reviews of the TPP-related empirical literature provided in Appendices 11.1 and 11.2. The literature that has applied such approaches to soft innovations using proxy measure of such innovation is then explored. The returns to some exemplars of soft innovation that illustrate impact upon firm performance are then provided before conclusions are drawn.

11.2 Standard approaches to modelling the impact of innovation on firm performance: productivity

The most prevalent approach to modelling the impact of innovation upon firm performance (see Griliches [1995]) is to assume that the output technology of the firm can be represented via a production function written as Equation (11.1)

$$Q(t) = F(K(t), L(t), T(t)) \tag{11.1}$$

where $Q(t)$ is value added in time t, $K(t)$ is capital services employed in time t, $L(t)$ is labour services employed in time t, and $T(t)$ is the state of the firm's technology in time t. It is common to allow that Equation (11.1) takes the form of a Cobb–Douglas production function and can be written (assuming constant returns to scale) as Equation (11.2)

$$Q(t) = A(t) . K(t)^{\alpha} . L(t)^{1-\alpha} \tag{11.2}$$

where α is a predetermined coefficient and $A(t)$, often called total factor productivity (TFP), incorporates the technology term.[1] In the literature this term may be considered as either (a) exogenous when it is often written as $Ae^{\lambda t}$; or (b) endogenous and determined by firm behaviour. In the latter case it has been represented in the past by measures such as the number of (functional) innovations introduced, new process technologies employed, number of organizational innovations introduced, number of skilled and/or educated workers employed, but most commonly is modelled as either some function of R&D expenditure or

---

[1] For the latest estimates of TFP in the United Kingdom, see Goodridge (2008) where TFP growth is calculated as 0.8% p.a. between 1997 and 2006.

the numbers of patents applied for or granted. The modelling may relate $A(t)$ to current values of R&D, $R(t)$ or allow for some stock effects and relate $A(t)$ to current and past values of R&D usually with depreciation rates in the 15 to 25 per cent per annum range. Relating to past values of R&D allows the possibility that R&D expenditure today may affect firm performance in the future.

There are various ways to estimate Equation (11.2). One is to estimate the equation econometrically using data on $Q(t)$, $K(t)$, $L(t)$, and, for example considering that $A(t) = Be^{\mu R(t)}$, thus generating estimates of α and μ and then TFP. This route allows also that one may obtain a measure of the impact of R&D on output (as a measure of firm performance) such as $\delta Q(t)/\delta R(t)$. Early work, however, argued that if the economy was perfectly competitive, then α and $1 - \alpha$ would equal the shares of capital and labour in national income, which are available data. In that case Equation (11.1) is estimated by calculating either TFP as in Equation (11.3) or the growth of TFP as in Equation (4)

$$A(t) = Q(t)/(K(t)^{\alpha} \cdot L(t)^{1-\alpha}) \tag{11.3}$$

$$\mathrm{dlog}\, A(t) = \mathrm{dlog}\, Q(t) - \alpha\, \mathrm{dlog}\, K(t) - (1 - \alpha)\mathrm{dlog}\, L(t) \tag{11.4}$$

Where the expression $\mathrm{dlog}X(t)$ indicates the time derivative of the natural log of the variable which measures the growth rate of the variable. Equation (11.4) indicates that the rate of growth of TFP equals the growth in output that is not due to increases in the capital or labour input and is taken as measure of the contribution of innovation or technology to output growth. One may also manipulate this equation to measure the contribution of TFP growth to labour productivity (output per unit of labour) growth.

It would appear that in principle there is no reason why the total factor productivity term $A(t)$ should not also encompass soft innovation as defined here, however most empirical literature to date has used R&D and/or patent counts to measure innovation and, as discussed above, soft innovation can neither be patented nor will be properly counted in R&D. Thus, although there is considerable empirical work relating firm performance to patents and R&D, these two measures will give little insight into the impact of soft innovation as such. However, as the results are informative in a general sense in terms of methods and approaches, a survey of empirical results relating productivity to R&D and/or patents is provided in Appendix 11.1.

11.3 Standard approaches to modelling the impact of innovation on firm performance: profitability[2]

The literature recognizes a number of different ways in which the relationship between technological effort and profitability of the firm can be formulated. The early industrial organization literature was built largely upon the structure–conduct–performance (S–C–P) paradigm, the basic principle of which is that the economic performance of firms in an industry is a function of the conduct of buyers and sellers which, in turn, is a function of the industry structure (Mason 1939; Bain 1956). It is assumed that in long-term equilibrium perfectly competitive markets will result in the optimal (welfare maximizing) allocation of resources in an economy (Samuelson 1965, ch. 8). However, the long-term run equilibrium will only arise in the absence of entry barriers. In the absence of entry barriers, profits are eliminated by the entry of new firms as the industry moves towards the long-term equilibrium. With entry barriers excess profits are possible and may be realized if there is appropriate conduct. One may note that the underlying theoretical structure implicitly assumes that causality runs from innovation towards profitability. This S–C–P paradigm has been much criticized (often because of its static nature).

An alternative, the efficiency paradigm, conceives of competition as a process rather than as an abstraction employed to evaluate whether optimal conditions are obtained under static conditions. The process approach argues that economic conditions affecting any industry are, for all practical purposes, never in static equilibrium. Forces within the economy move resources towards equilibrium but because there are imperfections in the world, including imperfect foresight and positive transaction costs, a static equilibrium is never reached (Alchian 1950; McGee 1985). Conceptualizing competition as a process allows one to recognize (*a*) that above normal profits can be earned in a competitive environment; (*b*) entry barriers are not a prerequisite for the realization of excess profits; and (*c*) competition only guarantees that prices will move towards the competitive level, not that they will ever achieve that level.

Firms that possess more skill and/or luck in anticipating changes in demand and technology will be able to earn above-average profits (Kirzner

[2] As part of their doctoral research, two of my students, Amid Mourani and Eleonora Bartolini, have under my supervision explored the literature on the link between innovation and profitability. It is on their work that this section and the related Appendix 11.2 is primarily built.

1973). However, above-average profits act as a signal that a reallocation of resources may allow other firms to take advantage of changes in demand or technology. Therefore, above-average profits invite entry and/or an increase in the capacity of incumbent firms (Jacobsen 1988). Proponents of the efficiency paradigm view above-average returns as a reward to effective competition (Brozen 1979; Demsetz 1973; Schumpeter 1942). The efficiency paradigm, like the S–C–P approach, also recognizes the importance of a firm's relative ability to take advantage of scale and scope economies, product differentiation, and focus opportunities in determining profitability. In fact, activities that allow a firm to lower cost or create price inelasticity from differentiation may result in both short run and long run competitive advantage in the efficiency paradigm (Teece 1982). According to the 'firm efficiency view' (Demsetz 1973; Peltzman 1977), causality runs from profits to market structure in that efficient firms grow and capture large shares of the market.

In an alternative dynamic approach, Mueller (1990) considers profitability and its persistence in a Schumpeterian dynamic framework driven by creative destruction. Here innovation creates monopoly which creates profits, and profits create imitators until a state of normalcy returns, only to be followed by new innovations and a repeat of the cycle. This approach emphasizes firms' characteristics as more important than industry characteristics in determining profit persistence.

Within the existing literature there is some conflict as to whether the link between profitability and innovation goes from the latter to the former or in the opposite direction. The evolutionary approach considers both these mechanisms as being present and self-reinforcing over time. According to their seminal contributions, Nelson and Winter (1982, 2002) argue that the technological context in which firms operate is crucially characterized by path dependency, bounded rationality, and high uncertainty. Under these assumptions, a firm's performance is affected, on the one hand, by past economic and innovation performance, which also determine the 'actual' stock of resources and competencies; on the other hand, it is affected by the ability to identify new opportunities to be adopted and commercialized in the future. Thus, profitability and innovative performance are dynamically related, and the empirical investigation of any causal relationship between the two becomes more difficult.

As discussed in earlier chapters, industrial organization theory often predicts that innovation should decline with competition, as more competition reduces the monopoly rents that reward successful innovators. Dasgupta and Stiglitz (1980) model R&D activity at the firm level recognizing the importance of relations with the other agents in the market, on both the supply and demand sides. In their model firms are profit-maximizing agents and are allowed to choose both R&D expenditure to determine costs and output. Firms are assumed to have Cournot conjectures: a given agent does not react to the other agents' decisions. Assuming free entry, the model predicts (*a*) when the degree of concentration in industries is low, industry-wide R&D effort is positively correlated with concentration which in turn is positively correlated with the degree of monopoly (the price–cost margin); (*b*) that optimal R&D expenditure and R&D expenditure per firm increase with the size of the market but decrease with the costs associated with R&D technology if demand is elastic and increase with increasing costs if demand is inelastic; and (*c*) there may be excessive duplication of research effort in a market economy in the sense that industry-wide R&D expenditure exceeds the socially optimal level even though cost-reduction is lower. In particular, an industry may be characterized by a very low degree of concentration (i.e. a large number of firms) and at the same time engage in a great deal of social waste. In conclusion, although the analysis suggests the existence of a positive correlation between concentration and R&D expenditure, nothing can be said about the causality of this relationship, as both concentration and R&D are endogenous to the model.

Finally, there is a literature on profitability and innovation as reflected in diffusion activity. The literature is limited (see Stoneman 2002), but for example Reinganum (1981) shows that if the value of adopting a cost-reducing, capital-embodied process innovation declines with the number of firms which have already adopted it, then the firms adopt the new technology in sequence so that it is 'diffused' into the industry over time. This diffusion is due purely to strategic behaviour (firms are assumed to be identical and information regarding the value of the innovation is perfect). The implication is that leaders make greater profits. Reinganum also argues that if the demand function is linear, an increase in the number of firms in the industry leads firms to delay adoption. In contrast Quirmbach (1986) predicts that adoption will be delayed if there are few users in a concentrated industry and they adopt cooperative behaviour.

There are a large number of existing empirical studies on profitability and innovation that are potentially worth mentioning. Although these could be extended to encompass soft innovation, they primarily use R&D and/or patents as an indicator of innovation which as stated above are poor indicators of soft innovation. The detail is thus included as a separate Appendix 11.2.

11.4 Soft innovation and firm performance: the evidence from copyrights, trademarks, design, and the PIMS database

The general underlying message of the sections above (and associated appendices) is that innovation is an important determinant of firm performance. The empirical literatures discussed thus far, however, primarily employ proxies that tend to be restricted to measures of functional innovation such as patents, R&D, or sometimes organizational innovation. The message of this book is however that there is another type of innovation, soft innovation, and it is the purpose of this chapter to concentrate on the returns to such innovation. There is much less work that uses proxies that may measure soft innovation. Four bodies of work do, however, merit some attention, relating specifically to copyrights, trademarks (which Mendonca et al. [2004] recommend as a proxy for innovative effort), design expenditures, and the PIMS database. As already stated in earlier chapters, however, the proxy measures may reflect soft innovation but not just soft innovation. They are most likely to reflect both soft and functional innovative activity. The following subsections look at these relevant literatures. It is particularly worth noting that if soft innovation activities do impact upon firm performance, then studies that look only at functional innovation will give biased estimates of the impact of such innovation on firm performance.

11.4.1 *Returns to copyright*

Greenhalgh and Rogers (2007) have, in addition to work cited above and in the appendices, also reviewed the literature of the impact of copyrights on the profitability of firms. Overall, they argue that there is very little evidence on the value of copyright (see also Chapter 10). They note that empirical analysis of the value of copyright is hampered in the United Kingdom and Europe by the fact that there is no legal requirement to register creative work. There are, however, some US-based studies, e.g. Landes and Posner (2003), who looked at the 1910–91 period when copyright did require registering and renewal, and who concluded that around 80 per cent of copyright had little economic value. Png and Wang (2006) look at the impact of copyright extensions on the production of movies in Organization for Economic Cooperation and Development (OECD) countries, finding that extension from fifty to seventy years after the author's life did increase production by around 10 per cent. Baker and Cunningham (2006) looked at the effect on the market value of firms of US federal court decisions that broadened copyright and found one ruling that raised the market value of firms by around 0.2 to 0.45 per cent (or $4 million to $8 million). Mazeh and Rogers (2006) also found that plaintiffs in copyright disputes have higher market values than a peer group of similar firms. Overall, however, there is very little evidence on the value of copyright.

11.4.2 *Returns to trademarks*

Greenhalgh and Rogers (2007) also survey work on the value of trademarks. Seethamraju (2003) analyses the value of trademarks in 237 US firms from selected industries for the period 1993–7, finding a positive role for trademarking on sales and market values. A study of 300 Australian firms in the period 1989–2002 by Griffiths et al. (2005) found that the stock of trademarks was a significant determinant of profits, but with a smaller impact than either patents or registered designs. The value of a trademark was rising over their data period. Greenhalgh and Rogers (2007*a*) analyse a large sample of publicly quoted UK firms for the 1996–2000 period. Their results indicate that stock market values are positively associated with R&D, patents, and trademark activity of firms. They find larger differences between firms with and without trademarks for firms in the services sector than for manufacturing. They also find bigger differences in the impact on Tobin's q when the services firm is applying for European Community marks, rather than just applying for UK marks.

Greenhalgh and Rogers (2007*a*) also investigate the relationship between trademarks and productivity levels and growth rates for both quoted and unquoted firms, using a value added production function. The results indicate that firms that trademark have significantly higher value added than non-trade markers (by between 10% and 30% across all firms). In addition higher trademark intensity has some positive association with productivity growth in services, but the results are relatively weak in manufacturing. Finally they also find that, in the short run, higher trademark activity by rivals in the same industry reduces the firm's value added. However, in their subsequent analysis they are led to conclude that positive spillovers negate market stealing effects to give a net positive impact of rivals' trademarks on a firm's productivity and of rivals' patents on the firm's market value.

11.4.3 *Returns to design*

The DTI (2005) review of the contribution of design to economic performance argues that there is some strong empirical evidence of a positive link between design and firm performance. They quote as evidence that Gemser and Leenders (2001) in a study of Dutch firms found that integrating industrial design into new product development projects had a significant and positive influence on company profits, turnover, and export sales; and that the impact of design on performance may differ by sector being much stronger in precision instruments, where design use was less mature, than in furniture where use of design was mature.

Haskel et al. (2005) assess the impact that expenditure on design has on firm performance using the Community Innovation Survey. Firms are grouped according to their productivity and turnover in order to assess whether more productive firms with higher growth tend to be more innovative or have higher expenditure on innovative activities, including design. They show that more innovative firms tend to have higher growth in turnover and productivity but there appears to be no simple (univariate) relationship between expenditure on design and firm performance. Haskel et al. (2005) also consider how expenditure on design affects the probability of innovating and productivity growth in a multivariate setting, i.e. controlling for other factors. They find that firms with higher design intensity have a greater probability of carrying out product innovation, but are not more likely to carry out process innovation. Importantly, they find a positive association between design expenditure and firm productivity growth. While difficult to prove that spending on design causes productivity increases, this finding lends support to the findings of previous research, much of which is based on case study analysis rather than statistical evidence.

Bruce et al. (1995) show that 60 per cent of their sample of 178 UK-funded design projects could be defined as commercially successful (measured by positive financial returns on investment). Around one-half of all projects for which export information was obtained saw some international trade benefit. Whyte et al. (2002) show that around one-half of actual export sales made by winners of the 'Queens Award for Exports' could be directly attributed to their investment in design. Sentance and Clarke (1997) find that design-intensive industries and firms are much more active in export markets. Their estimates suggest that had UK manufacturing invested one-third less in in-house design the growth rate in manufacturing would have been 0.3 per cent less per year over the period 1986–96.

Surveys of UK firms carried out for the Design Council (2005a) find that rapidly growing companies attach much greater weight to design than average growth companies. Separate research for the Design Council (2005b) showed sixty-three design-intensive companies outperformed the FTSE by more than 200 per cent over 1994–2004. Bessant et al. (2005) provide a broad overview of the evidence on design and business perform-ance. Based on this, they argue that 'there is clear evidence of the contri-bution and therefore potential for design to affect competitiveness'.

Swann and Birke (2005) undertake a detailed empirical and conceptual analysis of the innovation–design–performance link and cite several stud-ies that show – typically through case study work, but sometimes also through survey work – that design is an important source of innovation in its own right, and that one should not make the assumption (common amongst many economists, though not all) that most innovations eman-ate from R&D. They also argue that although these studies suggest a strong correlation between design input and firm performance, establishing clear causality is difficult. The multifaceted nature of design makes it difficult to isolate its impact from more traditional factors affecting performance, such as market conditions or investment.

11.4.4 *The PIMS database*

The Profit Impact of Market Strategy (PIMS) database was introduced in Chapter 3 as a potential source of data on soft innovation. This database represents a large-scale study designed to measure the relationship between business actions and business results. The project was initiated in the mid-1960s and since 1975 has been maintained by the Strategic Planning Institute. The data covers the characteristics of the market en-vironment, the state of competition, the strategy pursued by each business including innovation activity, and also business unit performance. For current purposes the data set is useful in that it uses definitions of innov-ation that are not restricted to the functional but also include soft aspects. The findings on the impact of innovation on performance thus, to some degree at least, reflect the impacts of soft innovation.

In brief, past studies using this database have found profit performance to be related to at least thirty-seven factors including market share, product quality, R&D expenditures, marketing expenditures, investment intensity, and corporate diversity. These factors included in a profit-level equation are reported to have explained close to 80 per cent of the variations in profit-ability among businesses in the PIMS database. In a review of PIMS-based research, Buzzell (2004) reports a consistently strong, positive association between quality and profitability. Quality may not exactly be the same as soft innovation but is close. Using structural equation modelling, Phillips et al. (1983) show that quality improvements lead to gains in market share as well as higher selling prices, while Hildebrandt and Buzzell (1991) show that quality improvement is the single most important source of gains in market share, which in turn favourably affects prices and various costs and, ultimately, profitability. Using an autoregressive model Jacobsen and Aaker (1987) explore year-to-year changes in returns on investment and similar relationships were observed.

Clayton and Carroll (1994), using pre-tax, pre-interest return on capital employed (ROCE) as a measure of profitability at the business unit level find a range of statistically significant 'drivers' of financial performance including relative quality (the strength of customer preference for goods and services), holding patents or proprietary know-how, and innovation, measured as the importance of new products in the revenue stream of a business compared to competitors. Innovation is equally powerful as a determinant of the ability of businesses to grow market share.

Although there is only weak direct correlation between R&D input and business growth, there are clear statistical links, inter alia, between R&D effort, the 'amount' of innovation achieved, and the creation of intellectual property (IP) advantages through patents or exclusive know-how; speed to market, and the success businesses have in maintaining high rates of innovation – that is a high proportion of new products in their sales mix; and innovation, IP, and the ability of businesses to achieve customer quality preference for their products and services. In Clayton (2003) the PIMS database was used specifically to look at firms in the service sector with similar findings. This may well be further confirmation that the results will also apply to soft innovation.

11.4.5 *Other evidence*

There is also some, apparently limited, literature from fields other than economics that has looked somewhat more systematically at the impact of aesthetic or design upon firm performance. Swan et al. (2005) argue that, from a global perspective, firms find it advantageous to develop products that visually communicate and appeal to a wide range of users and cite Yamamoto and Lambert (1994) who found that portraying a quality image and product integrity through pleasing aesthetics influences consumer product evaluation, even if the appearance has no bearing on the functional performance of the product. This highlights the value of capabilities that promote aesthetic semantics, that is visually communicate positive attributes about the product and the consumer, as well as inform consumers how to use the product, that is informative semantics. They also argue that a distinctive aesthetic capability can result in a competitive advantage. Although the aesthetic attributes of a product may be imitated, other more tacit aesthetic factors can sustain the competitive advantage. Bayus and Putsis (1999) look at product proliferation per se. Their empirical results for the personal computer industry over the period 1981–92 demonstrate that product proliferation has a negative impact upon net market share, that is any advantages from product innovation come from the characteristics of the product rather than purely from the number on the market. It has not, however, been possible to locate a wide-ranging survey of the impact of product aesthetics on firm performance.

11.5 The impact of soft innovation: a critical overview

It is obvious that there is a very large literature that theoretically suggests that innovation will have positive impacts upon the performance of innovating firms. There is less of it, but some literature that suggests that non-innovators will suffer from the innovation of others. These findings are sourced from many different modelling and even different disciplinary backgrounds. In most cases there is also considerable empirical support for these predictions. This is not to say of course that all innovations are successful, but instead to say that on an average innovation yields increases in productivity, profit, or growth. There is also literature to suggest how best to undertake innovation in order to generate positive benefits as opposed to being one of the many failures.

However, most of the literature, especially in economics, concentrates upon those measures of innovative behaviours that have dominated the literatures for so long. Thus there is a considerable body of results on the returns and impact of R&D and patents, which as we have previously argued reflect mainly product and process or functional innovation. Although there is less such emphasis in the management or marketing literatures the tendencies are still there.

It has been illustrated (in the Appendix 11.2) that there has been a small amount of work on organizational innovation, but when it comes to the soft innovations that are at the heart of this book the evidence is minimal. Although the arguments as to why innovation matters are the same, there is just no empirical evidence that is available for other types of innovations. It has been suggested that the impact of trademarks and design expenditures will give some insight. Although such literature is not large, it does suggest that design and trademarks yield, on average, positive returns, but these measures are not pure indicators of soft innovation. The literature on copyrights might be closer to suggesting whether soft innovation matters but there are difficulties in doing such work and empirical findings are sparse.

In the absence of any such body of work upon which to rely, this section considers whether the standard methods applied above can be usefully employed to look further at returns to soft innovation, and if not what else can be done. The key to any such discussion, as with most such issues, concerns the questions that one is trying to answer. It appears to be that the crucial question is 'What mean return on output, sales, or profitability, for example, will investment in soft innovation generate?'

It is not clear, however, that the standard techniques employed above actually answer this question. If one considers the production function or growth accounting approach, this answers the following question: 'Given current levels of innovative activity, what mean impact will an extra unit of innovation have on output (or profits or sales)?' In other words the technique provides an estimate of the mean marginal return to innovation. This is not necessarily the same as the mean of the average returns to innovation. An alternative way to express this view is that these techniques are primarily directed towards estimating marginal impacts, that is the impact of a little more innovation or a little less, and are not designed to make 0–1 comparisons in which one measures the performance of the firm with current innovation activity versus zero innovation activity. The analysis thus will only provide insight into the returns to innovation at the margin. For economists the marginal return is important, for that may be compared with marginal costs and decisions made as to whether to invest more or less in innovation. However, one should not read the results as estimates of the average return to innovation. If one wishes to estimate the mean average return to innovation, then different techniques will be required.

A second major problem with the above approaches is that in trying to answer what the impact of a little more or a little less innovation is, they are vague as to what is the counterfactual, that is what will happen in the absence of a little more or a little less. It seems to be that the counterfactual is often taken to be a continuation of the status quo. It is informative that if one considers Equation (11.4), which states that if capital and labour input do not change, in the absence of TFP growth output stays the same. Such an approach might in some cases be appropriate in marginal analysis but is probably not appropriate when looking at average returns. If one is seeking to evaluate the returns to an innovative project the appropriate method would seem to imply comparisons of returns with the project in place compared to returns in the absence of the project. However, returns in the absence of the project will not necessarily be the returns realized prior to undertaking the project. The counterfactual may involve other firms innovating and reducing returns, other shocks to the firm, or even investment in alternative projects.

The nature of the counterfactual may be particularly important when trying to evaluate the impact of soft innovations in some of the creative industries which produce products that are durables but which consumers will generally only purchase once. I am thinking here for example of books, CDs, and computer games. In these industries as time proceeds and the individual product variant is purchased the market for that variant gets smaller and smaller. In the absence of innovation the market may become saturated and sales and profitability will fall to zero. To employ a counterfactual that reflects a continuation of the status quo would be quite inappropriate. In fact, techniques that did employ such a counter-factual would considerably underestimate the impact of innovation upon firm performance. It may well therefore be the case that estimates above relating to soft innovation (although few in number) cast a negative bias upon the impact of soft innovation on firm performance.

The literature employing the approaches discussed above has also rec-ognized a number of other problems. These may encompass specific issues such as what estimation procedures are appropriate if markets are not competitive, directions of causality (see above), and international spill-overs. A major issue raised by Griliches (1995) is that over time much of the growth in output and productivity has taken place in what are labelled 'hard to measure' sectors and as such many of the results may not be reliable. Sectors may be hard to measure because the outputs are not marketed (e.g. government and health), the markets are imperfect (e.g. because of unregulated copying), the inputs are difficult to measure (IT services), or because innovation in inputs and outputs may not be properly reflected in empirical constructs employed. This latter effect may alternatively be seen as particular problems with the correct adjust-ment of prices for quality change and the resultant quality adjustment of output without which the results will be biased.

It would appear that soft innovation may well be concentrated in these hard-to-measure sectors. Thus, for example, the Intellectual Property Rights (IPR) regimes may not well protect soft innovations and thus their market sales will be poor estimates of their importance. Alternatively soft innovations may be important in service sectors where output is notoriously difficult to measure. Nevertheless, perhaps more than any-thing, soft innovations may not be taken account of in the quality adjust-ment of prices and as such measures of output and productivity will be biased. The most commonly employed methods in statistical offices to quality adjust price indices are either hedonic or chaining methods. Both attempt to provide measures of changes in prices over time for goods of a given 'quality'. In my experience, however, 'quality' in these exercises refers always to functional characteristics and not to aesthetic character-istics. Any soft innovation would thus not be reflected in the price indexes employed and in such circumstances any results will be biased.

Related to quality adjustment is the issue of vertical and horizontal product innovation. Implicitly, the standard approaches consider that product innovation is of the vertical type and that the new is (generally functionally) better than the old. As argued above, however, much product innovation will involve horizontal and not vertical differentiation, where the new may only be preferred by some. It is not at all clear that the standard models are capable of dealing with horizontal innovations. For them to do so would require that product price indexes reasonably quickly reflected changes in the product variant composition of total sales. It is not at all clear that official statistics do so.

11.6 The impact of soft innovation on firm performance: some examples

In the absence of many results related to the impact of soft innovation and also in the light of the issues raised in the last section, this section pro-vides, in a non-random way, some examples of returns to particular ex-amples of soft innovations. It should not be taken that these examples are typical, but they are chosen to illustrate the considerable returns that can be earned from soft innovation and, as such, illustrate that soft innovation can have considerable impacts on firm performance.

It has been observed in the literature that many innovations actually fail to make a return because they do not sell or they are technological failures or the costs and revenues just do not lead to a surplus. For example, according to Fredericks and McLaughlin (1992) 50 per cent of launched product innovations in the food industry are taken off the market in their first year, as they do not meet performance objectives. In a useful review McNamara, Weiss, and Wittkopp (2003) consider the relevant literature in the context of the food industry as to why this might be. Factors that they isolate as conducive to success include high quality of product development, synergy between R&D and marketing, and better products. It is not our intent to explore these determinants of success here to any great extent and the reader is thus referred to, for example, Hauser, Tellis and Griffin (2005). The point to make is that by looking at successes the material below is not claiming to measure typical returns.

11.6.1 *Films*

When first released, a new film is a horizontal innovation. The earnings of that film over its lifetime will reflect both the market value of that innovation and the impact upon the producing studio's revenues and profits. There are a number of lists of the world's top grossing films, few of which agree with any other. In Table 11.1 we reproduce one such list sourced from www.the-movie-times. The real advantage of this list is that it also provides some estimates of the movie budget and thus provides some (probably not

Table 11.1 Top grossing films

	Movie	Year	Budget (million)	World BO (million)
1	*Titanic*	1997	$200	$1,835.0
2	*LOTR: The Return of the King*	2003	$94	$1,129.2
3	*Pirates of the Caribbean: Dead Man's Chest*	2006	$225	$1,065.7
4	*Harry Potter and the Sorcerer's Stone*	2001	$130	$968.7
5	*Pirates of the Caribbean: At World's End*	2007	$200	$961.0
6	*Harry Potter and the Order of the Phoenix*	2007	$150	$938.5
7	*Star Wars: Episode I – The Phantom Menace*	1999	$110	$925.5
8	*The Lord of the Rings: The Two Towers*	2002	$94	$920.5
9	*Jurassic Park*	1993	$63	$920.0
10	*Shrek 2*	2004	$75	$912.0
11	*Harry Potter and the Goblet of Fire*	2005	$140	$892.2
12	*Spider-Man 3*	2007	$258	$890.9
13	*Harry Potter and the Chamber of Secrets*	2002	$100	$866.4
14	*The Lord of the Rings: The Fellowship of the Ring*	2001	$109	$860.7
15	*Finding Nemo*	2003	$94	$853.2
16	*Star Wars: Episode III*	2005	$115	$850.0
17	*Independence Day*	1996	$75	$813.1
18	*Spider-Man*	2002	$139	$806.7
19	*Star Wars*	1977	$11	$797.9
20	*Shrek the Third*	2007	$160	$794.6
21	*Harry Potter and the Prisoner of Azkaban*	2004	$130	$789.8
22	*Spider-Man 2*	2004	$200	$784.0
23	*The Lion King*	1994	–	$771.9
24	*The Da Vinci Code*	2006	$125	$758.2
25	*E.T.*	1982	–	$757.0

Source: www.the-movie-times.com/thrsdir/alltime.mv?adjusted + ByAG

Table 11.2 Revenues, Star Wars films

Rank	Rank in constant $	Change	Title	USA box office	Constant $
2	3	−1	*Star Wars*	$460,935,665	$1,472,637,907.35
23	14	9	*Star Wars: Episode V – The Empire Strikes Back*	$290,158,751	$681,123,828.64
19	18	1	*Star Wars: Episode VI – Return of the Jedi*	$309,125,409	$600,234,512.62
5	24	− 19	*Star Wars: Episode I – The Phantom Menace*	$431,065,444	$500,656,729.38
7	49	− 42	*Star Wars: Episode III – Revenge of the Sith*	$377,864,535	$377,864,535.00
18	58	− 40	*Star Wars: Episode II – Attack of the Clones*	$310,675,583	$334,059,766.67

Source: blogcritics.org/archives/2005/08/12/161245.php

very accurate) data on the contribution of each best-seller to profits. Revenue multiples of the highest grossing films are approaching ten times budgets.

Table 11.2 shows, from an alternative source, revenue in 2005 (in 2005 prices) from the Star Wars films. This illustrates that the impact of a concept can extend beyond a single innovation into a series of related innovations (line extension in marketing terms). The total revenue approaches $2.2 billion.

11.6.2 Books

As with films, a new book title upon launch is a soft horizontal innovation. Although Chapter 4 reports on the patterns of innovations in books there seems to be limited consistent data available on book revenues earned. However, a particularly outstanding phenomenon has been the Harry Potter books and the resulting spin-off in terms of films and computer games, etc. Indicative of the revenues and profits generated by the Harry Potter books is that *Forbes* magazine estimated the earnings of J. K. Rowling, the author in 2005, as £41 million (Dan Brown, author of *The Da Vinci Code*, generated £48 million). When typically the author only receives in royalties about 8–10 per cent of the revenues (sourced by The Author, September 1998) this suggests a huge total sales income. Bloomsbury, the publisher of Harry Potter series, stated (Sabbagh 2008) that sales in its children's division had increased 261 per cent to £98.2 million from £27.4 million in 2006, a year in which there was no new Harry Potter title. The company said that the 'main contributor' to the £70.8 million improvement was sales of *Harry Potter and the Deathly Hallows*.

11.6.3 *Budget air travel*

The third example is somewhat different – budget airlines. The budget airline concept involves passengers being provided with less space, less convenient airports, poorer in-flight catering, less flexibility, reduced baggage capacity, etc. compared to previous airline travel concepts. The aesthetic of the air travel experience (or the sensory experience) is reduced. This was a soft vertical product innovation, but an innovation reflecting a reduction in product quality. The success of the product resulted from the fact that the price was reduced by more than the quality (enabled by process innovations related to booking and turnaround times) which made the product attractive to many more potential flyers.

The obvious example of budget air travel is Easy Jet. The company was established on 18 October 1995 and started operations on 10 November 1995 with two aircrafts. By September 2006 its fleet of aircraft had grown to 122 aircraft and its network covered 262 routes and 74 airports in 21 countries. Passenger numbers were 33 million. In 2007 it had passenger revenue of £1,626 million and made a profit of £191.3 million before tax (source: www.easyjet.com).

11.6.4 *Plastic surgery*

Although plastic surgery or cosmetic surgery may be undertaken for many reasons, it seems to be completely acceptable to consider it as an aesthetic product for at least some customers. Product innovations in the sector can thus reasonably be called soft innovations. The US expenditures on cosmetic surgery and non-surgical procedures in 2004 was estimated at $9.4 billion. In the United Kingdom in 2004, the market was estimated to be £225 million, the number of procedures undertaken rose by 60 per cent compared to 2003 and 15,019 women underwent surgery. The global breast-implant market (which was the first sector of the market to take off in the United States) is estimated alone to be worth around $650 million per annum (www.moneyweek.com/file/2838/carving-out-a-profit-from-cosmetic-surgery). A particular innovation was the use of botulinum toxin (botox) which smoothes out wrinkles. On 15 April 2002, the FDA announced the approval of botulinum toxin type A (botox cosmetic) to temporarily improve the appearance of moderate-to-severe frown lines between the eyebrows (glabellar lines). California-based company Allergan reported sales of $705 million for Botox in 2004 – up 25 per cent from 2003. The shares of this company trade on a forward price-to-earnings (p/e) ration of twenty-six times.

11.6.5 *DVDs*

New pre-recorded DVDs are innovations similar to new films and new books. Profits from DVDs can be huge with studios getting $12 per disk sold (http://www.businessweek.com/magazine/content/05_28/b3942101. htm). The British Video Association, the industry trade association (see www.bva.org.uk), estimates that 248 million DVDs were sold in the United Kingdom in 2007 with the value of the DVD market being worth more than twice as much as the peak of £893 million achieved by VHS in 1998. Since DVD was launched, ten years ago, 50,000 titles have been released into the market. Examples that illustrate the potential returns to a successful DVD include:

In 2000 *Gladiator* was the first DVD to sell over 100,000 copies in one week. In 2001 the film sold a million copies.

In 2006 *Pirates of the Caribbean* became the fastest-selling DVD of all time, with 1.5 million copies sold in its first week of release.

In 2007 *Casino Royale* was the best-selling title of the year, with almost three million copies sold.

The *Shawshank Redemption* appeared in the best-selling title charts of both 1998 and 2008.

11.6.6 *Cirque du Soleil*

Cirque du Soleil is a major Quebec-based organization providing high-quality artistic entertainment. Although it started as a group of only twenty street performers in 1984, by 2008 the company had almost 4,000 employees from over forty different countries, including 1,000 artists. Its declared mission is to invoke the imagination, provoke the senses, and evoke the emotions of people around the world. It is thus very much an examplar of soft innovation. In 2008, Cirque du Soleil will present eighteen shows simultaneously throughout the world. Close to 80 million spectators have seen a Cirque du Soleil show since 1984 and close to 10 million people saw a Cirque du Soleil show in 2007. Cirque du Soleil has not received any grants from the public or private sectors since 1992. Estimated annual revenue exceeded US$600 million (cirquedusoleil.com).

11.6.7 *The Eden Project*

The Eden Project is a charitable large-scale environmental complex located in Cornwall in a reclaimed china clay pit. The complex comprises a number of domes that house plant species from around the world, with each emulating a natural biome. It describes itself as

a project which successfully combines ecology, horticulture, science, art and architecture. It provides an informative and enjoyable experience while promoting ways to maintain a sustainable future in terms of human global dependence on plants and trees. The exhibits include over one hundred thousand plants representing five thousand species from many of the climate zones of the world.

The project opened to the public on 17 March 2001, and has experienced a total capital investment of £140 million. The Eden Annual Review 2006/7 reports annual visitor numbers of just under 1.2 million and visitor admissions revenue of £8.7 million in 2006/7 with total visitor revenue of £16.09 million.

11.6.8 *The London Eye*

Like the Eden Project the London Eye (see www.londoneye.com) offers a sensory experience and may thus be considered a soft innovation. The London Eye is essentially a Ferris wheel in the centre of London, offering views up to forty kilometres in all directions. It opened in March 2000. British Airways was the main sponsor of the London Eye until February 2008 and up until November 2005 were joint shareholders with Marks Barfield Architects and The Tussauds Group. The London Eye is the United Kingdom's most popular paid-for visitor attraction, visited by over 3.5 million people every year.

In 2004 revenue was £38.6 million, an increase of 5 per cent over 2003. In November 2005 British Airways sold its stake in the London Eye to The Tussauds Group for £95 million, with the new owner also assuming the £175 million debt the Eye owed the airline. It is now part of the Blackstone Group.

11.7 Conclusions

This chapter has explored the impact of soft innovation on firm performance. Despite considerable theoretical and empirical evidence that the more traditional types of innovation matter to firm performance in terms of profits, value added, sales, etc. there is little existing evidence to reflect the importance of soft innovation. Attempts were made to interpret some of the evidence relating, inter alia, to the impact of copyrights, trademarks, and designs as reflecting, at least in part, the impact of soft innovation. These exercises indicate that soft innovation does yield positive pay-offs to firms, but there is considerable doubt as to whether the existing methods will give a true picture of that impact.

Using some high-profile examples it was also illustrated how soft innovation can and has yielded significant returns. The examples are neither randomly chosen nor definitive. They do, however, exemplify that soft innovation can be an important contributor to firm performance. Thus, just as it has been shown above that soft innovation is widespread and extensive, although generally ignored in the analysis of innovation, it has now been shown that soft innovation can generate significant returns. These arguments reinforce the view that soft innovation merits more attention both in terms of analysis and in terms of policy.

The positive pay-off to soft innovation may also throw some doubt upon the validity of analyses of pay-offs that concentrate upon TPP innovation alone. In such studies, if soft innovation is excluded or ignored, the pay-offs to such innovation will be attributed to TPP innovation and the estimates will be biased as a result.

PRODUCTIVITY, R&D, AND PATENTS: AN EMPIRICAL OVERVIEW[3]

There is now a very large amount of literature that attempts to measure the impact of R&D on firm productivity. One can divide past econometric studies into two categories: those that estimate the effect of R&D spending on output or productivity (production function studies) and those that estimate the effect on production costs (cost function studies). Studies that use the production function approach, more prevalent in the empirical literature, have at least two variants: cross-sectional studies, which examine the levels of variables in different firms or industries at a single point in time; and time-series studies, which consider changes in variables over time. The best-regarded results are those based on panel data (time series of cross sections) at the firm level.

The earliest research to examine the impact of R&D on productivity centred on individual industries within manufacturing, and especially in agriculture, used cross-sectional data and generally found that R&D had a positive and significant effect on productivity growth in the sector being examined (e.g. Mansfield [1965]; Minasian [1969], and Griliches [1973]). Later studies included more industries, more firms in a single industry, or more firms in more industries, although mainly in the manufacturing sector, typically with use of cross-sectional data in an equation, such as Equation (11.3) above. Generally the results confirmed the role of R&D as a significant contributor to differences in productivity levels across firms (examples include Griliches [1980, 1986], Schankerman [1981], Cuneo and Mairesse [1984], Griliches and Mairesse [1984], and Jaffe [1986]).

Cross-sectional studies have also analysed how R&D impacts upon growth rates. Using data for individual firms, estimates of the R&D elasticity vary, depending on the sample, from about 0.05 to 0.60, with central estimates from about 0.10 to 0.20 (Griliches 1988; Mairesse and Sassenou 1991. The elasticity estimates are, by and large, statistically significant. Estimates of the elasticity with respect to R&D using time-series data are generally much lower and often the coefficients are not significant (see Mairesse and Sassenou [1991] and Hall and Mairesse [1995]). In a statistical

---

[3] As part of his doctoral research and under my supervision Amid Mourani has surveyed this literature, and it is upon his survey that this appendix relies.

sense, that result is not surprising since the R&D data has much more variation in the cross-sectional dimension than in the time-series dimension.

It is also commonly found that disparities in the measured impact of R&D are greater across industries than the differences across firms in the same industry or across the same industries in different countries. Allowing for this generally reduces the estimated rate of return to R&D and thus its significance. In particular, several studies have found that R&D performed in 'scientific' or 'research-intensive' industries (such as chemicals, pharmaceuticals, computers, and electronics) produces higher returns than R&D carried out in other manufacturing sectors (see Griliches [1984], Odagiri [1983], Cuneo and Mairesse [1984], Griliches and Mairesse [1984], Englander et al. [1988], Hall [1993a], and Wang and Tsai [2003]). Although the elasticity of R&D is generally positive and significant for scientific firms, it is generally smaller and often statistically insignificant for non-scientific firms. The same is true for the rate of return to R&D investment.

Overall these studies reach the conclusion that R&D does matter, that it impacts on productivity and productivity growth and that the estimated elasticity of output with respect to R&D varies from about from 3 to 56 per cent. Despite this we do have a remaining concern that the literature has not adequately resolved the directions of causality in the models tested. In particular, does R&D affect firm performance or is firm performance the determinant of R&D? Baumol and Wolff (1983) tackled causality in terms of a two-way relationship between productivity growth and the scale of R&D activity and showed that while the scale of R&D activity affects the rate of growth of productivity in manufacturing, that rate of growth, in turn, affects the relative cost of R&D and, hence, its demand. Mairesse et al. (1999), using panel data for French, Japanese, and US scientific firms, investigate the causal relationship of cash indicators (sales and cash flow) with investment and R&D across the three countries. Using a final sample of 156 firms for France, 221 firms for Japan, and 204 firms for the United States, they show that the cash-flow coefficient in the R&D regression is strongly positive in the United States and very small in the other countries, thus suggesting that future R&D is highly dependant on past cash flow in the US economy. Conversely, the impact of R&D on future cash flow is almost nil in Japan and much higher in the United States and France. There is only evidence for strong bivariate causality in the US scientific sector. Considering total sales, the results suggest that in each country future R&D is highly dependant on past sales, although in the US economy the coefficient is larger. Evidence for the impact of past R&D on future sales is more controversial, as the impact is positive and significant (although small) only in the United States, whereas it is negative (and small) in France, and non-significant in Japan.

Rouvinen (2002) explores Granger causality between R&D and productivity using an unbalanced panel data based on fourteen industries in twelve OECD countries. He concludes that R&D Granger causes TFP, but not vice versa, and that the potency of R&D also varies in timing and magnitude. Frantzen (2003) analysed the causality between productivity and domestic and foreign R&D using panel data on twenty-two manufacturing sectors in fourteen OECD countries during the period 1972–94. His results show that, although there are feedbacks, both on average and in a clear majority of sectors, the causation runs mainly from the R&D variables to TFP rather than the other way around. Lööf and Heshmati (2004) examine the interaction between sets of financial indicators represented by investments in R&D and tangible capital on a set of performance variables including sales, value added, profit, cash flow, capital structure and employment in R&D, and physical capital investments. Empirical results are based on a large panel data set of Swedish manufacturing firms over the period 1992–2000. Their results show a large and highly significant causal influence from sales to R&D but not the reverse causality. The feedback from profit on R&D is mostly positive, however only weakly significant or insignificant. The causal relationship between employment and R&D turned out to be fragile and insignificant. Reeves and Smith (2006) use industry-level data to investigate the relationship between R&D and productivity in the United Kingdom. They use a Cobb–Douglas approach and find that R&D boosts TFP growth at the industry level and that R&D increases TFP growth in some industries.

The literature using patent measures of innovation is somewhat thinner than that using R&D measures. Greenhalgh and Rogers (2007) have reviewed the literature of the impact of patents on productivity in firms. They report that, building upon early work by Griliches (1984) in the United States, Bloom and Van Reenen (2002) employ a database of over 200 UK firms for the period 1968–96, and using both simple patent counts and patents weighted by citations measure a significant and positive effect of patents on TFP (as measured by a real sales variable), implying that TFP will rise 3 per cent if total patent stocks are doubled. Greenhalgh and Longland (2005) use a larger UK panel database for 1986–94 period and relate firms' net output (measured by value added) to the number of new patents registered in three geographical domains, the United Kingdom, European Union, and United States, and by trademarks registered in the United Kingdom. They find that firms that register trademarks and patents, and who carry out R&D, are more productive; however, the immediate productivity benefits appear to be fairly short-lived. Cross-section analysis indicates that differences in productivity are associated with the presence of R&D and IP activity in both high- and low-tech firms, and firms which do not participate in any of these innovative activities are persistent laggards. They suggest that firms need to continually renew their intangible assets stocks to improve both their production technology and product offering. This result is claimed to be similar to conclusions of survey work on US firms in the high-tech semiconductor industry by Hall and Zeidonis (2001).

PROFITABILITY, R&D, PATENTS, AND DIFFUSION: THE EMPIRICAL EVIDENCE

There are a large number of empirical studies on profitability and innovation that are potentially worth mentioning.[4] Existing studies use various different measures of innovation and profitability. For example some studies have looked at equity values (e.g. Zantout and Tsetsekos [1994]), whereas others have addressed R&D effects on profitability more directly (e.g. Jaffe [1986], Megna and Mueller [1991], and Geroski et al. [1993] among many others).

It is generally found that the market value of a manufacturing firm in the United States is strongly related to its knowledge assets as partly conveyed by the usual R&D measure, although according to Hall (1993) the relative valuation of R&D assets declined in the United States during the 1980s (but increased again in the mid-1990s; Hall [1998]). Zantout and Tsetsekos (1994) found that in addition to having a direct positive impact on the value of its own shares, a firm's announcements of new R&D projects also exert downward pressure on the share value of competitors.

Most papers find empirical evidence of a significant positive association between R&D (or patents, or innovations) and the accounting profit of the firm (see Geroski et al. [1993], Leiponen [2000], Holger [2001], Hanel and St-Pierre [2002], and Lööf and Heshmati [2005]). For example, Geroski et al. (1993) relate profit margins to market shares, industry concentration, import intensity, the interaction between sales and concentration and innovation using a panel of 721 large UK firms over the period 1972–83. Although they see a link between profitability and innovation, they cannot be sure of the direction of causality. Leiponen (2000) used a panel of 209 Finnish manufacturing firms over the period 1985–93 and generalized method of moments (GMM) to investigate the effects of education and innovation on profitability (net profit margins). The author finds positive effects on profitability. Hanel and St-Pierre (2002) employed a sample of 278 Canadian firms from the COMPUSTAT II database to link the profitability of sales of the firm to market share, the price elasticity of demand, the physical capital intensity of firm, the R&D capital intensity of firm (R&D Stock of Knowledge), and other variables. Their

---

[4] This appendix relies upon the work of two doctoral students of mine, Eleanora Bartolini and Amid Mourany.

results did not reject the hypothesis that R&D has a direct, positive effect on profitability.

Loof and Heshmati (2005) examined the interaction between investments in R&D and tangible capital and a number of performance variables including sales, value added, profit, cash flow, capital structure, and employment using a large panel data set of Swedish manufacturing firms over the period 1992–2000. Their results showed evidence of weak feedback effects from performance to investment.

From a managerial perspective, benchmark studies by Schmalensee (1985) and Rumelt (1991) show that industry effects do not matter significantly in explaining a firm's performance. Studies by Roberts (1999, 2001) and Hawawini, Subramanian, and Verdin (2002), addressing profit persistence and its determinants, emphasize that firm-specific effects explain a larger proportion of profitability than total industry effects. Geroski et al. (1993) obtained a result that the long-term effect of innovation on a firm's profitability is positive, significant, and insensitive to the estimation method used. That there are permanent differences between innovative and non-innovative firms due to specific skills accumulated by the former is also confirmed by Cefis and Ciccarelli (2005).

Roberts (1999) finds support for the expected relationship between high innovative propensity and sustained superior profitability, but no support for a link between persistence and the ability to avoid competition. Roberts (2001) develops a framework for firm-level profit persistence that embraces product innovation, competitor imitation, and the prospect that several product innovations may be embodied within a single firm. The author stresses the need for a shift from the firm level to the sub-firm level of analysis in the study of relations between innovation activity and profitability.

Although a number of studies have examined the relationship between productivity and R&D spillovers, few have examined the relation between R&D spillovers and profitability. Hanel and St-Pierre (2002) define different kinds of technological externalities and explore their effects on a firm's profitability. The effects of the knowledge spillover variable are found to be negative and significant, indicating that the potential positive effect of knowledge dissemination on profits may be counteracted by the negative effect of competition, which encourages other firms to imitate and to erode their rivals' profitability. However, the interaction between the knowledge spillover variable and the R&D variable is positive and significant, indicating that the returns to a firm's R&D is increased by the spillovers. This result is in accordance with Jaffe (1986) (see also Cohen and Levinthal [1989]). On the contrary, the market spillover variable has a positive effect on profitability, thus suggesting that a firm's performance may be directly affected by knowledge incorporated into capital goods.

In interpreting empirical results of the kind mentioned above there has been increasing focus on the causality direction of any relationship between firm performance and innovation. Cainelli, Evangelista, and Savona (2006) explore the relationship in services using a longitudinal firm-level data set. The results presented show that innovation is positively affected by past economic performance, and that innovation activities have a positive impact on both growth and productivity. Furthermore, productivity and innovation act as self-reinforcing mechanisms, which further boosts economic performance. Leiponen (2000) uses a panel of 209 Finnish manufacturing firms over the period 1985–93 and a GMM to investigate the effects of education and innovation on profitability (net profit margins). The author finds positive effects on profitability. Lööf and Heshmati (2006) use a panel of Swedish manufacturing firms between 1992 and 2000 in order to test for Granger Causality between R&D investment and financial performance variables, namely gross profits, cash flows, and sales. In addition, they try to assess whether the hypothesized relationship is transitory or permanent. They use two main sources of data: the first is the innovation survey (CIS) for the years 1996, 1998, and 2000, which contains information on firms' R&D activity during the period 1992–2000; the second is a panel covering the entire period and with data on R&D investments and other economic and financial variables at firm level. The results of the causality tests show, surprisingly, the lack of influence of both profitability on R&D investments, and of R&D on profitability. These results are also confirmed when the estimations are performed by firm size: The two-way relationship between R&D and profitability remains weak and insignificant for both small to medium-sized enterprises (SMEs) and large firms.

Battisti, Mourani, and Stoneman (2007), using a twelve-year panel on 650 large R&D performing firms in the United Kingdom, find significant results indicating that causality runs from R&D to TFP to profitability. Overall, the evidence suggests that there are links between R&D and the profitability of firms and it is reasonable to conclude that innovation impacts positively upon firm profitability. However the links are complex and not necessarily unidirectional.

The literature using patents as a measure of innovation is thinner. Greenhalgh and Rogers (2007) have reviewed that literature, and this section relies heavily upon that review. Initially looking at the impact of patents on the market value of firms as measure of present and future profitability impacts, Hall, Jaffe, and Trajtenberg (2005) use a sample of over 6,000 publicly traded manufacturing firms for the period 1965–95, and relate the value of the firm (defined as the value of equity plus debt) to the value of tangible and intangible assets proxied by a variable representing citation-weighted stocks of patents. It is found that the R&D stock is more closely correlated with market value than either patents or citations, but even after controlling for firms' R&D, the citation variable is associated with increased market value. Bloom and Van Reenen (2002) also examine the role that patents play in determining the market value of large UK firms. They find that patents positively affect market value and the effect is quicker than the effect on productivity measures. McGahan and Silverman (2006) also explore the impact of IPRs on rival firms. They find that positive spillover effects dominate negative market-stealing effects in the competition between rivals in the same industry.

Only a few studies have tried to analyse the relationship between profitability and the adoption of new technology. In my own previous work with various collaborators (see Stoneman [2002]) there is not only considerable evidence that technology adoption leads to increased profitability, but also evidence that the increase in profitability may also reflect synergies in the case of multiple technology adoption, and that adoption by one firm may have negative spillover (creative destruction) effects on other adopters and non-adopters. The effects may however decrease over time and as usage increases.

The above analysis concerns the general impact of innovation on firm performance, it being clear that what is largely in the mind of the researchers is innovation in the traditional functional sense (basically product and process innovation). Battisti and Stoneman (2007a) have also looked at the impact of organizational innovation upon firm performance. Using data from the fourth UK Community Innovation Survey they first find that there is considerable correlation between the use of technological and organizational innovations in the United Kingdom. Employing principle components analysis they split the UK population of firms into three clusters. The first cluster is made up of firms with only limited use of both technological and organizational innovations, the second cluster of firms with medium use of both, and the third with firms exhibiting high level of usage of both. Table A11.2.1 is indicative of the firms' own evaluation of the importance of innovation in the different clusters. There is a strong suggestion of the relevance of both technological and organizational innovation to firm performance.

Table A11.2.1 Inter-cluster distribution of the percentage of firms who ticked each of the four options (row %)

	Cluster			
	1	2	3	Total (firm count)
Turnover affected by the introduction of products new to market	9.1	35.4	55.5	100 (2,359)
Turnover affected by the introduction of products new to the enterprise	9.6	37.8	52.6	100 (3,182)
Turnover affected by the introduction of significantly improved products	8.6	36.7	54.7	100 (2,916)
Turnover affected by products unchanged or marginally modified	10.4	39.0	50.6	100 (4,189)

Source: Battisti and Stoneman (2007a)

12

Soft Innovation and Government Policy

12.1 Introduction

The objectives of this chapter are to explore the rationales for government intervention in the soft innovation process, the tools or instruments available for intervention, and the potential pay-offs to intervention. The means by which this objective is pursued is very similar to that used when discussing intervention in the process of TPP innovation. However, the emphases differ with the chapter being built to a considerable extent upon the findings in earlier chapters relating to the soft innovation process, normative outcomes, IPR, etc.

In the discussion of functional or TPP innovations the policy literature has tended to follow two main paths. The first path is built on the concept of market failures in the sense that it argues and explores whether markets fail to provide the appropriate private incentives to innovate and as a result there is (usually but not always) insufficient innovation taking place. If market failures are found, then intervention can be considered as a corrective action. The second main path pursued is the more political argument based on international comparisons. Here politicians tend to see innovation as good and thus more innovation as better, especially if their economy is low in the international innovation league tables. Such a political view may then lead to intervention to 'improve' performance. Clearly the two approaches provide different rationales and may also yield different prescriptions as to where intervention is necessary and what instruments are required.

The two approaches tend to come together in the literature on national systems of innovation. When market failure is discussed, the failure being considered is usually in the particular product market being considered. Thus, one might ask whether there is market failure in the provisions of, for example, a biotechnology product such that the private incentives to produce such a product are too small because there are problems in appropriating the potential profits to be gained from such investments. However, there are other markets in which firms operate, for example labour markets and capital markets. As discussed in Chapter 9, if the capital market does not provide risk capital, then innovation may be constrained to a welfare suboptimal level. Alternatively if there are insufficient skills being generated in the labour market, then this may also slow innovation. Problems in markets such as these tend to be considered as part of the institutional environment; the environment in discussions of innovations being called the national system of innovations (Nelson 1993). The market failure approach and the politician's approach both accept the importance of the system of innovation. They may, however, differ in their views as to whether, and if so why, the system of innovation is 'failing'.

Primarily taking a UK perspective, this chapter will consider both the market failure and the international comparisons justifications for policy in the soft as opposed to functional innovation context. The two policy approaches therefore concern: (*a*) Do markets operate sufficiently well in providing incentives to soft innovation and if not why not? (ii) Does the performance of the United Kingdom (or any other country) bear reasonable comparison with the performance of competing countries, and if not why? If the findings are negative, then policy instruments and their impact will be considered. Much of the argument on market failure will be built upon the analysis presented in earlier chapters.

There is a considerable literature on technology policy or innovation policy (see, e.g., Diederen et al. [1999] and Stoneman [1987, 1995]). Much of that literature tends to concentrate upon the R&D end of the innovation spectrum at the expense of the diffusion end and has also been primarily concerned with manufacturing rather than other sectors of the economy. NESTA (2008), however, points out that the service sector is now the largest in most economies and as such merits more attention (and goes on to provide a discussion of policy issues relating to the service sector). However, the prime concern here is policies with respect to soft innovation on which there is no specific policy literature. This chapter mainly, therefore, builds on the general rather than any specific literature (although a particular paper, Fathom [2007] on public-backed investment funds for the creative industries covers some similar grounds to this chapter).

12.2 Market failures

It has long been considered by economists that market failures are prevalent in the innovation process so that the private incentives to innovate may not well match the social incentives to innovate and as such government intervention can often be justified. There are a number of different lines in this argument but, pursuing the chapter structure used above, the analysis can start by looking at the incentives to soft innovate in the absence of risk and appropriability problems. From there diffusion will be considered, after which risk, appropriability, and IPR problems are introduced.

12.2.1 *Incentives to variety*

It was argued above that the nature of soft innovation is such that a preferred means of analysis is in models of markets with differentiated products. In such models the welfare issue is whether such markets provide too little or too great an incentive to product or variety proliferation. The different models have different normative predictions. In some scenarios expenditure on developing variety may be too low. In others it may be too great. In conjunction with the literature on TPP innovation this suggests that on this issue there is no general finding to be carried forward (see Chapter 7). The conclusion of Lancaster's (1990) survey is still a useful summary of the position:

There is much disagreement on an important policy issue – whether particular market structures produce more or less variety than is optimal. The conclusion in this regard varies from model to model, and in the more complex models, from situation to situation. A fair statement, however, is that most of the models predict that the monopolistic competition equilibrium will give more than optimal variety under most circumstances, and that protected monopoly will gives less variety than is optimal. There seems to be no clear cut answer to such a question as whether an oligopolistic structure of multiproduct firms, or a monopolist attempting to deter entry, will result in more or less than the optimal degree of variety.

As with many fields of economics, one is left in a position that says that there may be market failures but it all depends. It suggests that in some cases there may be a reason for government intervention on the grounds that there are insufficient incentives to variety, but the analysis has to be situation-specific and general recommendations are unlikely. If there are market failures, it still leaves open the issue of appropriate instruments. Most analysis would recommend taxes or subsidies to correct such market failures although the specificity required here may make this impractical. The effectiveness of taxes and subsidies as a means to stimulate soft innovation is considered below.

12.2.2 Spillovers, network effects, and externalities

Commonly market failure may result from spillovers, network effects, and externalities. Soft innovation is no exception. Spillovers may be across firms or between firms and consumers. In general, even with IPR, an innovating firm cannot appropriate the whole social benefit derived from its innovative activity. Thus, one firm may open up a market into which other firms follow, for example Star Wars created a market for science fiction films which was exploited by Battlestar Galactica. The fact that consumers may increase their consumer surplus from innovation is another clear example of this. Network effects may for example be factors such as how early releases on DVD stimulated the building up of a network of DVD rental outlets. Externalities is a general name for other such similar effects not encompassed by these examples, for example how one firm's determination of a standard may assist all future consumers in the choice of appropriate technology.

However spillovers, network effects, and externalities are only reasons for government intervention if they are not market intermediated. Their presence alone is not important. What matters is whether they drive a wedge between the social and private incentive to the inventor. Thus, for example, through increased future sales the firm may have sufficient incentive to develop and impose standards on the industry, or by exploiting the 'brand' the Star Wars producers had sufficient incentive to continue their series of films. The only externalities that matter are those that are not market intermediated. Thus, for example, if one firm's behaviour yields information to other firms, then that is a non-market intermediated externality that may need correction.

If there are non-intermediated spillovers and externalities of this kind, then there will be rationales for subsidy and/or tax incentives (see below) or in certain cases even institutional intervention by, for example, standards setting. Standards setting is, however, no simple matter and the reader is referred to David and Greenstein (1990) for fuller details.

12.2.3 The diffusion of soft innovation

The discussion in Chapter 8, drawing on both the general literature and a consideration of soft innovations, went beyond the usual statement that fastest is best and isolated a number of factors that may cause the diffusion path to differ from that which is welfare optimal. Market failure in the diffusion process can result from (*a*) common pool issues, (*b*) supply industry market structures, (*c*) mistaken expectations as to future technology improvement, (*d*) information spillovers, and (*e*) a lack of agreed technology standards.

Policies that are usually discussed in the diffusion context tend to be information provision and subsidy policies (see Stoneman and Diederen [1994], although rarely are these justified in terms of market failure. Although, in the presence of positive externalities from use, tax incentives or subsidies could be justified. Moreover, if information deficiencies and associated risk do limit diffusion to a suboptimal extent, then information provision policies may also be justified. However, it is clear that the actors in the economy may react to these policies in that, for example, in the face of subsidies, suppliers may increase prices and in the face of information provision suppliers may cut private provision. There may thus be forces at work that counteract the policy. Having said this, however, such arguments are usually only applied to functional innovation. They should also be applied to soft innovation.

There may also be reasons for interventions in standard setting for soft innovation. It has been noted, however, that such policies may be difficult to devise and perhaps ineffective (see David and Greenstein [1990]). First it could be that the path towards an inferior standard takes some time to be established before it is noticed that intervention is required, especially if there is no clear a priori picture of what is best, and, if realization is late, then it may be very difficult to overcome the inherited network externalities. In addition if the intervention creates widows and orphans left with standards that are no longer supported in the market, the popularity of decision makers may well be adversely affected.

12.2.4 *Risk, uncertainty, insurance, and missing markets*

In Chapter 9 a variety of issues surrounding missing (insurance) markets and the availability of finance for innovation were considered as market failures. The findings suggested that the innovative activity of small and medium enterprises (SMEs) especially in high-tech sectors is constrained by financial factors. There may thus be a case for government provision of finance for innovation and this is considered further below. However, it was also argued that there were some missing markets for the provision of high-risk capital and the correction of missing markets may also be considered as a policy tool.

Kaivanto and Stoneman (2007) consider a form of possible government-backed funding to support innovation, called Sales Contingent Claims (SCC)-backed finance, that offers firms a different risk–return profile compared with debt and equity instruments, may rank higher in the firms pecking order, does not require collateral, and will not entail loss of control – all characteristics that would make it attractive to many borrowers. Such finance offers loans for projects which are only repaid if the project is successful. Kaivanto and Stoneman (2007) show that SCC-backed finance is not generally available in the private market, especially to SMEs. There is a missing market problem as a result of the nature of the uncertainty faced by firms and moral hazard. High-tech SMEs undertaking innovation especially may face such uncertainty.

However, there are prior examples of governments offering SCC-based schemes for project-specific finance in a number of countries, often in the aerospace industry. These schemes tend to show that SCC-backed finance is attractive to innovators and moreover facilitates innovation. In addition, there is sufficient evidence from existing schemes that there is nothing inherently unworkable in SCC-based schemes and that obvious issues such as moral hazard, actions in the face of bankruptcy, and takeover can all be tackled successfully.

On the basis of the above, Kaivanto and Stoneman (2007) thus propose that, in order to further stimulate innovation and growth in the SME sector, governments could establish institutions to provide guarantees to underwrite the private provision of SCC-backed funding to existing SMEs. It is, however, noted that the situation where SCCs are most attractive to firms and also where there is least likely to be a market is where risks are greatest and/or there is a particular balance of idiosyncratic to systematic uncertainty. This implies that government involvement is more appropriate in some circumstances than in others. The argument is that any such scheme should therefore largely be confined to the high-risk sectors of the economy, these essentially being the high-tech sectors. The evidence also suggests that SMEs in higher-risk sectors are also the firms facing the greatest financial constraints. The Kaivanto and Stoneman (2007) proposition can easily be extended to cover soft innovations and in particular very risky projects in, for example, the film industry, which generally lie outside the activities usually being addressed in such discussions.

12.2.5 *Intellectual property rights*

Chapter 10 theoretically and empirically explored the justification and operation of four different institutional IPR mechanisms within the soft innovation context. Three of the mechanisms, copyrights, design rights, and trademarks are particularly applicable to soft innovation (as well as TPP innovations) but the fourth, patents, are not applicable to soft innovations.

The four mechanisms are not regarded widely to be of prime importance as a means to protect IP. In some circumstances there are other non-institutional means by which such property may be protected, for example secrecy and/or lead time. However, in cases where there is no excludability, the different mechanisms do offer some protection. It might even be that in certain circumstances the institutional mechanisms (from a social point of view) are to be preferred to market mechanisms because of the information that they reveal.

All IPR mechanisms work through providing a stimulus to creativity and innovation by providing the inventor with monopoly rights that may be exploited to yield a return. The cost, however, is that the use of the monopoly power means a cost to society equal to the monopoly welfare loss. The latter static inefficiency has to be traded off against the gain in dynamic efficiency. The trade off between social cost and private return is however not a simple one, and issues that have merited consideration include: (*a*) the standing-on-shoulders effect whereby, because institutional IPR mechanisms require revealing technological knowledge, one inventor's discoveries may provide the foundation for discoveries by others and, to the extent that this happens and the original inventor receives no reward for this, then there will be underinvestment in invention and discovery; (*b*) the mechanisms are of the winner-takes-all type which leads to common pool problems and although they may stimulate innovation they may stimulate it too much because of rent seeking; and (*c*) creative destruction arguments, which have been more extensively pursued in the new growth theory field, in case a new technology is introduced, part of the return to the innovator comes from a reduced return to the incumbent, and as society is not concerned with such allocative issues there may be over-incentive to innovate.

Although such issues as well as aspects of the breadth of protection have been addressed in the literature relating to the optimal life for IP, the picture on a theoretical level is by no means clear. On the empirical level there is some evidence that institutional protection does stimulate innovation, but there seems little that relates this to the social costs incurred.

The recent review of the IPR system in the United Kingdom, Gowers (2006), has looked at the operation of the system and generally gives it a clean bill of health. The common problem of the different mechanisms is, however, that enforcement is in the hands of the holder of the IPR and enforcement can be prohibitively expensive. The extent of protection offered may thus be limited. Gowers (2006) has already offered policy recommendations in this area and the UK government has promised action on enforcement (DCMS, 2008). The Department for Culture, Media and Sports, in reaction to Gowers (2006), set up a Creative Industries Forum on Intellectual Property in 2008.

12.2.6 Competition and monopoly

One of the long-standing arguments in the economics of innovation concerns whether market power stimulates or deters innovative behaviour. In other words does monopoly power act as a market failure? Clearly an answer to this can inform antitrust policy. However, it has been argued that either (*a*) the question is irrelevant in that market structure and innovations are determined simultaneously and neither is causal to the other; or (*b*) that given creative destruction, it is contestability of the market that matters and not the existing structure. Taking this further, from a creative destruction perspective, monopoly per se does not deter further innovation, only a lack of contestability does so. For the purposes of innovation policy, therefore, governments do not need to control monopolies. As long as the market is contestable, the economy will, given appropriate IPR mechanisms, generate its own incentives to further innovation and the eradication of any incumbent's monopoly.

Antitrust policy, the main thrust of which is to prevent abuses of dominant positions (as in Article 82 of the Treaty of Rome) and promote contestability would seem to be taking the appropriate policy stance. From this perspective, market power is the means by which the return that induces the innovation is generated and it is thus desirable. What is not desirable is that current market power should be used to prevent further innovation by limiting market contestability. Policy should worry less about current market positions and concentrate instead on ensuring contestability. However, although contestability yields a greater incentive to innovate, whether it will generate the social optimum will depend on the nature of competition in the invention-producing industry as well as, inter alia, the particular characteristics of the IPR schema in place.

12.2.7 *An overview of market failure issues*

The market failure approach suggests many reasons why, left unaided, markets may not generate welfare optima. These arguments are often quite standard in the field of product and process innovation but it has been argued here that they also apply to soft innovation and may be similarly used as justification for intervention in that process (although in addition attention has been drawn several times above to the link between soft innovation and product differentiation). However, often the outcomes in markets are very situation-specific and thus general policy recommendations are not immediately forthcoming. In fact where policies are suggested (e.g. tax incentives), these are either (*a*) the same policies as will be suggested by the international comparisons approach considered below; or (*b*) already in place to some degree (e.g. IPR mechanisms).

Fathom (2007) has also explored the possible role of market failure in the creative industries. They argue that the creative industries operate in an environment that involves, inter alia, increasing returns, information asymmetries, and large uncertainties that may generate 'market failure', causing restriction of the supply of capital to creative content producers. The issues are the same as above even if the emphases are different. They conclude, however, with a tentative finding that it is too early to determine that these market failures necessitate public intervention in the form of the backing of a dedicated fund for the industry.

12.3 International comparisons

The other ground by which government intervention in the innovation process is justified is in terms of international comparison. On the TPP side it is believed on the basis of the literature reviewed in Chapter 11 that TPP innovation yields considerable benefits in terms of wealth and prosperity and, as such, government would prefer higher rather than lower ranking in comparisons of international productivity and R&D. They will thus pursue policies to achieve this. The difference between this and the market failure argument is that this takes little note of the social costs of achieving any improvements.

In Chapter 11 it has also been shown that, although the picture is not fully clear, soft innovation can be an important contributor to firm performance and can generate significant returns. If soft innovation in the United Kingdom lags behind that in other countries, then there is a case for government intervention on these grounds.

The problem in undertaking international comparisons of soft innovation performance is the metric to be used. Throughout this volume the issue of what methods one might use to measure soft innovation has been addressed and has put some emphasis on trademarks, copyrights, and design rights. However, copyrights are not always recorded and are thus not particularly useful. Headcounts of trademarks and design rights are useful but, as stated before, they do not only measure soft innovation, they will also reflect some functional or TPP innovation. Even so, they are probably the best measures currently available. Such measures do not, however, reflect the diffusion of innovation and thus diffusion-related issues are put aside in this section.

In addition to the data in Chapter 3, Table 12.1 presents some data on trademark application filings in the offices of seven countries. These may have been filed by either a national or overseas resident. Similar data is represented graphically in Figure 12.1 for five countries. A particular problem with this data is time inconsistency arising from the introduction of the European trademarking system during the sample period.

There may be many arguments about the international comparability of such data. For example: Should one use the raw data or should one consider trademarks proportional to gross domestic product (GDP) or some other measure? Looking at absolute numbers, this data reflects the US dominance for most of the period and the decline of Japan (between 1990 and 2000 Japanese registrations fell while all others increased); however the most obvious feature is that from 2001 China took the lead in registering trademarks (with 85 per cent registered by residents) and since that time has been increasing that lead. There appear to be no obvious disparities to be seen in the data between the major European economies.

Table 12.2 presents some international data on registrations of industrial designs by countries. The data refers to 2000. Once again international

Table 12.1 Trademark applications filed, by country, 1990–2005

Country	1990	2000	2004	2005
France	95,091	111,792	73,654	8,602
Germany	–	97,337	74,197	80,091
Italy	–	58,999	7,950	8,833
Japan	171,726	145,834	135,979	135,990
Sweden	11,920	16,651	13,800	1,472
UK	39,632	85,578	35,564	36,998
US	127,346	292,464	248,406	264,510

Source: www.wipo.int

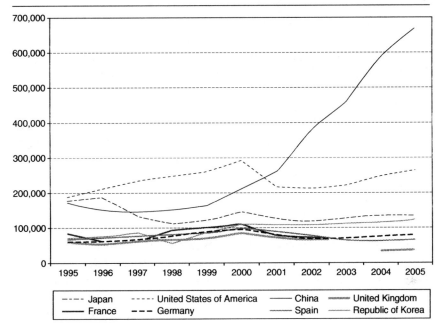

Figure 12.1 Total number of trademark application filings in eight trademark offices since 1995

Table 12.2 Registrations for industrial designs filed during 2000

Australia	4,255
Austria	5,092
Canada	3,416
China	50,120
Denmark	1,399
Finland	962
France	7,694
Germany	71,375
Hong Kong	2,898
Italy	2,429
Japan	38,496
Spain	3,644
Sweden	2,340
Switzerland	1,070
UK	9,380
USA	18,292

Source: www.wipo.int

comparability is not clear, nor is it clear whether such data should be taken relative to the size of the economy. The absolute data reveals that Germany, China, and Japan are the leaders, followed by the United States, the United Kingdom, and France. There are some irregular patterns for the European countries in 2004/5 which are attributed here to the introduction of online European design registration system.

Further international comparisons of this kind could be explored. Howkins (2001, p. 116) provides some useful international comparative data on the creative industries (using a definition that includes R&D, publishing, toys and games, and software within sector). See Table 12.3. The United Kingdom appears to have a relatively small presence. However, Hutton et al (2007), using OECD data argue (p. 40) that the United Kingdom is a world leader in the creative industries, with a greater share of GDP (approaching 6 per cent) coming from such industries than other nations. They also argue that UNESCO estimates suggest that the United Kingdom is the world's biggest exporter of cultural (a slightly different concept) goods. UNCTAD data, on the other hand, shows that the United Kingdom is only fourth in the ranking of top ten exporters of creative goods in 2005 (see Table 12.4).

Further indicators such as the number of Oscars won (comparable perhaps to Nobel Prizes), the number of Nobel Prizes for literature and even economics may also be indicative of soft innovation activity. Such

Table 12.3 International comparisons, creative industries, total sales (1999; $billions)

	Global	USA	UK
Advertising	45	20	8
Architecture	40	17	2
Art	9	4	3
Crafts	20	2	1
Design	140	50	27
Fashion	12	5	1
Film	57	17	3
Music	70	25	6
Performing arts	40	7	2
TV and radio	195	82	8
Video games	17	5	1
Publishing	506	137	16
R&D	545	243	21
Software	489	325	56
Toys and games	55	21	2
Total	2,240	960	157

Source: Howkins (2001 p. 116)

Table 12.4 Creative goods, top ten exporters among developed economies, 2005 (all creative industries and crafts)

Exporter	Value* (fob $million)	World (%) Total
World	335,494	100.00
Developed economies	196,109	58.45
Developing economies	136,231	40.61
Economies in transition	3,154	0.94
Italy	28,008	8.35
USA	25,544	7.61
Germany	24,763	7.38
UK	19,030	5.67
France	17,706	5.28
Canada	11,377	3.39
Belgium	9,343	2.78
Spain	9,138	2.72
Netherlands	7,250	2.16
Switzerland	6,053	1.80

Source: UNCTAD (2008) page 292.
* free on board

comparisons are all fraught with data difficulties and suffer in terms of data availability compared to the TPP field. Even so, the above data does not suggest that the United Kingdom cannot improve its performance and as such one might argue that intervention could be desirable.

12.3.1 *Barriers to innovation*

Even if one reads the international comparative data given above as indicating that intervention is desirable in order to speed up soft innovation in the United Kingdom, the international comparisons give no reasons as to why innovation in the United Kingdom is slower than elsewhere and thus no obvious guide for policy instruments. One way to approach an answer to why the patterns are as seen might be to look at the constraints that limit soft innovation in the United Kingdom. Some such data from the Community Innovation Survey (CIS) might be useful for this purpose – at least for comparison within Europe. There have now been several runs of the CIS in each of the European countries, and within these surveys are questions relating to barriers to innovation. Using such data is not, however, without problems. First, as it has been argued above, the CIS instrument, if strictly responded to according to the definitions, would not effectively reflect soft innovation activity. One has to either consider that soft and TPP innovation are limited by similar constraints or that, in answering the questions, respondents did not follow the guidelines strictly. There is, however, no suitable alternative data source. We thus use the CIS returns but consider the responses to be indicative rather than definitive. Second, most CIS responses involve self-identified constraints on innovation, the interpretation of which is not straightforward. A basic problem is that a reported constraint (such as, e.g., that the cost of capital is too high) may just be another way of saying that the demand curves for capital is downward sloping (as discussed in Canepa and Stoneman [2007]). Thus the constraint information is only indicative.

Data on barriers to innovation from the UK CIS 4 (also known as the 2005 UK Innovation Survey) is presented in Table 12.5. This data apparently reveals that high or medium important barriers to innovation primarily relate to risks, innovation costs, cost of finance, availability of finance, lack of qualified personnel, market domination, and uncertainty. This is a fairly wide list. However, this data relates to all sectors and thus includes functional as well as soft innovation. The DTI (2006) argue that the data also indicates that the creative industries rate most barriers higher than other industries, and although the barriers are ordered in the same way, lack of qualified personnel ranks higher than other industries.

Table 12.5 Ratings of constraints faced, percentage of all enterprises, CIS 4

	Not			
	Important	**Low**	**Medium**	**High**
Cost factors				
Excessive perceived economic risks	50	17	20	13
Direct innovation costs too high	51	15	20	15
Cost of finance	49	20	19	12
Availability of finance	52	22	15	11
Knowledge factors				
Lack of qualified personnel	50	23	19	8
Lack of info on technology	55	30	13	3
Lack of info on markets	55	29	13	3
Market factors				
Market dominated by established enterprises	52	21	18	9
Uncertain demand for innovative goods or services	52	21	19	8
Other factors				
Need to meet UK Government regulations	56	19	14	12
Need to meet EU regulations	60	18	12	10

Source: DTI (2006)

Table 12.6 Proportion of enterprises regarding potential barriers to innovation as 'high', UK Innovation Survey, 2007 (percentage of all respondents)

Size of enterprise (employees)	10–250	250+	All
Costs factors			
Direct innovation costs too high	10	12	10
Excessive perceived economic risk	8	10	8
Cost of finance	9	7	9
Availability of finance	7	6	7
Knowledge factors			
Lack of qualified personnel	6	4	6
Lack of information on markets	2	3	2
Lack of information on technology	2	2	2
Market factors			
Dominated by established enterprises	6	7	6
Uncertain demand	5	6	5
Other factors			
UK regulations	7	7	7
EU regulations	6	5	6

Source: Robson and Haigh (2008)

In the first findings from the 2007 UK Innovation Survey, see Table 12.6, although the data does not separate the large part of the sample that relates to the creative industry, the proportion of respondents who gave a high rating to each category of constraint is lower than in CIS4, but cost factors were still regarded as of major significance with market factors, regulations, and labour supply also being constraining. A quarter of non-innovators responded that the above-mentioned constraints were strong enough to stop them innovating, although the main reasons why firms did not innovate was that they considered it not necessary due to market-related conditions.

On the basis of these findings the sections below concentrate upon policies and instruments directed at cost and personnel factors with some limited comment upon market and other factors.

12.4 Policy instruments

12.4.1 *Tax incentives to soft innovation*

A major constraint to innovation as indicated by the CIS data is that the costs of innovation may be too high. A possible reaction to this is to provide tax incentives that will reduce the costs. It was also argued above that there may be market failures in the soft innovation process which mean that private returns to innovation may be too low, in which case tax incentives may again be called for. In most countries there are already systems in place that give preferential tax treatment to R&D spending and many countries are extending their R&D incentive schemes.[1] From April 2000 SMEs (and later larger companies also) in the United Kingdom were given a favourable tax treatment for R&D spending.[2] To qualify, that spending must either constitute an advance in the field and/or resolve scientific or technological uncertainty. Although the government made a number of changes to the R&D tax regime since its introduction in 2000, the rules largely exclude expenditures on soft innovation (i.e. design costs, the costs of making films, music, videos, games, etc.) that are the equivalent in the soft innovation process to the R&D expenditure on TPP innovation.[3] Such exclusion will not only not encourage soft innovation, but is also likely to bias firms' innovative activity away from soft innovation and towards R&D-based innovation. It has been shown that there is a social

[1] For example in France in the 2007 Finance Act their R&D credit was made of two components: a variation component equal to 40% of the differential in R&D-qualifying expenses between the year and the average of the two preceding years and a volume component equal to 10% of the qualifying R&D expenses of the year. The total of these two components was limited to €16 million ($23.6 million). From 2008 the R&D credit is enhanced in that the €16 million ($23.6 million) limitation is eliminated; the variation component is also eliminated, and the volume component raised to 30% of the qualifying R&D expenses of the year (up to €100 million of expenses, reduced to 5% over this threshold); if the company has R&D credits for the first time in a relevant year (e.g. 2008) or has not had R&D credits in the five years preceding the relevant year, the 30% rate will increase to 50% in the relevant year (e.g. 2008) and 40% in the following year (2009) provided that the company is not related to an entity which benefited from the credit system in any of these preceding five years.

[2] The R&D tax credits are now available to companies throughout the United Kingdom with further enhancements to the credits were announced in the 2007 Budget. R&D Tax Credits are the biggest single funding mechanism for business R&D provided by the government. The cost of support claimed increased from £0.4 billion in 2002/3 to £0.5 billion in 2003/4 and £0.6 billion in both 2004/5 and 2005/6. Of the total expenditure to date, expenses under the SME scheme totalled £1.01 billion and claims including cashback and tax deduction totalled £0.18 billion; total claims thus equated to about 18% of this expenditure. Expenditure under the large company scheme totalled £5.7 billion and claims £0.43 billion; claims equated to about 7.5% of this expenditure (www.berr.gov.uk/dius/innovation/randd/randd-tax-credits/page11350)

[3] For the purposes of the tax credit, R&D is defined as a project which seeks to, for example (a) extend overall knowledge or capability in a field of science or technology; or (b) create a process, material, device, product, or service which incorporates or represents an increase in overall knowledge or capability in a field of science or technology; or (c) make an appreciable improvement to an existing process, material, device, product, or service through scientific or technological changes; or (d) use science or technology to duplicate the effect of an existing process, material, device, product, or service in a new or appreciably improved way (e.g. a product which has exactly the same performance characteristics as existing models, but is built in a fundamentally different manner) and will be considered R&D for tax purposes *if* the project seeks to achieve an advance in overall knowledge or capability in a field of science or technology, not a company's own state of knowledge or capability alone (www.hmrc.gov.uk/randd).

return to soft innovation and thus such a bias is not desirable. An initial recommendation is thus to extend the favourable tax treatment of R&D to the soft innovation-related expenditures.

In fact some such subsidies already exist (e.g. with respect to film production). In the United Kingdom (www.hmrc.gov.uk/films/reforms.htm) from 2006 films with budgets of up to £20 million are entitled to government subsidies worth up to £4 million a film if the film is culturally British, intended to be shown in cinemas, and at least 25 per cent of the total qualifying production expenditure is incurred on filming activities which take place within the United Kingdom. The subsidies are paid directly to producers on completion, who receive a 50 per cent tax waiver on their production costs if the film makes a profit and 20 per cent of the budget if it does not. Ireland also has a (different) scheme to stimulate film production. It also has tax incentive schemes for artists (www.citizensinformation.ie/ . . . /tax/income-tax/exemption_from_income_tax_for_artists?).

Canoy et al. (2005) indicate that governments also intervene in the market for books through laws concerning prices of books, grants for authors and publishers, lower value-added tax, public libraries, and education in order to stimulate the diversity of books on offer, increase the density of retail outlets, and to promote reading. On the basis of a review of the different ways by which countries differ they suggest that there is in fact little need for government intervention.

The main issue is whether the incentives work. Hall and Van Reenen (2000) surveyed the econometric evidence on the effectiveness of fiscal incentives for R&D, describing the various systems previously operating in different OECD countries and their impact on the user cost of R&D. They conclude that a dollar in tax credit for R&D stimulates a dollar of additional R&D. Griffith et al. (2001) investigated the economic impact of the new UK R&D tax credit using existing econometric estimates of the tax–price elasticity of R&D, and the effect of R&D on productivity. They find that in the long run, the increase in GDP far outweighs the costs of the tax credit. The short-term effect is far smaller, with value added only exceeding cost if R&D grows at or below the rate of inflation.

Work on the impact of R&D tax credits continues. Koga (2003), for example, looks at the Japanese system and finds a positive effect. Lokshin and Mohnen (2007) examine the impact of the Dutch R&D fiscal incentive programme, known as WBSO, on R&D capital formation. An econometric model is estimated and they find evidence that the R&D incentive programme in the Netherlands has been effective in reducing the user cost of R&D and in stimulating firms' investment. There are also further studies for, for example, New Zealand (Sawyer 2004), the United States (Wu 2005), and Canada (Czarnitzki et al. 2004) that offer similar results. Although most such studies do see some small impact of the R&D incentives, none consider them an extension to soft innovation. Belief in a positive pay-off from use of such incentives to soft innovation must thus be considered as a matter of faith rather than certainty.

12.4.2 Project funding

Prior to the introduction of tax incentives to R&D in the United Kingdom much financial support for innovation was provided through funding for projects. Over time the move away from support for near market research and also the growing dissatisfaction with schemes that required civil servants to pick winners meant that such project funding is now a rarity. However, such policies are still worthy of consideration as a means to stimulate soft innovation when costs are too high or the project is too risky.

In fact policies of this kind to stimulate soft innovation are claimed to be already in place in the United Kingdom. In England, the Arts Council is the primary body investing in the Arts, and between 2006 and 2008 was to invest £1.1 billion of public money from the government and the National Lottery in supporting the Arts. The Council states that it is within its ambition that 'arts and creativity will continue to play a significant part in injecting innovation and enterprise into the economy' (www. artscouncil.org.uk) and the Council will contribute to developing and sustaining the creative economy by funding for risk investment in new work and new talent that stimulates connections between the subsidized and commercial creative industries; supporting arts education activities to foster creative thinking at all life stages; funding R&D linking arts with other aspects of the economy, such as industry and science; and investing in new business models, leadership development, and in partnerships to develop creative clusters and build regional prosperity and sustainable communities.

There may be a rationale for extending such schemes within the Arts. It also appears, however, that such schemes do not currently extend outside the Arts and the creative industries into, for example, industrial design and there may be some advantage therefore in extending current coverage. There is still, however, an issue as to whether such schemes work. There is only limited evidence on this. Busom (2000) shows in a sample of 154 Spanish R&D active firms in 1988 that public funding (totalling

39 per cent in aggregate of all R&D) did increase aggregate innovative effort, but in about 30 per cent of the sample complete crowding out of private funding could not be ruled out. Gorg and Strobl (2007) show that in a large sample of Irish manufacturing firms, in 1999–2002, for domestic firms small government grants served to increase private R&D expenditure, while too large a grant may crowd out private R&D spending; there is no impact on foreign-owned establishments. Using data on Israeli manufacturing firms in the 1990s Lach (2002) finds evidence that government subsidies stimulated the R&D of small firms but had a (non-significant) negative effect on the R&D of large firms. Aerts and Schmidt (2008), on the other hand, test whether public R&D subsidies crowd out private R&D investment in Flanders and Germany, using firm-level data from the Flemish and German part of the Community Innovation Surveys (CIS III and IV). The results clearly indicate that the crowding-out hypothesis can be rejected as funded firms are significantly more active in R&D than non-funded firms. Gonzalez and Pazo (2008) similarly cannot find crowding-out effects in Spanish data. Their main conclusions indicate the absence of 'crowding-out', either full or partial, between public and private spending and that some firms – mainly small and operating in low technology sectors – might not have engaged in R&D activities in the absence of subsidies.

12.4.3 *Finance for innovation*

Past discussion regarding financial barriers has tended to emphasize institutional heterogeneity across countries. It has often been pointed out that in the United Kingdom (and the United States) the market for corporate control encourages lack of trust, short termism, and short-term strategic reactions to adversity, whereas the more bank-based system in the rest of Europe and Japan encourages trust building between financiers and innovators over time, long-term arrangements, and a more long-term horizon especially in strategic decision making. One cannot necessarily say that one system is better than another. The systems are different (see Stoneman [2001]), but that difference may well impact upon the need for policy and/or the policies to be instituted. Thus, for example, much of the literature suggests that financial constraints are more important where there is a market for corporate control, and thus policies may be needed to counteract this. On the other hand, in bank-based systems there may be a conservative behavioural bias that may merit counteraction.

In the United Kingdom, the availability and cost of finance are considered in the CIS results to be major constraining factors to innovation. The

CIS surveys may be taken to indicate that firms feel constrained in their ability to raise finance for innovation and probably, therefore, for soft innovation. Most finance for investment in the United Kingdom comes from internal sources but the main concern is usually taken to be external sources of finance either being not available or being too expensive. For innovation activities external sources may include trade credit, new equity (including venture capital), and debt of varying duration with varying terms. There is no apparent cause why similar reasoning should not also encompass soft innovation.

Over the years, there have been many policy interventions intended to address the financial constraints that firms undertaking innovation have faced (especially SMEs). Those that are especially relevant are, in particular: (*a*) finance guarantees for SMEs, and (*b*) support for greater provision of venture capital. The purpose of both has been to make finance either cheaper or more readily available to SMEs. It would appear, however, that these schemes are already largely open to soft innovation.

The former schemes are exemplified by a scheme operated by the European Investment Fund where 'loan guarantees support enterprises with growth potential with up to 1,000 employees. Under this window, the EIF issues partial guarantees (directly or indirectly) to cover portfolios of loans'.[4] In the United Kingdom, the Small Firms Loan Guarantee Scheme provides lenders with a government guarantee against default in certain circumstances. The cost of the guarantee is 2 per cent per year on the outstanding amount of the loan, payable to Department of Business, Enterprise and Regulatory Reform (DBERR) quarterly. The main features and criteria of the scheme include: a guarantee to the lender covering 75 per cent of the loan amount, for which the borrower pays a 2 per cent premium on the outstanding balance of the loan; the ability to guarantee loans of up to £250,000, and with terms of between two and ten years; availability to qualifying UK businesses with an annual turnover of up to £5.6 million; available to businesses in most sectors and for most business purposes, although there are some restrictions (www.berr.gov.uk/bbf/enterprise-smes/info-business-owners/access-to-finance/sflg/page37607). Clearly this scheme is available for investment in soft innovation.

With regard to the latter (venture capital), both national and EU-wide initiatives have been implemented over a number of years to encourage the development of a larger early-stage venture capital industry and to boost the supply of venture capital (OECD 1997). In the United Kingdom

---

[4] http://www.eif.org/Attachments/productdocs/sme_gf_summary.pdf (page 1).

the government has established Regional Venture Capital Funds, an England-wide programme to provide risk capital finance in amounts up to £500,000 to SMEs which demonstrate growth potential. The government's intervention is designed to be the minimum necessary to stimulate private sector investors to provide small-scale risk finance for SMEs with growth potential (www.berr.gov.uk/ . . . /info-business-owners/access-to-finance/ regional-venture-capital-funds/page37596). Again this scheme is available for soft innovation.

A third form of intervention considered above on the grounds of market failure is in terms of launch aid for soft innovation and in particular the extension of a scheme such as that available for the aerospace industry to smaller firms pursuing soft innovation in risky sectors including the creative industries. This may be a policy gap that needs filling.

12.4.4 Labour markets

The CIS surveys suggest that the creative industries employ larger numbers of arts and science graduates and also are more constrained by the availability of skilled labour. This would suggest that labour market intervention might speed soft innovation. Labour markets tend not to be free markets in that they are often regulated and there is also considerable argument politically as to who should pay for education and/or training. There are then further arguments as to how the training should be directed – towards the general or towards the specific. One might well accept the argument that a greater availability of skilled labour would stimulate innovation but it is (a) not necessarily the case that the market will generate such an increase; and (b) not necessarily the case that the resulting downward pressure on wages will be welcome by the already qualified. In the current context the real policy lesson is that soft innovation is also important and, as such, education and training policies that are skewed towards the functional rather than the aesthetic are not necessarily to be preferred.

12.4.5 Product market factors

The CIS results indicate that market factors are a barrier to innovation. Interpretation of the responses is by no means obvious but to the extent that it has already been argued on other grounds that contestability in markets is to be encouraged, the arguments in favour of policies upon this line are to be reinforced. Georghiou (2007) particularly stresses the role of government as a buyer in product markets and the possible use of procurement strategies and influence in order to lead and encourage innovation. There may be only a limited extent to which government can be a buyer of soft innovation, but clearly in terms of buildings and architecture, advertising, public relations, health services, and many other areas there are many possibilities in this area. Some realization of the potential influence that purchasing patterns might have would be a useful beginning.

12.4.6 *Standards and regulations*

Regulations, either European Union- or United Kingdom-based, are singled out in the CIS survey as barriers to innovation. There is no reason why this should not also be relevant to soft innovation. There are many types of regulations with many rationales for their existence. The most relevant here are probably standards relating to compatibility. These we have discussed above. A fuller discussion of standard-setting problems can be found in David and Greenstein (1990), who argue that government regulatory bodies may have an interest in standards setting for many reasons, either because some government agency (*a*) holds authority to regulate the industry's firms; (*b*) perceives that the result of standardization activity affects important national goals, such as protecting domestic employment or maintaining defence capabilities; (*c*) concludes that voluntary industry-wide standardization activities have had an effect that is improperly stifling market competition. In addition, much of the research on network externalities and coordination problems has suggested that intervention by a central government can solve one or another externality problem. Arguments for central government intervention can also be based on the observation that adoption of a good with a network externality confers a public good on all subsequent adopters. Such justifications are as relevant to soft as to other innovations.

12.5 Arts and science

The arguments above regarding government intervention have been built on a view of soft innovation that values such activities because of the economic welfare (the sum of consumer and producer surplus) that they generate. This economic approach is not uncontentious, as has already been discussed in Chapter 2 to some degree when trying to resolve the issue of when a soft innovation is significant. Of particular importance is a set of views that value art more in terms of 'art for art's sake' and embody different values, beliefs, and foundations to those implicit or explicit above. The art for art's sake view is that art and aesthetic advances cannot be valued like margarine or washing powder, and that one can never measure the value of beauty or artistic achievement by price alone (and especially one cannot expect the market price to be a true valuation). Art is argued to have its own inherent aesthetic value.

Such a view may be used as a separate basis for policy intervention. Thus, for example, the Arts Council states its ambition to be (*www. artscouncil.org.uk*)

to put the arts at the heart of national life and people at the heart of the arts. Our aim is for everyone in the country to have the opportunity to develop a rich and varied artistic and creative life. We will ensure that more high quality work reaches a wider range of people – engaging them as both audience and participants. We will support artists and arts organisations to take creative risks and follow new opportunities.

This is not an economically driven agenda; rather it is a culturally driven agenda. The view is that cultural activity is the sign of a civilized society and, as the United Kingdom is a civilized society, the government should support art and, by implication, soft innovation. The intention here is not to argue with such approaches to validating policies. Instead, it is to be argued that, even if the driving forces for government investment in the arts is as just stated, it may well still be that the pay-offs are more than might have been intended. In order to do, some parallels are drawn with the literatures that (*a*) distinguish between science and technology, and (*b*) which try to value the output of science.

There is a considerable literature that attempts to distinguish between science and technology. A particular view is provided by Dasgupta and David (1994), which considers that science is an activity pursued by scientists in the search for self-gratification and peer esteem, whereas technology is an activity pursued for profits. Any individual may be a technologist one day and a scientist the next, depending on the driving forces behind current activities. A useful distinction in the soft innovation field between 'high art' (corresponding to science) and 'the rest' (corresponding to technology) may then lessen the argument between the economic approach to soft innovation and the 'art for art's sake' school. High art might be considered as driven similarly to how science is driven (i.e. by peer esteem and self-gratification) with incentives to innovate that are less financial and more personal. At the other end, profit and other economic incentives may be more important for, for example, 'the rest', design, 'low art', and industrial soft innovation.

Pursuing the analogy with science also leads to a further realization of the value of high art. Following the literature on the value of basic science, one could argue that there are other outputs from the high art process that might have value in addition to the embodied beauty or artistic achievement. The outputs from basic research commonly listed (see Salter and Martin [2001]) include:

1. Increases in the stock of useful knowledge.
2. The output of trained skilled graduates.
3. New scientific instrumentation and methodologies.
4. Improved networks and social interaction.
5. Increases in the capacity for scientific and technological problem solving.
6. The creation of new firms.

Such measures of the productivity of scientific activity allow it to be argued that the outputs from high art, although it is not driven by economic incentives, similarly include increases in the stock of (aesthetic) knowledge, skilled artists, methodologies, networks, capacity for problem solving, and new economic activities. Policies to stimulate high art and research and university activities in the arts may well thus pay off, for example, in terms of loosening up the labour market. Further pay-offs would include especially the output of information, knowledge, and foundations for future work. Clarification of the outputs from high art is thus of particular relevance if public support is to be discussed.[5]

In England the Arts Council is the primary body investing in the arts. The Council (www.artscouncil.org.uk) pursues an artistic-driven agenda (see above) but also states that 'arts and creativity will continue to play a significant part in injecting innovation and enterprise into the economy', and it will contribute to developing and sustaining the creative economy by funding for risk investment in new work and new talent that stimulates connections between the subsidized and commercial creative industries; supporting arts education activities to foster creative thinking at all life stages; funding R&D linking arts with other aspects of the economy, such

---

[5] A related issue is whether economic incentives are such that the market will support those ideas of greatest artistic merit and if it does not then this is a market failure. In our view it may or may not, probably not, but even if it does not this is not a problem of market failure in the sense normally considered by economists.

as industry and science; investing in new business models, leadership development, and in partnerships to develop creative clusters and build regional prosperity and sustainable communities.[6]

In the United Kingdom, the Arts and Humanities Research Council (AHRC) supports (university) research within a subject domain from traditional humanities subjects, such as history, modern languages, and English literature, to the creative and performing arts (www.ahrc.ac.uk). It funds research and postgraduate study within the United Kingdom's higher education institutions. In addition, on behalf of the Higher Education Funding Council for England, it provides funding for museums, galleries, and collections that are based in, or attached to, higher education institutions in England. It has an annual budget of more than £75 million, funding about 550–600 research awards and about 1,500 postgraduate awards.

The AHRC states four strategic aims: (*a*) to promote and support the production of world-class research in the arts and humanities; (*b*) to promote and support world-class postgraduate training designed to equip graduates for research or other professional careers; (*c*) to strengthen the impact of arts and humanities research by encouraging researchers to disseminate and transfer knowledge to other contexts where it makes a difference; and (*d*) to raise the profile of arts and humanities research and to be effective.

They also state that disseminating the knowledge and understanding generated by arts and humanities research is a key element of their mission, capturing business interactions, which are of importance to the arts and humanities research base, within broader knowledge engagement; knowledge transfer with a business and economic focus, as well as knowledge interaction with other audiences, including the public and voluntary sectors. It allows, for example, knowledge interaction with the museums and galleries and heritage sectors to be captured, as too is research that informs public policy and the enhancement of civil society; the potential for knowledge transfer in high-quality content derived from arts and humanities research for print, films, digital and broadcasting media, as well as experiencing the outcomes of research through contemporary exhibitions and performances. This broader definition thus encompasses public engagement and understanding.

---

[6] It is not clear, however, how any conflict between artistic importance and market relevance are to be solved.

Clearly such statements illustrate that the economic vale of basic research in the arts and humanities is realized but in such statements the weighting of the strengths of artistic and market forces is not clear.

12.6 Conclusions

This chapter has explored policy issues relating to soft innovation. Two complimentary approaches to the question have been taken. The first approach relied upon market failure as a guide to determining where policy may be needed. Building upon the chapters above, it is clear that the literature is not particularly definitive as to where intervention is desirable. There are a variety of results in the literature but they do not provide a clear overall picture.[7] Even so, some discussion was provided as to (*a*) the need for tax incentives to innovation, (*b*) the optimal design of antitrust policies, (*c*) correction for missing markets, (*d*) diffusion-related policies, and (*e*) changes to the intellectual property regime.

International comparative performance provided an alternative rationale for intervention. However, the selection of policy levers or instruments had to be based upon the results of a recent CIS survey which will not necessarily well reflect soft innovation. This led to the discussion of tax incentives, project funding, loan guarantee schemes, venture capital, and other schemes for financing soft innovation, labour market policies, and policies orientated towards standards and compatibility and also contestability in product markets.

Finally, the issue of the economic benefits arising from the 'art for art's sake' agenda was raised, it being argued that the pay-off to such activities may be valued in a way similar to how science may be valued.

The underlying theme throughout has been that soft innovation is important to the economy. This is not totally accepted in policy circles, although the recent Sainsbury Review of Science and Innovation in the United Kingdom (H. M. Treasury 2007) shows a growing realization of the importance of the closely related service sector: '[W]e need to understand better how innovation takes place in the very different industries which make up the services sector, so that the Departments for Innovation, Universities and Skills (DIUS) and for Business, Enterprise and Regulatory Reform (DBERR) can apply their current policy initiatives

---

[7] Fathom (2007) covers similar ground but without any resulting clear policy recommendation.

more effectively' (p. 5). Even with such emphasis, although some policies (e.g. the loan guarantee scheme and the regional venture capital schemes) may already apply to soft innovations, most other policies are not orientated towards (if they do not specifically exclude) soft innovation activities. For this there is no justification and policy changes ought to be put in place to reflect this. Recent policy initiatives in the United Kingdom, however (see DCMS [2008]), do not go far down this route. In addition to promised action on IP enforcement and a number of exploratory investigations and pilot studies, these recent initiatives just involve small sums of funding in support of collaborative R&D and some technology transfer networks.

In the presence of a wide and well-funded set of policies in support of TPP innovation, to not encourage soft innovation may not only deter potentially advantageous routes of growth and development in the economy, but also bias the transfer of resources away from soft innovation towards TPP innovation where the economy-wide pay-off may be less.

13

Conclusions and Future Prospects

13.1 Introduction

More than fifty years ago, Solow (1957) showed that the major determinant of changes in labour productivity in the US economy was not increases in factor inputs but, rather, an unexplained component that has generally been called technological change. The result has been refined over the years and extended to many other countries, but the finding that the main source of economic growth and prosperity is technological change or innovation continues to be a core finding. As a result there has grown a large, and still developing, academic literature addressing the issue of innovation and also growing policy concern in most economies regarding the stimulation of innovation in order to improve growth and efficiency.

To date, however, the main concept of innovation has primarily centred around the functional, scientific, or technological. This view is mostly incorporated in OECD manuals that are guiding the collection of data on innovation and are widely used internationally. Earlier work emphasized product and process (TPP) innovation in new goods, and then goods and services. The significance of new products and processes was to be judged on the basis of improvements in functionality. These definitions provided the foundations for considerable advances in our knowledge of the extent, nature, and drivers of innovation. Later amendments have introduced the concept of organizational innovation but only recently has this been studied in depth (see Battisti and Stoneman, [2009]).

The emphasis on functionality (and to some degree science and technology) has served the subject well. However, apart from some occasional papers here and there, another type of innovation which includes the artistic, formal (as in the contrast between form and function), or aesthetic, has been ignored in the mainstream literature, largely, it might seem, because such innovation is not encompassed by a definition based upon functionality. Here, that type of innovation has been called soft innovation and has been defined to encompass changes in goods and services that primarily impact upon sensory or intellectual perception and aesthetic appeal rather than functional performance.

Soft innovation mainly concerns product innovation and product differentiation. Emphasizing product differentiation allows that innovation may (*a*) involve changes that are horizontal in nature, and as such soft innovation may involve differences from the status quo and not just improvements, which is quite different from the standard approach where improvements in functionality would require any new product to be a vertical improvement; or (*b*) vertical in nature, but in the absence of a functionality requirement, instead of innovation requiring an improvement in quality as in the standard definition, soft innovation may involve reductions in quality rather than just improvements (if price also falls more than proportionately).

The emphasis on product differentiation also means that economic analysis designed for exploring (static) models in differentiated markets can be brought to bear upon dynamic questions related to innovation. Innovation in terms of new product launches in such markets may reflect either movements towards or changes in the equilibrium. Although models of vertical differentiation have been used to some degree in the past to look at innovation, this bringing together of two associated fields represents a step forward. In addition, the application of models of horizontal differentiation has to be new as previously the introduction of new goods that showed horizontal differentiation was not considered innovation.

Two main types of soft innovation are detailed: the first involving changes in products in the creative industries and the second involving changes in the aesthetic dimensions of products in other industries. Examples analysed include the launch of new books, recorded music, and games titles, for the former and the launch of new food, pharmaceutical, and financial services products as examples of the latter. Soft innovation includes marketing innovation as currently defined by the OECD, and it is also argued that it can be extended to encompass changes in product attributes such as brand image. Speculatively it was also suggested that the launch of new generic products may be soft innovations, although the literature has tended to consider these as imitations rather than innovations. Soft innovation is separate from and does not impinge upon organizational innovation.

In order to study soft innovation further, four main issues have been explored, these being the core of the economic analysis of innovation.

1. The measurement of the rate and extent of soft innovation.
2. The determinants of the rate and direction of soft innovation.
3. The impacts of soft innovation.
4. Policy, considering whether there is a rationale for government intervention in the soft innovation processes.

In the earlier chapters these issues have been considered in turn.

13.2 The extent of soft innovation

In a series of chapters looking at both the macro and micro levels several potential indicators of the extent of soft innovation were discussed. At the macro level the indicators included the numbers of creative employees in different sectors, the extent of design activity, and headcounts of registered trademarks. The difference between the latter and indicators of R&D spending was considered as potentially the most useful on account of both concept and data availability. The analysis of the data indicated that the extent of soft innovation in the creative and other industries was extensive and in terms of headcounts of employees probably greater that that indicated by measures of formal R&D activity. Indicators such as trademarks and the ratio of trademarks to patents suggest that soft innovative activity is also growing faster than TPP activity.

At the industrial level, whereas TPP innovation was concentrated in a few industrial sectors (mainly manufacturing and utilities), soft innovation was widely spread in the economy. This indicated firstly that most sectors revealed some innovative activity but this has not been obvious because soft innovation has not been studied. Secondly, the apparent balance in innovative effort between sectors is much more even than reliance upon measures of TPP innovation alone would suggest.

At the micro level, industry-specific indicators relating to the numbers of new product variants introduced were the preferred measure of soft innovation, with certain advantages relating to the identification of the rate of significant innovation being claimed for a specific measure that tracked the share of the sales of bestsellers that were recently introduced to the market. In the creative sectors where data was available on product launches this could be calculated for two of the three cases studied in depth. Outside the creative sector, where the separation of soft innovations from others was more difficult, other less clear indicators had to be used.

At the micro level, in the creative sector, the indicated rates of innovation were very high, with very considerable numbers of new titles being launched and rates of churn of the bestsellers in the studied markets being very fast, reflecting a pattern quite different to the usual suggestion that innovation occurs at a rate of about 2.5 per cent per annum (as measured by labour productivity growth). There was some suggestion that the rate of soft innovation as indicated by churn has been speeding up in some markets but not all. Outside the creative sector the measurement of soft innovation is hampered by data availability. Once again, however, it was possible to observe extensive soft innovation as reflected in new product launches that did not reflect changed functionality. This was especially prevalent in the food industry but also could be found in banking and pharmaceuticals. The study of generics in pharmaceuticals suggested that soft innovation activity may be the larger part of such activity in that industry. The data did not enable one to conclude whether the rate of soft innovation here was getting faster.

The data at different levels of aggregation therefore indicates that rates of soft innovation are high and that such innovation is widespread and extensive. It has thus been argued that the failure of the traditional literature to ignore such innovation causes much innovation activity in the economy to be missed. This is not to argue that TPP innovation is not important, for it is, both in itself and as a basis for much soft innovation. However, to concentrate solely on TPP innovation and to ignore soft innovation provides only a limited and biased picture of total innovative activity.

13.3 The determinants of the rate and direction of innovation

Although useful in many ways, the standard literature on the determinants of technological innovation has been found to not be completely suitable to the analysis of soft innovation. This is primarily due to (a) the fact that soft innovation is mainly concerned with the introduction of new product variants and thus models with differentiated products are most appropriate; and (b) partly to do with difficulties in conceptualizing, in the context of soft innovation, a basic component of standard models that relates the extent of any advance to expenditure on R&D.

The chapters above have considered innovation and diffusion in several different models with differentiated products. A number of different scenarios that reflect some of the characteristics of products that may embody soft innovation have been discussed. These include issues such as whether production and innovation coincide, whether the product is durable or not, whether the service flow requires hardware and software, and whether there are standards and compatibility issues. Of particular interest (because it fits the examples of books, recorded music, and video games) is the consideration of models where product variants are usually only bought once and continuation of the market requires continual launching of new variants.

Although demand (diffusion) and supply were considered separately, it was emphasized that the market outcome reflects the interaction of both and their separate treatment is just a matter of ease of analysis. Considerations of uncertainty (and optimal launch strategies) as well as appropriability and IPR were also undertaken. The several models provide predictions that are not easy to summarize; however, the list of factors shown to be important in the innovation process includes the level and particularly changes in costs of generating and developing innovations, fixed costs of production, variable production costs, the number of suppliers, uncertainty and reactions to it, rivalry and excludability, the institutional IPR environment, the allocation of buyers' preferences, buyers' knowledge bases, buyers' price and technology expectations, and the nature of the product.

A prime reason for undertaking such theoretical analysis is that in addition to indicating what matters and why, such models also enable predictions on whether unaided, free markets will generate a welfare optimal outcome. If not, then government intervention might be considered desirable. The theoretical analysis shows that, as with much analysis concerned with TPP innovation, there is no guarantee that free markets will produce a welfare optimal outcome. The outcome may involve either too much or too little innovation.

The market failure thus identified can come from a number of sources. One general source is that there are positive or negative externalities in the market that drive a wedge between private and social incentives. Other factors such as creative destruction effects and the standing-on-shoulders effects also have a role to play. Considerations of uncertainty (and optimal launch strategies) as well as appropriability and IPR extend such arguments to matters of missing markets and the need for, and effectiveness of, different means of protecting IPR. It was found that although it is generally argued that institutional mechanisms for protecting IPR are essential, this may not always be so. Moreover, in discussing appropriability and such rights it has to be realized that there is a trade off in welfare terms between the gains to free riders from unauthorized and unpaid-for copying and the profit gains to suppliers from protection.

Overall market failure in the soft innovation process was considered to be very plausible. However, it was less clear as to whether this meant the incentives were too great or too small.

13.4 The impacts of soft innovation

Throughout this volume it has been argued that the importance of a new soft innovation should be considered in terms of its impact upon economic welfare, this being made up of consumer and producer surplus. Although this is an approach that has been used in several US studies of particular (TPP) innovations it has not been common practice in the wider literature on TPP innovations where functional improvement has been the dominant characteristic.

In order to operationalize this approach in the micro-level studies, the impact of an innovation on economic welfare has been proxied by its sales or market share. It is, of course, realized that sales will also reflect prices and that is not taken account of in this approach but the alternative of estimating a fully specified demand system for each industry is beyond the resources available.

In addition, however, some attempt has been made to look in more detail at the impact of soft innovation on firm performance as a proxy for producer surplus. Again it was shown that the existing literature, not surprisingly, is dominated by TPP-based approaches. Although it was shown that such approaches can and have been applied to soft innovations using soft innovation proxies such as headcounts of trademarks, it was argued that such approaches are not ideal. Instead a number of successful soft innovations were presented as examples that show that soft innovation may stimulate firm performance and increase producer surplus.

13.5 Government policy

Given the potential benefits of soft innovation, it is natural to consider whether government can speed up or extend such activity. However, this is not necessarily desirable for welfare. The real issue concerns whether markets will or will not, unaided, produce the welfare optimal outcome.

The literature considered in Part II of the book shows that this question cannot be answered irrefutably in either direction. Market failure is thus not a strong ground on which to base policy intervention. Alternatively, international comparisons of soft innovation performance may be used by governments as a basis for policy. It is shown that the United Kingdom is not the international leader (although not a major laggard) in soft innovation. However, if intervention is to be based on relatively poor international performance, the problem is in getting a handle on why domestic performance is not good enough. Looking at returns of the Community Innovation Survey provides some insight into the barriers to innovations and may be argued to support certain policy interventions, but it is pointed out that the CIS may give an unclear picture of soft innovation activities. There is also only limited evidence on the potential effectiveness of policies. Some comments are also made on government support on the grounds of art for art's sake.

Even so, it has been argued that there may be a foundation for supporting several policies such as tax incentives, to soft innovation, government funding of soft innovation projects, government finance for soft innovation, labour market intervention, stimulating market contestability, and facilitating the setting of standards.

In the recent past, the UK policy (and that of many other countries) has associated innovation with science and technology and R&D and has devised policies aimed at these. This approach excludes consideration of soft innovation, although soft innovation is a major part of the innovation map. Policy now needs to be rebalanced to include the total of innovative activity and not just part.

13.6 Future research

At the end of a piece of work such as this it is traditional to discuss where research might go next. There are three main paths that seem obvious as ways forward. The first is more to do with promotion than research and encompasses the dissemination of the idea that soft innovation is important, extensive, capable of economic analysis, and merits considerably more attention than has been the case in the past. This, to a considerable extent, depends upon the second point which is that more data is needed to better measure soft innovation and its prevalence. This will require the development of new metrics. Thirdly, there are considerable possibilities for further analysis of soft innovation. This could involve further development of the link between models of product differentiation and innovation and further particular consideration of how to model the costs of developing new technologies. If there are advances on these three fronts, then (*a*) general knowledge of soft innovation in particular, and innovation as a whole will be improved; (*b*) our ability to measure, track, and internationally compare the soft innovation process will be enhanced; and (*c*) further progress may also be made in policy advice and intervention.

References

D. Acemoglu (2009), *Introduction to Modern Economic Growth*, Oxford: Princeton University Press and Oxford University Press.

R. Acharya and T. Zeisemer (1996), 'A closed economy model of horizontal and vertical product differentiation: The case of innovation in biotechnology', *Economics of Innovation and New Technology*, 4, 245–64.

K. Aerts and T. Schmidt (2008), 'Two for the price of one? Additionality effects of R&D subsidies: A comparison between Flanders and Germany', *Research Policy*, 37, 5, 806–22.

P. Aghion and P. Howitt (1992), 'A model of Growth through creative destruction', *Econometrica*, 60, 2, 323–51.

—— —— (1997), 'A Schumpeterian perspective on growth and competition', *in* D. M. Kreps and K. F. Wallis (eds.), *Advances in Economics and Econometrics: Theory and Applications*, Vol. 2, Cambridge University Press, pp. 279–317.

—— M. Dewatripont, and J. C. Stein (2005), *Academic Freedom, Private-Sector Focus, and the Process of Innovation*, NBER Working Paper No. W11542, August.

—— , T. Fally, and S. Scarpetta (2007), 'Credit constraints as a barrier to entry and post entry growth of firms', *Economic Policy*, 52, 731–72.

A. Alchian (1950), 'Uncertainty, evolution and economic theory', *Journal of Political Economy*, 58, 211–21.

A. Ali (1994), 'Pioneering versus incremental innovation: Review and research propositions', *Journal of Product Innovation Management*, 11, 1, 46–61.

H. H. Ali, S. Lecocq, and M. Visser (2008), 'The impact of gurus: Parker Grades and En Primeur wine prices', *Economic Journal*, 118, 529, F158–74.

American Bar Association (2007), *Intellectual Property and Antitrust Handbook*, Chicago, IL: ABA.

R. Andari, H. Bakhshi, W. Hutton, A. O'Keeffe, and P. Schneider (2007), *Staying Ahead, the Economic Performance of the UK's Creative Industries*, London: The Work Foundation.

C. Anderson (2006), *The Long Tail*, New York: Hyperion.

C. Antonelli (1997), 'The economics of path-dependence in industrial organization', *International Journal of Industrial Organization*, 15, 6, 643–75.

M. Armstrong (2006), 'Competition in two sided markets', *Rand Journal of Economics*, 37, 3, 668–91.

K. J. Arrow (1962*a*), 'Economic welfare and the allocation of resources for invention', *in* R. R. Nelson (ed.), *The Rate and Direction of Inventive Activity*, Princeton, NJ: Princeton University Press, pp. 609–25.

—— (1962*b*), 'The economic implications of learning by doing', *The Review of Economic Studies*, 29, 3, 155–73.

W. B. Arthur (1989), 'Competing technologies, increasing returns and lock-in by historical events', *Economic Journal*, 99, 106–31.

O. Ashenfelter (2008), 'Predicting the quality and prices of Bordeaux Wine', *Economic Journal*, 118, 529, F174–84.

J. S. Bain (1956), *Barriers to New Competition*, Cambridge, MA: Harvard University Press.

M. Baker and B. Cunningham (2006), 'Court decisions and equity markets: Estimating the value of copyright protection', *The Journal of Law and Economics*, 49, 567–96.

H. Bakhshi, E. McVittie, J. Simmie, et al. (2008), *Creating Innovation: Do the Creative Industries Support Innovation in the Wider Economy*, NESTA Research Report, February.

D. W. Barnes (2006), 'A new economics of trademark', *Northwestern Journal of Technology and Intellectual Property*, 5, 1, http://www.law.northwestern.edu/journals/njtip/v5/n1/2.

A. Barroso (2007), 'Advertising and consumer awareness of a new product', Job Market Paper, CEMFI, C/Casado del Alisal 5, 28014, Spain.

F. M. Bass (1969), 'A new product growth for model consumer durables', *Management Science*, 15, 5, 215–27.

P. Basu and A. Guariglia (2002), 'Liquidity constraints and firms investment return behaviour', *Economica*, 69, 563–82.

G. Battisti and P. Stoneman (2000), 'The role of regulation, fiscal incentives and changes in tastes in the diffusion of unleaded petrol in the UK', *Oxford Economic Papers*, 52, 2, 326–56.

—— —— (2007), 'How innovative are UK firms: The synergistic effects of innovations', presented at a CIS user's conference, DTI Innovation Conference 1/12/06, London: The British Academy.

—— —— (2009), 'How innovative are UK firms? Evidence from the CIS4 on the synergistic effects of innovations', *British Journal of Management*, 2009.

—— A. Mourani, and P. Stoneman (2007), *Devising a Methodology for an Innovation Scoreboard*, presented at an EU conference, Seville.

W. Baumol and E. N. Wolff (1983), 'Feedback from productivity growth to R&D', *Scandinavian Journal of Economics*, 85, 2, 147–57.

B. L. Bayus and W. P. Putsis (1999), 'Product proliferation: An empirical analysis of product line determinants and market outcomes', Available at SSRN: http://ssrn.com/abstract = 244098 or DOI: 10.2139/ssrn.244098.

J. Beath, Y. Katsoulacos, and D. Ulph (1995), 'Game theoretic approaches', *in* P. Stoneman (ed.), *Handbook of the Economics of Innovation and Technological Change*, Oxford: Blackwell Basil.

References

P. D. Bennett (ed.) (1995), *American Marketing Association Dictionary of Marketing Terms*, Second Edition, Lincolnwood, IL: NTC Business Books.

R. Bentley, C. P. Libo, H. A. Herzog, and M. W. Hahn (2007), 'Regular rates of popular culture change reflect random copying', *Evolution and Human Behavior*, 28, 151–8.

S. T. Berry and J. Waldfogel (2001), 'Do mergers increase product variety? Evidence from radio broadcasting', *The Quarterly Journal of Economics*, 116, 3, 1009–25.

—— J. Levinsohn, and A. Pakes (1993), 'Applications and limitations of some recent advances in empirical industrial organization: Price indexes and the analysis of environmental change', *American Economic Review Papers and Proceedings*, 83, 241–6.

D. Besanko and R. R. Braeutigam (2008), *Microeconomics*, Third Edition, New York: Wiley.

S. M. Besen and L. J. Raskind (1991), 'An introduction to the law and economics of intellectual property', *The Journal of Economic Perspectives*, 5, 1, 3–27.

J. Bessant, J. Whyte, and A. Neely (2005), *DTI Think Piece Management of Creativity and Design Within the Firm*, London: Advanced Institute for Management (AIM) and Imperial College.

J. Bessen and E. Maskin (2000), 'Sequential innovation, patents and imitation', Department of Economics WP no 00 = 01, Cambridge, MA: Massachusetts Institute of Technology.

B. Bianchi and F. Bartolotti (1996), *On the Concept of Formal Innovation*, European Regional Science Association, 36th European Congress, ETH, Zurich, August.

N. Bloom and J. Van Reenen (2002), 'Patents, real options and firm performance', *Economic Journal*, 112, C97–116.

S. Bond, H. Harhoff, and J. Van Reenen (1999), *Investment, R&D and Financial Constraints in Britain and Germany*, IFS Working Paper No. 99/5.

—— J. A. Elston, and J. B. Mairesse Mulkay (2003), 'Financial factors and investment in Belgium, France, Germany and the United Kingdom: A comparison using company panel data', *The Review of Economics and Statistics*, 85, 153–65.

A. Bowness (1989), *The Conditions of Success: How the Modern Artist Rises to Fame*, Walter Neurath Memorial Lectures, London: Thames and Hudson.

N. Bradley (2007), *Marketing Research, Tools and Techniques*, Oxford: Oxford University Press, 2007.

R. Brealey and S. Myers (2003), *Principles of Corporate Finance*, Seventh Edition, New York: McGraw-Hill.

T. F. Bresnahan (1986), 'Measuring spillovers from technical advance: Mainframe computers in financial services', *American Economic Review*, 76, 4, 742–55.

—— and R. J. Gordon (eds.), (1997), *The Economics of New Goods*, Chicago, IL: University of Chicago Press.

R. Brozen (1979), 'Antitrust and the theory of concentrated markets', *in Industrial Concentration and the Market System*, Chicago, IL: American Bar Association, pp. 90–120.

M. Bruce, S. Potter, and R. Roy (1995), 'The risks and rewards of design investment', *Journal of Marketing Management*, 11, 403–17.

E. Brynjolfsson (1995), 'The contribution of information technology to consumer welfare', *Information Systems Research*, 7, 3, 281–300.

—— Y. Hu and M. D. Smith (2003), 'Consumer surplus in the digital economy: Estimating the value of increased product variety at online booksellers, Paper 176, *Management Science*, 49, 11.

—— —— —— (2006), From niches to riches, anatomy of the long tail, *MIT Sloan Management Review*, 47, 4, 67–71.

—— —— and D. Simester (2007), 'Goodbye Pareto principle, hello long tail: The effect of search costs on the concentration of product sales', Available at SSRN: http://ssrn.com/abstract = 953587.

S. Bulli (2008), *Business Innovation Investment in the UK*, London: Department for Innovation Universities and Skills.

I. Busom (2000), 'Empirical evaluation of the effects of R&D subsidies', *Economics of Innovation and New Technology*, 9, 2, 111–48.

D. Buzzell (2004), 'The PIMS program of strategy research A retrospective appraisal', *Journal of Business Research*, 57, 5, 478–83.

G. Cainelli, R. Evangelista, and M. Savona (2006), 'Innovation and economic performance in services: A firm-level analysis', *Cambridge Journal of Economics*, 30, 435–58.

A. Canepa and P. Stoneman (2003), 'Financial constraints to innovation in the UK and other European countries: Evidence from CIS2 and CIS3', *CIS User Group Conference: Modelling Innovation*, London: DTI Conference Centre.

—— —— (2007), 'Financial constraints to innovation in the UK: evidence from CIS2 and CIS3', *Oxford Economic Papers*, Advance Access, published online on December 6, 2007, doi:10.1093/oep/gpm044.

—— —— (2005), 'Financing constraints in the inter firm diffusion of new process technologies', *The Journal of Technology Transfer*, 30, 2, 159–69.

M. Canoy, T. C. van Ours, and R. Van de Ploeg (2005), *The Economics of Books*, CESIFO, Working Paper No. 1414.

R. Cappetta, P. Cillo, and A. Ponti (2006), 'Convergent designs in fine fashion: An evolutionary model for stylistic innovation' *Research Policy*, 35, 9, 1273–90.

J. Carey (2005), *What Good Are the Arts ?* London: Faber and Faber.

R. Carpenter and B. C. Petersen (2002*a*), 'Is the growth of small firms constrained by internal finance?', *The Review of Economics and Statistics*, 84, 298–309.

—— —— (2002*b*), 'Capital market imperfections, high tech investments and new equity financing', *Economic Journal*, 112, F54–72.

J. P. Caulkins, R. F. Hartl, P. M. Kort, and G. Feichtinger (2007), 'Explaining fashion cycles: Imitators chasing innovators in product space', *Journal of Economic Dynamics and Control*, 31, 5, 1535–56.

R. Caves (2000), *Creative Industries, Contracts Between Art and Commerce*, Cambridge, MA: Harvard University Press.

References

E. Cefis and M. Ciccarelli (2005), 'Profit differentials and innovation', *Economics of Innovation and New Technology*, 14, 43–61.

D. C. Chisholm, M. S. Mcmillan, and G. Norman (2006), *Product differentiation and film programming choice: Do first-run movie theatres show the same films?* NBER Working Paper No. W12646.

J. P. Choi (1997), 'Herd behavior, the penguin effect and the suppression of informational diffusion: An analysis of informational externalities and payoff interdependency', *Rand Journal of Economics*, 28, 3, 407–25.

T. Clayton (2003), 'Service innovation – aiming to win from service innovation', *in* J. Tidd (ed.), *Organisational Responses to Technological Opportunities*, London: Imperial College Press 2003.

T. Clayton and C. Carroll (1994), 'Building business for Europe, evidence from Europe & North America on intangible, factors behind growth, competitiveness and jobs', Final report to the European Commission by PIMS Associates Ltd. and the Irish Management Institute.

M. T. Clements and H. Ohashi (2005), 'Indirect network effects and the product cycle: Video games in the US, 1994–2002', *Journal of Industrial Economics*, LIII, 4.

W. Cohen (1995), 'Empirical studies of innovative activity and performance' *in* P. Stoneman (ed.), *Handbook of the Economics of Innovation and Technological Change*, Oxford: Blackwell Basil.

W. Cohen and D. Levinthal (1989), 'Innovation and learning: The two faces of R&D', *The Economic Journal*, 99, 397, 569–96.

J. M. Connor (1981), 'Food product proliferation: A market structure analysis', *American Journal of Agricultural Economics*, 63, 4, 607–17.

F. Cornelli and M. Schankerman (1996), *Optimal Patent Renewals*, STICERD Suntory Discussion Paper No. EI/13, London School of Economics and Political Science.

T. Cowen (2000), *In Praise of Commercial Culture*, Cambridge, MA: Harvard University Press.

—— (2006), *Good and Plenty: The Creative Successes of American Arts Funding*, Princeton, NJ: Princeton University Press.

G. Cox (2006), *Cox Review of Creativity in Business: Building on the UK's Strengths*, HM Treasury, December (www.hm-treasury.gov.uk/cox).

P. Cuneo and J. Mairesse (1984), 'Productivity and R&D at the firm level in French manufacturing', *in* Z. Griliches (ed.), *R&D, Patents, and Productivity*, Chicago, IL: University of Chicago Press, pp. 375–92.

D. Czarnitzki, P. Hanel, and J. M. Rosa (2004), *Evaluating the Impact of R&D Tax Credits on Innovation: A Microeconometric Study on Canadian Firms*, ZEW Discussion Paper No. 04–77.

P. Dasgupta (1987), 'The economic theory of technology policy: An introduction' *in* P. Dasgupta and P. Stoneman (eds.), *Economic Policy and Technological Performance*, Cambridge: Cambridge University Press, pp. 7–23.

—— and P. Stoneman (eds.) (1987), *Economic Policy and Technological Performance*, Cambridge: Cambridge University Press.

P. Dasgupta and J, Stiglitz (1980), 'Industrial structure and the nature of innovative activity', *Economic Journal*, v, 90, no, 358, 1980, pp. 266–93.

—— and D. A. Paul (1994), 'Toward a new economics of science', *Research Policy*, 23, 5, 487–521.

P. David, and T. Olsen (1986), 'Equilibrium dynamics of diffusion when incremental technological innovations are foreseen', *Ricerche Economiche*, 40, 4, 738–70.

—— and S. Greenstein (1990), The economics of compatibility of standards: A survey, *Economics of Innovation and New Technology*, 1, 3–41.

S. Davies (1979), *The Diffusion of Process Innovations*, Cambridge: Cambridge University Press.

H. Demsetz (1973), 'Industry structure, market rivalry and public policy', *Journal of Law and Economics*, 16, 1–9.

V. Denicolo (2007), 'Do patents over compensate innovators', *Economic Policy*, 52, 679–713.

Department of Culture Media and Sports (2006), *Creative Industries Economic Estimates Statistical Bulletin*, September, London: DCMS.

—— (2008), *Creative Britain: New Talents for the New Economy*, London: DCMS.

Department of Trade and Industry (2005), *Creativity, Design and Business Performance*, DTI Economics Papers, No. 15, November, London: DTI.

—— (2006), *Innovation in the UK: Indicators and Insights*, Occasional Paper No. 6, July, London: DTI.

Design Council (2005*a*), *Design in Britain, 2004–2005*, London.

Design Council (2005*b*), *Design Index: The Impact of Design on Stock Market Performance*, London.

P. Diederen, P. Stoneman, O. Toivanen, and A. Wolters (1999), *Innovation and Research Policies: An International Comparative Analysis*, Cheltenham: Edward.

A. K. Dixit (1988), 'A general model of R&D competition and policy', *Rand Journal of Economics*, 19, 3, 317.

—— and R. Pindyck (1994), *Investment Under Uncertainty*, Princeton, NJ: Princeton University Press.

—— and J. E. Stiglitz (1977), 'Monopolistic competition and optimum product diversity', *American Economic Review*, 67, 297–308.

T. Donoghue, S. Scotchmer, and J. H. Thisse (1998), 'Patent breadth, patent life and the pace of technological progress', *Journal of Economics and Management Strategy*, 7, 1, 1–32.

G. Dosi, C. Freeman, R. Nelson, G. Silverberg, and L. Soete (1988), *Technical Change and Economic Theory*, London: Pinter Publishers.

C. Elliott (2004), Vertical product differentiation and advertising, *International Journal of the Economics of Business*, 11, 1, 37–53.

A. S. Englander, R. Evenson, and M. Hanazaki (1988), 'R&D, innovation, and the total factor productivity slow down', *OECD Economic Studies*, 11, 8–42.

D. Fantino (2008), *R&D and Market Structure in a Horizontal Differentiation Framework*, Bank of Italy Temi di Discussione (Working Paper), No. 658.

Fathom Financial Consulting (2007), Understanding the rationale for publicly backed investment funds in the creative content industries, a report prepared for NESTA, http://www.nesta.org.uk/assets/Uploads/pdf/Working-paper/fathom_paper.pdf.

R. C. Feenstra (1988), 'Gains from trade in differentiated products: Japanese compact trucks' *in* R. Feenstra, *Empirical Methods for International Trade*, Cambridge, MA: MIT Press.

Financial Times (2007), 'Food movement gathers pace', 01 September 2007, p. 3.

D. Frantzen (2003), 'The causality between R&D and productivity in manufacturing: An international disaggregate panel data study', *International Review of Applied Econometrics*, 17, 2, 125–46.

P. J. Fredericks and E. W. McLaughlin (1992), *New Product Procurement: A Summary of Buying Practices and Acceptance Criteria at U.S. Supermarket Chains*, Cornell University, Department of Agricultural Economics, College of Agriculture & Life Sciences, Ithaca, New York, Working Paper 92–12.

J. L. Funk (2007), Technological change within hierarchies: The case of the music industry, *Economics of Innovation and New Technologies*, 16, 1, 1–16.

D. W. Galenson (2005), *Who Are the Greatest Living Artists? The View from the Auction Market*, NBER Working Paper No. W11644, October.

F. Galindo-Rueda (2007), 'Developing an R&D satellite account for the UK: A preliminary analysis', *Economic and Labour Market Review*, 1, 12, 19–29.

D. Gantchev (2004), 'The WIPO guide to surveying the economic contribution of the copyright industries', *Review of Economic Research on Copyright Issues*, 1, 1, 5–16.

P. A. Geroski (1995), 'Markets for technology: Knowledge, innovation and appropriability', *in* P. Stoneman (ed.), *Handbook of the Economics of Innovation and Technological Change*, Oxford: Blackwell.

—— (2000), 'Models of technology diffusion', *Research Policy*, 29, 4–5, 603–25.

—— S. Machin and J. Van Reenen (1993), 'The profitability of innovative firms', *Rand Journal of Economics*, 24, 198–211.

G. Gemser and M. A. A. M. Leenders (2001), 'How integrating industrial design in the product development process impacts on company performance', *The Journal of Product Innovation Management*, 18, 28–38.

L. Georghiou (2007), *Demanding Innovation: Lead Markets, Public Procurement and Innovation*, NESTA Provocation No. 2, London: NESTA.

V. Ginsburg and D. Throsby (2006), *Handbook of the Economics of Art and Culture*, North Holland: Elsevier.

R. Goettler and R. Shachar (2001), 'Spatial competition in the network television industry', *Rand Journal of Economics*, 32, 4, 624–56.

X. Gonzalez and C. Pazo (2008), 'Do public subsidies stimulate private R&D spending?', *Research Policy*, 37, 3, 371–89.

A. Goodacre and I. Tonks (1995), 'Finance and technological change', *in* P. Stoneman (ed.), *Handbook of the Economics of Innovation and Technological Change*, Oxford: Blackwell, pp. 298–341.

P. Goodridge (2008), 'Multi factor productivity estimates for 1997–2006', *Economic and Labour Market Review*, 2, 1, 42–8.

A. Goolsbee and A. Petrin (2001), 'The consumer gains from direct broadcast satellites and the competition with cable television', *National Bureau of Economic Research Working Paper W8317*, Cambridge, Massachusetts.

H. Gorg and E. Strobl (2007), 'The effect of R&D subsidies on private R&D', *Economica*, 74, 215–234.

A. Gowers (2006), *The Gowers Review of Intellectual Property*, December 2006, www.hm-treasury.gov.uk/media/6/E/pbr06_gowers_report_755.pdf.

L. Green, I. Miles J. Rutter, and J. As (2007), *Hidden innovation in the creative sectors*, NESTA Working Paper, London: NESTA.

C. A. Greenhalgh and M. M. Rogers (2007a), *The Value of Intellectual Property Rights to Firms*, Oxford: St Peter's College, Oxford Intellectual Property Research Centre.

—— —— (2007b), *Trade Marks and Performance in UK Firms: Evidence of Schumpeterian Competition Through Innovation*, Oxford Intellectual Property Research Centre, Working Paper 300, March.

—— and M. Longland (2005), 'Running to stand still? The value of R&D, patents and trade marks in innovating manufacturing firms', *International Journal of the Economics of Business*, 12, 3, 307–28.

S. M. Greenstein (1994), '*From superminis to supercomputers: Estimating surplus in the computing market*', Working Paper No. 4899, Cambridge, MA: NBER.

—— and G. Ramey (1988), 'Market structure, innovation and vertical product differentiation', *International Journal of Industrial Organization*, 16, 3, 285–311.

R. Griffith, S. Redding and J. Van Reenen (2001), 'Measuring the cost-effectiveness of an R&D tax credit for the UK', *Fiscal Studies*, 22, 3, 375–99.

W. Griffiths, P. Jensen, P. E. Webster (2005), *The Effects on Firm Profits of the Stock of Intellectual Property Rights*, Melbourne Institute Working Paper 4/05.

Z. Griliches (1957), 'Hybrid corn an exploration in the economics of technological change', *Econometrica*, XXV, 501–22.

—— (1973), Productivity and Research 1973, in Conference on an Agenda for Economic Research on Productivity (sponsored by the National Commission on Productivity, Washington, DC, April 1973), Washington, DC: U.S. Government Printing Office, 1974, 0-522-283, pp. 26–30.

—— (1980), 'Patents and R&D at the firm level: A first report (with A. Pakes)', *Economics Letters*, 5, 1980, 377–81.

—— (1984), *R&D Patents and Productivity*, Chicago, IL: University of Chicago Press, 1984.

—— (1986), 'Productivity, R&D, and basic research at the firm level in the 1970s', *The American Economic Review*, 76, 141–54.

—— (1988), 'Productivity and technical change' (with E. Berndt), Program Report in *NBER Reporter*, Spring.

References

Z. Griliches (1995), 'R&D and productivity: econometric results and measurement issues', *in* P. Stoneman (ed.), *Handbook of the Economics of Innovation and Technical Change*, Oxford: Blackwell.

—— and J. Mairesse (1984), 'Productivity and R&D at the Firm Level' *in* Z. Griliches, ed., *R&D, Patents, and Productivity*, Chicago, IL: University of Chicago Press, 339–74.

G. M. Grossman and E. Helpman (1991), *Innovation and Growth in the Global Economy*, Cambridge, MA: MIT Press.

H. Hagtvedt and V. M. Patrick (2008), 'Art infusion: The influence of visual art on the perception and evaluation of consumer products', *Journal of Marketing Research*, XLV, 379–89.

B. Hall (1993*a*), 'The stock market's valuation of R&D investment during the 1980s', *American Economic Review*, 83, 259–64.

—— (1993*b*), 'Industrial R&D during the 1980s: Did the rate of return fall?', *International Economic Review*, 27, 2, 265–84.

—— (1998), *Innovation and Market Value, Paper Prepared for the NIESR Conference on Productivity and Competitiveness*, London, February 5–6.

—— (2002), 'The financing of research and development', *Oxford Review of Economic Policy*, 18, 35–51.

—— and J. Mairesse (1995), 'Exploring the relationship between R&D and productivity in French manufacturing firms', *Journal of Econometrics*, 65, 263–93.

—— and J. Van Reenen (2000), 'How effective are fiscal incentives for R&D? A review of the evidence', *Research Policy*, 29, 4–5, 449–69.

—— and R. Ziedonis (2001), 'The effects of strengthening patent rights on firms engaged in cumulative innovation: Insights from the semiconductor industry', *in* G. Libecap (ed.), *Entrepreneurial Inputs and Outcomes: New Studies of United States, Vol. 13 of Advances in the Study of Entrepreneurship, Innovation, and Economic Growth*, Amsterdam: Elsevier.

—— A. Jaffe, and M. Trajtenberg (2005), 'Market value and patent citations' *Rand Journal of Economics*, 36, 16–38.

P. Hanel and A. St-Pierre (2005), 'Effects of R&D spillovers on the profitability of firms', *Review of Industrial Organization*, 20, 305–22.

J. Haskel (2007), 'Measuring Innovation and Productivity in a knowledge based service Economy', *Economic and Labour Market Review*, 1, 7, 27–31.

—— M. Cereda, G. Crespi, and C. Criscuolo (2005), *Creativity and Design Study for DTI Using the Community Innovation Survey*, DTI Think Piece, Queen Mary, University of London, AIM, University of Sussex, OECD.

J. Hauser, G. J. Tellis, and A. Griffin (2005), 'Research on innovation: A review and agenda for marketing science', Special Report, Marketing Science Institute, pp. 110–52.

J. A. Hausman (1997*a*), 'Valuation of new goods under perfect and imperfect Competition' *in* T. F. Bresnahan and R. J. Gordon (eds.), *The Economics of New Goods*, The University of Chicago Press, Chicago, IL, pp. 209–37.

—— (1997b), 'Valuing the effect of regulation on new services in telecommunications', *Brookings Papers on Economic Activity, Microeconomics*, pp. 1–38.

—— (1999), Cellular telephone, new products and the CPI, *Journal of Business and Economic Statistics*, 17, 2, 188–94.

—— and G. Leonard (2002), 'The competitive effects of a new product introduction: A case study', *Journal of Industrial Economics*, 50, 3, 237–64.

G. Hawawini, V. Subramanian, and P. Verdin (2002), 'Is performance driven by industry-or firm-specific factors? A new look at the evidence', *Strategic Management Journal*, 24, 1–16.

H. M. Treasury (2007), *Intangible Investment and Britain's Productivity, Treasury Economic Working Paper No. 1*, London: H. M. Treasury.

H. M. Treasury (2007), *The Sainsbury Review of Science and Innovation: The Race to the Top*, London: HMSO.

P. Higgs, S. Cunningham, and H. Bakhshi (2008), *Beyond the Creative Industries*, NESTA Technical Report, London, January.

L. Hildebrandt and R. Buzzell (1991), *Product Quality, Market Share, and Profitability: A Causal Modeling Approach*, Working Paper 91–045, Cambridge, MA: Harvard Business School.

T. J. Hoban (1998), Improving the success of new product development, *Food Technology*, 52, 1, 46–9.

E. Holger (2001), 'Patent applications and subsequent changes of performance: Evidence from time-series cross-section analyses on the firm level', *Research Policy*, 30, 143–57.

S. Hong, M. Shepherd, D. Scoones, and T. T. Wan (2005), 'Product-line extensions and pricing strategies of brand-name drugs facing patent expiration', *Journal of Managed Care Pharmacy*, November/December, 11, 9, 746–54.

N. W. Horne (1991), 'The user – the missing link in IT research and development' *Engineering Management Journal*, 1, 5, 224–26.

H. Hotelling (1929), 'Stability in competition', *Economic Journal*, 39, 41–57.

House of Commons (2007), *New Media and the Creative Industries*, Select Committee on Culture, Media and Sport, Fifth Report, London.

J. Howkins (2001), *The Creative Economy: How People Make Money from Ideas*, London: Penguin.

R. G. Hubbard (1998), 'Capital market imperfections and investment', *Journal of Economic Literature*, 36, 193–225.

R. M. Hurt and R. M. Schuchman (1966), 'The economic rationale of copyright', *The American Economic Review*, 56, 1/2, 421–32.

M. Hutter and D. Throsby (2008), 'Value and valuation in art and culture introduction and overview' *in* M. Hutter and D. Throsby (eds.), *Beyond Price: Value in Culture, Economics, and the Arts*, New York: Cambridge University Press.

W. Hutton (2007), *Staying Ahead: The Economic Performance of the UK's Creative Industries*, June, London: The Work Foundation.

References

N. Ireland and P. Stoneman (1986), 'Technological diffusion, expectations and welfare', *Oxford Economic Papers*, June, pp. 283–304.

R. Jacobsen (1988), 'The persistence of abnormal returns', *Strategic Management Journal*, 9, 415–30.

—— and D. A. Aaker (1987), The strategic role of product quality, *Journal of Marketing*, 51, 4, 31–44.

A. Jaffe (1986), 'Technological opportunity and spillovers of R&D: Evidence from firm's patents, profits and market value', *American Economic Review*, 76, 984–1001.

C. Jones (1999), 'Growth: With or without scale effects?', *American Economic Review P&P*, 82, 139–44.

—— and J. Williams (2000), 'Too much of a good thing? The economics of investment in R&D', *Journal of Economic Growth*, 5, 66–85.

K. Kaivanto (2004), *Spin offs, externalities and the economic justification of public expenditure on R&D*, Lancaster University, United Kingdom, January.

—— and P. Stoneman (2007), 'Public provision of sales contingent claims backed finance to smes: A policy alternative', *Research Policy*, 36, 5, 637–51.

P. Kanavos, J. Costa-Font, and E. Seeley (2008), 'Competition in off patent drug markets: Issues regulation and evidence', *Economic Policy*, 45, 499–544.

M. Karshenas and P. Stoneman (1993), 'Rank, stock, order and epidemic effects in the diffusion of new process technologies: An empirical model', *Rand Journal of Economics*, I, 24, 4, 503–28.

—— —— (1995), 'Technological diffusion' *in* P. Stoneman (ed.), *Handbook of the Economics of Innovation and Technological Change*, Cambridge: Blackwell.

M. L. Katz and C. Shapiro (1986), 'Technology adoption in the presence of network externalities', *Journal of Political Economy*, 94, 4, 822–41.

R. Kennedy (2002), 'Strategy fads and competitive convergence: An empirical test for herd behaviour in prime time television programming', *Journal of Industrial Economics*, L, 1, 57–84.

I. M. Kirzner (1973), *Competition and Entrepreneurship*, Chicago, IL: University of Chicago Press.

T. Koga (2003), 'Firm size and R&D tax incentives', *Technovation*, 23, Issue 7, 643–648.

A. Kolah (2002), *Essential Law for Marketers*, Oxford: Butterworth Heineman.

M. Kretschmer and P. Hardwick (2007), *Authors' Earnings from Copyright and Non-copyright Sources: A Survey of 25,000 British and German Writers*, Dorset, UK: Bournemouth University, Centre for Intellectual Property and Management.

S. Lach (2002), 'Do R&D subsidies stimulate or displace private R&D; evidence from Israel', *Journal of Industrial Economics*, L, 4, 369–90.

J. J. Laffont (1988), *Fundamentals of Public Economics*, Cambridge, MA: MIT Press.

K. Lancaster (1990), 'The economics of product variety: A survey', *Marketing Science*, 9, 3, 189–206.

W. M. Landes and R. A. Posner (1987), 'Trademark law: An economic perspective', *Journal of Law and Economics*, 30, 2, 265–309.

—— —— (2003), *The Economic Structure of Intellectual Property Law*, Cambridge, MA: Harvard University Press.

A. Leiponen (2000), 'Competencies, innovation and profitability of firms', *Economics of Innovation and New Technology*, 9, 1–24.

P. Leslie (2004), 'Price discrimination in Broadway theater', *Rand Journal of Economics*, 35, 3, 520–41.

R. Levin, A. Klevorick, R. Nelson, and S. Winter (1987), 'Appropriating the returns from industrial research and development', *Brooking Papers on Economic Activity*, 3, 783–820.

P. Lin and K. Saggi (2002), 'Product differentiation, process R&D, and the nature of market competition', *European Economic Review*, 46, 1, 201–11.

D. Lindsay (2002), *The Law and Economics of Copyright, Contract and Mass Market Licenses*, Research Paper prepared for the Centre for Copyright Studies Ltd, May, ACN 058 847 948.

B. Lokshin and P. Mohnen (2007), *Measuring the Effectiveness of R&D Tax Credits in the Netherlands*, UNU-MERIT Working Papers, Maastricht Economic and Social Research and Training.

H. Lööf and A. Heshmati (2006), *Investment and Performance of Firms: Correlation or Causality? Working Paper Series in Economics and Institutions of Innovation 72*, CESIS – Centre of Excellence for Science and Innovation Studies, Royal Institute of Technology.

P. D. Lopes (1992), 'Innovation and diversity in the popular music industry 1969–1990', *American Sociological Review*, 57, 56–71.

S. Lutz (1996), *Vertical Product Differentiation and Entry Deterrence*, CEPR Discussion Paper, 1455, London: CEPR.

Madakom (2001), *Innovations report* 2001, Köln.

J. Mairesse and M. Sassenou (1991), *R&D and productivity: A survey of econometric studies at the firm level*, NBER Working Papers Series 3666.

J. Mairesse, B. Hall, L. Branstetter, and B. Crepon (1999), 'Does cash flow cause investment and R&D? An exploration using panel data for French, Japanese, and United States scientific firms', *in* D. B. Audretsch and A. R. Thurik (eds.), *Innovation, Industry Evolution, and Employment*, Cambridge: Cambridge University Press.

E. Mansfield (1963*a*), 'Intrafirm rates of diffusion of an innovation', *The Review of Economics and Statistics*, XLV, 348–59.

—— (1963b), 'The speed of response of firms to new techniques', *Quarterly Journal of Economics*, 77, 2, 290–309.

—— (1965), 'Rates of return from industrial research and development', *American Economic Review*, 55, 110–22.

—— (1968), *Industrial Research and Technological Innovation*, New York: Norton.

—— (1985), 'How rapidly does new industrial technology leak out?', *Journal of Industrial Economics*, 34, 217–23.

H. M. Markowitz (1987), *Mean-Variance Analysis in Portfolio Choice and Capital Markets*, Oxford: Basil Blackwell.

References

J. A. Marzal and E. T. Esparza (2007), 'Innovation assessment in traditional industries: A proposal of aesthetic innovation indicators', *Scientometrics*, 72, 1, 33–57.

E. S. Mason (1939), 'Price and production policies of large-scale enterprise', *American Economic Review*, Supplement 29, 2, 61–74.

Y. Mazeh and M. Rogers (2006), 'The economic significance and extent of copyright cases: An analysis of large UK firms', *Intellectual Property Quarterly*, 12, (4), 404–20.

A. McGahan and B. Silverman (2006), 'Profiting from technological innovation by others: The effect of competitor patenting on firm value', *Research Policy*, 33, 1222–12.

J. McGee (1985), Strategic groups: A bridge between industry structure and strategic management, *in* H. Thomas and D. Gardner (Eds.), *Strategic Marketing and Management*, New York: Wiley, pp. 293–313.

K. McNamara, C. Weiss, and A. Wittkopp (2003), *Market Success of Premium Product Innovation: Empirical Evidence from the German Food Sector*, Working Paper FE 0306: University of Kiel, Department of Food Economics and Consumption Studies.

P. Megna and D. C. Mueller (1991), 'Profit rates and intangible capital', *Review of Economics and Statistics*, 73, 632–42.

S. Mendonca, T. Pereira, and M. Godinho (2004), 'Trademarks as an indicator of innovation and industrial change', *Research Policy*, 33, 1385–404.

J. Metcalf (1988), 'The diffusion of innovations: An interpretive study', *in* G. Dosi, C. Freeman, R. Nelson, G. Silverberg, and L. Soete (eds.), *Technical Change and Economic Theory*, London: Pinter Publishers.

J, Minasian (1969), 'Research and Development, Production Functions and Rates of Return', *American Economic Review*, 55, 80–5.

Mintel (2006), *Breakfast Cereals Report* Mirtel International Group Ltd.

M. Morrin and S. Ratneshwar (2000), 'The impact of ambient scent on evaluation, attention, and memory for familiar and unfamiliar brands', *Journal of Business Research*, 49, 2, 157–65.

D. C. Mueller (ed.) (1990), *The Dynamics of Company Profits: An International Comparison*, Cambridge: Cambridge University Press.

T. Mukoyama (2006), 'Rosenberg's "learning by using" and technology diffusion', *Journal of Economic Behavior & Organization*, 61, 1, 123–44.

National Science Foundation (2007), *Research and Development Bolsters U.S, Economic Growth*, Press Release, 07–129.

R. R. Nelson (ed.) (1993), *National Innovation Systems: A Comparative Analysis*, Oxford: Oxford University Press.

—— and S. G. Winter (1982), *An Evolutionary Theory of Economic Change*, Cambridge, MA and London: Belknap Press of Harvard University Press.

—— —— (2002), 'Evolutionary theorizing in economics', *Journal of Economic Perspectives*, 16, 2, 23–46.

NESTA (2006), *The Innovation Gap; Why Policy needs to reflect the reality of innovation in the UK*, London: NESTA.

—— (2007), *The Hidden Innovation Report*, London: www.nesta.org.uk/hidden-innovation.

—— (2008), *Taking Services Seriously, How Policy Can Stimulate the Hidden Innovation in the UK's Service Economy*, London: NESTA.

A. Nevo (2001), *New Products, Quality Changes and Welfare Measures Computed from Estimated Demand Systems*, Working Paper W8425, Cambridge, MA: National Bureau of Economic Research.

Y. H. Noh and G. Moschini (2006), 'Vertical product differentiation, entry-deterrence strategies, and entry qualities', *Review of Industrial Organization*, 29, 227–52.

W. Nordhaus (1969), *Invention, Growth and Welfare*, Cambridge, MA: MIT Press.

H. Odagiri (1983), 'R&D expenditures, royalty payments and sales growth in Japanese manufacturing corporations', *The Journal of Industrial Economics*, 32, 1, 61–71.

OECD (1997), *Government Venture Capital for Technology Based Firms*, OECD/GD(97) 201, Paris: OECD.

—— (2002), *Proposed Standard Practice for Surveys of Measurement of Research and Experimental Development*, Third Edition, Paris: DSTI, OECD.

—— (2006), *The Measurement of Scientific and Technological Activities: Proposed Guidelines for collecting and Interpreting Technological Innovation Data*, Third Edition Paris: Commission Eurostat.

Office of National Statistics (2007*a*), *Gross Domestic Expenditure on Research and Development, 2005*, Newport: National Statistics, March.

—— (2007*b*), *R&D in UK Businesses, 2005, Business Monitor, MA14*, Newport: National Statistics, January.

A. Pakes (1986), 'Patents as options: Some estimates of the value of holding European patent stocks', *Econometrica*, 54, 755–85.

N. R. Pandit, G. Cook and G. M. P. Swann (2002), 'A comparison of clustering dynamics in the British broadcasting and financial services industries', *International Journal of the Economics of Business*, 9, 2, 195–224.

K. Pavitt (2000), *Technology, Management and Systems of Innovation*, Cheltenham: Edward.

S. Peltzman (1977), 'The gains and losses from industrial concentration', *Journal of Law and Economics*, 20, 229–63.

R. A. Petersen and D. G. Burger (1975), 'Cycles in symbol production: The case of popular music', *American Sociological Review*, 40, 158–73.

A. Petrin (2002), Quantifying the benefits of new products: The case of the minivan, *Journal of Political Economy*, 110, 4, 705–29.

L. W. Phillips, D. R. Chang, and R. D. Buzzell (1983), Product quality, cost position and business performance: A test of some key hypotheses, *Journal of Marketing*, 2, 26–43.

M. Piirainen (2001), *Design and Business Performance – Assessing the Impact of Product Design on Business Performance*, Helsinki: Faculty of International Business, Helsinki School of Economics and Business Administration.

R. Pindyck and D. L. Rubinfeld (1998), *Microeconomics*, Upper Saddle River, NJ: Prentice Hall.

References

R. Pitkethly (2007), *UK Intellectual Property Awareness Survey, 2006*, Intellectual Property Office, www.ipo.gov.uk/ipsurvey.

I. P. L. Png (2006), 'Copyright: A pleas for empirical research', *Review of Economic Research on Copyright Issues*, 3, 2, 3–13.

—— and Q. Wang (2006), *Copyright Duration and the Supply of Creative Work*, Singapore: National University of Singapore.

V. Postrel (2004), *The Substance of Style: How the Rise of Aesthetic Value Is Remaking Commerce, Culture, and Consciousness*, New York: HarperCollins.

J. Prašnikar and T. Škerlj (2006), 'New product development and time to market in the generic pharmaceutical industry', *Industrial Marketing Management*, 35, 6, 690–702.

J. Prince (2007), *Repeat Purchase Amid Rapid Quality Improvement: Structural Estimation of Demand for Personal Computers*, Available at SSRN: http://ssrn.com/abstract = 917865.

H. C. Quirmbach (1986), 'The diffusion of new technology and the market for an innovation', *Rand Journal of Economics*, 17, 33–47.

G. B. Ramello and F. Silva (2006), 'Appropriating signs and meaning: The elusive economics of trademarks', *Industrial and Corporate Change*, 15, 6, 937–63.

P. Roberts (1999), 'Product innovation, product market competition and persistent profitability in the US pharmaceutical industry', *Strategic Management Journal*, 20, 655–70.

R. Reeves and J. Smith (2006), 'The link between R&D and productivity in the UK', *Bank of England Working Paper Series*, January 2006.

J. Reinganum (1981), 'Market structure and the diffusion of new technology', *Bell Journal of Economics*, 12, 618–24.

M. Reisinger (2004), *Vertical Product Differentiation, Market Entry, and Welfare*, Discussion Papers in Economics No. 479, Munich: University of Munich, Department of Economics.

R. Rob and J. Waldfogel (2007), 'Piracy on the silver screen', *Journal of Industrial Economics*, LV, 3, 379–95.

P. W. Roberts (1999), 'Product innovation, product-market competition and persistent profitability in the U.S. pharmaceutical industry', *Strategic Management Journal*, 20, 655–70.

—— (2001), 'Innovation and firm-level persistent profitability: A Schumpeterian framework', *Managerial and Decision Economics*, 22, 239–50.

S. Robson and G. Haigh (2008), 'First findings from the UK Innovation Survey 2007', *Economic & Labour Market Review*, Vol, 2, No 4, 47–53.

J. C. Rochet and J. Tirole (2006), Two-sided markets: A progress report, *Rand Journal of Economics*, 37, 645–67.

E. M. Rogers (2003), *Diffusion of innovations*, Fifth Edition, New York: Free Press.

P. Rouvinen (2002), 'R&D-productivity dynamics: Causality, lags, and dry holes', *Journal of Applied Economics*, 5, 1, 123–56.

R. P. Rumelt (1991), 'How much does industry matter?', *Strategic Management Journal*, 12, 167–85.

M. Rysman (2007), 'An empirical analysis of payment card usage', *Journal of Industrial Economics*, LV, 1, 1–36.

D. Sabbagh (2008), 'Bloomsbury profit to fade without Harry Potter or JK Rowling', *The Times*, April 2.

G. Saloner and A. Shephard (1995), 'Adoption of technologies with network effects: An empirical examination of the adoption of automated teller machines', *Rand Journal of Economics*, 26, 3, 479–501.

S. Salop (1979), 'Monopolistic competition with outside goods', *Bell Journal of Economics*, 10, 141–56.

A. Salter and B. Martin (2001), 'The economic benefits of publicly funded basic research: a critical review', *Research Policy*, 30, 3, 509–32.

P. A. Samuelson (1965), *Foundations of Economic Analysis*, Valley Forge, MA: Atheneum.

P. Samuelson (2004), 'Should economics play a role in copyright law and policy?', *University of Ottawa Law & Technology Journal*, 1, 1, available at SSRN: http://ssrn.com/abstract = 764704.

A. J. Sawyer (2004), *Potential Implications of Providing Tax Incentives for Research and Development in NZ, A Report for the Royal Society of New Zealand*.

M. Schankerman (1981), 'The effect of double counting and expensing on the measured returns to R&D', *Review of Economics and Statistics*, 63, 3, 454–8.

F. M. Scherer (2006), 'The evolution of music', *in* V. A. Ginsburgh and D. Throsby (eds.), *Handbook of the Economics of Art and Culture*, North Holland: Elsevier.

R. Schmalensee (1985), 'Do markets differ much?', *The American Economic Review*, 75, 3, 341–51.

J. A. Schumpeter (1942), *Capitalism, Socialism and Democracy*, New York: Harper.

—— (1950), *Capitalism, Socialism and Democracy*, Third Edition, New York: Harper-Collins.

J. Sedgwick (2002), 'Product differentiation at the movies: Hollywood 1946–1965', *Journal of Economic History*, 62, 676–05.

C. Seethamraju (2003), 'The value relevance of trademarks', *in* J. Hand and B. Lev (eds.), *Intangible Assets: Values, Measures and Risks*, Oxford: Oxford University Press.

K. Seim (2006), 'An empirical model of firm entry with endogenous product type choices', *Rand Journal of Economics*, 37, 3, 619–40.

A. Sentance and J. Clarke (1997), *The Contribution of Design to the UK Economy*, London: Design Council.

A. Shaked and J. Sutton (1982), 'Relaxing price competition through product differentiation', *Review of Economic Studies*, 49, 3–14.

—— —— (1983), 'Natural oligopolies', *Econometrica*, 51, 5, 1469–83.

B. C. Shine, J. Park, and R. S. Wyer Jr. (2007), 'Brand synergy effects in multiple brand extensions', *Journal of Marketing Research*, 44, 4, 663–70.

References

R. Siebert (2003), *The Introduction of New Product Qualities by Incumbent Firms: Market Proliferation Versus Cannibalization*, CIG Working Papers number SP II 2003–11, Wissenschaftszentrum Berlin (WZB).

S. Simeons and S. De Costar (2006), *Sustaining Generic Medicines Markets in Europe*, Leuven: Katholieke Universiteit Leuven, Research Centre for Pharmaceutical Care and Pharmaco-economics, April.

P. Siriwongwilaichat (2001), *Technical Information Capture for Food Product Innovation in Thailand*, Massey University, New Zealand, PhD Thesis.

R. Solow (1957), 'Technical change and the aggregate production function', *Review of Economics and Statistics*, 39, 312–20.

A. T. Sorensen (2007), 'Best seller lists and product variety', *Journal of Industrial Economics*, LV, 4, 715–38.

Statistics New Zealand (2006), *Cultural Indicators for New Zealand*, Wellington, 2006.

B. Stewart-Knox and P. Mitchell (2003), 'What separates the winners from the losers in new food product development?', *Trends in Food Science & Technology*, 14, 58–64.

J. Stiglitz and A. Weiss (1981), 'Credit rationing in markets with imperfect information', *American Economic Review*, 71, 393–410.

P. Stoneman (1981), 'Intra-firm diffusion, Bayesian learning and profitability', *Economic Journal*, 91, 375–88.

—— (1987), *The Economic Analysis of Technology Policy*, Oxford: Oxford University Press.

—— (1989), 'Technological diffusion, vertical product differentiation and quality improvement', *Economic Letters*, 31, 277–80.

—— (1990), 'Technological diffusion, horizontal product differentiation and adaptation costs', *Economica*, 57, 49–62.

—— (1991), 'Copying capabilities and intertemporal competition between joint input technologies: CD vs. DAT', *Economics of Innovation and New Technology*, 1, 3, 233–41.

—— (ed.) (1995), *Handbook of the Economics of Innovation and Technological Change*, Oxford: Blackwell.

***—— (2001), *Heterogeneity and Change in European Financial Environments*, EIFC – Technology and Finance Working Papers 7, United Nations University: Institute for New Technologies.

—— (2002), *The Economics of Technological Diffusion*, Oxford: Blackwell.

—— (2005), *Creative Destruction and Underinvestment in R&D: Did Arrow Point the Wrong Way*, Presented at a conference in Manchester in December 2005 celebrating the contribution of John Barber to the development and implementation of technology policy in the UK.

—— and G. Battisti (2009), 'The diffusion of new technology', *in* B. H. Hall and N. Rosenberg (eds.), *Handbook of the Economics of Technical Change*, North Holland: Elsevier.

—— and P. Diederen (1994), Technology diffusion and public policy, *Economic Journal*, 104, 918–30.

—— and M. Y. Kwon (1996), 'Technology adoption and firm profitability', *Economic Journal*, 106, 952–62.

***J. Sutton (1986), 'Vertical product differentiation: Some basic themes', *American Economic Review*, Papers and Proceedings, 393–8.

K. S. Swan, M. Kotabe, and B. B. Allred (2005), 'Exploring robust design capabilities, their role in creating global products, and their relationship to firm performance', *Journal of Product Innovation Management*, 22, 2, 144–64, doi:10.1111/j.0737–6782.2005.00111.x.

P. Swann and D. Birke (2005), *How Do Creativity and Design Enhance Business Performance? A Framework for Interpreting the Evidence*, 'Think Piece' for DTI Strategy Unit, Final Report.

L. N. Takeyama (1994), 'The welfare implications of unauthorized reproduction of intellectual property in the presence of demand network externalities', *The Journal of Industrial Economics*, 42, 2, 155–66.

D. J. Teece (1982), 'Towards an economic theory of the multiproduct firm', *Journal of Economic Behaviour and Organization*, 3, 39–63.

B. Tether (2003), 'The sources and aims of innovation in services: Variety between and within sectors', *Economics of Innovation and New Technology*, 12, 6, 481–506.

—— (2006), *Design in Innovation*, A report to the DTI.

The Economist (2005), 'This sceptered aisle', 4 Aug 2005.

J. Theeuwes (2004), 'The economic contribution of the copyright based sector in the Netherlands', *Review of Economic Research on Copyright Issues*, 1, 1, 65–9.

D. Throsby (2001), *Economics and Culture*, Cambridge: Cambridge University Press.

J. Tirole (1988), *The Theory of Industrial Organization*, Cambridge, MA: MIT Press.

R. Towse (2004), *Assessing the Economic Impacts of Copyright Reform on Performers and Producers of Sound Recordings in Canada*, Report Commissioned by Industry Canada, strategis.ic.gc.ca/epic/site/ippd-dppi.nsf/en/ip01108e.html.

M. Trajtenberg (1989), 'The welfare analysis of product innovations, with an application to computed tomography scanners', *Journal of Political Economy*, 97, 444–79.

—— (1990), *The Economic Analysis of Product Innovation: The Case of CT Scanners*, Cambridge, MA: Harvard University Press.

P. Tufano (2003), 'Financial innovation', *in* R. Constantinides, M. Harris, and R. Stulz (eds.), *Handbook of the Economics of Finance*, Volume 1, Part 1, North Holland: Elsevier, pp. 307–35.

UNCTAD (2008), *Creative Economy Report, 2008*, United Nations http://www.unctad-xii.org/en/Programme/Other-Events/Creative-Africa/Launch-of-the-Creative-Economy-Report/Notification/ < http://www.unctadxii.org/en/Programme/Other-Events/Creative-Africa/Launch-of-the-Creative-Economy-Report/Notification/.

M. R. Veall (1992), 'Brand/product innovation and the optimal length of trademark/patent protection', *Economics Letter*, 40, 491–6.

A. Venkatesh and L. A. Meamber (2006), 'Arts and aesthetics: Marketing and cultural production', *Marketing Theory*, 6, 1, 11–39.

References

J. Vickers (1986), 'The evolution of market structure when there is a sequence of innovations', *The Journal of Industrial Economics*, XXXV, 1–12.

J. Wang and K. Tsai (2003), *Productivity Growth and R&D Expenditure in Taiwan's Manufacturing Firms*, NBER Working Paper 9724, National Bureau of Economic Research.

H. Watzke and L. Saguy (2001), 'Innovating R&D innovation', *Food Technology*, 55, 5, 174–88.

P. Westhead and D. J. Storey (1997), 'Financial constraints on the growth of high-technology small firms in the United Kingdom', *Applied Financial Economics*, 7, 197–201.

C. M. White (1976), 'The concept of social saving in theory and practice', *The Economic History Review*, XX1X, 82–100.

J. Whyte, A. Salter, D. Gann, and A. Davies (2002), *Investing in Design to Improve, Export Potential*, Sussex: SPRU, University of Sussex.

R. Winger and G. Wall (2006), *Food Product Innovation, a Background Paper*, Rome: Food and Agricultural Organisation of the United Nations, UNCTAD *Creative Economy Report, 2008*, United Nations.

S. J. Winter (2006), 'The logic of appropriability: From Schumpeter to Arrow to Teece', *Research Policy*, 35, 8, 1100–6.

Y. Wu (2005), 'The effects of state R&D tax credits in stimulating private R&D expenditure: A cross-state empirical analysis', *Journal of Policy Analysis and Management*, 24, 4, 785–802.

M. Yamamoto and D. R. Lambert (1994), 'The impact of product aesthetics on the evaluation of industrial products', *Journal of Product Innovation Management*, 11, 309–24.

A. Yiannaka and M. Fulton (2006), 'Strategic patent breadth and entry deterrence with drastic product innovations', *International Journal of Industrial Organisation*, 24, 177–202.

Z. Z. Zantout and G. P. Tsetsekos (1994), 'The wealth effects of announcements of R&D expenditure increases', *The Journal of Financial Research*, 17, 205–16.

M. Zhang (2002), *Stardom, Peer-to-Peer and the Socially Optimal Distribution of Music*, Cambridge, MA: MIT, Sloan School of Management.

Index

Index